1000
Japanese Knitting & Crochet Stitches

THE ULTIMATE BIBLE FOR NEEDLECRAFT ENTHUSIASTS

TUTTLE Publishing

Tokyo | Rutland, Vermont | Singapore

Knitting can be a mysterious activity. The same knitted shape can take on many
forms, depending on the choice of color, pattern and materials.

This collection of 1000 knitting and crochet stitches shows the stitches as symbols,
placed in a gridded chart. For knitted stitches, each box of the grid is a stitch.
Next to the chart is a photo of each stitch, so it's easy to see
how the chart relates to the completed stitch.

Use the stitches in this book to create original knitted and crocheted garments,
and when you want to try various arrangements of the fabrics.

CONTENTS

KNITTING

CROCHET

ABOUT THE CHARTS
Before using this book, please read this section

All charts and symbols are shown as viewed from the front side–that is,
the chart is a visual representation of the knitted or crocheted fabric.
The row numbers are given at the right edge of the chart, and the stitch
numbers at the bottom. Odd-numbered rows (right sides) are worked reading
from right to left across the row. Even-numbered rows (wrong sides)
are worked reading from left to right, reversing the stitches so they
will appear correct on the right side of the fabric. For crochet charts,
the directions of the rows are indicated by arrows.

The numbers at the bottom of the chart tell you how many
stitches are in one pattern repeat, and the numbers at the
right edge tell you how many rows in each repeat.
Note that the stitches and rows are numbered only as far as the repeat.
In addition, one pattern repeat is outlined with heavy lines,
so it's easy to see how to repeat a stitch pattern.

The knitting charts don't include setup rows. When making an item,
if you have started with ribbing, begin the new stitch pattern at row 1.
If you're beginning from a cast-on, work the cast-on and a return row first,
then begin the new stitch pattern at row 1.

INTRODUCTION

For years, "1000 Stitch Patterns" has been a go-to reference for Japanese designers and knitters. The volume contains charted instructions for 700 knitting and 300 crochet stitch patterns, some of them quite unusual.

Originally published in 1992, the book is a compilation of stitch patterns from a variety of publications from Nihon Vogue, one of Japan's largest craft publishers. Knitting and crochet charts and symbols in the '80s and '90s were not quite as standardized as they are now, so you'll find some minor variations among the charts. Where there's a variation, you'll also find an explanation.

Read through this introduction before you start a project. It provides important information about interpreting the charts, finding pattern repeats, and understanding the symbols that represent stitches.

KNITTING CHART BASICS

The stitch patterns in this book are presented as charts, using symbols to describe each stitch. It's as if the chart is a drawing of what your finished knitting will look like. Japanese charts don't have keys (though there may be supplementary explanation, like an unusual symbol); they also don't offer hints, like placing the numbers for wrong-side rows on the left. The charts are organized by type, such as cables or mosaic stitches.

The single most important thing to remember is that *the chart shows the right side of the work.* Each symbol shows what the stitch will look like on the right side, not necessarily what you have to execute to get there. Each chart has a close-up photo to give you a visual reference of what the pattern looks like when complete.

If you're knitting back and forth:

- On the right side (RS), read the chart from right to left, in the same sequence as you work the stitches. In general, odd-numbered rows are the RS, and even-numbered rows are WS. In this book, every row is charted.
- On the reverse ("wrong") side (WS), read the chart from left to right, reversing the execution of the stitches so they show up correctly on the right side. For example, to create a knit stitch on the right side, purl on the wrong side.
- Aside from knits, purls and yarnovers, relatively few stitches are worked on the reverse side. In this volume, when an increase or decrease is worked on both RS and WS, the definition gives you both versions. If only one definition is provided, the stitch is only worked on the RS.

If you're knitting in the round:

- Read every row from right to left. There's no need to reverse stitches.

STITCH AND ROW REPEATS

Notice that the boxes in the bottommost row and the rightmost column of every chart contain numbers. Those boxes aren't stitches; they contain the stitch and row counts of the pattern repeat. Stitch 1 and row 1 are not necessarily in the lower-right corner, either; the pattern may begin a few stitches in or a few rows up. Look carefully before you begin.

It's also important to keep in mind that the chart as shown may include more than one pattern repeat. Look for notations to find the repeat. First, the number of stitches and rows is stated right next to each chart. Second, the stitches and rows are only numbered as far as the repeat. If you want to repeat a pattern across a set number of stitches, perhaps for a scarf, be sure to repeat only the numbered stitches and the numbered rows. Most charts include a heavier line around the repeat, but it can be difficult to see. In a few cases, you may need to adjust the increases or decreases at the sides of the first and last repeats to maintain your stitch count. If a double decrease is the first or last stitch in the repeat, for instance, you may need a single decrease for the first or last repeat to keep the number of increases equal to the number of decreases.

Row 1 is not counted as the cast-on row, unlike some other stitch dictionaries. In most cases, the pattern begins in row 1, so your cast-on row will lie below row 1, possibly with a purl-back row as well–knitter's choice. There may also be a couple of setup rows, where row 1 of the repeat begins a row or two higher in the chart.

If there are some stitches to the right of numbered stitch 1, you may want to include them as a mirror image to the left of the last pattern repeat for symmetry.

Find a good way to keep your place in the chart. You may want to highlight wrong side rows, or draw arrows to remind you which way each row is worked. You may also want to draw a line around the pattern repeat with a contrast colored marker. Tools such as highlighter tape can be a lifesaver when following a complex chart.

A few charts include more than one stitch pattern with row repeats that don't match. For instance, in chart #201, stitch pattern A (marked in the bracket at the top) has a 6-row repeat, while pattern B has a 10-row repeat. You'll have to keep track of each repeat separately, because the 6-row repeat doesn't evenly divide into the 10-row repeat.

Be sure to check for insets at the top and footnotes at the bottom of your chosen chart. Top insets normally show how a bobble or leaf is worked. Footnotes tell you whether a blank box is a knit, purl, or no-stitch (see charts #76 to #78, for instance). A footnote may also define a particular symbol.

KNITTING SYMBOL BASICS

The technical section that follows (pp. 8 to 29) illustrates and defines the basic symbols used to represent stitches. You'll find that, once familiar with the basics, you can interpret more complex symbols by looking at their component parts. The symbols used in Japanese stitch charts are standardized. If you've used Japanese charts before, you're probably accustomed to many of these symbols.

The explanations in the technical section were expanded in this translation to provide additional information about certain types of stitches. They describe the principles behind how the symbols are drawn, so you can begin to figure out a new or complex symbol by examining its component parts. Cables, slip and brioche stitches in particular come in so many variations over differing numbers of rows and stitches that a table defining each one would be large and hard to use. Once you know the principles on which the stitches are constructed, you can interpret a stitch that you may not have seen before.

There's also a new table of additional symbols (pp. 323 to 327). An unusual symbol that appears more than once in the book is probably in this table, with some exceptions for cables, slip and brioche stitches.

If an unusual symbol appears in only one chart, on the other hand, you'll normally find a footnote to explain it.

You may have to look in a couple of places to find the definition of a given symbol. Unfortunately, the original book didn't illustrate everything, because it was assumed that a Japanese knitter knew the standardized symbols and most of their combinations. We hope that the explanations here will help to interpret or "parse" the symbols–both for this book and for Japanese charts that you may find in other sources.

For an unfamiliar symbol:

1. Check whether it's illustrated in the technical section (pp. 8 to 29), or whether the further explanations tell you how to figure out its meaning.
2. Check the table of additional symbols (pp. 323 to 327).
3. Check the footnotes of the chart itself.
4. At the back of the technical section (pp. 30 to 32), there are additional notes about some of the more unusual symbols and techniques.

The technical section includes only one way to work a particular symbol, but experienced knitters often know more than one way to accomplish something. The symbol ⟨✕⟩, for instance, can be worked either as "slip 1, knit 1, pass slipped stitch over" (the definition used by most Japanese books) or as "slip 1, slip 1, knit 2 together through back loop." The result is the same: a left-leaning single decrease. As long as you get the same result, feel free to use an alternate method when you are more comfortable.

CROCHET CHART BASICS

Just like knitting, crochet stitch patterns are comprised of combinations of basic stitches. The stitch pattern charts are not shown in a grid, but drawn to more closely resemble the finished work; a fan-style pattern, for instance, will be drawn along a curve.

- On the right side (RS), read the chart from right to left, in the same sequence that you work the stitches. Next to the first few row numbers in each chart, you'll see tiny arrows indicating the direction of work. This gives crocheters an advantage, because knit charts don't include the arrows.
- On the reverse (or "wrong") side (WS), read the chart from left to right. Work each symbol as show; unlike knitting, there's no need to reverse operations. Because crochet stitches look much alike on both sides, you may want to mark your RS as you work. This is particularly important in a stitch pattern like those in charts #857 to #866, where a finished row consists of two "passes," one in each color.

Pay close attention to all the markings on the charts. Watch for row numbers, arrows showing the direction of rows, standing or turning chains as transitions between rows, and other hints that will help you to work the pattern.

CROCHET SYMBOL BASICS

The crochet world has largely adopted the Japanese crochet symbols. Most of the symbols used here will probably be familiar to crocheters. Throughout this book, American terminology is used; Japanese crocheters use American terms when they translate to English.

The crochet technical section (pages 232 to 242) describes the symbols for the basic stitches. An experienced crocheter probably already knows most of these symbols.

Watch for some unusual patterns, such as the "wrapped" stitches in charts #827 to #834. Non-standard stitches and symbols are explained with their charts.

KNITTING SYMBOLS AND METHODS

Most knitting symbols are standardized according to guidelines of the Japan Industrial Standards Committee; these are usually referred to as the JIS symbols. This book also uses some symbols that are not included in the JIS. Notice that some basic symbols may be combined to explain specific operations. For instance, the addition of a "purl dash" below the symbol for "knit through back loop" indicates "purl through back loop."

All of these illustrations show how to work a stitch on the right side of the work.
In a few cases, the WS operation is described but not illustrated.

Abbreviations used in this section:

RN = Right needle

LN = Left needle

CN = cable needle

RS = Right side of work

WS = Wrong side of work

St = Stitch

K = Knit

P = Purl

Inc = Increase

Dec = Decrease

YO = Yarn over

Ktbl = Knit through the back loop

Ptbl = Purl through the back loop

Sl = Slip

Wyib = With yarn in back of work

Wyif = With yarn in front

K2tog = Knit 2 together

K3tog = Knit 3 together

K2togtbl = Knit 2 together through the back loops

P2tog = Purl 2 together

P2togtbl = Purl 2 together through the back loops

Psso = pass slipped stitch over

SKP = Slip 1 knitwise, knit 1, pass slipped stitch over

SK2P = Slip 1 knitwise, k2tog, pass slipped stitch over

SSK = [Slip 1 knitwise] twice, return 2 st to LN, k2togtbl

SSP = [Slip 1 knitwise] twice, slip 2 stitches back to LN, then p2togtbl

CDD = Slip 2 sts together knitwise, k1, pass the 2 slipped sts over

M1 = Make one: with tip of RN, pick up the strand of yarn before the next stitch on LN and ktbl

BASIC STITCHES

☐ KNIT (K) ON RS, PURL (P) ON WS

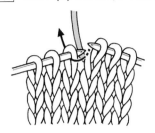 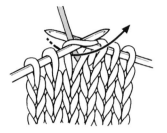 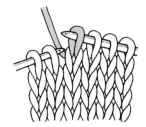

❶ With yarn in back, insert RN into next st on LN from front to back.

❷ Wrap yarn over RN, and bring it through loop as shown by the arrow.

❸ Drop st off LN. Knit st complete. On WS, work this symbol as purl.

☐ PURL (P) ON RS, KNIT (K) ON WS

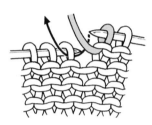 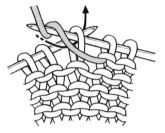 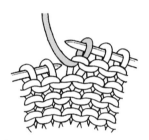

❶ With yarn in front, insert RN into next st on LN from back to front.

❷ Wrap yarn over RN as shown and bring it through.

❸ Drop st off LN. Purl st complete. On WS, work this symbol as knit.

☒ TWISTED KNIT ST (KTBL, OR KNIT THROUGH BACK LOOP)

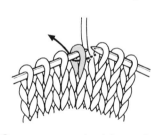 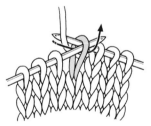 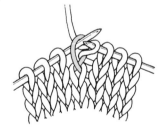 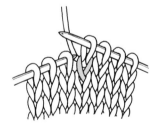

❶ Insert RN into back loop of next st on LN as shown.

❷ Wrap yarn over RN.

❸ Bring yarn through loop as shown.

❹ Twisted knit st complete. On WS, purl through the back loop. Note: this symbol is also used for the m1 increase.

☒ TWISTED PURL ST (PTBL, OR PURL THROUGH BACK LOOP)

 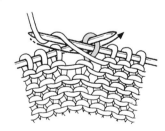 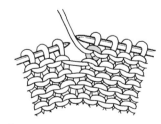

❶ Insert RN into back loop of next st on LN as shown, in the direction of the arrow.

❷ Wrap yarn over RN, and bring through loop as shown.

❸ Twisted purl st complete. On WS, knit through the back loop.

⊡ YARNOVER (YO)

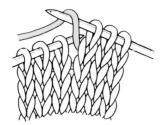 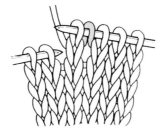 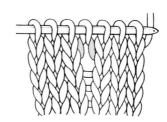

❶ From front, wrap yarn over RN as shown.

❷ K the next st.

❸ Continue in pattern on next row, working over the yo. On WS, work yo in the same way (front to back).

Decreases

⊠ SLIP 1, K1, PASS SLIPPED ST OVER (SKP)

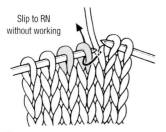 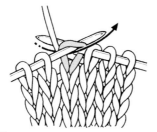 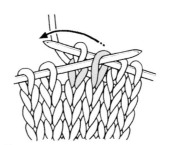 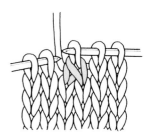

Slip to RN without working

❶ Insert RN into next st on LN as if to knit, slip it to RN.

❷ Knit next st on LN.

❸ With tip of LN, lift slipped st over the k st as shown.

❹ Skp complete. On WS, ssp.

⊠ SLIP 2, CHANGE POSITION, PURL 2 TOGETHER (SSP)

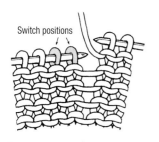 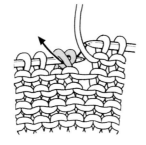 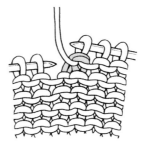 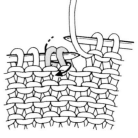

Switch positions

❶ Change the positions of the next st on LN so that st 1 crosses to the left over st 2.

❷ Insert RN into both stitches together, from right to left, as shown.

❸ Wrap yarn over RN and bring it through both sts (p2tog).

❹ *Alternate method (p2 togtbl):* Insert RN through the back legs of the next 2 sts together, as shown, and p2togtbl (purl 2 together through back loop). On WS, skp.

⊠ KNIT 2 TOGETHER (K2TOG)

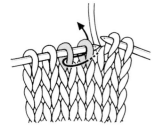 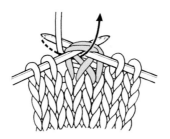 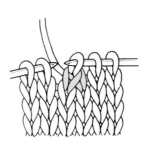

❶ Insert RN into next 2 sts on LN together as shown.

❷ Wrap yarn over RN and k both together.

❸ K2tog complete. On WS, p2tog.

⊿ PURL 2 TOGETHER (P2TOG)

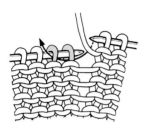 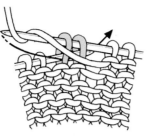 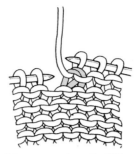

❶ Insert RN into next 2 sts on LN together.

❷ Wrap yarn over RN and bring through both.

❸ P2tog complete. On WS, k2tog.

⊼ CENTERED DOUBLE DECREASE (CDD)

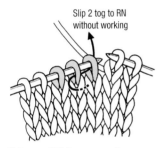 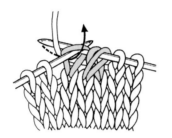 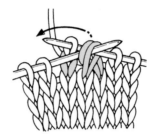 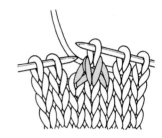

Slip 2 tog to RN without working

❶ Insert RN into next 2 sts on LN together as if to knit, and slip both to RN.

❷ Wrap yarn over RN.

❸ With tip of LN, pass 2 sl sts over together.

❹ CDD complete.

⊼ LEFT DOUBLE DECREASE (SK2P)

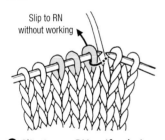 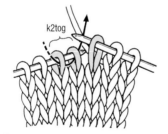 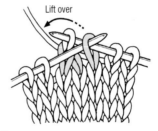 

Slip to RN without working

k2tog

Lift over

❶ Slip 1 st to RN as if to knit.

❷ K2tog the next 2 sts on LN.

❸ With tip of LN, pass the sl st over.

❹ Sk2p complete. On WS, sl 1 kwise, sl 2 tog kwise, insert tip of LN into all 3 sts from right to left, slip all 3 sts back to LN and p3tog

⊼ KNIT 3 TOGETHER (K3TOG OR RIGHT DOUBLE DECREASE)

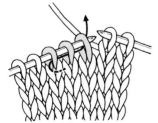 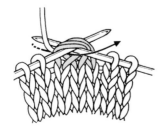 

❶ Insert RN into next 3 sts on LN together as if to knit.

❷ Wrap yarn over RN and bring through.

❸ K3tog complete. On WS, purl 3 together.

⚹ LEFT QUADRUPLE DECREASE (LQD)

To work on WS: do not work the next 5 sts, but pass sts 2, 3, 4 and 5 over st 1, then purl st 1.

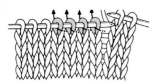 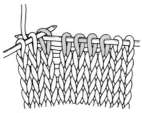 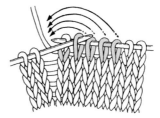 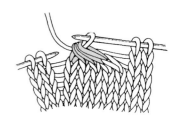

❶ With tip of RN, slip the next 4 sts on LN knitwise, one at a time, to RN.

❷ K 5th st.

❸ One at a time, pass the sl sts over the k st.

❹ LQD complete.

Note: symbol may be elongated as shown below.

Increases

⊬ RIGHT LIFTED INCREASE IN KNIT

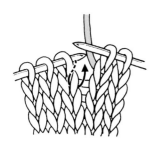 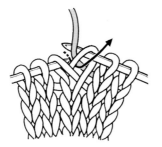 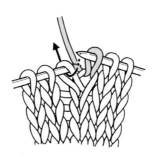 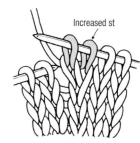

Increased st

❶ With tip of RN, pick up knitwise the right leg of the st in the row below next st on LN knitwise as shown.

❷ K lifted st.

❸ K next st on LN.

❹ Right lifted inc complete.

⊬ RIGHT LIFTED INCREASE IN PURL

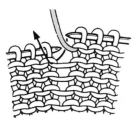 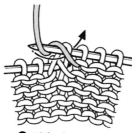 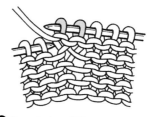

❶ With tip of RN, pick up the purl bump of the st in the row below next st on LN from top to bottom as shown.

❷ P lifted st.

❸ P next st on LN.

⊾ LEFT LIFTED INCREASE

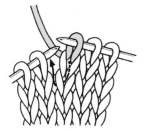 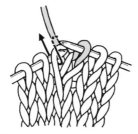 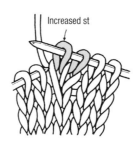

Increased st

❶ K next st on LN. Then, with tip of RN, pick up the left leg of the st two rows below the st just worked. Place it on LN.

❷ K lifted st.

❸ Left lifted inc complete. On WS, work left lifted increase in purl.

⌐ LEFT LIFTED INCREASE IN PURL

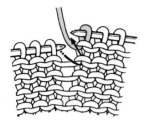

❶ P next st on LN. Then, with tip of LN, pick up the left leg of the st two rows below the st just worked.

❷ P lifted st.

❸ Left lefted inc in purl complete.

  **MAKE 3 FROM 1 WITH YO CENTER**

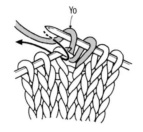

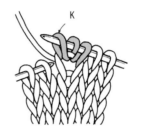

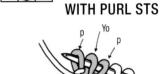 **MAKE 3 FROM 1 WITH PURL STS**

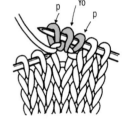

❶ K 1, but do not remove st from LN.

❷ Yo, then k the same st again. Remove from LN.

❸ Make 3 from 1 complete.

❹ On WS, p, yo, p into same st.

 MAKE 3 FROM 1 WITH P CENTER

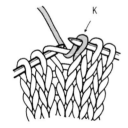

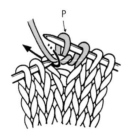

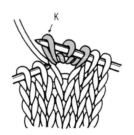

❶ K1, but do not remove st from LN.

❷ P into the same st, but do not remove from LN.

❸ K into the same st. Remove from LN.

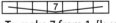 To make 5 from 1, k, yo, k, yo, k into same st.

To make 7 from 1, [k, yo] 3 times, k into same st.

⌧ CROSS 1 TO LEFT

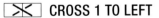

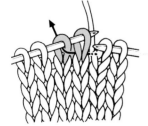

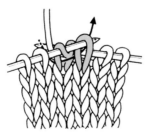

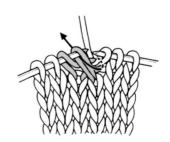

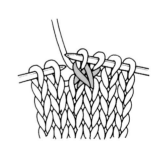

❶ Insert tip of RN from the back into second st on LN, as shown.

❷ K second st; do not remove from LN.

❸ K first st on LN.

❹ Move both sts to RN.

⊠ CROSS 1 TO LEFT: ALTERNATE METHOD

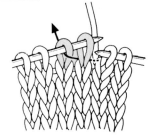 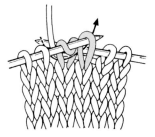 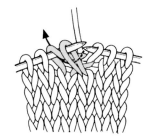 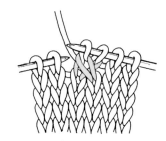

❶ Insert tip of RN into second st on LN from behind, as shown.

❷ K second st; do not remove from LN.

❸ K2tog tbl with both sts on LN.

❹ Completed st.

⊠ CROSS 1 TO LEFT OVER PURL

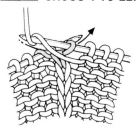 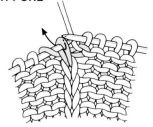 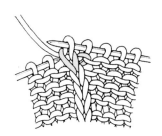

❶ Insert tip of RN from the back into second st on LN, as shown, bringing leg of st from behind; wrap yarn over RN and p second st.

❷ K first st on LN.

❸ Move both sts to RN. On WS, exchange the positions of the next 2 sts, crossing st 1 over st 2; p st 2, then k st 1 (chart 10 only)

⊠ CROSS 1 TO RIGHT

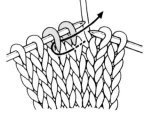  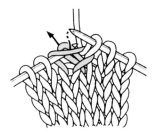 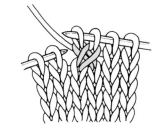

❶ Insert tip of RN knitwise from the front into second st on LN .

❷ Wrap yarn over RN and k second st; do not remove from LN.

❸ Insert tip of RN knitwise into first st on LN and k.

❹ Move both sts to RN.

⊠ CROSS 1 TO RIGHT: ALTERNATE METHOD

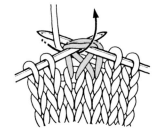 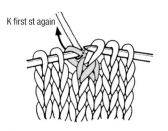 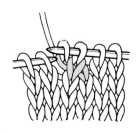

❶ K2tog; do not remove from LN.

❷ K first st again, as shown.

❸ Completed st.

CROSS 1 TO RIGHT OVER PURL

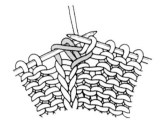

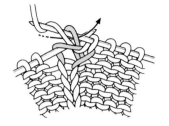

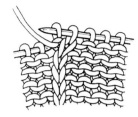

❶ Insert tip of RN knitwise from the front into second st on LN; wrap yarn over RN and k second st; do not remove from LN.

❷ P first st on LN.

❸ Move both sts to RN. On WS, exchange the positions of the next 2 sts, crossing st 2 over st 1; k st 2, then p st 1.

MORE ABOUT CROSSED STITCH SYMBOLS

Crossed stitches involve two stitches: one over another, to the right or to the left. The symbol covers two boxes. The way the symbol is drawn gives you the key:

- The stitch drawn with an unbroken line lies in front when the stitch is complete.
- The stitch drawn with a broken line lies in back. If there's a purl dash next to this line, the stitch in back is a purl.
- For example, this is the symbol for a one-over-one cross to the right:
- When the unbroken line is straight, it's a knit stitch.
- The stitch in front may also be a twisted knit stitch, such as this one: The stitch in back is a plain knit.
- The stitch in back may also be a purl stitch, in which case you'll see the "purl dash" next to it:
- Sometimes two twisted stitches cross:

The stitches in front may be plain knits, purls, or twisted knit stitches. The stitches in back may also be knits, purls, or twisted stitches. Twisted-stitch crosses from this book are shown in the Additional Symbols table on pp. 323-327.

There are several ways to work crossed stitches. These illustrations showed you two methods:

- Work the second stitch, then work the first
- Work the second stitch, then work two together

Crossed stitches can also be worked in at least two more ways:

- Use a cable needle
- Exchange the positions of the two stitches ("cabling without a cable needle") before working them.

Cable Stitches

CABLE 2 TWISTED KTBL OVER 2 K TO THE LEFT

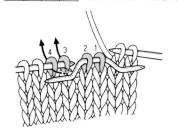
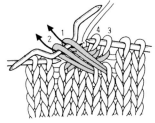
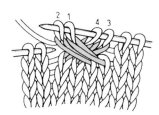

❶ Place 2 sts on CN and hold to front; k2.

❷ K2tbl from CN.

❸ Completed left cable.

CABLE 2 TWISTED KTBL OVER 2 K TO THE RIGHT

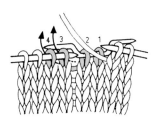
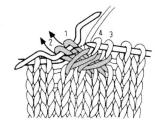
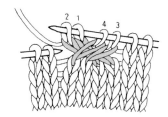

❶ Place 2 sts on CN and hold to back; k2.

❷ K2tbl from CN.

❸ Completed right cable.

5-ST CABLE TO THE LEFT WITH CENTER PURL

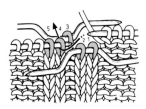
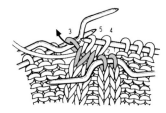
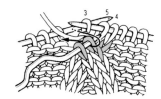

❶ Place 2 sts on CN, hold to front; place next st on another CN, hold to back.

❷ K2, then p1 from back CN.

❸ K2 from front CN.

5-ST CABLE TO THE RIGHT WITH CENTER PURL

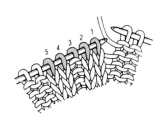

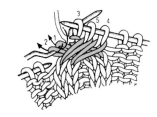
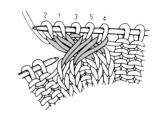

❶ Place 2 sts on CN, hold to back, place next st on another CN, hold to back.

❷ K2, then p1 from second CN.

❸ K2 from first CN.

❹ Completed right cable.

MORE ABOUT CABLE STITCH SYMBOLS

Although these illustrations showed only four cable stitches, the Additional Symbols table (pp. 323-327) includes many more. Like crossed stitches, cable stitch symbols are drawn to look like the stitches they represent. To decode a cable symbol:

- Count how many stitches are involved in total. This may be an even or odd number. Examples:

  6-stitch cable, crossing to the right

  3-stitch cable, with 2 stitches crossing to the left over 1 stitch

- Check how many stitches cross other stitches, and which way they lean. Cables aren't always 2-over-2 or other even numbers. The book includes some that are 3-over-1, 3-over-5 and other variations. This seven-stitch cable has 3 stitches crossing to the left over 4 stitches.

- As with crossed stitches, those drawn with an unbroken line lie in front when the stitch is complete, and those with broken lines lie in back. You can also see, from where each line begins and ends, where a given stitch will end up: it may start in position 3 and end in position 1, for instance. There may also be a purl at the center of the cable. Here's an example of a 5-stitch cable with a purl at the center:

This one requires 2 cable needles: place 2 on a CN, hold to back; place 1 on another CN, hold to back; knit 2; purl 1 from second CN, then knit 2 from first CN.

- Cables may be worked with knits, purls, and twisted stitches. On some of the smaller charts, it may be hard to see the purl dashes for the stitches lying behind. Check the next row to see whether the stitch is a knit, purl or ktbl.

Two twisted knit stitches crossed over   two regular knit stitches

Two twisted knit stitches crossed over   one purl stitch (note the "purl dash" on the third stitch)

PASS 1 ST OVER TO RIGHT

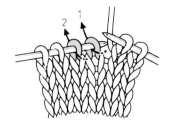

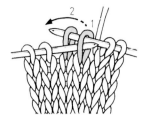

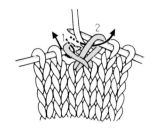

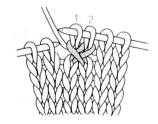

❶ Slip 2 sts to RN knitwise.

❷ Use tip of LN to lift the first over the second (without dropping it).

❸ Replace both sts on LN, then k both sts in their new positions.

❹ Completed pass 1 to left.

PASS 1 ST OVER TO RIGHT

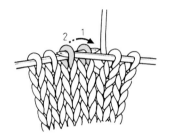

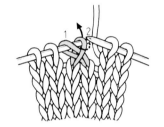

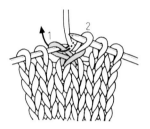

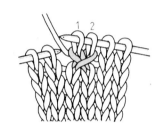

❶ With tip of LN, lift 2nd st over first st on LN (without dropping it).

❷ Replace st on LN.

❸ K both sts in their new positions.

❹ Completed pass 1 to right.

Slip Stitches

SLIP ST WYIB

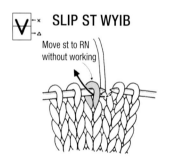

Move st to RN without working

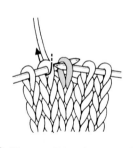

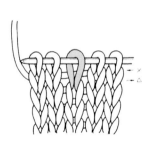

VARIATION: SLIP P ST WYIB

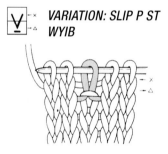

❶ With yarn in back, insert tip of RN into next st as if to purl.

❷ Slip st to RN without working it.

❸ K subsequent sts.

❹ When the st to be slipped is a p, slip in the same way.

SLIP ST WYIF

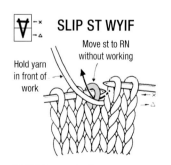

Move st to RN without working

Hold yarn in front of work

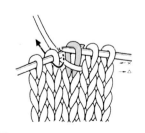

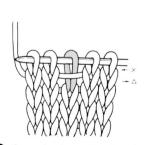

VARIATION: SLIP P ST WYIF

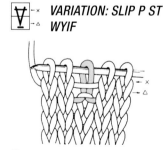

❶ With yarn in front, insert tip of RN into next st as if to purl.

❷ Slip st to RN without working it. K next st.

❸ Slipped st has a "bar" on front of work.

❹ When the st to be slipped is a p, slip the same way.

MORE ABOUT SLIP STITCH SYMBOLS

This book introduces a range of slip stitches. The basics are illustrated in this section. Please read through this additional explanation. It will help you understand how to interpret variations on the basic slip stitches when you encounter them.

- A slip st is worked over at least two rows. On the first row, you work the stitch and on the second, you slip it. The first illustration on p. 18 shows the stitch slipped with yarn in back (wyib), so that the unworked strand of yarn doesn't show on the front of the work. The second illustration shows the stitch slipped with yarn in front (wyif), so the unworked strand does show.

 Basic slip stitch over 2 rows with yarn in back

 Basic slip stitch over 2 rows with yarn in front

- The symbol for the slip st is an elongated "V". Think of it this way: the bottom tip of the V is worked in pattern (k, p or yo); this stitch is where the maneuver starts, but it's not slipped yet. The top of the "legs" of the V is the completion of the slip—it's the last row where you slip. So when a stitch is slipped over three, four or more rows: work the st at the bottom tip of the V, and slip it over the appropriate number of rows. Examples:

 Knit st slipped over 3 rows (chart 85)

 Purl st slipped over 5 rows (chart 86)

- Keep yarn in back of RS, unless it's charted as wyif. For slip sts wyib when working back and forth, be careful to keep the unworked yarn at the back of the work—meaning you'll slip wyif when WS is facing you.

- Slip sts may be crossed: see the method on p. 25. If crossing a slip st over more than two rows, it's easiest to slip the st in its original position until you reach the row above completion (that is, above the end of the legs of the V), then move the st to its new position. Examples:

 Sl the 3rd st over 3 rows. On row 4, use a CN to move it to the new position and work in contrast color. (Chart 79)

 Sl the 2 sts for 5 rows. On row 6, change their positions to cross and work them in contrast color. (Chart 83)

Brioche Stitches

° BRIOCHE KNIT ST OVER 3 ROWS

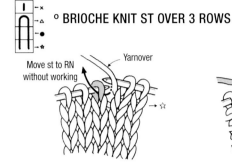

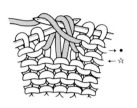

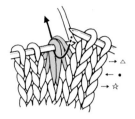

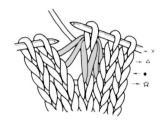

❶ Lay the yarn over RN as shown, front to back, and slip the first st purlwise.

❷ On the next row, lay the yarn over RN as shown, front to back, and slip the sl st from the previous row and the strand of yarn over it purlwise to RN.

❸ On final row, k under all strands.

❹ 3-row brioche st complete.

BRIOCHE PURL ST OVER 3 ROWS

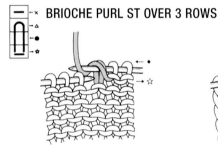

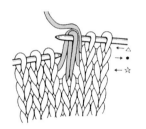

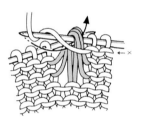

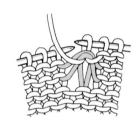

❶ Slip 1st st purlwise to RN, then lay the yarn over RN as shown, front to back.

❷ On the next row, lay the yarn over RN as shown, front to back, and slip the sl st from previous row and the strand of yarn over it purlwise to RN.

❸ On final row, p under all strands together.

❹ 3-row brioche p st complete.

BRIOCHE KTBL OVER 3 ROWS

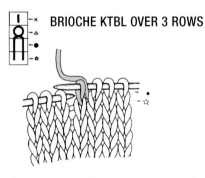

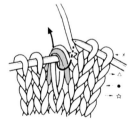

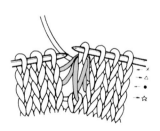

❶ Lay the yarn over RN as shown, front to back, then insert RN into back loop of the st to twist, and slip it to RN.

❷ On the next row, lay the yarn over RN as shown, front to back, and slip the sl st from the previous row and the strand of yarn over it purlwise to RN.

❸ On final row, k under all strands.

❹ 3-row brioche ktbl complete.

MORE ABOUT BRIOCHE STITCH SYMBOLS

Brioche stitches are somewhat similar to slip stitches, because they lift a stitch from one row to the next, but they're worked a bit differently. Instead of slipping a st wyif or wyib, you lay the working yarn over the st to be slipped. Brioche symbols look like an arch, as illustrated on p. 20. Only a couple are illustrated below, but many more appear in the charts in this book.

- A brioche st is worked over at least 2 rows. The st in the first row (at the bottom end of the legs of the arch) is worked normally. In the next row, lay the working yarn over the RN and sl the st, so that 2 loops are on the RN (see illustrations). For a two-row brioche st, complete it on the third row by working under both the paired yo and sl st.

- The rounded top of the arch is the last row slipped; the brioche st is completed when you knit into it in the next row. So if your brioche st extends over three, four or more rows, continue to sl the sts, laying the working yarn over the st each time, until you reach the row above the top of the arch. Examples:

3-row brioche knit (chart 36)

4-row brioche purl (chart 45)

To compare the techniques and results of slip sts and brioche sts, try working charts 82, 86 or 90, which use both slip and brioche methods.

- How to read, so you can parse them out if unfamiliar:
- In the row at the bottom end of the "legs," sl the st knitwise, at the same time laying the working yarn over the top of the st
- On the next row, sl the st again, again laying the working yarn over the st
- Sl for as many rows as indicated: 2 or 3 rows are the most common in this book, but some are longer.
- When you reach the row above the "arch," work under all the strands to finish the lift.

Variety Stitches

⟨QJ⟩ BACKWARD LOOP (E-WRAP) INCREASE

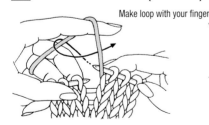

Make loop with your finger

❶ With tip of RN, go behind yarn and catch strand in the direction of the arrow.

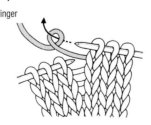

❷ Insert tip of RN into the loop as shown.

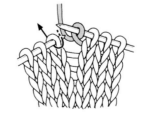

❸ K next st.

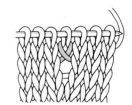

❹ Completed backward loop increase.

DOUBLE-WRAPPED KNIT ST

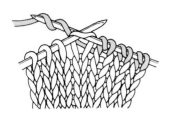

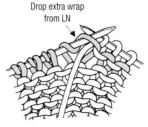

Drop extra wrap from LN

VARIATION: TRIPLE-WRAPPED KNIT ST

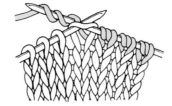

❶ On knit side, insert RN into next st, wrap yarn twice around RN, and bring through the st.

❷ On purl side, insert RN as if to purl, wrap yarn twice around RN, and bring both loops through the st.

❸ Insert RN into next st, wrap yarn three times around RN, and bring through the st.

LIFTED PURL

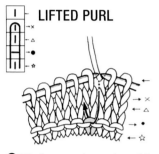

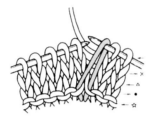

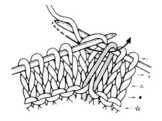

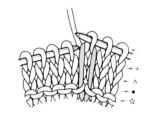

❶ Work sts as charted until 2 rows above the p st. With tip of RN, pick up the "bump" of the p st from beneath, in the direction of the arrow.

❷ Picked-up st on RN.

❸ K the next st on LN, bringing yarn through both that st and the picked-up purl st.

❹ Completed lifted purl.

CROSSED LIFTED PURL

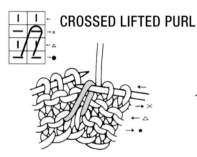

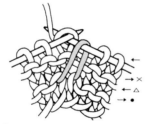

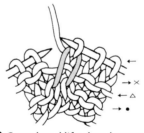

❶ Work sts as charted until 2 rows above the p st. With tip of RN, pick up the *downward-facing* part of the purl bump (between the next 2 sts).

❷ K the next st on LN and bring the st through both the st and the picked-up st.

❸ Completed lifted and crossed purl.

WRAPPED KNOT ST

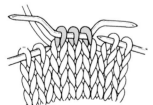

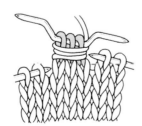

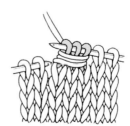

❶ K 3, then place 3 sts on CN.

❷ Wrap the working yarn around these 3 sts counter-clockwise (from back to front). Drop yarn in back.

❸ Move the 3 sts to RN without working them. Note that both the number of sts wrapped, and the number of wraps, may vary. Count the number of sts involved, and wrap as many times as the tiny numeral at left.

ONE ST PULLED OUT TO LEFT

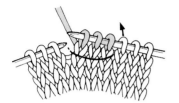 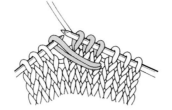 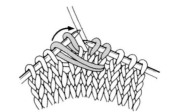 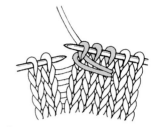

❶ Insert tip of LN into space between the 3rd and 4th sts on RN as shown, front to back.

❷ Wrap yarn over LN and pull out a loop.

❸ Slip 1st st on RN to LN purlwise. With tip of RN, pass the pulled-out loop over the st.

❹ Move st back to RN.

ONE ST PULLED OUT TO RIGHT

K the next 2 sts. Note that the sts involved may be knits, purls or a combination.

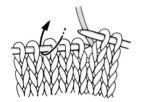  

❶ Insert tip of RN into space between the 3rd and 4th sts on LN as shown, front to back.

❷ Wrap yarn over RN and pull out a loop, then insert tip of RN into next st on LN.

❸ Knit loop and st together, then k2 to complete.

PULLED-OUT ST WITH RIGHT-LEANING DEC ON NEXT ROW

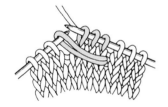 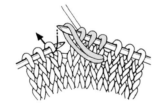  

❶ On the first row, insert tip of LN into space between the 3rd and 4th sts on RN as shown, front to back; wrap yarn over LN and pull out a loop.

❷ K the next st.

❸ On the next row, p2tog the pulled-out loop with the st next to it.

❹ Completed st shown on RS.

PULLED-OUT ST WITH LEFT-LEANING DEC ON NEXT ROW

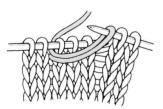 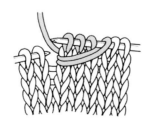 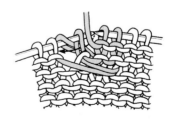 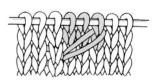

❶ On the first row, insert tip of RN into space between the 3rd and 4th sts on LN as shown, front to back; wrap yarn over RN and pull out a loop.

❷ K the next 3 sts.

❸ On the next row, insert tip of RN into the next st and the pulled-out loop, as shown by the arrow, and p2tog.

❹ Completed st shown on RS. Note that the sts involved may be knits, purls or a combination, and a different number of sts may be called for (as in chart #146).

⊏⊏⊣⊣ㅇ YO PASSED OVER TO LEFT

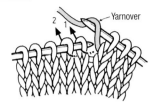 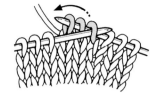 

❶ Yo, then sl the next 2 sts on LN to RN knitwise, one at a time.

❷ With tip of LN, lift the yo over those 2 sts.

❸ K the next st and continue.

ㅇ⊢⊢⊢⊐ YO PASSED OVER TO RIGHT (WORKED ON WS)

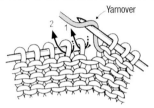 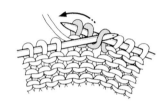 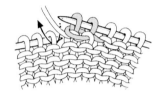 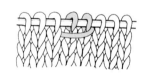

❶ Yo, then sl the next 2 sts on LN to RN purlwise, one at a time.

❷ With tip of LN, lift the yo over those 2 sts.

❸ P the next st and continue.

❹ Completed st shown on RS.

⊏⊢○⊢⊐ PASSED-OVER KNOT ST TO THE LEFT

 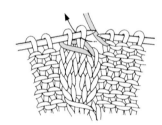 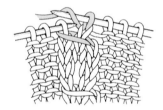 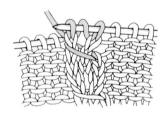

❶ Sl 3 sts purlwise from LN to RN. Insert tip of LN into the third st on RN, lift it over the first 2 sts and let it drop.

❷ K next st.

❸ Yo.

❹ K next st.

⊢⊢○⊢⊐ PASSED-OVER KNOT ST TO THE RIGHT

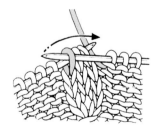 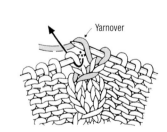 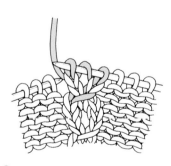

❶ Insert tip of RN into third st on LN; lift it up and over the first 2 sts and let it drop.

❷ K, yo.

❸ K.

PASSED-OVER SLIP ST TO THE LEFT

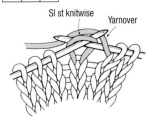

SI st knitwise   Yarnover

Lift over

❶ Yo, then insert RN into next st knitwise and sl it.

❷ K the next 2 sts. With tip of LN, lift the slipped st over the 2 st just worked.

❸ Completed st.

 PASSED-OVER SLIP ST TO THE RIGHT

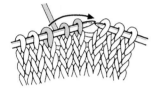 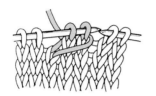  

❶ K2, then return them to LN. Insert tip of RN into the 3rd st.

❷ Lift 3rd st over the 2 st just worked.

❸ Return those 2 st to RN and yo.

❹ Completed st.

 SL ST BELOW CROSSED LEFT

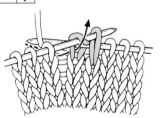 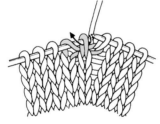 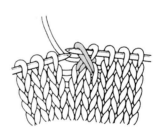

❶ Insert tip of RN knitwise into 2nd st on LN from behind, as shown. Do not work the 1st st.

❷ K the 2nd st, then sl 1st st purlwise to RN.

❸ Slip both sts to RN.

SL ST BELOW CROSSED RIGHT

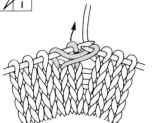 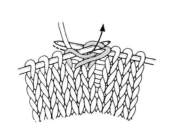 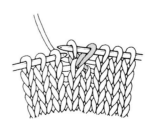

❶ Insert tip of RN purlwise into 2nd st on LN from the front, as shown, without working it.

❷ K first st on LN.

❸ Slip both sts purlwise to RN.

✕ DEC 3, THEN INC 3 (VARIATION ON "BLACKBERRY" OR "TRINITY" STITCH)

✕ VARIATION

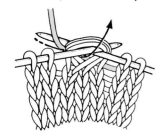

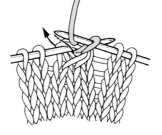

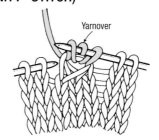

❶ K3 tog. Do not remove from LN.

❷ Yo, then K3 tog again with the same sts.

❸ Completed st.

❹ K3tog (the st marked 3). Without removing from LN, pick up the other 2 sts just worked and k them (sts marked 1 and 2).

PULLED-UP LOOP

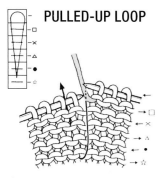

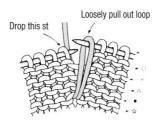

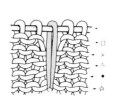

❶ Insert tip of RN, from front to back, into the center of the st 4 rows below the next st on LN (counting to the tip of the "V").

❷ Wrap yarn over RN, and loosely pull out a loop to the front. Drop the next st from LN.

❸ Completed st.

TRIPLE PULLED-UP LOOPS

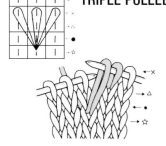

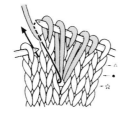

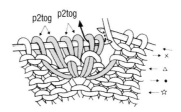

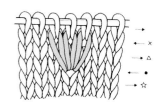

❶ K 1, then insert tip of RN, from front to back, into the center of the st 3 rows below the next st on LN (counting to the tip of the "V"). Loosely pull out a loop.

❷ K next st, then pull out another loop from the same place] twice = 6 loops.

❸ On next row, p2tog 3 times, joining each loop with the st next to it on the left.

❹ Completed st.

DOUBLE PULLED-UP LOOPS

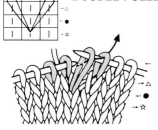

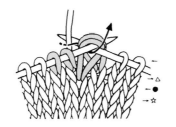

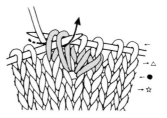

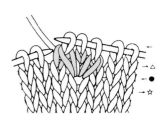

❶ Sl 1 to RN. Insert tip of RN, from front to back, into the center of the st 2 rows below the next st on LN. Loosely pull out a loop

❷ K2tog the loop with the sl st.

❸ K1. Pull out another loop from the same place.

❹ SSK this loop with the st to its left.

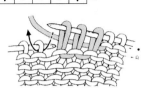

PULLED-UP SLIP STITCHES (ALSO CALLED BUTTERFLY STITCH)

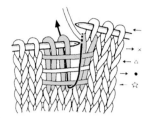

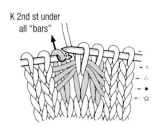

K 2nd st under all "bars"

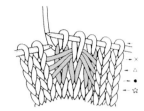

❶ K all sts on row 1. On row 2 (WS), sl 3 purlwise with yarn in back (at RS of work).

❷ On row 3 (RS), sl the same 3 sts wyif. On row 4 (WS), sl the same 3 sts wyib. On row 5 (RS), k 1st st, then bring tip of RN under all 3 "bars" and k 2nd st.

❸ K 3rd st.

❹ Completed butterfly st
Note: in chart #8, there is only one row of sl wyif

STACKED CENTERED DOUBLE DECS (CDD) (USED ONLY IN CHART 337)

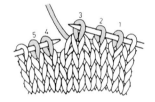

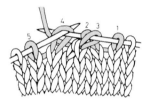

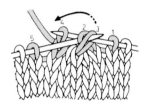

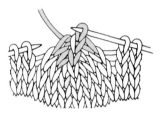

❶ Work one CDD: sl 2 tog knitwise, k1, p2sso. Completed st on RN is st 3.

❷ Return sts 2 and 3 to RN. Sl those 2 tog knitwise, k st 4.

❸ Pass sts 3 and 2 over st 4.

❹ Return sts 4 and 1 to LN, sl those 2 tog knitwise, k st 5, then pass sts 4 and 1 over it.

Bobbles

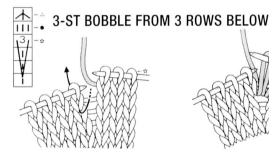

3-ST BOBBLE FROM 3 ROWS BELOW

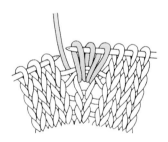

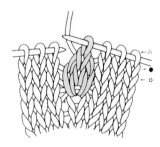

❶ Work in stockinette to the row with the numeral "3." Insert tip of RN, from front to back, into the center of the st 3 rows below the next st on LN. (Note that the "V" is not a slip st in this case.)

❷ Loosely pull out a loop of yarn, yo, loosely pull out another loop from the same place.

❸ Let next st on LN drop off.

❹ On next row (WS), p these 3 sts. On following row (RS), work these 3 sts as CDD. Note: there are several variations of this bobble: it may be worked over more rows, the background sts may be purls (as in chart #74), and the final decrease may be k3tog.

• 5-ST BOBBLE FROM 3 ROWS BELOW, COMPLETED ON WS

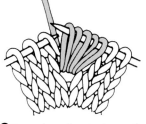  

❶ Work in stockinette to the row with the numeral "5." Insert tip of RN, from front to back, into the center of the st 3 rows below the next st on LN. (Note that the "V" is not a slip st in this case.)

❷ Loosely pull out a loop of yarn, yo, loosely pull out another loop from the same place, yo, loosely pull out a third loop.

❸ Let next st on LN drop off.

❹ On next row (WS), insert a crochet hook through all 5 sts and draw through a st, then place it on RN." Note: there are several variations of this bobble: it may be worked over more rows, the background sts may be purls, and the final decrease may be right-leaning, left-leaning or centered.

5-ST BOBBLE OVER 5 ROWS

  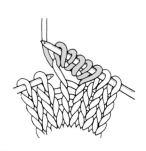 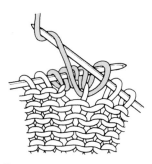

❶ Make 5 sts from 1 as follows: k next st but do not remove from LN.

❷ Yo, k same st again, do not remove from LN.

❸ Yo, k same st again, move st to RN. 5 sts made.

❹ Turn work and p5.

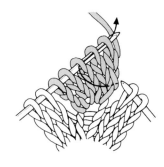 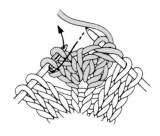 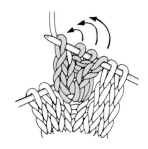 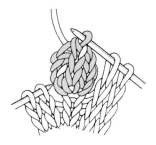

❺ Turn work and k5, turn work and p5. Then insert tip of RN knitwise into sts 1, 2 and 3 together (arrow). Sl these 3 to RN.

❻ K2tog sts 4 and 5.

❼ Pass the 3 sl sts over.

❽ Completed bobble. Note: similar bobbles may be worked with 3, 5 or 7 sts, and with more or fewer short rows.

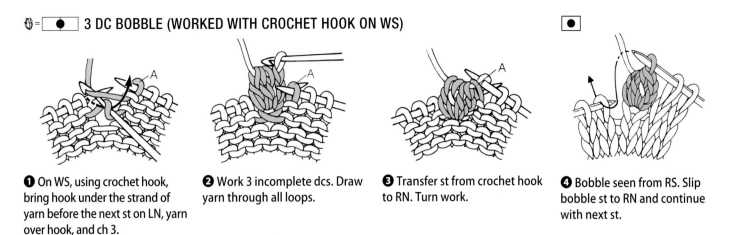

3 DC BOBBLE (WORKED WITH CROCHET HOOK ON WS)

❶ On WS, using crochet hook, bring hook under the strand of yarn before the next st on LN, yarn over hook, and ch 3.

❷ Work 3 incomplete dcs. Draw yarn through all loops.

❸ Transfer st from crochet hook to RN. Turn work.

❹ Bobble seen from RS. Slip bobble st to RN and continue with next st.

This bobble is explained on p. 327 of the Additional Symbols table. Here, you see how it is worked onto the WS of a knitted fabric.

MORE ABOUT BOBBLES

A "bobble" is a knot of yarn, worked into one stitch, that appears on the surface of the knitted fabric. It's usually formed by increasing into a stitch, working one or two short rows over the new stitches, then decreasing them away. (An increase that extends over several rows usually makes a "leaf.")

In this book, bobbles are coded with a heavy black dot. Some are footnoted next to the chart; those that appear more frequently are defined in the Additional Symbols table (pp. 323-327). Both knit and crocheted bobbles are included. Like knit bobbles, crocheted bobbles are worked into a single stitch, but with a crochet hook.

Because each bobble fits in a single stitch, feel free to substitute bobbles to suit your preferences.

STITCH PATTERN NOTES

Pattern 33

⬜️ RS: k3tog   WS: p3tog

⬜️ RS: sl2kp   WS: sssp

⬜️ RS: left lifted inc with yarnover between new st and original st (p. 12)
WS: right lifted inc with yarnover between new st and original st (p. 13)

⬜️ RS: right lifted inc with yarnover between new st and original st (p. 12)
WS: left lifted inc with yarnover between new st and original st (p. 13)

Patterns 79–106 These use slip and brioche stitches of varying heights. Both knits and purls are slipped; some are crossed; and several combine sl sts with brioche. See p. 19 and 21 to understand how to interpret the slip and brioche symbols. Color changes are indicated by letters along the right edges of the charts.

Pattern 159

⬜️ = wrap yarn twice (see p. 22)

 = on second row: lift the 2 double-wrapped sts over the 5 purls and drop them (similar to p. 25, passed the opposite way.)

Pattern 322

 = WS: purl, wrapping yarn 3 times around needle

⬜️ = Sl 5 sts from LN to RN, dropping extra wraps; sl elongated sts back to LN and k5tog, but do not remove sts from LN, yo, k5tog the same 5 sts again, yo, k5tog the same 5 one more time and move to RN.

Patterns 408–556 These consist primarily of cable patterns. Be sure to read through the introductory material (p. 17) about how to interpret cable symbols.

Pattern 434

 = place 3 st on CN, hold to back; k1, p first st from CN; k1, p second st from CN; k1, p third st from CN

 = place 3 st on CN, hold to front; p1, k first st from CN; p1, k second st from CN; p1, k 3rd st from CN

 = place 1 st on CN, hold to back, k1; place another st on CN, hold to back, k1; place a third st on CN, hold to back, k1;p3 from CN

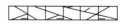 = place 1 st on CN, hold to front, p1; place another st on CN, hold to front, p1; place a third st on CN, hold to front, p1; k3 from CN

Patterns 574–580 These use a slightly unusual technique that is a variation of slipped stitches. Make the inverted "U" stitches by picking up the downward-facing purl bump from three rows below. See p. 21 for an illustrated explanation.

Patterns 581–615 These provide more colorwork. All are worked in stockinette stitch. The symbols in the charts represent colors rather than stitch manipulations.

Patterns 616–631 These are mosaic stitches. Mosaic patterns are worked in garter stitch, with 2 rows of one color at a time. Stitches are slipped with the yarn in back of the work to show the contrast color on top. For all of these, slip as if to purl with yarn at the back of the RS (slip wyib on RS, slip wyif on WS).

Patterns 632–638 These use an unusual method of creating a lacy pattern. Instead of a yarnover, you use the tip of the RN to pick up the strand of yarn between the last st worked and the next st, and knit or purl the strand without twisting it—unlike the m1 increase. This new stitch will lean to the right or left depending on the placement of the corresponding decrease. The symbols used are:

◻️ RS: pick up the strand between the last st and the next st and knit it. WS: pick up the strand between the last st and the next st and purl it.

◻️ RS: pick up the strand between the last st and the next st and purl it.

◻️ RS: pick up the strand between the last st and the next st and knit it. WS: pick up the strand between the last st and the next st and purl it.

◻️ RS: pick up the strand between the last st and the next st and purl it.

Patterns 639–645 These provide more colorwork in stockinette stitch. The symbols in the charts represent colors rather than stitch manipulations.

Patterns 646–649 These four patterns create surface decorations on the knitted fabric. Background stitches are all stockinette. Strips of knitting in contrast colors are worked on one row, then secured on a later row. Two of the patterns also use tuck stitches.

For a printable pdf of this page visit https://tuttlepublishing.com/1000-japanese-knitting-crochet-stitches

Pattern 646

- On row 5, at the point where you begin the strip, work 2 sts in main color (MC), then return them to LN and, with another needle or DPN, pick up 2 sts from below those sts in contrast yarn (CC). With separate needle, work the 2 sts indicated in CC for 6 rows of stockinette. Place these sts on a holder and leave the strip hanging at front of work.
- Pick up main color. With tip of RN, pick up the purl bumps of MC that are visible below the CC sts. Continue in MC. Make more strips where indicated, to row 8. When you reach the sts where the strip should attach, pick up the strip and work p2tog (k2tog if working in the round) with one st from the strip and one st of the main color, for 2 sts.
- Work the bobbles in main or contrast yarn as charted.

Pattern 647

- On Row 1, at the point where you begin the strip, work 3 sts in main color (MC), then return them to LN and, with another needle or DPN, pick up 3 sts from below those sts in contrast yarn (CC). With separate needle, work the 3 sts indicated in CC for 10 rows of stockinette. Place these sts on a holder and leave the strip hanging at front of work.
- Pick up main color. With tip of RN, pick up the purl bumps of MC that are visible below the CC sts. Continue in MC for 2 sts, then work another strip in CC.
- On row 5, at front of work, catch the two strips of CC by passing MC over them, between the two sts indicated.
- Work the crossed sts in MC where charted
- In row 9, work to the sts where the strip should attach, pick up the strip and work k2tog with one st from the strip and one st of the main color, for 3 sts.

Pattern 648

Work the indicated 5 sts in contrast color as 4-row tuck stitches:

- Drop MC and work 4 rows of stockinette in CC over 5 sts.
- On the 5th row of CC, join top of tuck to 5th row below as follows: With tip of RN, pick up the purl bump in MC behind the current st from 5 rows below. Place it on LN and k2tog with the first st of tuck.
- Repeat 4 more times to complete the tuck.

Pattern 649

= Work these 5 sts in garter st in CC for 20 rows.

- On row 1, work 3 sts in MC, then 5 sts in CC in garter for 20 rows. Leave this strip hanging on a holder at front of work, rejoin MC and pick up 5 sts at the base of the strip, and continue.
- In row 12, pick up the strip, twist it 180°, and secure it by working those sts as p2tog one st of CC with one st of MC on the indicated WS row (k2tog if working in the round).

= Work these 4 sts as 4-row tuck stitches in CC (see pattern 648).

Patterns 650–653 The four stitch patterns in this section are unusual and challenging. The patterns create a fabric similar to double knitting, with two layers in the patterned areas. On one side, we see a lacy pattern superimposed on reverse stockinette. On the other side, we see plain stockinette. The original Japanese book called this technique "reversible knitting." It could also be considered a type of double knitting. A more appropriate term might be "overlaid lace."

The basic technique: using two colors, background stitches (purls on RS) are worked with both yarns held together. For the lace patterning, the yarns are separated. The front yarn makes the lacy pattern, and the back yarn creates the background, which consists of reverse stockinette sts on RS. On the RS, all sts look like stockinette, some in a single color and some with both colors together.

Knitters have devised several ways to work this technique. It could be approached like double knitting, using one set of needles and slipping stitches around as necessary to make the lace pattern. It could also be done with two circular needles, each holding some of the stitches.

The technique described here was demonstrated by one of the technical experts from Nihon Vogue, the publisher of the original book. Most knitters will probably find it one of the easier methods.

Overlaid lace

Cast on to your selected needle with both colors held together. A return row is optional.

Have ready two DPNs in the same size (DPN1 and DPN2) for the lace patterning on RS rows. Your main needles are referred to as LN and RN.

- Slip all sts purlwise.
- Each vertical panel of lace is worked separately.
- Important: be careful to keep both strands of yarn between the two layers of knitted fabric.
- The sts keyed as reverse stockinette on RS are purled with both colors together.
- Front color means the yarn that's visible on the front of the fabric; back color means the yarn that forms the stitches behind it. Note that front and back colors swap across the row.
- The charts here don't include edge stitches, but you may want to add some.

Begin on RS. Work to the point where the colors divide. Begin with DPN1:

[Slip one st of front color to DPN1, slip one st of back color to RN] for the number of sts in the first lace panel—for chart 651, for instance, that's 7 sts. Now slip the 7 sts of back color back to LN. Slide the sts on DPN1 to the other end of DPN1. Using DPN2 and front color yarn, work the lace sts in front color. Set aside DPN1.

With back color, [purl a st from LN, then slip one st of front color from DPN2 to RN.] Repeat across the lace panel. Set aside DPN2.

With both colors together, purl the dividing sts that separate the first lace panel from the next.

Pattern 650

▨ = RS: work these sts with lighter yarn as charted, and purl the sts behind them with darker yarn; WS: purl the sts with lighter yarn as charted and knit the other sts in darker yarn.

▨ = RS: work these sts with darker yarn as charted, and purl the sts behind them with lighter yarn; WS: purl the sts with darker yarn as charted and knit the other sts in lighter yarn.

Pattern 651

▨ = RS: work these sts with darker yarn as charted, and purl the sts behind them with lighter yarn; WS: purl the sts with darker yarn as charted and knit the other sts in lighter yarn.

▨ = RS: work these sts with lighter yarn as charted, and purl the sts behind them with darker yarn; WS: purl the sts with lighter yarn as charted and knit the other sts in darker yarn.

Pattern 652

▨ = RS: work these sts with darker yarn as charted, and purl the sts behind them with lighter yarn; WS: purl the sts with darker yarn as charted and knit the other sts in lighter yarn.

▨ = RS: work these sts with lighter yarn as charted, and purl the sts behind them with darker yarn; WS: purl the sts with lighter yarn as charted and knit the other sts in darker yarn.

Pattern 653

▨ = RS: work these sts with darker yarn as charted, and purl the sts behind them with lighter yarn; WS: purl the sts with darker yarn as charted and knit the other sts in lighter yarn.

▨ = RS: work these sts with lighter yarn as charted, and purl the sts behind them with darker yarn; WS: purl the sts with lighter yarn as charted and knit the other sts in darker yarn.

Patterns 654–661 This section presents multi-colored patterns using lifted and slipped stitches. Stitches are slipped over varying numbers of rows, and some are twisted or crossed. Be sure to review the conventions for lifted and slipped sts (p. 19).

Patterns 662–676 These patterns provide designs for two-toned cable stitches. All are worked in cabled stockinette, with no other texture. Some also include stranded colorwork.
For the most part, you'll probably find it easiest to work the cables in stranded knitting, although the chart doesn't specify whether to use stranding or intarsia.

The cable crosses in this section are almost all 4 – over – 4, although #667 also has an unusual 6-st cable. See the technique section for a discussion of cable symbols (p. 17).

Patterns 677–684 The cabled stitches in this section (677 to 684) gain an added textural dimension through the use of short rows. The stitches to be crossed in front have two or more extra rows, making them stand out more than usual. Most of the cables are 2-over-2 or 3-over-3, but note that 678 also uses an unusual 2-over-4 cable.

Look carefully at the charts and you'll see short rows with arrows indicating the direction of work. Example: in 677, work the cable as follows:

- Work sts 1 to 6 as charted. Knit sts 6 to 8. Turn (arrow). Purl sts 6 to 8. Turn (arrow).
- Knit sts 6 to 8. Turn (arrow). Purl sts 6 to 8. Turn (arrow).
- Now work a 3-over-3 cable: place sts 6 to 8 on CN, hold to front, k3, k3 from CN. Follow the arrow to st 13 and continue in the same way

Patterns 685–700 The final section of knitted stitches (685 to 700) provides more examples of mosaic patterns, similar to 616–631. Alternate two rows each of two colors, slipping stitches over the contrast color as charted to produce color patterns. 685 to 692 are based on garter stitch, while 693 to 700 are based on stockinette stitch. For all of these, slip as if to purl with yarn at the back of the RS (slip wyib on RS, slip wyif on WS).

Patterns 857, 859–866 These stitches are primarily worked in interwoven crochet, where a row consists of one pass of each color—as if there were two active rows at once. The chart shows the work from the right side, so be sure to mark your right side and work the back-side rows so they appear correct on the right side. (Solid lines are the symbols that lie in front.) When changing colors, place a marker in the loop of the color you've finished to keep it from unraveling while you work the next color.

OVERALL STITCH PATTERNS ✥ Knit, purl and crossed stitches

The texture of the knitted fabric emerges from basic stitches such as knit and purl. The use of these two stitches creates varied yet simple patterns with a three-dimensional look.

Many stitch patterns in this section also include crossed and cabled stitches for additional texture. Be sure to read the discussion of cable symbols in the technique section (p. 17) to understand how to interpret them. There are crosses and cables with varying numbers of stitches, crossed in both directions. When you know the principles behind the symbols, you'll easily see how to work the stitch.

Some of these patterns also include slipped stitches or brioche stitches, so be sure to review the discussion of slip-stitch symbols on p. 19 and of brioche sts on p. 21. Bobbles are discussed on p. 29.

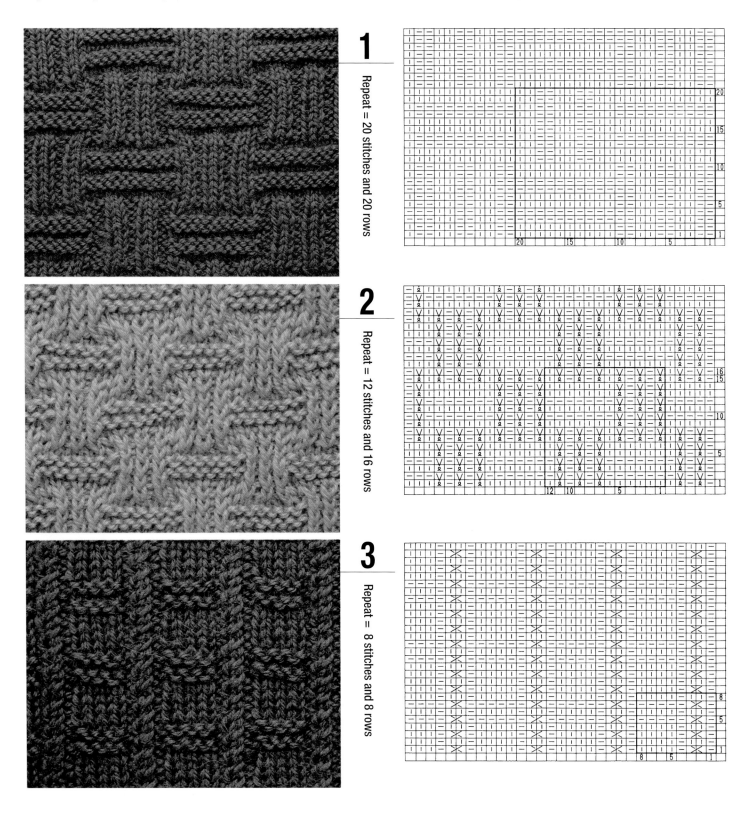

1 Repeat = 20 stitches and 20 rows

2 Repeat = 12 stitches and 16 rows

3 Repeat = 8 stitches and 8 rows

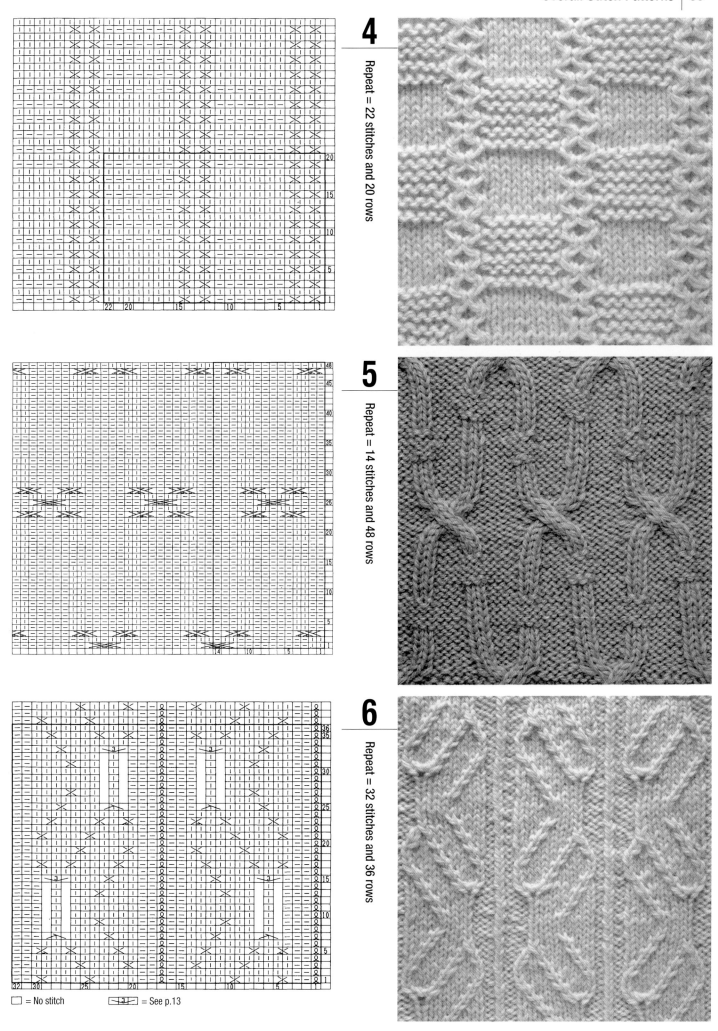

4

Repeat = 22 stitches and 20 rows

5

Repeat = 14 stitches and 48 rows

6

Repeat = 32 stitches and 36 rows

☐ = No stitch   ⊏3⊐ = See p.13

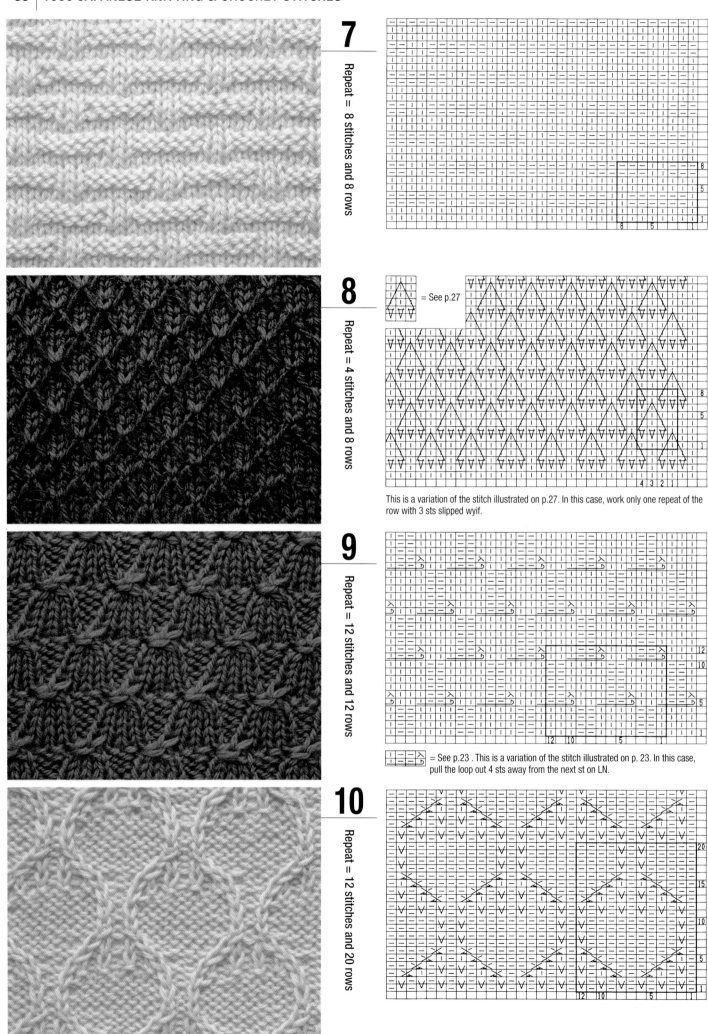

7

Repeat = 8 stitches and 8 rows

8

= See p.27

Repeat = 4 stitches and 8 rows

This is a variation of the stitch illustrated on p.27. In this case, work only one repeat of the row with 3 sts slipped wyif.

9

Repeat = 12 stitches and 12 rows

= See p.23 . This is a variation of the stitch illustrated on p. 23. In this case, pull the loop out 4 sts away from the next st on LN.

10

Repeat = 12 stitches and 20 rows

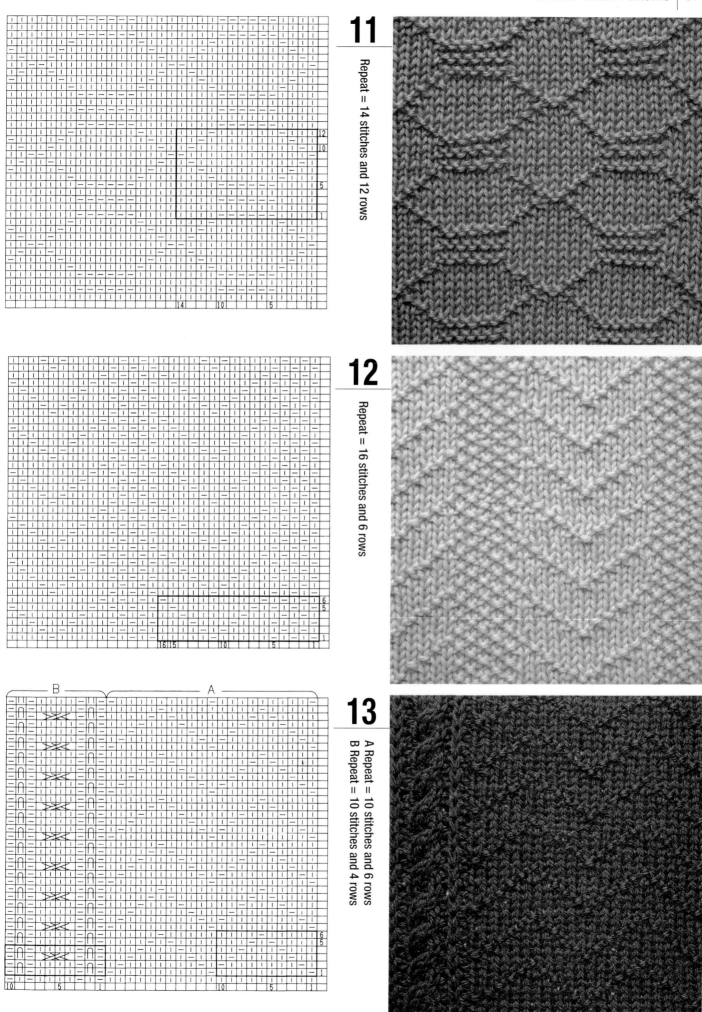

11

Repeat = 14 stitches and 12 rows

12

Repeat = 16 stitches and 6 rows

13

A Repeat = 10 stitches and 6 rows
B Repeat = 10 stitches and 4 rows

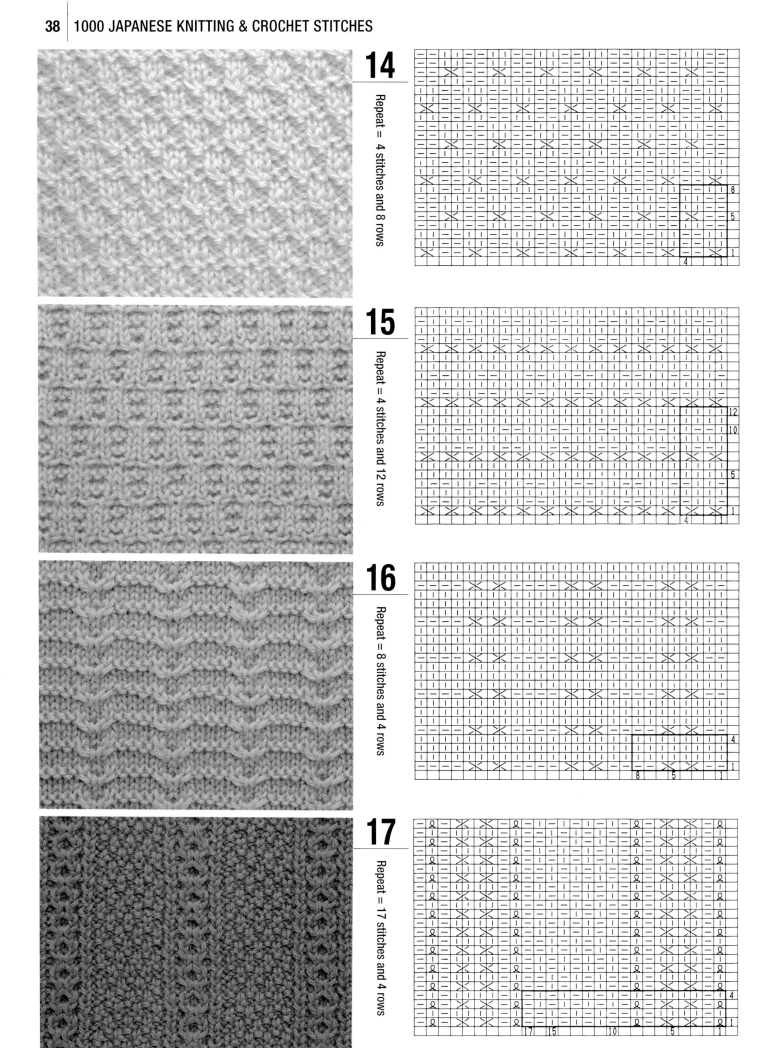

14

Repeat = 4 stitches and 8 rows

15

Repeat = 4 stitches and 12 rows

16

Repeat = 8 stitches and 4 rows

17

Repeat = 17 stitches and 4 rows

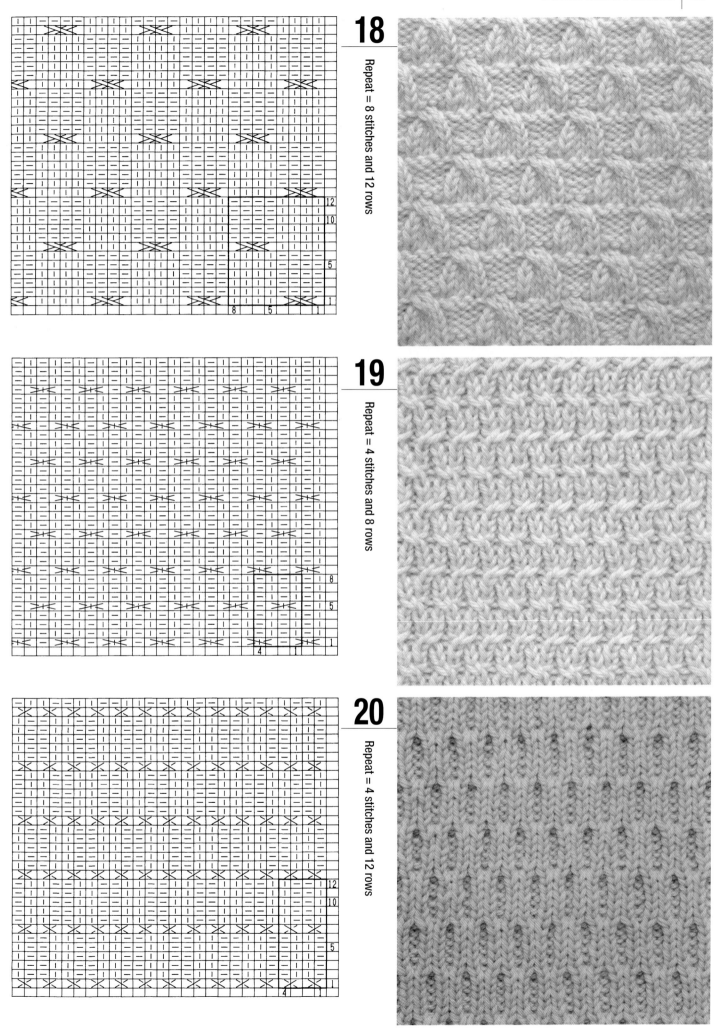

18

Repeat = 8 stitches and 12 rows

19

Repeat = 4 stitches and 8 rows

20

Repeat = 4 stitches and 12 rows

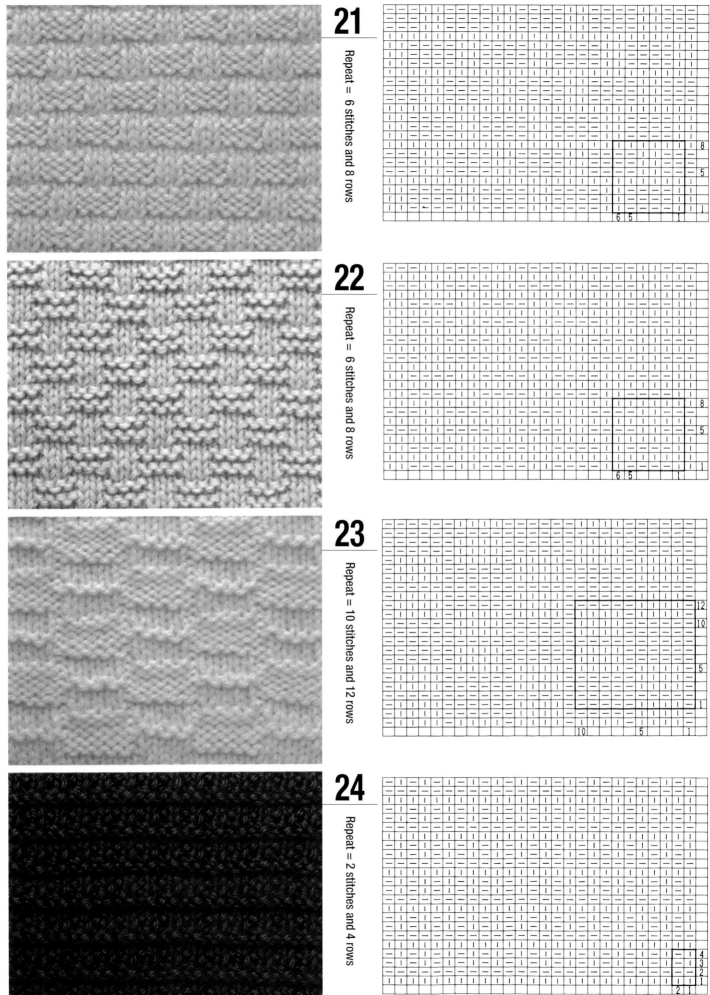

21

Repeat = 6 stitches and 8 rows

22

Repeat = 6 stitches and 8 rows

23

Repeat = 10 stitches and 12 rows

24

Repeat = 2 stitches and 4 rows

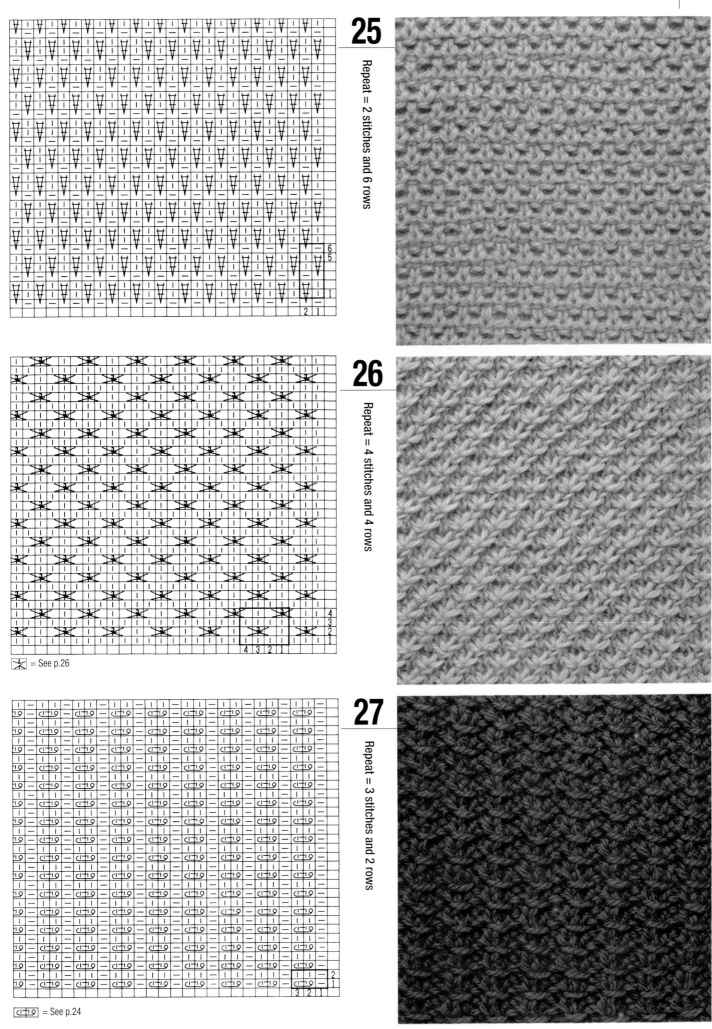

25

Repeat = 2 stitches and 6 rows

26

Repeat = 4 stitches and 4 rows

= See p.26

27

Repeat = 3 stitches and 2 rows

= See p.24

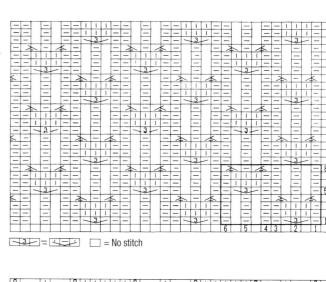

28

Repeat = 6 stitches and 8 rows

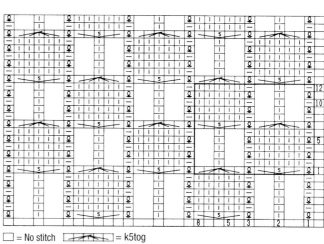

29

Repeat = 8 stitches and 12 rows

☐ = No stitch ⟨⟩ = k5tog

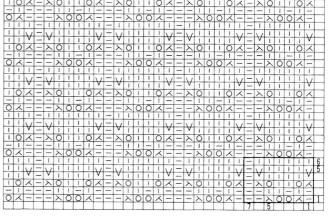

30

Repeat = 7 stitches and 6 rows

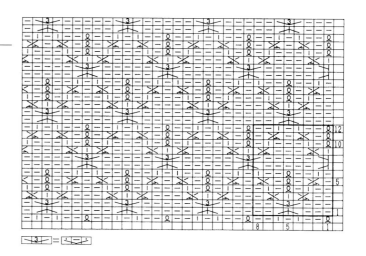

31

Repeat = 8 stitches and 12 rows

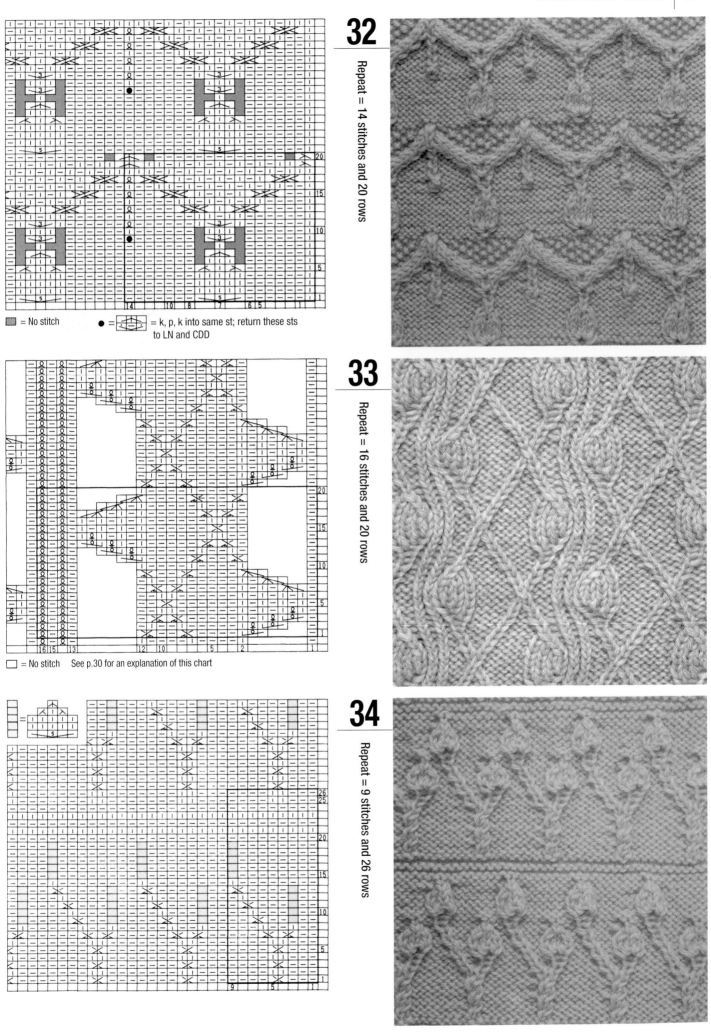

32

Repeat = 14 stitches and 20 rows

⬛ = No stitch   ● = = k, p, k into same st; return these sts to LN and CDD

33

Repeat = 16 stitches and 20 rows

☐ = No stitch   See p.30 for an explanation of this chart

34

Repeat = 9 stitches and 26 rows

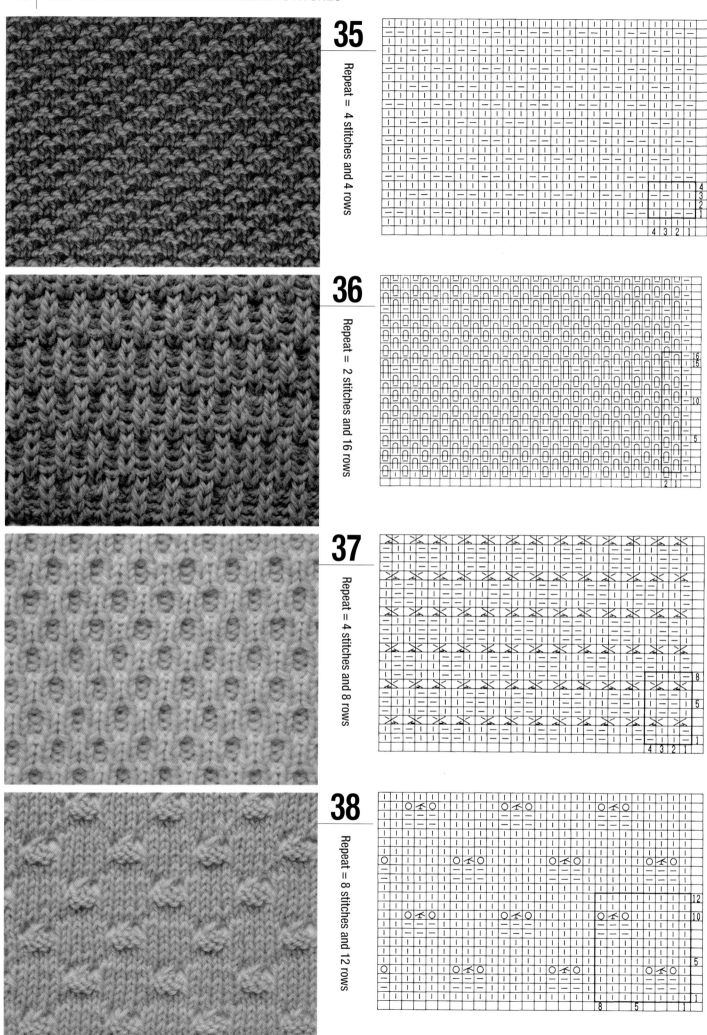

35
Repeat = 4 stitches and 4 rows

36
Repeat = 2 stitches and 16 rows

37
Repeat = 4 stitches and 8 rows

38
Repeat = 8 stitches and 12 rows

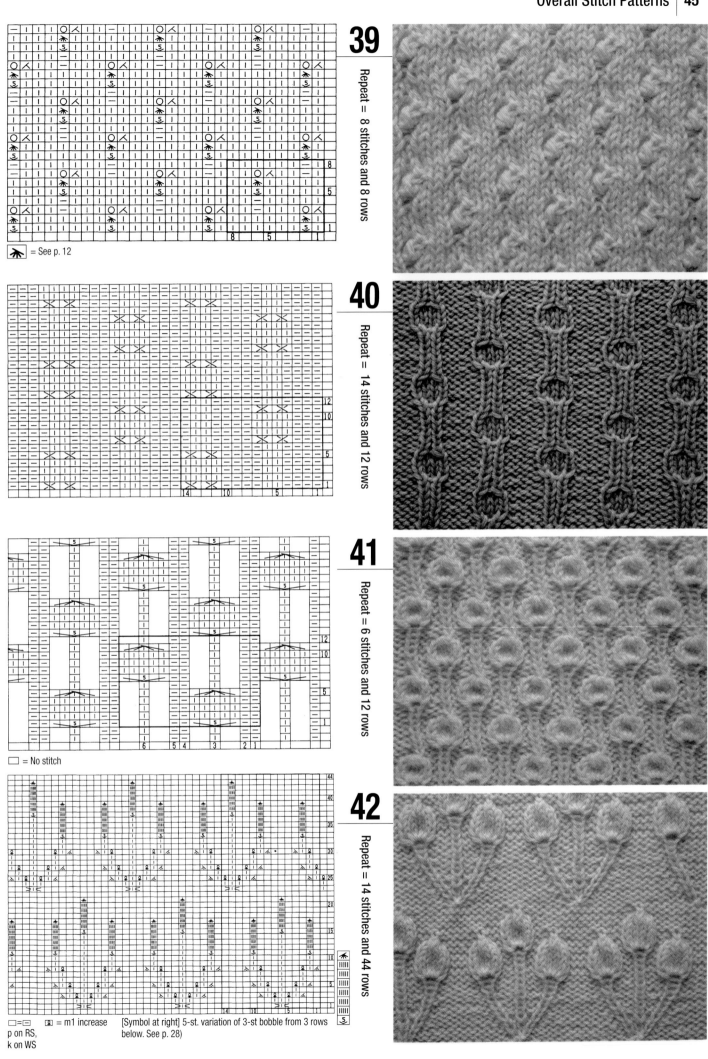

39

Repeat = 8 stitches and 8 rows

➤ = See p. 12

40

Repeat = 14 stitches and 12 rows

□ = No stitch

41

Repeat = 6 stitches and 12 rows

42

Repeat = 14 stitches and 44 rows

□ = □ = p on RS, k on WS   □ = m1 increase   [Symbol at right] 5-st. variation of 3-st bobble from 3 rows below. See p. 28)

43

Repeat = 6 stitches and 12 rows

= sl the st, letting extra yo drop to elongate

44

Repeat = 8 stitches and 16 rows

45

Repeat = 8 stitches and 16 rows

46

Repeat = 6 stitches and 12 rows

☐ = No stitch

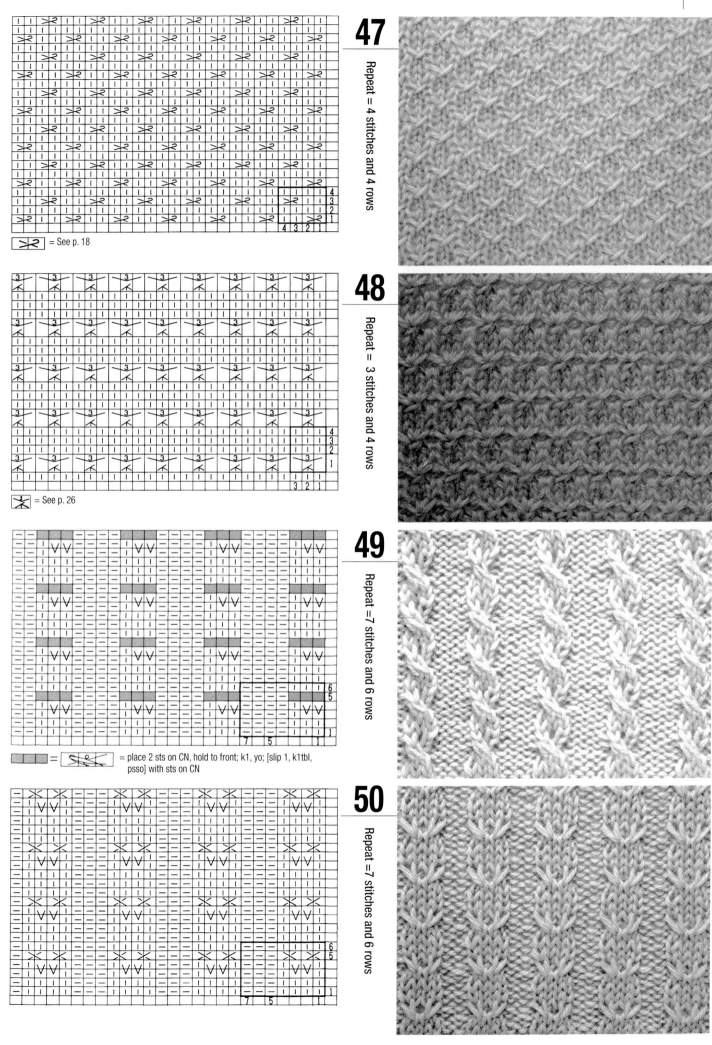

⟩⟨ = See p. 18

⟩⟨ = See p. 26

▢▢ = ⟨⟩ = place 2 sts on CN, hold to front; k1, yo; [slip 1, k1tbl, psso] with sts on CN

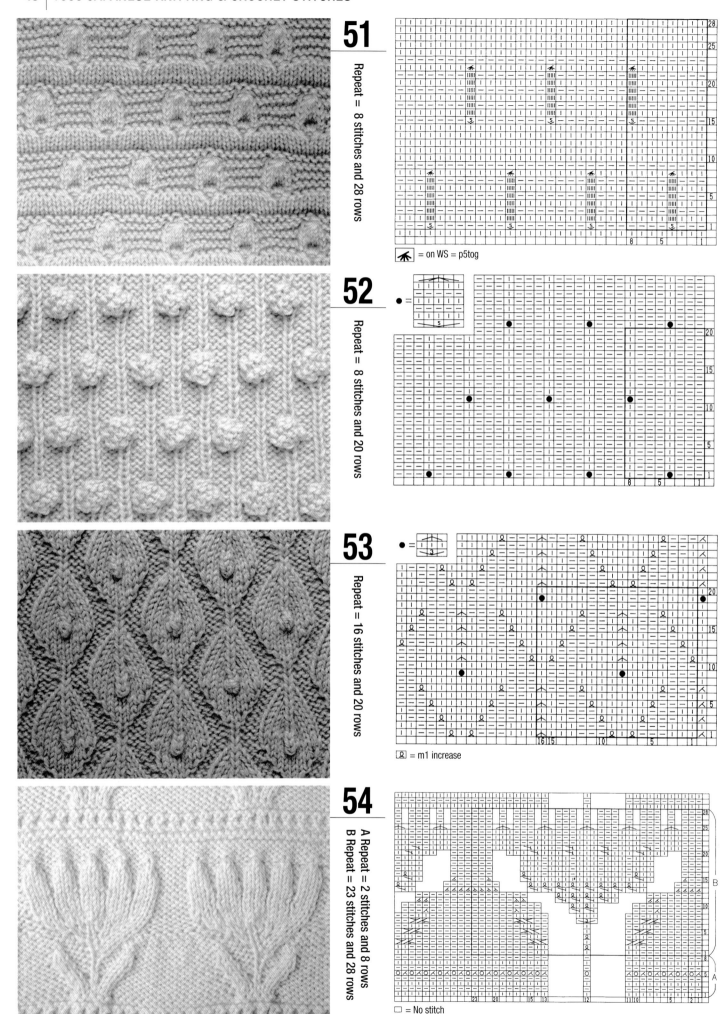

51

Repeat = 8 stitches and 28 rows

= on WS = p5tog

52

Repeat = 8 stitches and 20 rows

53

Repeat = 16 stitches and 20 rows

= m1 increase

54

A Repeat = 2 stitches and 8 rows
B Repeat = 23 stitches and 28 rows

□ = No stitch

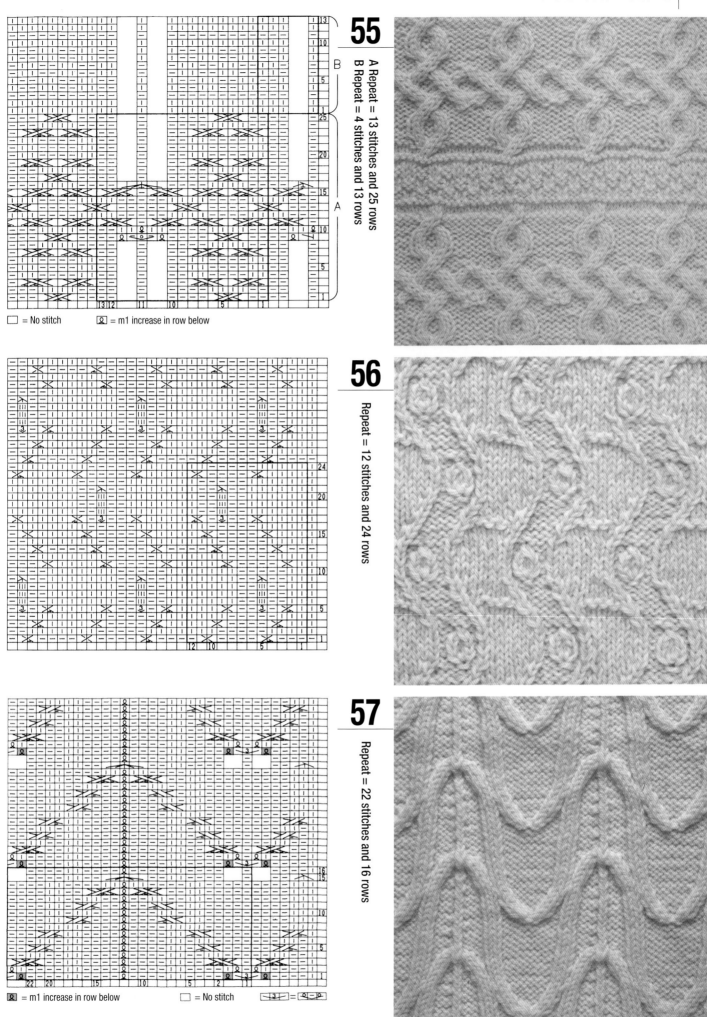

55

A Repeat = 13 stitches and 25 rows
B Repeat = 4 stitches and 13 rows

□ = No stitch   ♀ = m1 increase in row below

56

Repeat = 12 stitches and 24 rows

57

Repeat = 22 stitches and 16 rows

♀ = m1 increase in row below   □ = No stitch   = ♀—♀

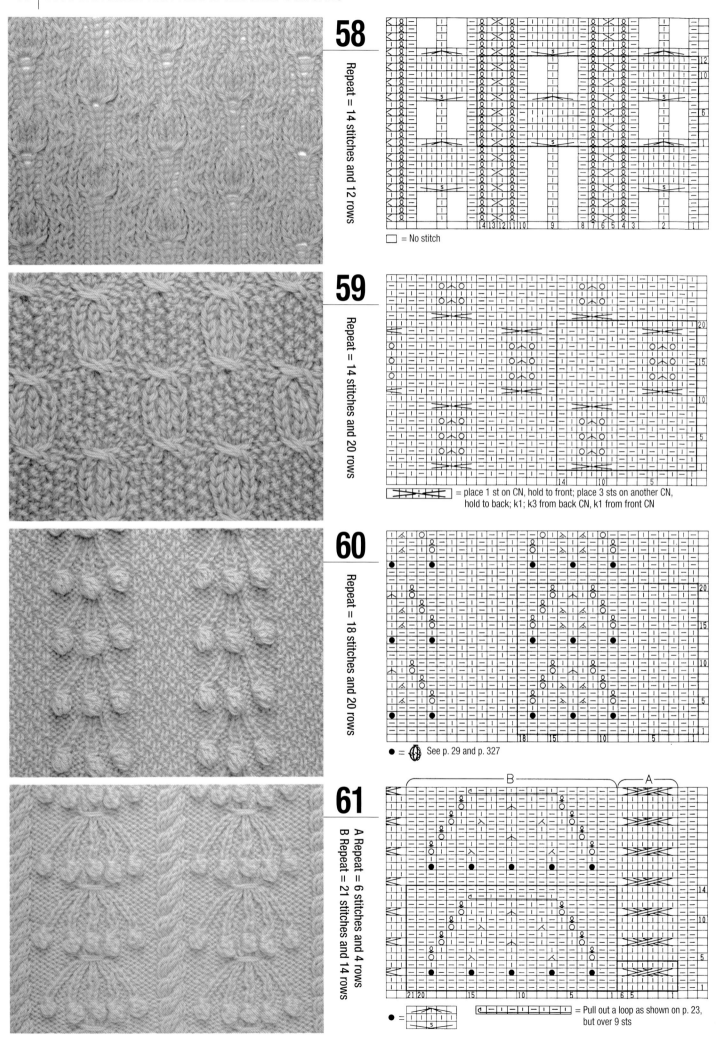

58

Repeat = 14 stitches and 12 rows

☐ = No stitch

59

Repeat = 14 stitches and 20 rows

= place 1 st on CN, hold to front; place 3 sts on another CN, hold to back; k1; k3 from back CN, k1 from front CN

60

Repeat = 18 stitches and 20 rows

● = See p. 29 and p. 327

61

A Repeat = 6 stitches and 4 rows
B Repeat = 21 stitches and 14 rows

● =

= Pull out a loop as shown on p. 23, but over 9 sts

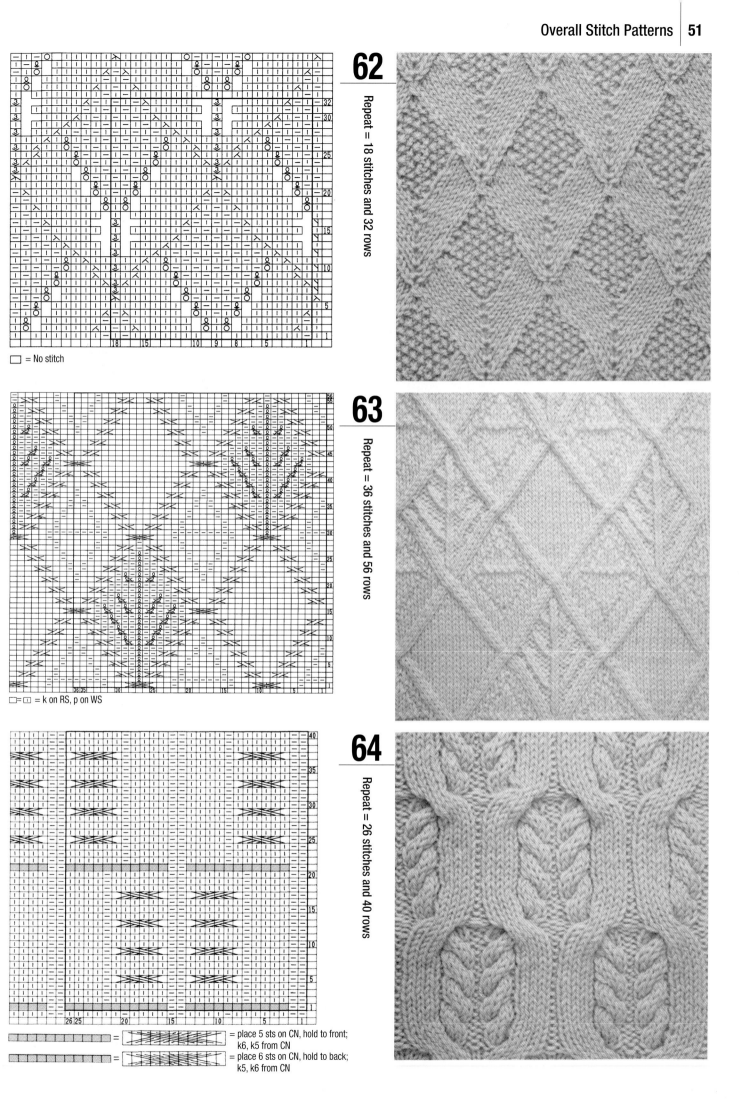

62

Repeat = 18 stitches and 32 rows

☐ = No stitch

63

Repeat = 36 stitches and 56 rows

☐ = 🔲 = k on RS, p on WS

64

Repeat = 26 stitches and 40 rows

= place 5 sts on CN, hold to front; k6, k5 from CN

= place 6 sts on CN, hold to back; k5, k6 from CN

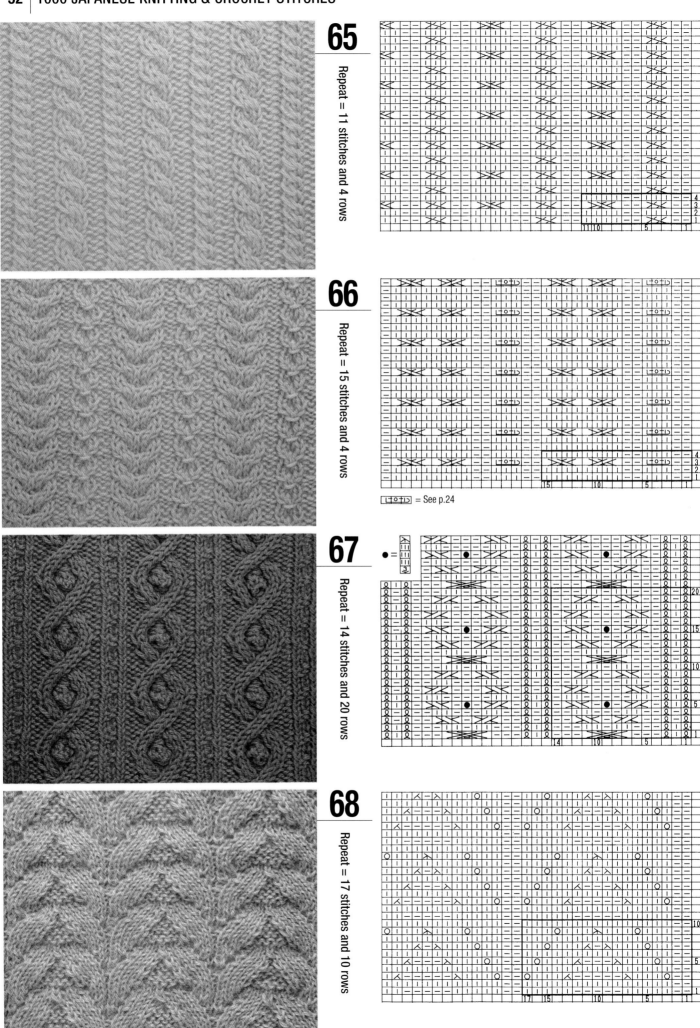

65 Repeat = 11 stitches and 4 rows

66 Repeat = 15 stitches and 4 rows

⌐┴○┴⌐ = See p.24

67 Repeat = 14 stitches and 20 rows

68 Repeat = 17 stitches and 10 rows

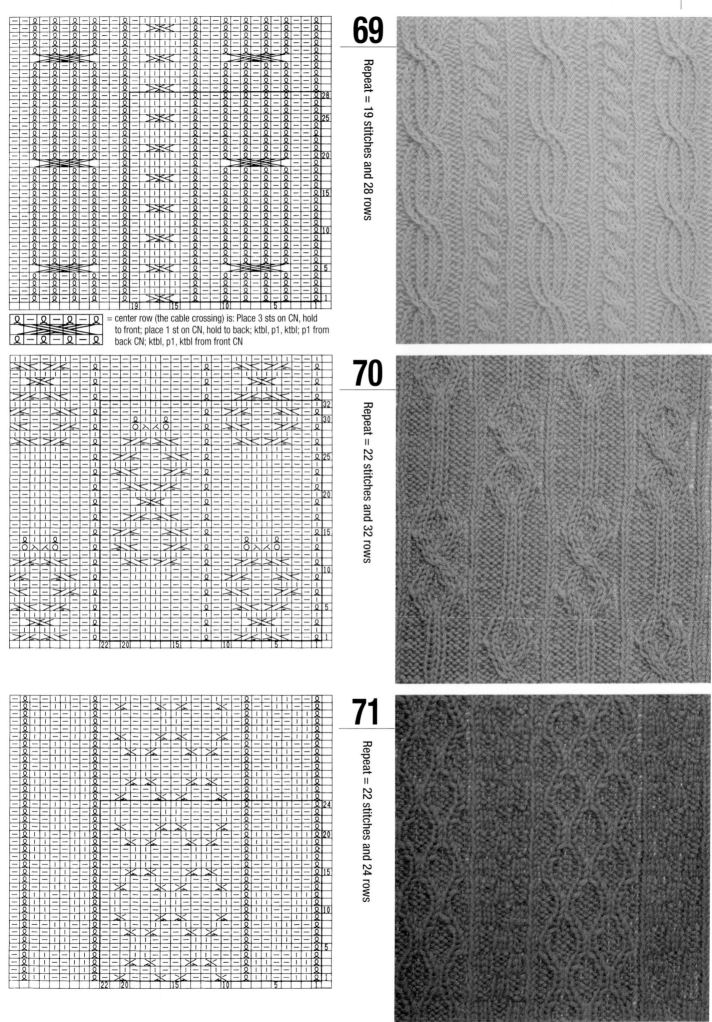

69

Repeat = 19 stitches and 28 rows

= center row (the cable crossing) is: Place 3 sts on CN, hold to front; place 1 st on CN, hold to back; ktbl, p1, ktbl; p1 from back CN; ktbl, p1, ktbl from front CN

70

Repeat = 22 stitches and 32 rows

71

Repeat = 22 stitches and 24 rows

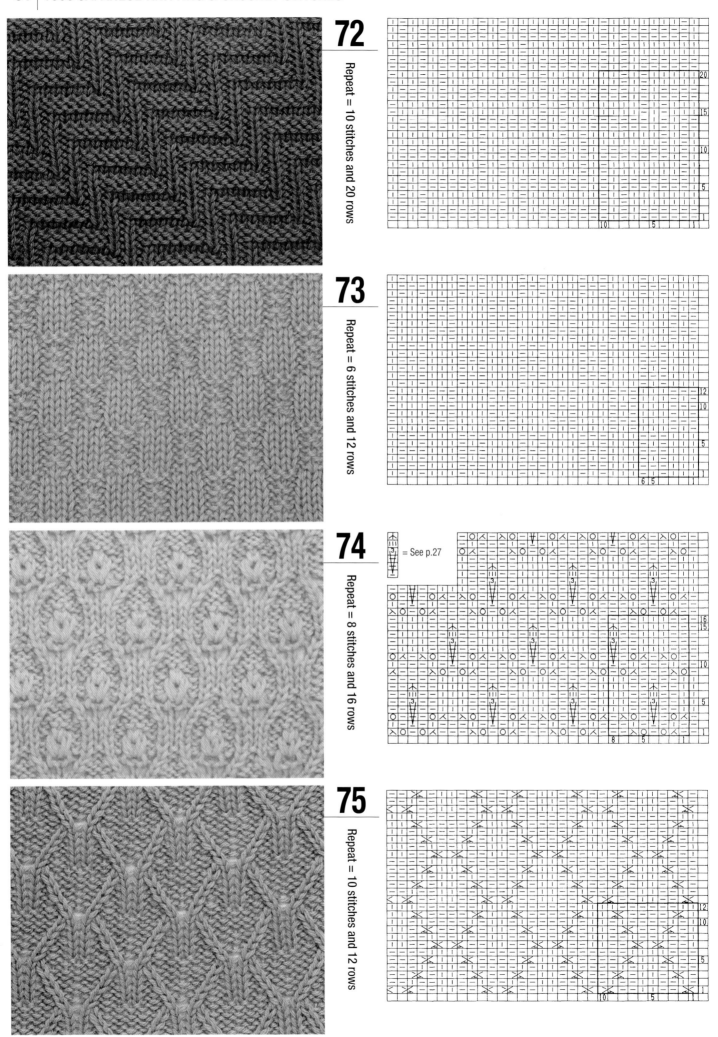

72

Repeat = 10 stitches and 20 rows

73

Repeat = 6 stitches and 12 rows

74

Repeat = 8 stitches and 16 rows

75

Repeat = 10 stitches and 12 rows

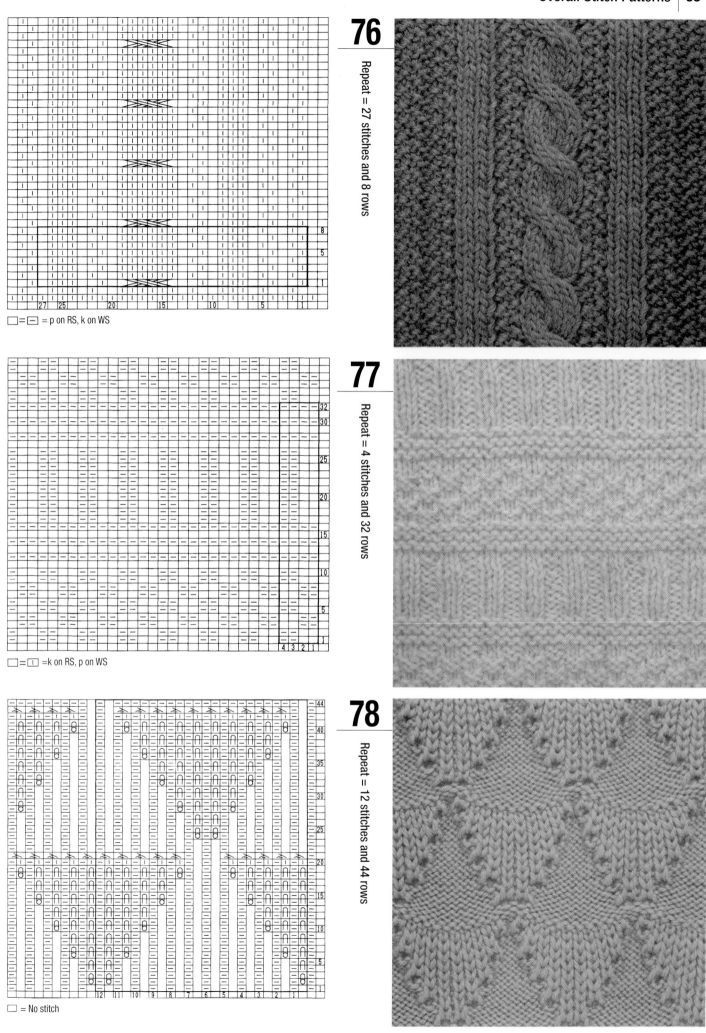

76

Repeat = 27 stitches and 8 rows

☐ = ⊟ = p on RS, k on WS

77

Repeat = 4 stitches and 32 rows

☐ = ⊡ = k on RS, p on WS

78

Repeat = 12 stitches and 44 rows

☐ = No stitch

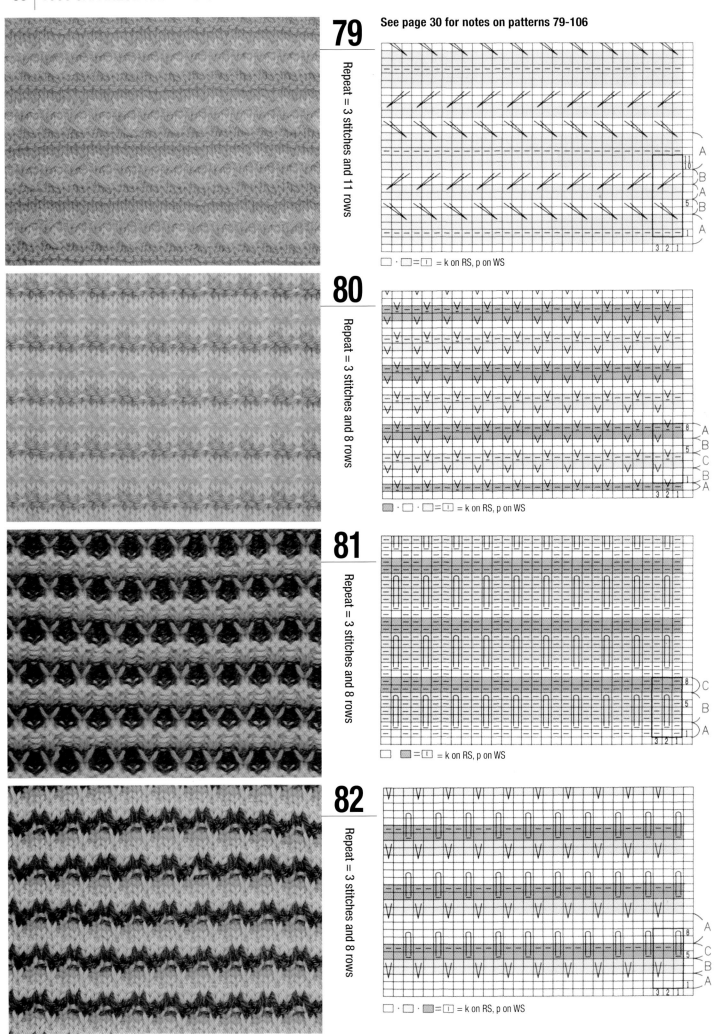

79

Repeat = 3 stitches and 11 rows

See page 30 for notes on patterns 79-106

☐ · ☐=☐ = k on RS, p on WS

80

Repeat = 3 stitches and 8 rows

☐ · ☐ · ☐=☐ = k on RS, p on WS

81

Repeat = 3 stitches and 8 rows

☐ ☐=☐ = k on RS, p on WS

82

Repeat = 3 stitches and 8 rows

☐ · ☐ · ☐=☐ = k on RS, p on WS

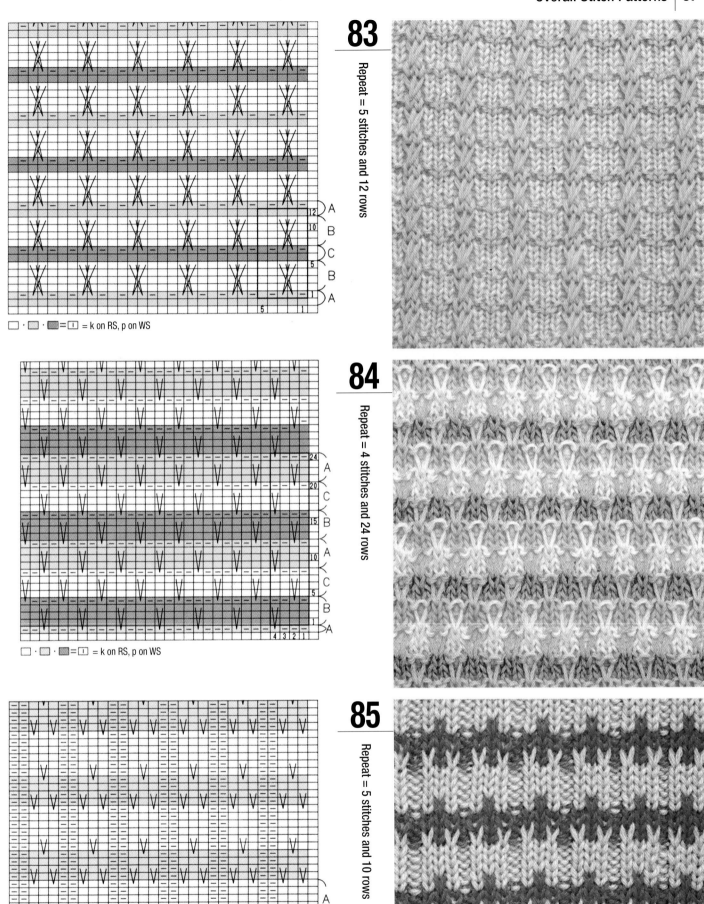

83

Repeat = 5 stitches and 12 rows

□ · □ · ▣ = ⊡ = k on RS, p on WS

84

Repeat = 4 stitches and 24 rows

□ · □ · ▣ = ⊡ = k on RS, p on WS

85

Repeat = 5 stitches and 10 rows

□ · □ = ⊡ = k on RS, p on WS

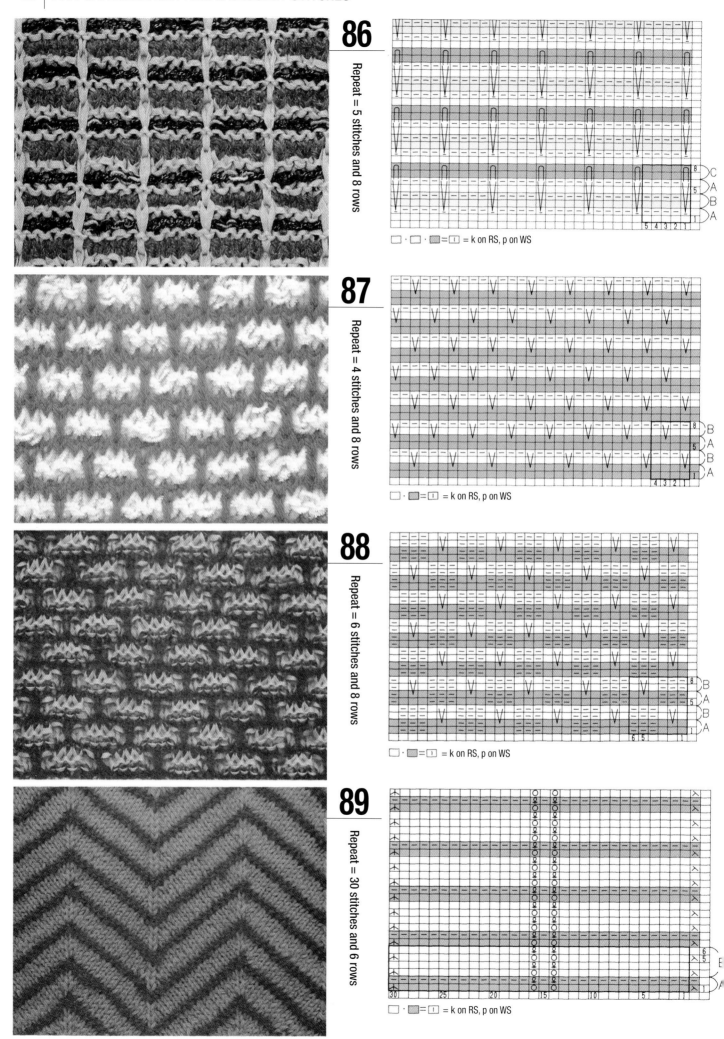

86

Repeat = 5 stitches and 8 rows

☐ · ☐ · ☐ = ☐ = k on RS, p on WS

87

Repeat = 4 stitches and 8 rows

☐ · ☐ = ☐ = k on RS, p on WS

88

Repeat = 6 stitches and 8 rows

☐ · ☐ = ☐ = k on RS, p on WS

89

Repeat = 30 stitches and 6 rows

☐ · ☐ = ☐ = k on RS, p on WS

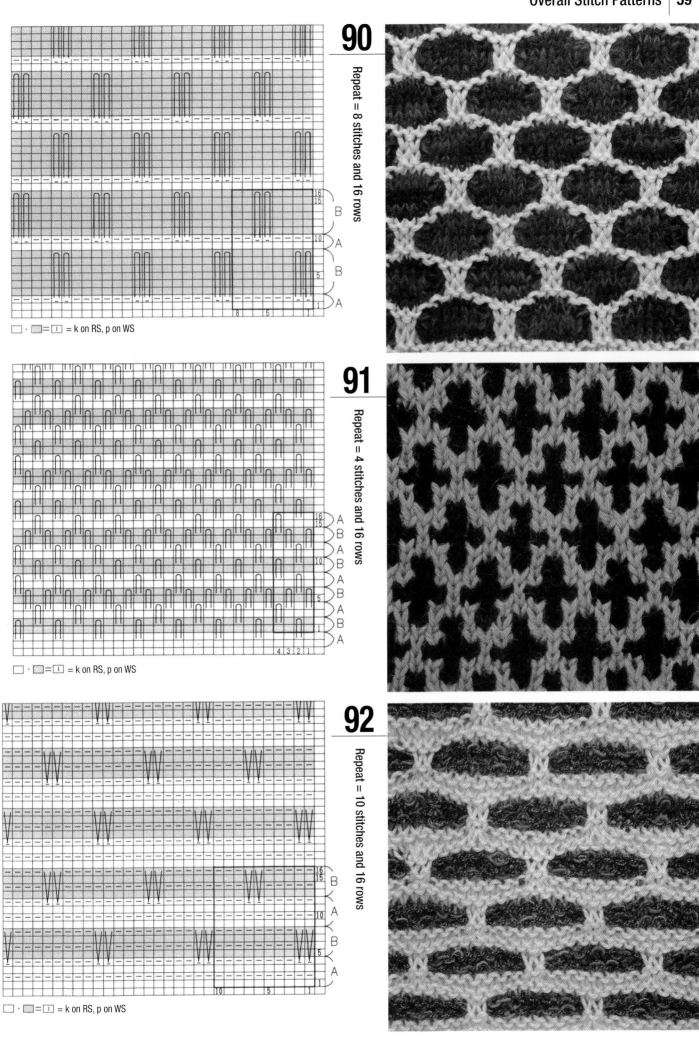

90

Repeat = 8 stitches and 16 rows

□ · □ = ⊡ = k on RS, p on WS

91

Repeat = 4 stitches and 16 rows

□ · □ = ⊡ = k on RS, p on WS

92

Repeat = 10 stitches and 16 rows

□ · □ = ⊡ = k on RS, p on WS

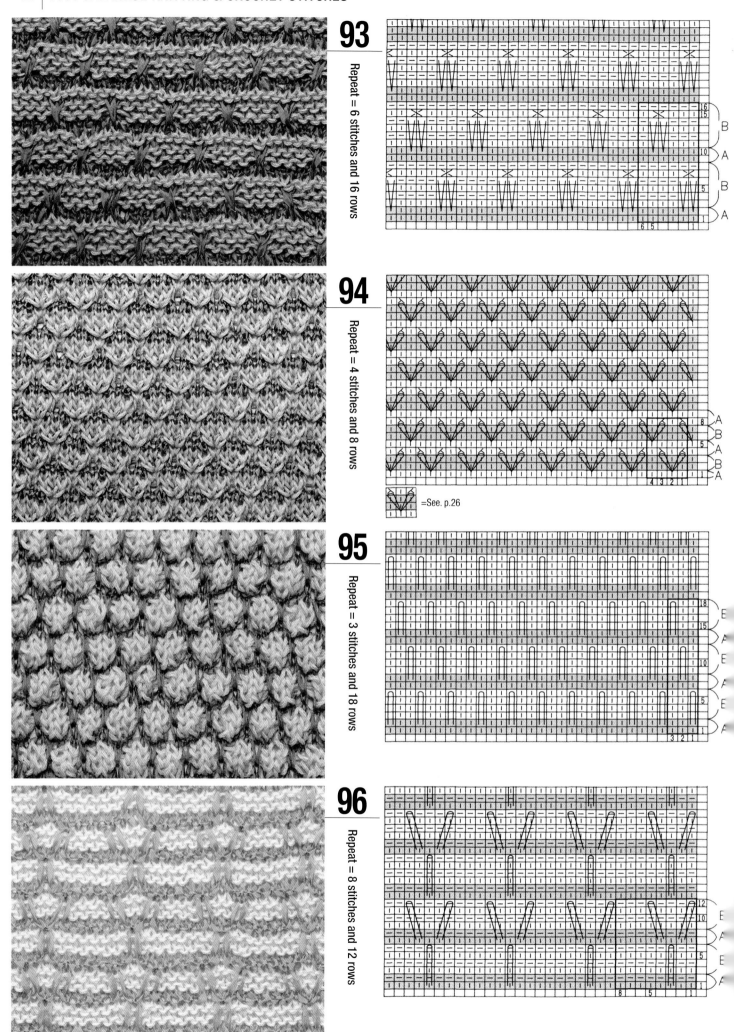

93

Repeat = 6 stitches and 16 rows

94

Repeat = 4 stitches and 8 rows

=See. p.26

95

Repeat = 3 stitches and 18 rows

96

Repeat = 8 stitches and 12 rows

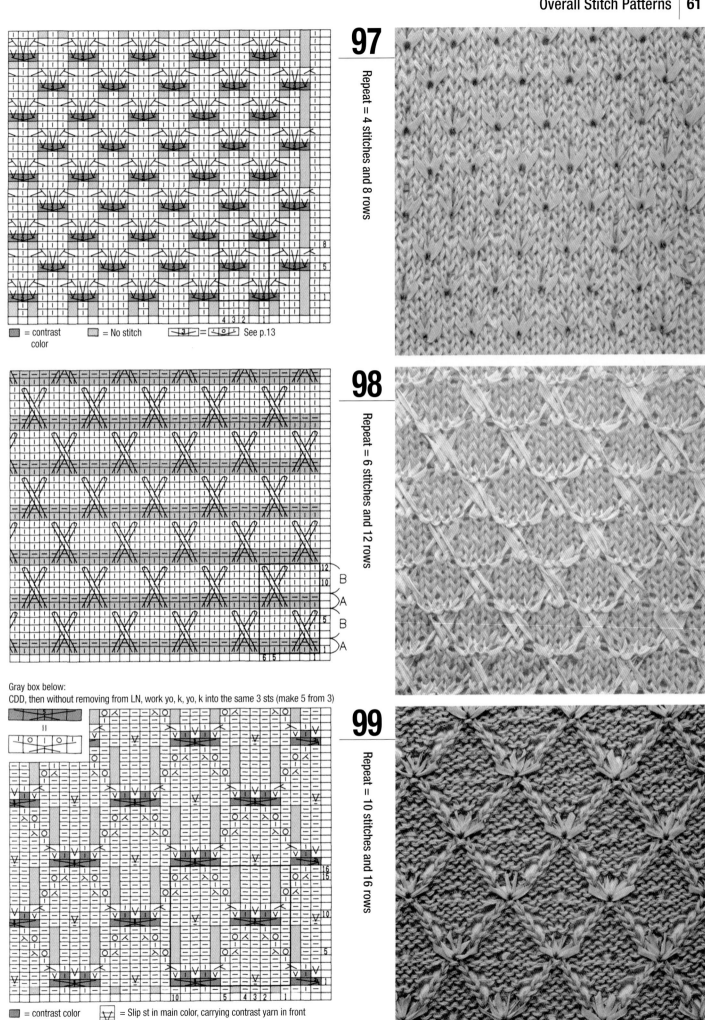

97

Repeat = 4 stitches and 8 rows

■ = contrast color   ■ = No stitch   ⊐3⊏ = ⌐⌐o⌐⌐ See p.13

98

Repeat = 6 stitches and 12 rows

Gray box below:
CDD, then without removing from LN, work yo, k, yo, k into the same 3 sts (make 5 from 3)

99

Repeat = 10 stitches and 16 rows

■ = contrast color   Ⅴ = Slip st in main color, carrying contrast yarn in front
□ = No stitch

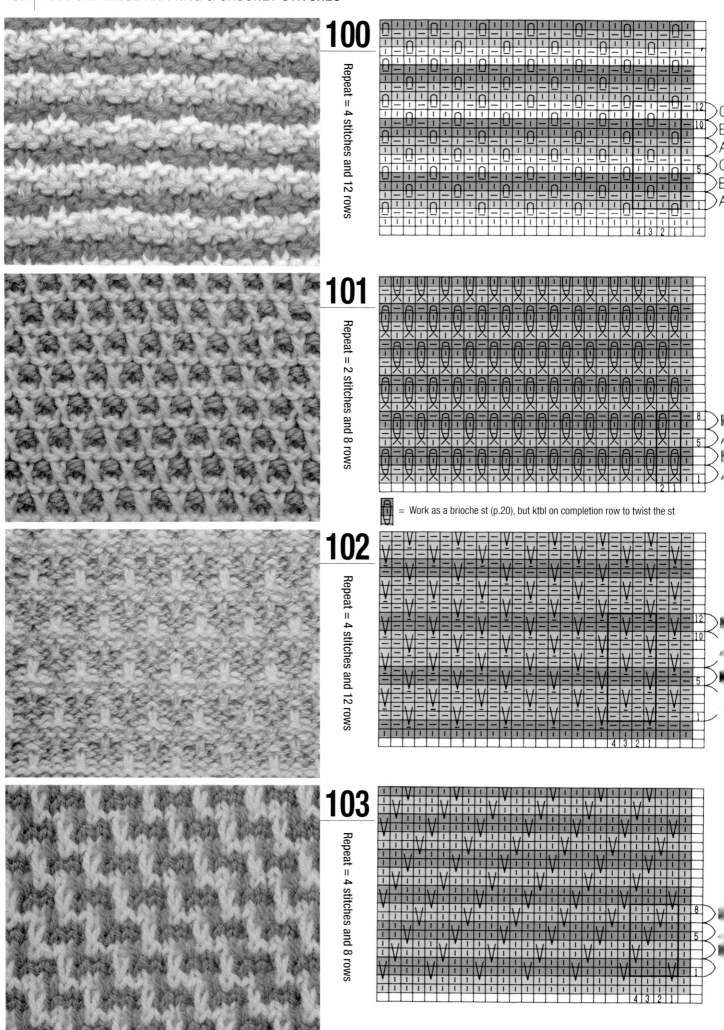

100

Repeat = 4 stitches and 12 rows

101

Repeat = 2 stitches and 8 rows

⬚ = Work as a brioche st (p.20), but ktbl on completion row to twist the st

102

Repeat = 4 stitches and 12 rows

103

Repeat = 4 stitches and 8 rows

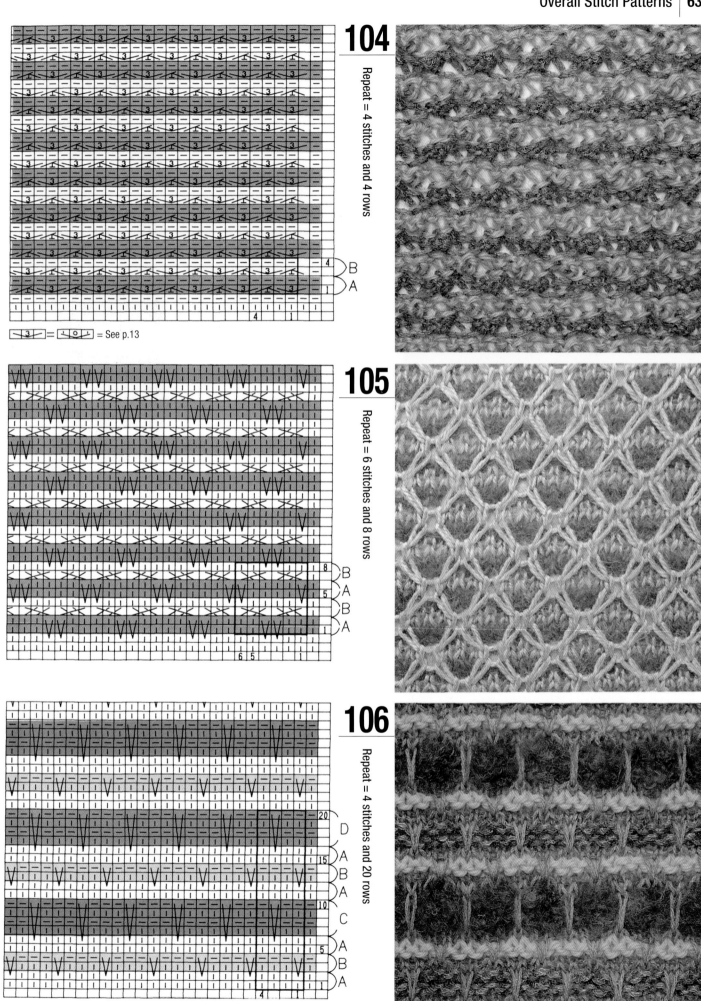

104

Repeat = **4** stitches and **4** rows

= See p.13

105

Repeat = **6** stitches and **8** rows

106

Repeat = **4** stitches and **20** rows

107

Repeat = 16 stitches and 20 rows

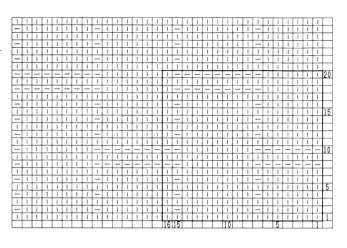

108

Repeat = 13 stitches and 22 rows

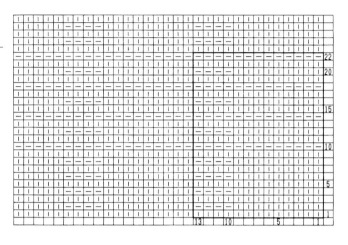

109

Repeat = 12 stitches and 4 rows

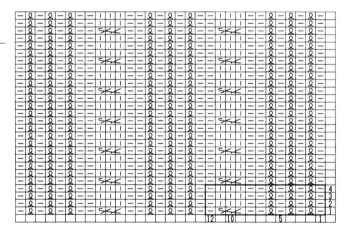

110

A Repeat = 2 stitches and 4 rows
B Repeat = 11 stitches and 6 rows
C Repeat = 20 stitches and 16 rows

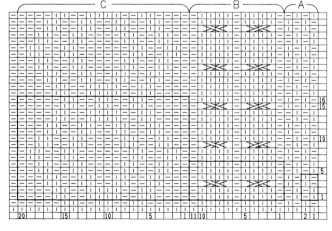

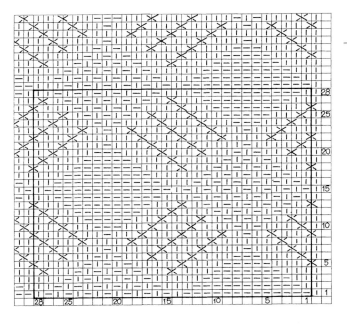

111

Repeat = 28 stitches and 28 rows

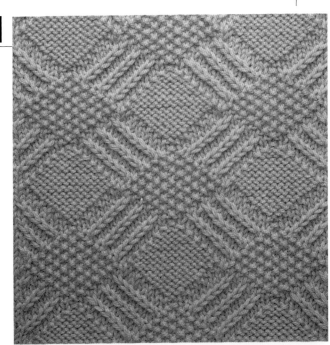

112

Repeat = 30 stitches and 20 rows

☐ = No stitch

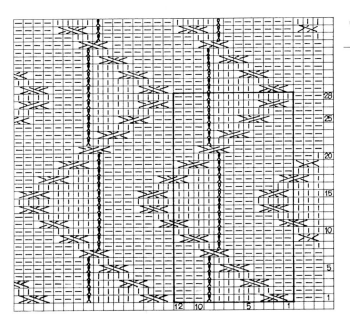

113

Repeat = 12 stitches and 28 rows

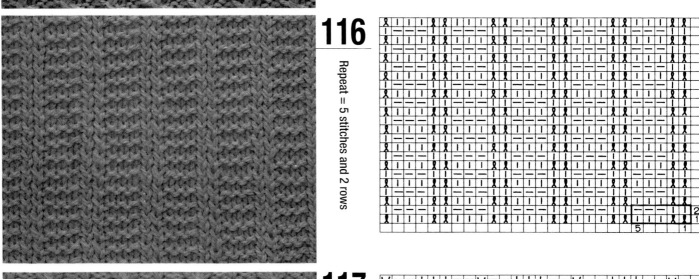

114

Repeat = 2 stitches and 2 rows

115

Repeat = 5 stitches and 4 rows

116

Repeat = 5 stitches and 2 rows

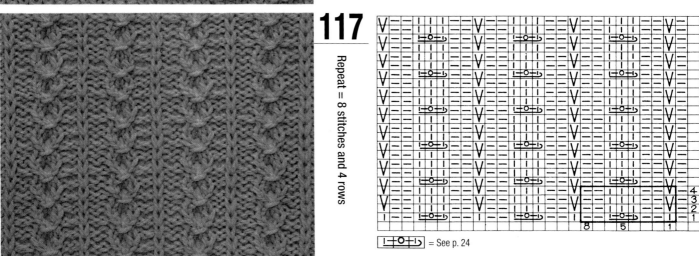

117

Repeat = 8 stitches and 4 rows

= See p. 24

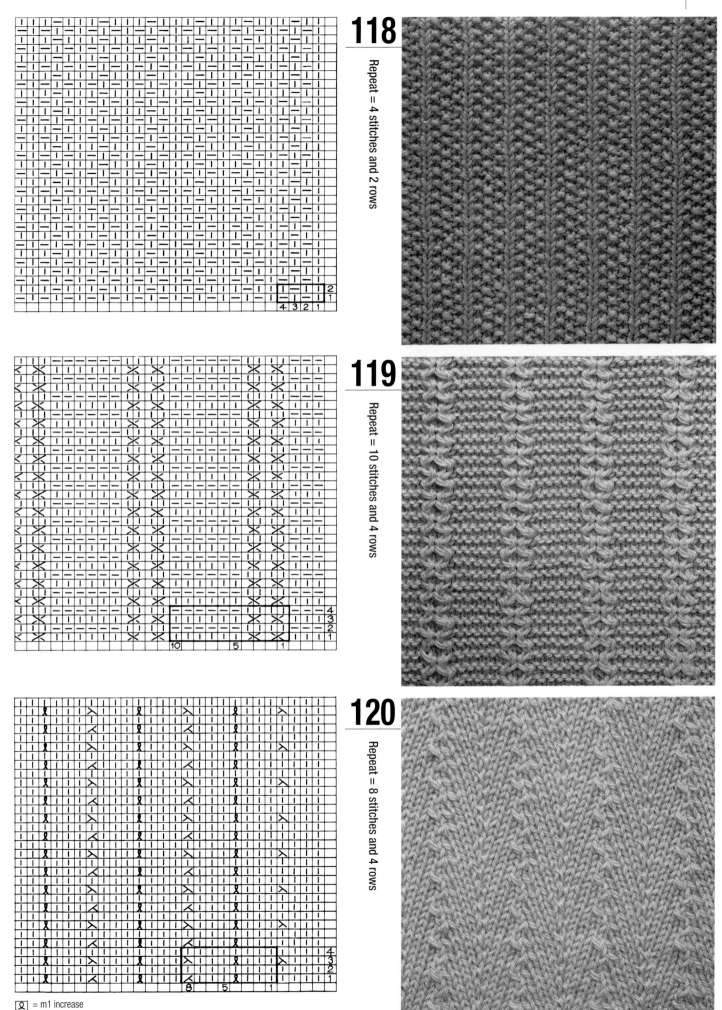

118

Repeat = 4 stitches and 2 rows

119

Repeat = 10 stitches and 4 rows

120

Repeat = 8 stitches and 4 rows

⚡ = m1 increase

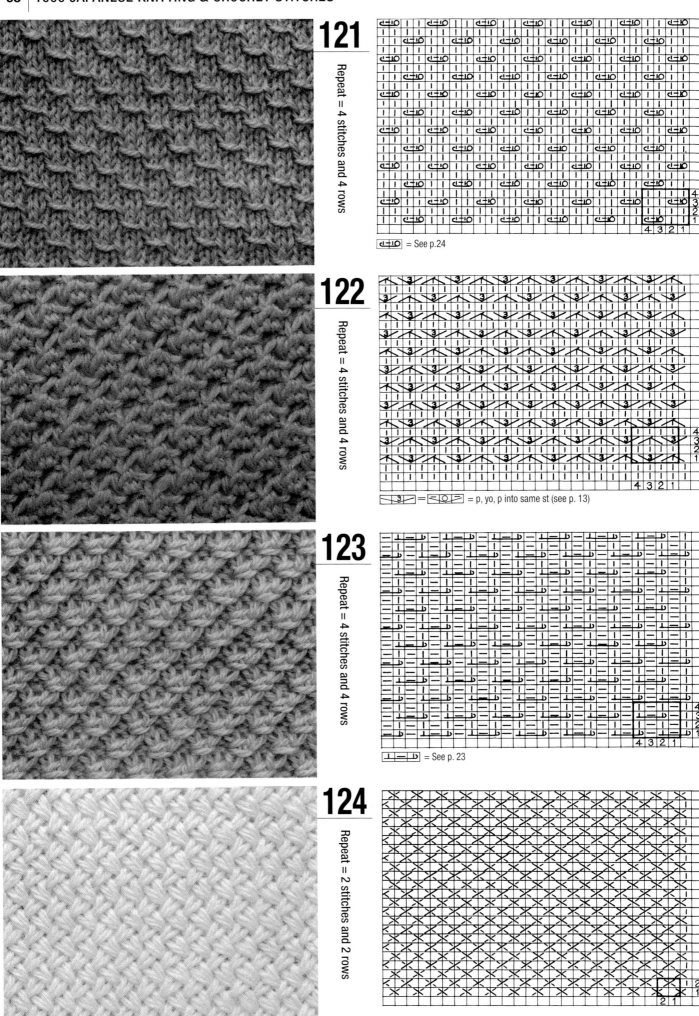

121

Repeat = 4 stitches and 4 rows

⊂⊥⊃ = See p.24

122

Repeat = 4 stitches and 4 rows

‾3‾ = ◁◯▷ = p, yo, p into same st (see p. 13)

123

Repeat = 4 stitches and 4 rows

⊥=⅃ = See p. 23

124

Repeat = 2 stitches and 2 rows

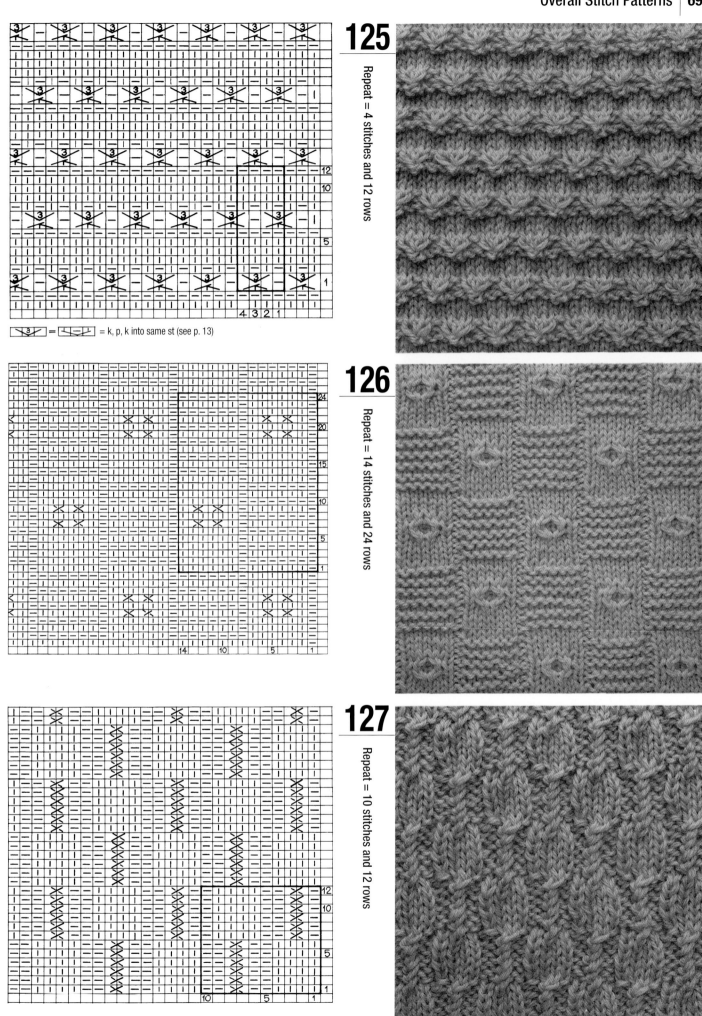

125
Repeat = 4 stitches and 12 rows

$\boxed{3}$ = k, p, k into same st (see p. 13)

126
Repeat = 14 stitches and 24 rows

127
Repeat = 10 stitches and 12 rows

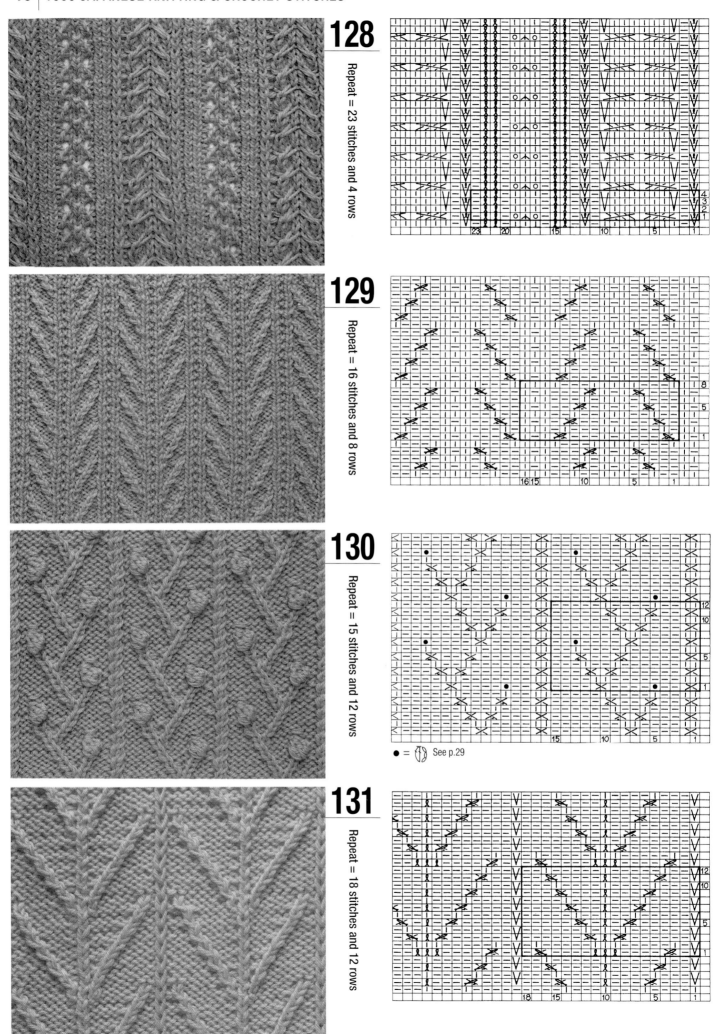

128
Repeat = 23 stitches and 4 rows

129
Repeat = 16 stitches and 8 rows

130
Repeat = 15 stitches and 12 rows

● = See p.29

131
Repeat = 18 stitches and 12 rows

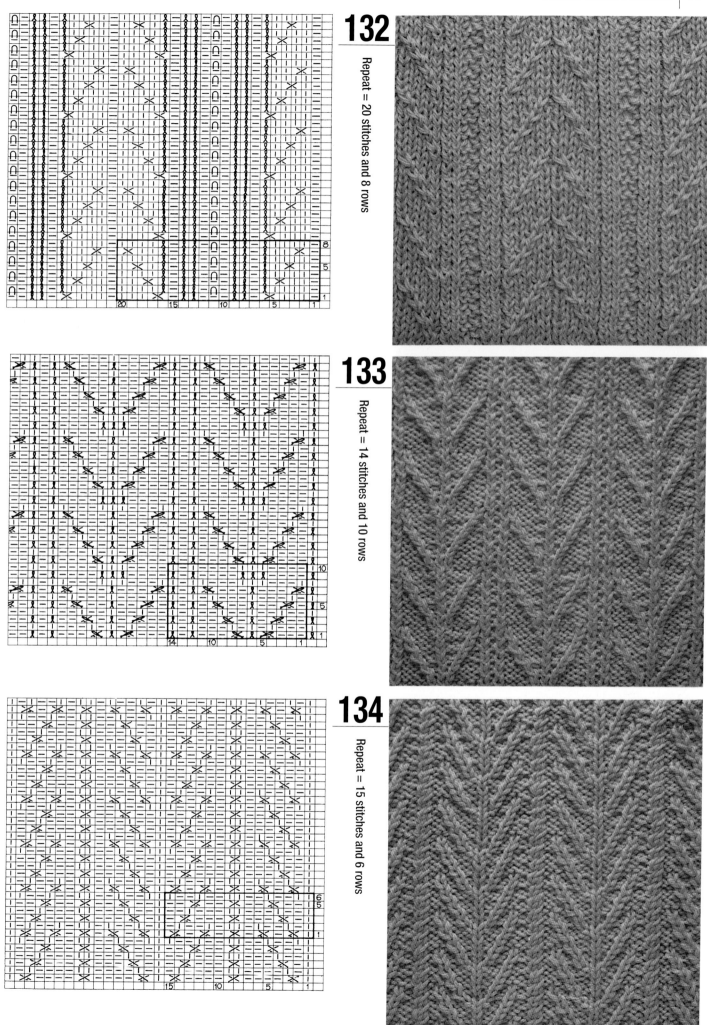

132

Repeat = 20 stitches and 8 rows

133

Repeat = 14 stitches and 10 rows

134

Repeat = 15 stitches and 6 rows

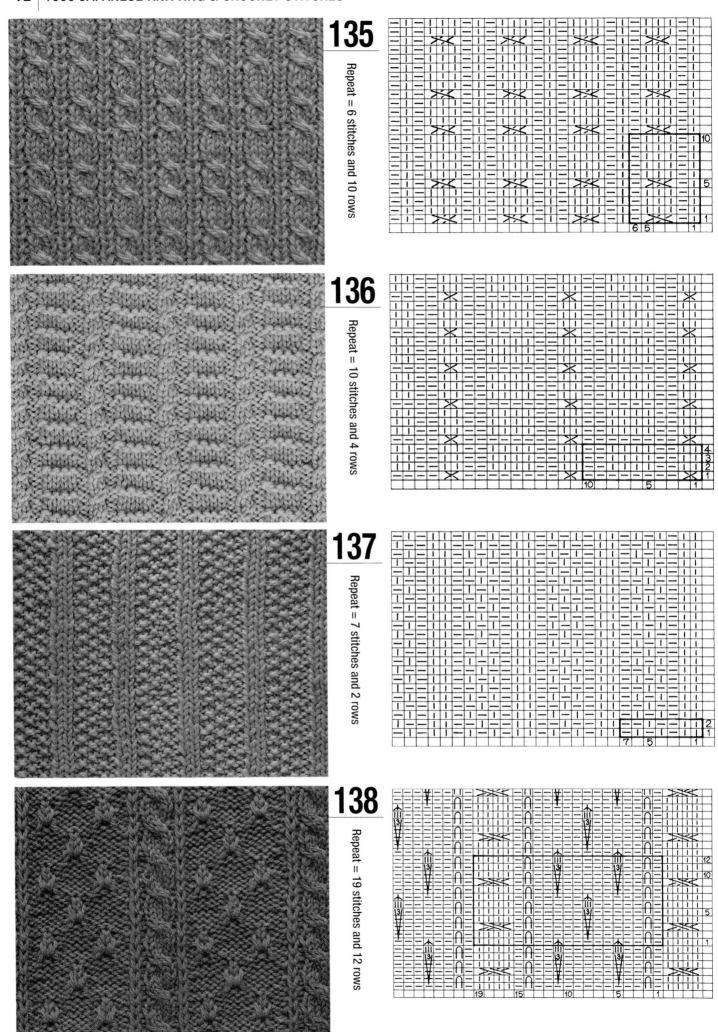

135

Repeat = 6 stitches and 10 rows

136

Repeat = 10 stitches and 4 rows

137

Repeat = 7 stitches and 2 rows

138

Repeat = 19 stitches and 12 rows

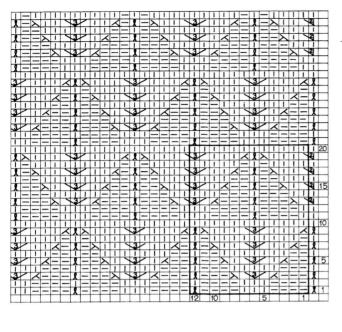

139

Repeat = 12 stitches and 20 rows

140

Repeat = 19 stitches and 38 rows

● = 🧶 See p.29

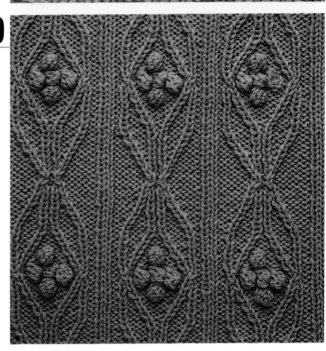

141

Repeat = 9 stitches and 12 rows

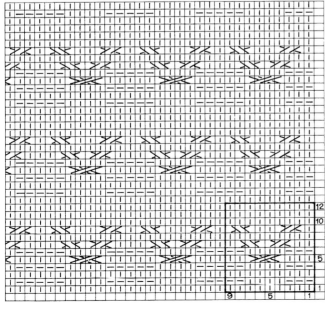

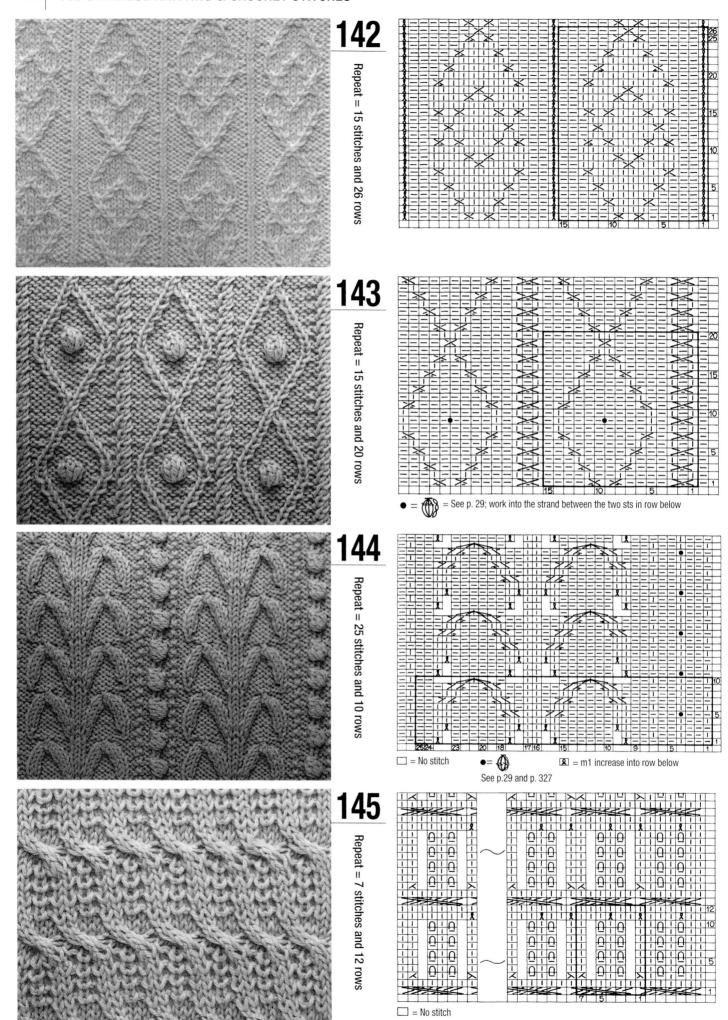

142

Repeat = 15 stitches and 26 rows

143

Repeat = 15 stitches and 20 rows

● = 🕸 = See p. 29; work into the strand between the two sts in row below

144

Repeat = 25 stitches and 10 rows

☐ = No stitch   ●= 🕸   🙎 = m1 increase into row below
See p.29 and p. 327

145

Repeat = 7 stitches and 12 rows

☐ = No stitch

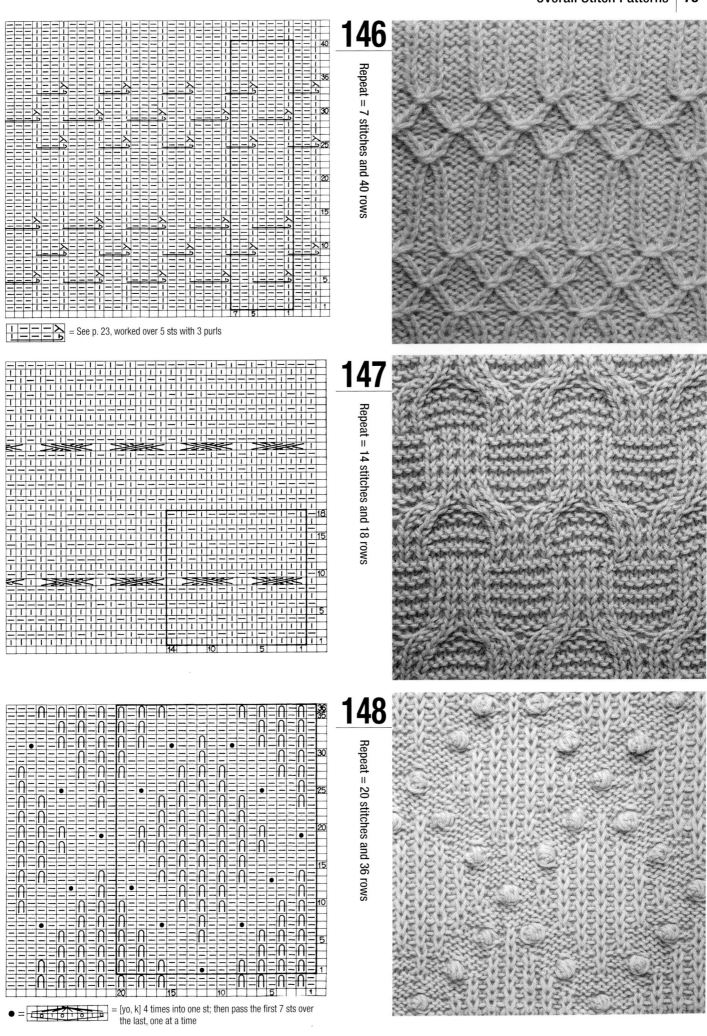

146

Repeat = 7 stitches and 40 rows

$\boxed{\begin{array}{c}| - - - ⅄ \\ | - - - ⅄\end{array}}$ = See p. 23, worked over 5 sts with 3 purls

147

Repeat = 14 stitches and 18 rows

148

Repeat = 20 stitches and 36 rows

● = $\boxed{}$ = [yo, k] 4 times into one st; then pass the first 7 sts over the last, one at a time

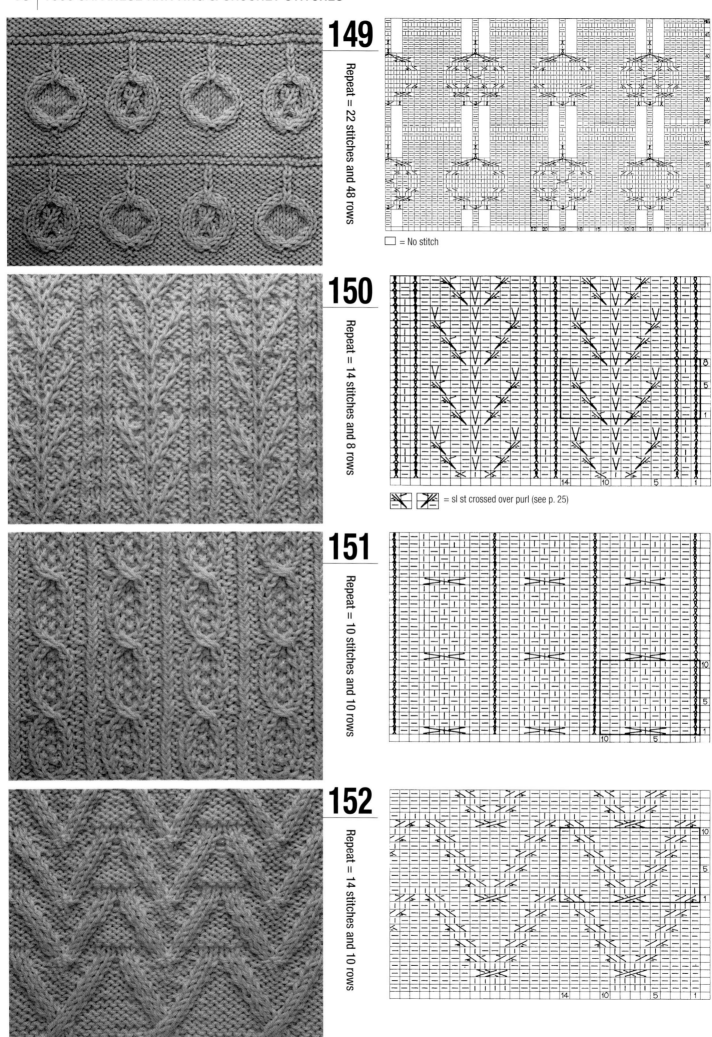

149

Repeat = 22 stitches and 48 rows

☐ = No stitch

150

Repeat = 14 stitches and 8 rows

⬚⬚ = sl st crossed over purl (see p. 25)

151

Repeat = 10 stitches and 10 rows

152

Repeat = 14 stitches and 10 rows

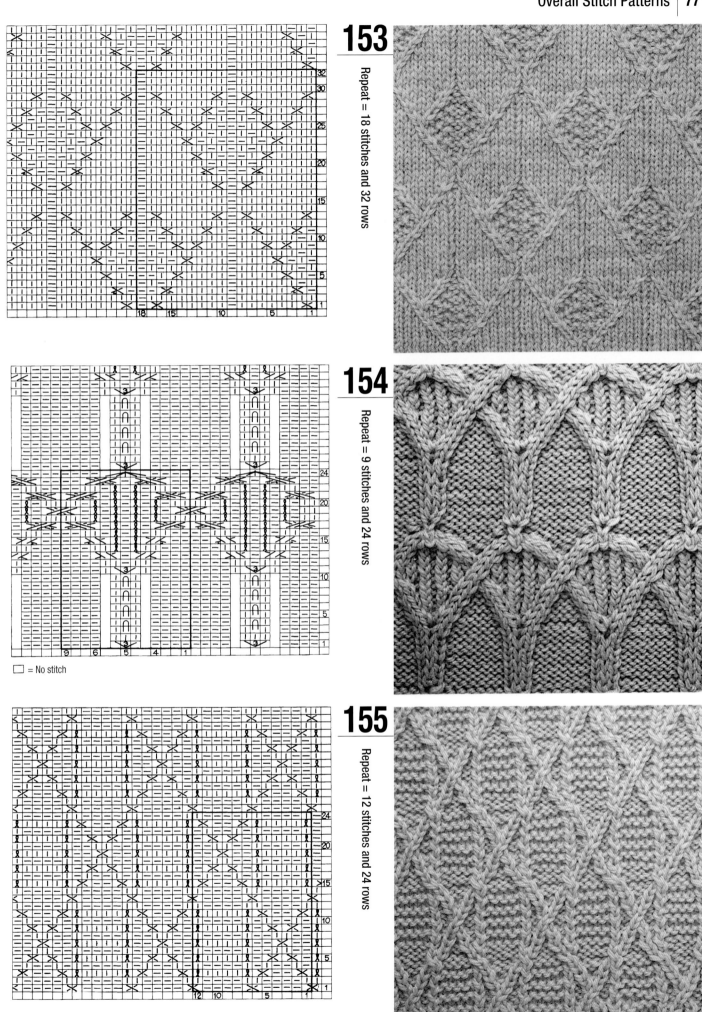

153

Repeat = 18 stitches and 32 rows

154

Repeat = 9 stitches and 24 rows

☐ = No stitch

155

Repeat = 12 stitches and 24 rows

156

Repeat = 10 stitches and 20 rows

□ = No stitch   = CDD, then without removing from LN, work yo, k, yo, k into the same 3 sts (make 5 from 3)

157

Repeat = 7 stitches and 8 rows

□ = No stitch

158

Repeat = 6 stitches and 12 rows

= wrap yarn twice (see p. 22)

159

Repeat = 6 stitches and 8 rows

□ = No stitch   = on second row: lift the 2 double-wrapped sts over the 5 purls and drop them (similar to p. 30)

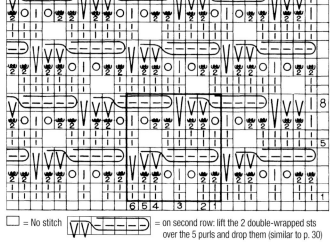

160

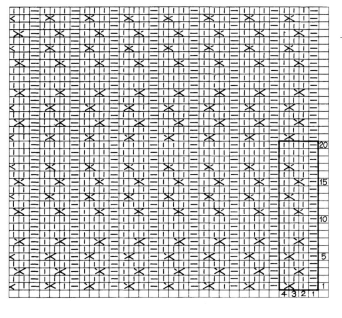

Repeat = 4 stitches and 20 rows

161

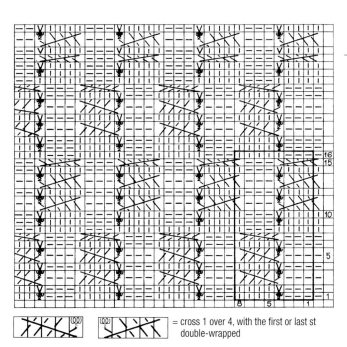

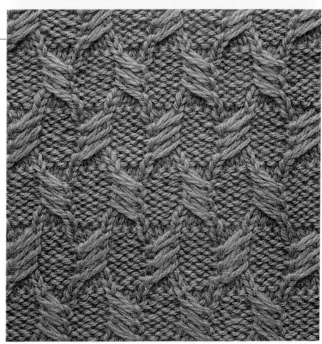

Repeat = 8 stitches and 16 rows

= cross 1 over 4, with the first or last st double-wrapped

162

Repeat = 24 stitches and 32 rows

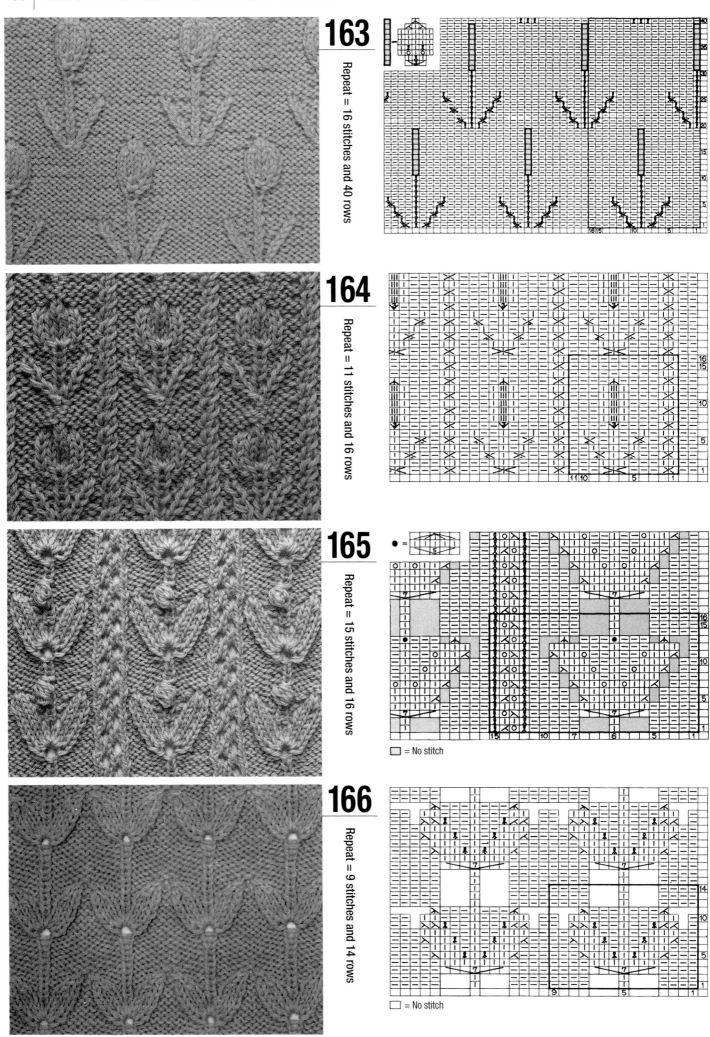

163

Repeat = 16 stitches and 40 rows

164

Repeat = 11 stitches and 16 rows

165

Repeat = 15 stitches and 16 rows

☐ = No stitch

166

Repeat = 9 stitches and 14 rows

☐ = No stitch

OPENWORK STITCH PATTERNS ✳ Floral, leaf and meandering stitches

Openwork stitches are created with yarnovers, increases and decreases. The patterns collected here may be complex, and result in elegant knitted fabrics. Choice of materials is an important factor in getting good results; your stitches will show better in smooth, monotone yarn.

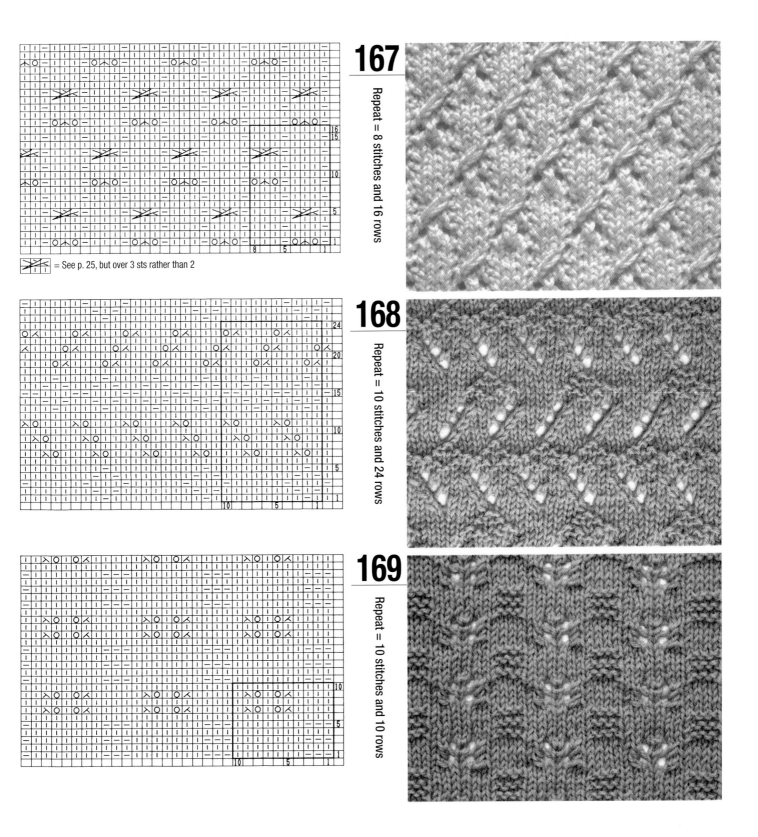

⤬ = See p. 25, but over 3 sts rather than 2

167 Repeat = 8 stitches and 16 rows

168 Repeat = 10 stitches and 24 rows

169 Repeat = 10 stitches and 10 rows

170

Repeat = 24 stitches and 24 rows

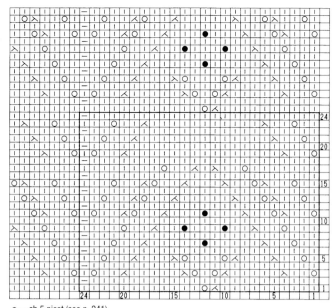

● = ch 5 picot (see p. 241)

171

Repeat = 21 stitches and 8 rows

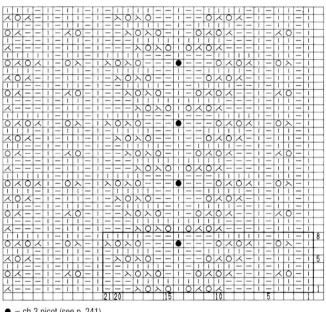

● = ch 3 picot (see p. 241)

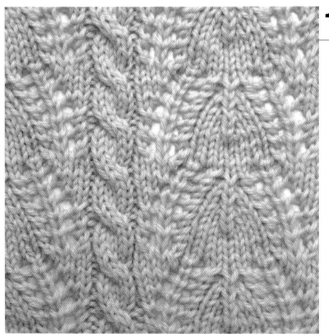

172

Repeat = 23 stitches and 12 rows

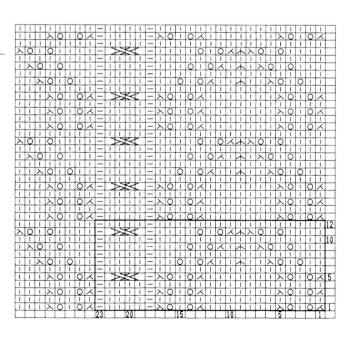

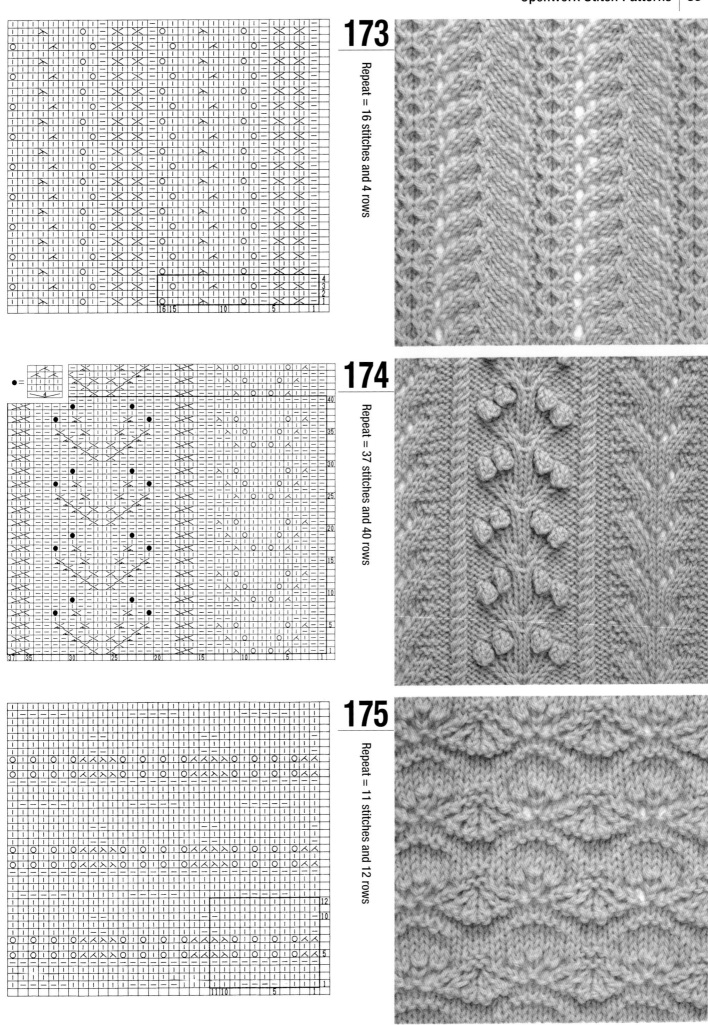

173

Repeat = 16 stitches and 4 rows

174

Repeat = 37 stitches and 40 rows

175

Repeat = 11 stitches and 12 rows

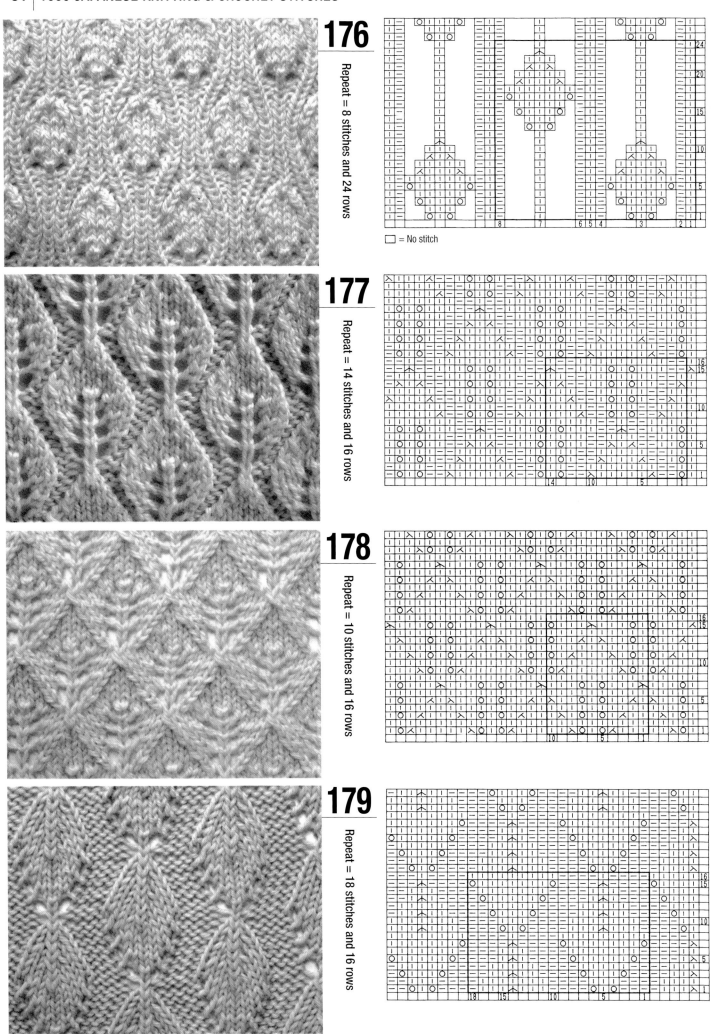

# 176
Repeat = 8 stitches and 24 rows

☐ = No stitch

# 177
Repeat = 14 stitches and 16 rows

# 178
Repeat = 10 stitches and 16 rows

# 179
Repeat = 18 stitches and 16 rows

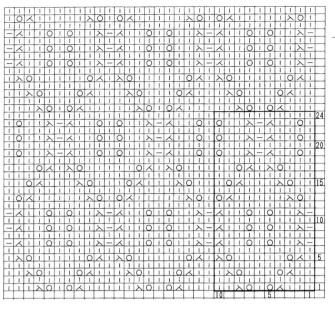

180

Repeat = 10 stitches and 24 rows

181

Repeat = 14 stitches and 16 rows

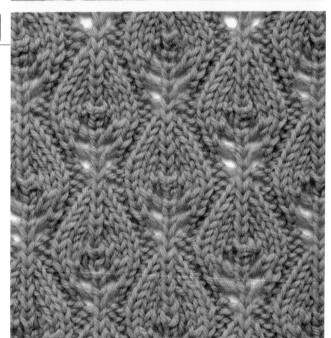

182

Repeat = 22 stitches and 32 rows

⊠ · ⊠ = work as m1 or m1p increase

183

A Repeat = 5 stitches and 4 rows
B Repeat = 9 stitches and 18 rows

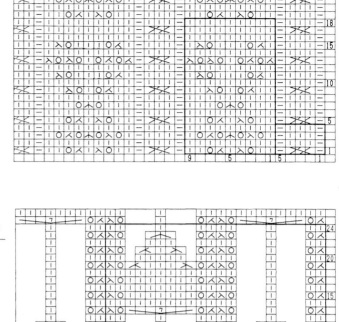

184

Repeat = 10 stitches and 24 rows

□ = No stitch

185

Repeat = 11 stitches and 20 rows

186

Repeat = 22 stitches and 12 rows

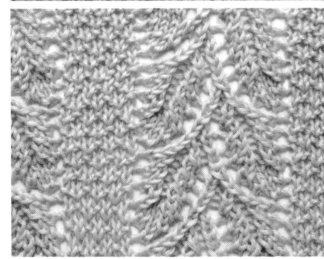

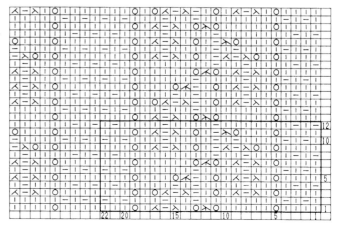

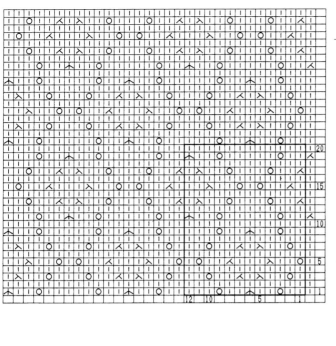

187

Repeat = 12 stitches and 20 rows

188

Repeat = 16 stitches and 28 rows

189

Repeat = 24 stitches and 24 rows

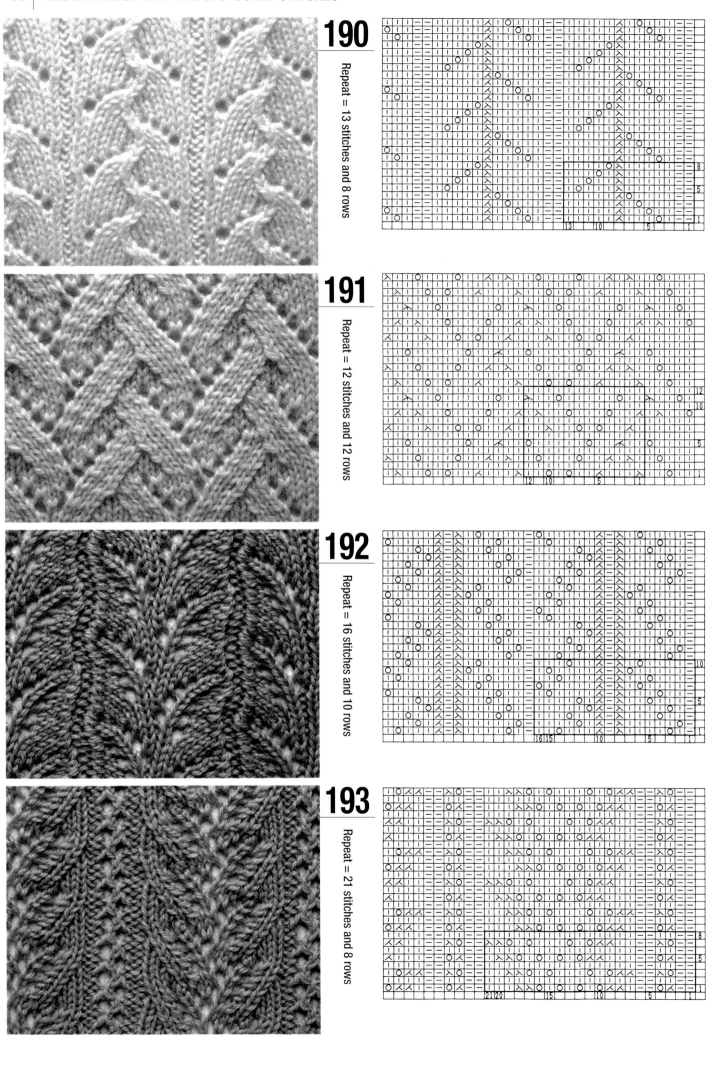

190

Repeat = 13 stitches and 8 rows

191

Repeat = 12 stitches and 12 rows

192

Repeat = 16 stitches and 10 rows

193

Repeat = 21 stitches and 8 rows

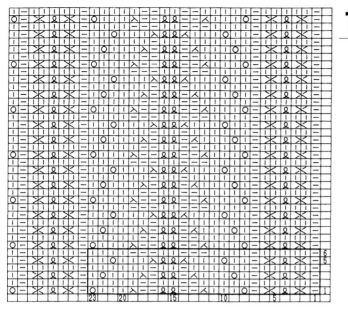

194

Repeat = 23 stitches and 6 rows

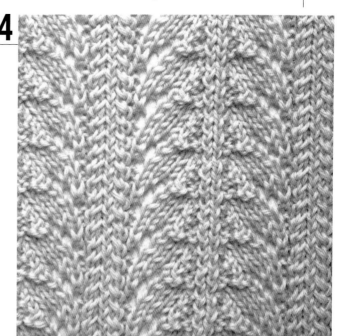

195

Repeat = 17 stitches and 8 rows

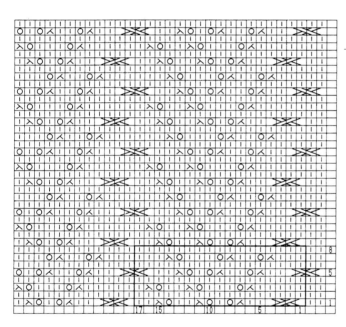

196

Repeat = 16 stitches and 24 rows

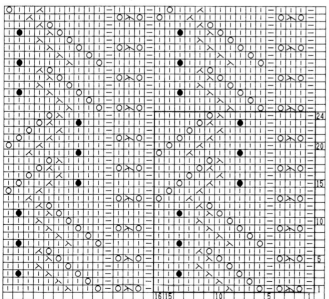

● = ch 5 picot (see p. 241)

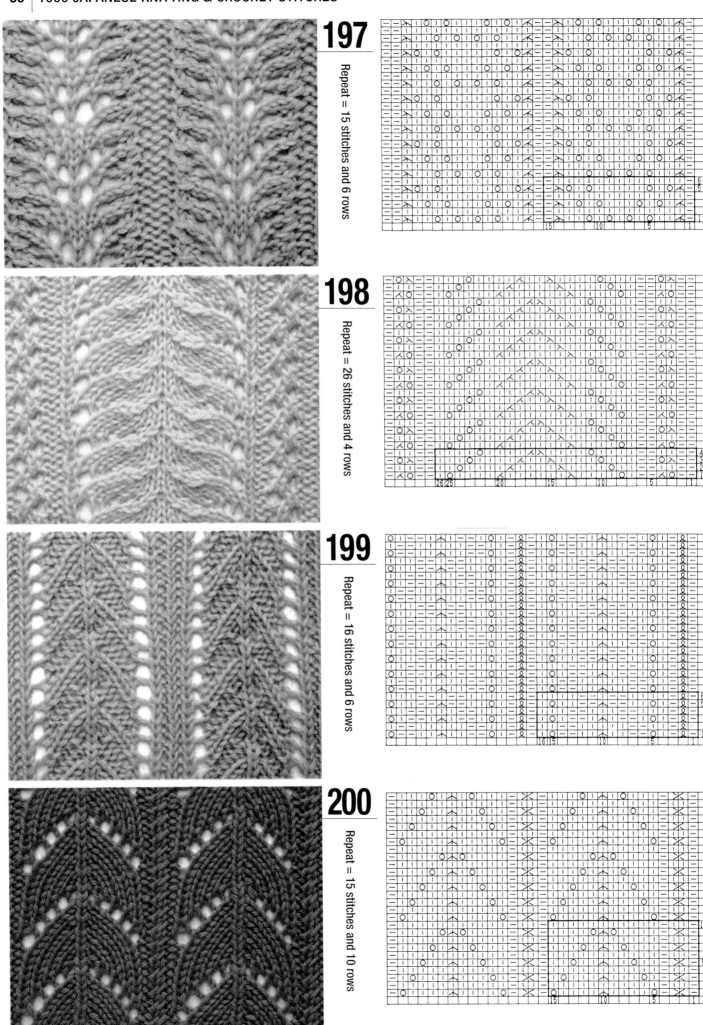

197

Repeat = 15 stitches and 6 rows

198

Repeat = 26 stitches and 4 rows

199

Repeat = 16 stitches and 6 rows

200

Repeat = 15 stitches and 10 rows

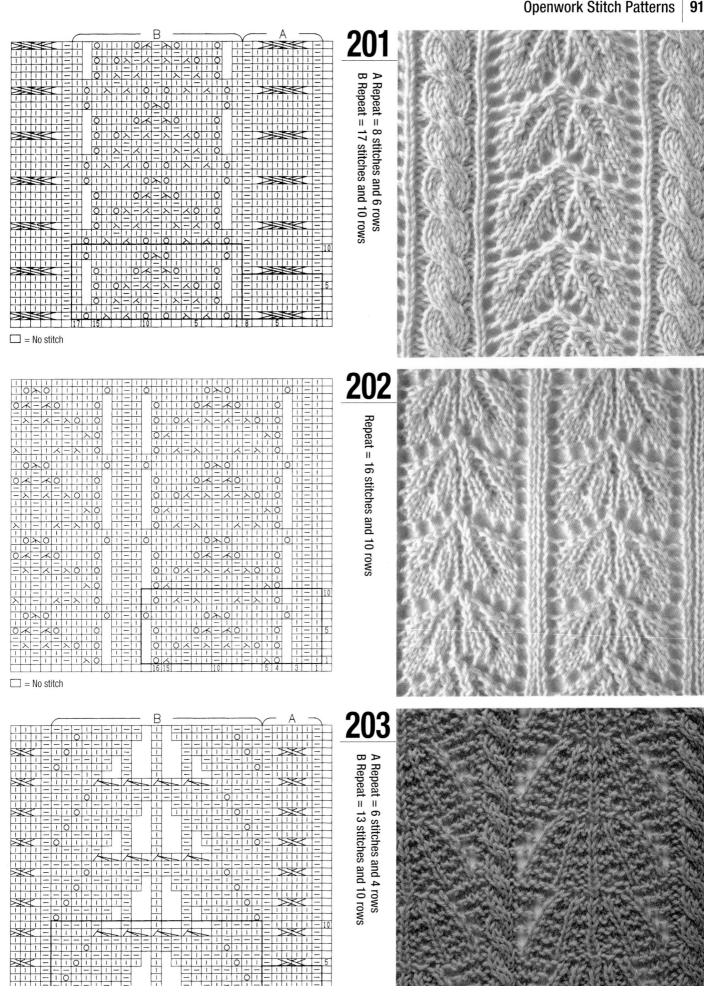

201

A Repeat = 8 stitches and 6 rows
B Repeat = 17 stitches and 10 rows

☐ = No stitch

202

Repeat = 16 stitches and 10 rows

☐ = No stitch

203

A Repeat = 6 stitches and 4 rows
B Repeat = 13 stitches and 10 rows

☐ = No stitch   ⟋⟋⟍ = k3tog

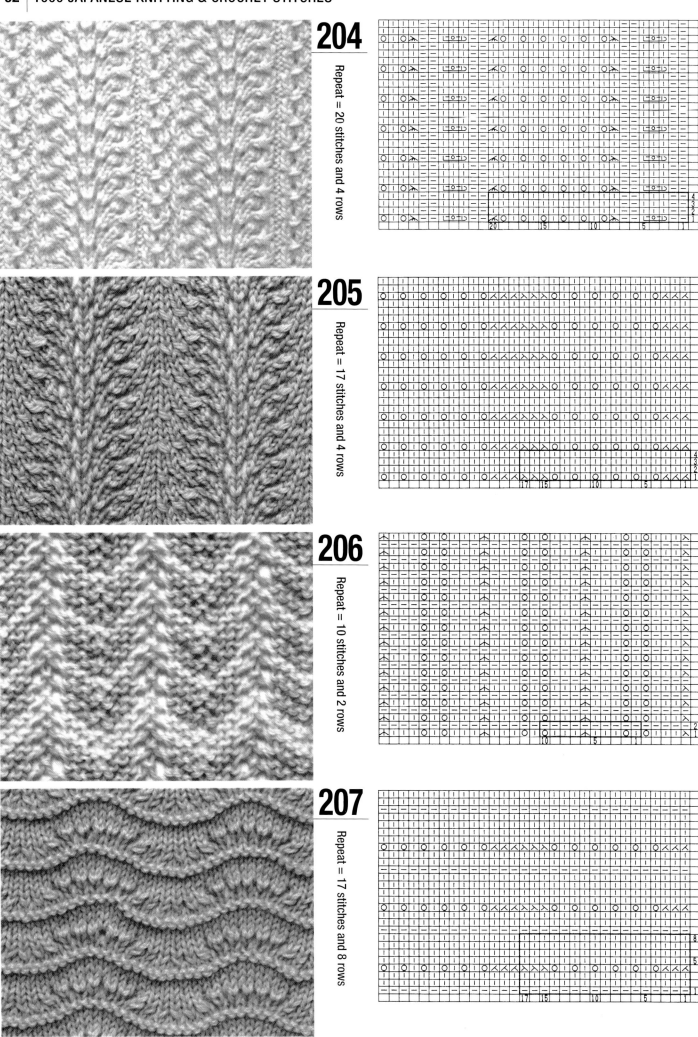

204
Repeat = 20 stitches and 4 rows

205
Repeat = 17 stitches and 4 rows

206
Repeat = 10 stitches and 2 rows

207
Repeat = 17 stitches and 8 rows

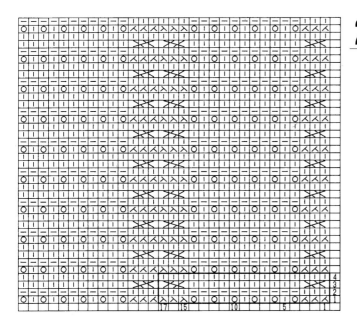

208

Repeat = 17 stitches and 4 rows

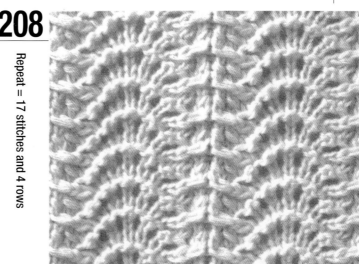

209

Repeat = 18 stitches and 6 rows

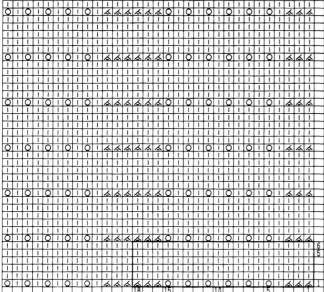

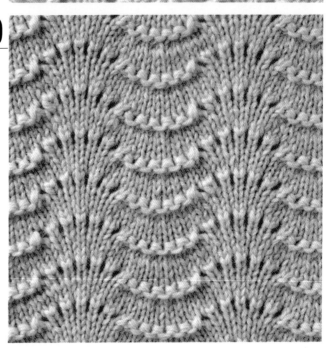

210

Repeat = 17 stitches and 4 rows

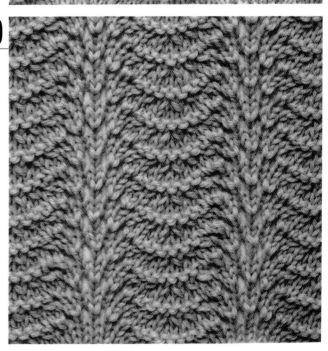

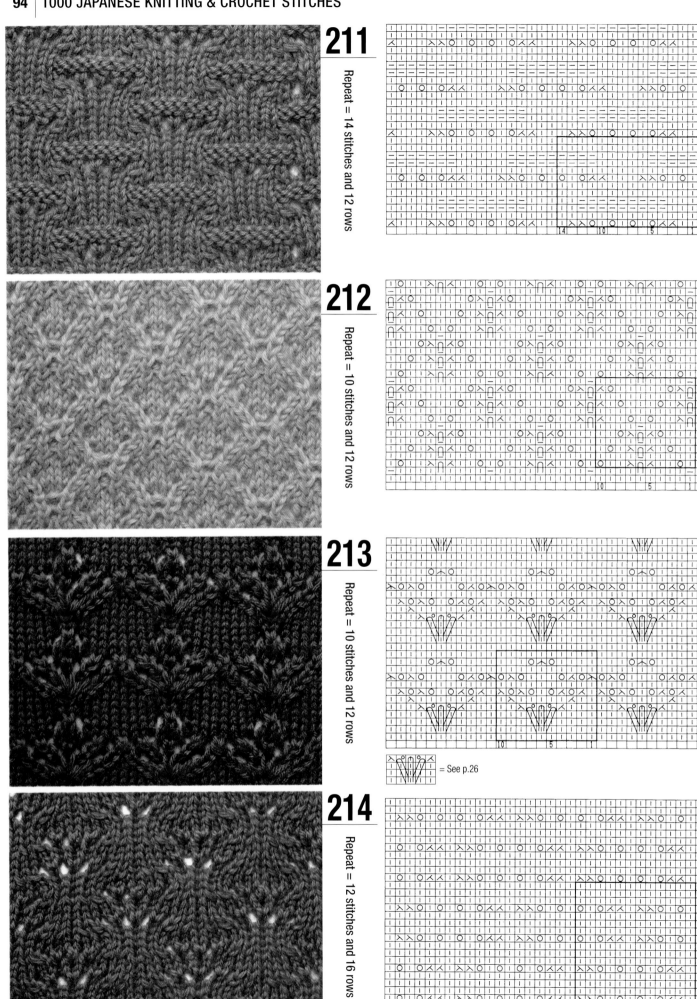

211

Repeat = 14 stitches and 12 rows

212

Repeat = 10 stitches and 12 rows

213

Repeat = 10 stitches and 12 rows

= See p.26

214

Repeat = 12 stitches and 16 rows

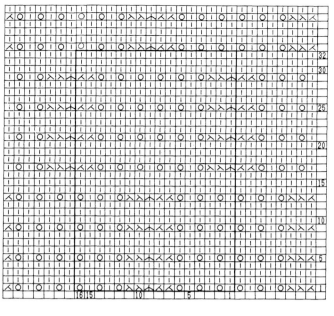

215

Repeat = 16 stitches and 32 rows

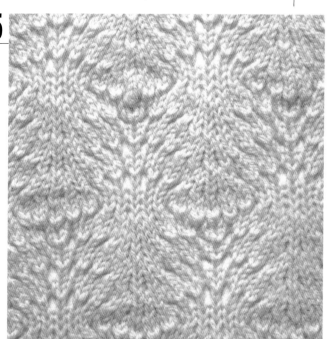

216

Repeat = 11 stitches and 10 rows

217

Repeat = 18 stitches and 16 rows

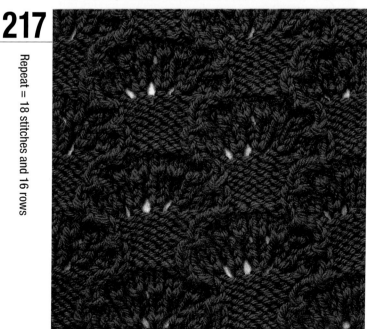

⋏ = k4tog   ⋏ = sl 3 knitwise, k1, p3sso

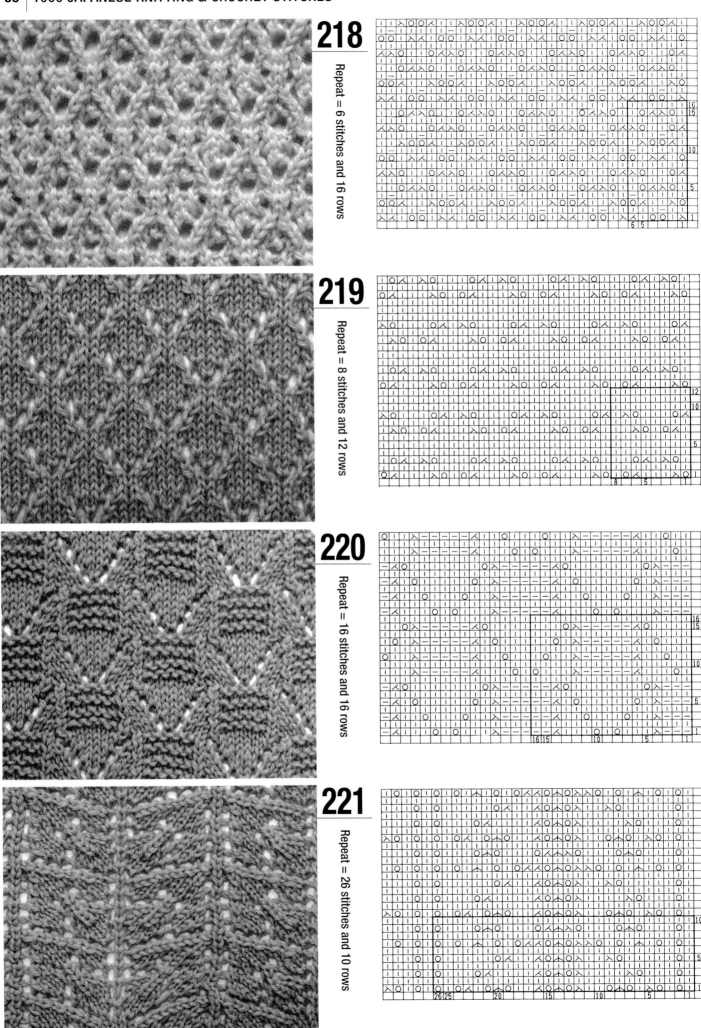

218

Repeat = 6 stitches and 16 rows

219

Repeat = 8 stitches and 12 rows

220

Repeat = 16 stitches and 16 rows

221

Repeat = 26 stitches and 10 rows

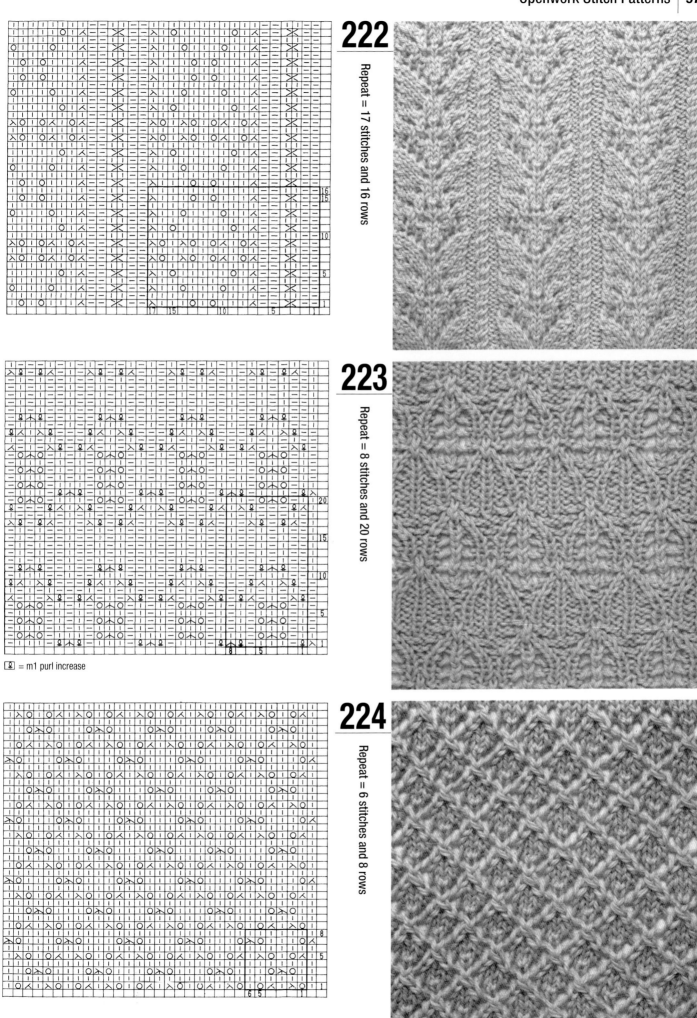

222

Repeat = 17 stitches and 16 rows

223

Repeat = 8 stitches and 20 rows

= m1 purl increase

224

Repeat = 6 stitches and 8 rows

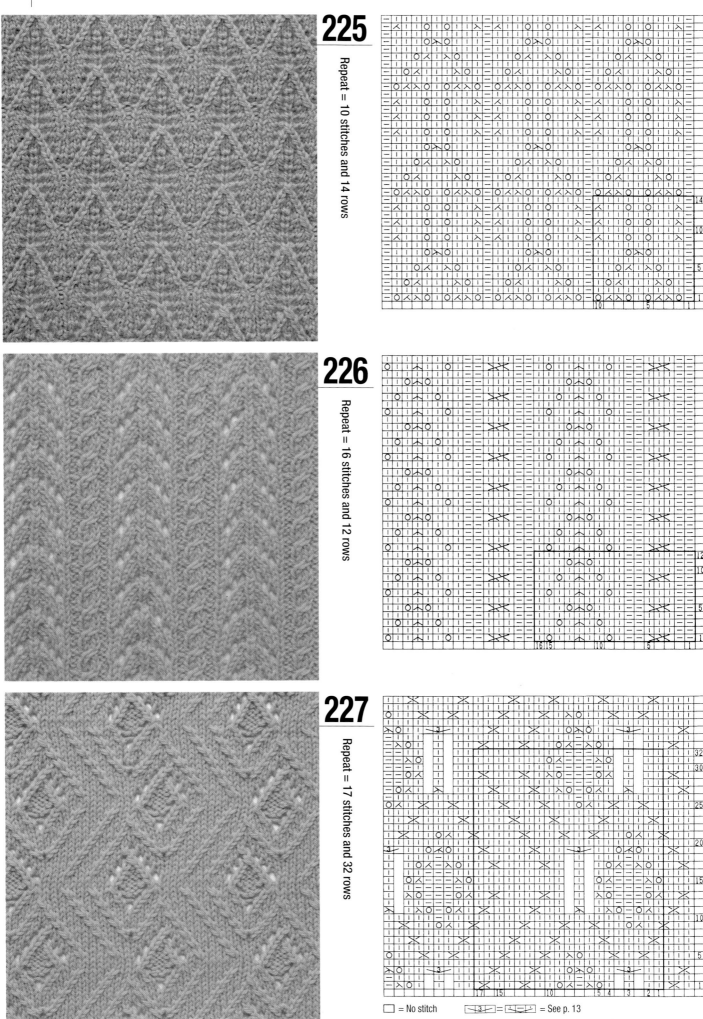

225

Repeat = 10 stitches and 14 rows

226

Repeat = 16 stitches and 12 rows

227

Repeat = 17 stitches and 32 rows

□ = No stitch   = See p. 13

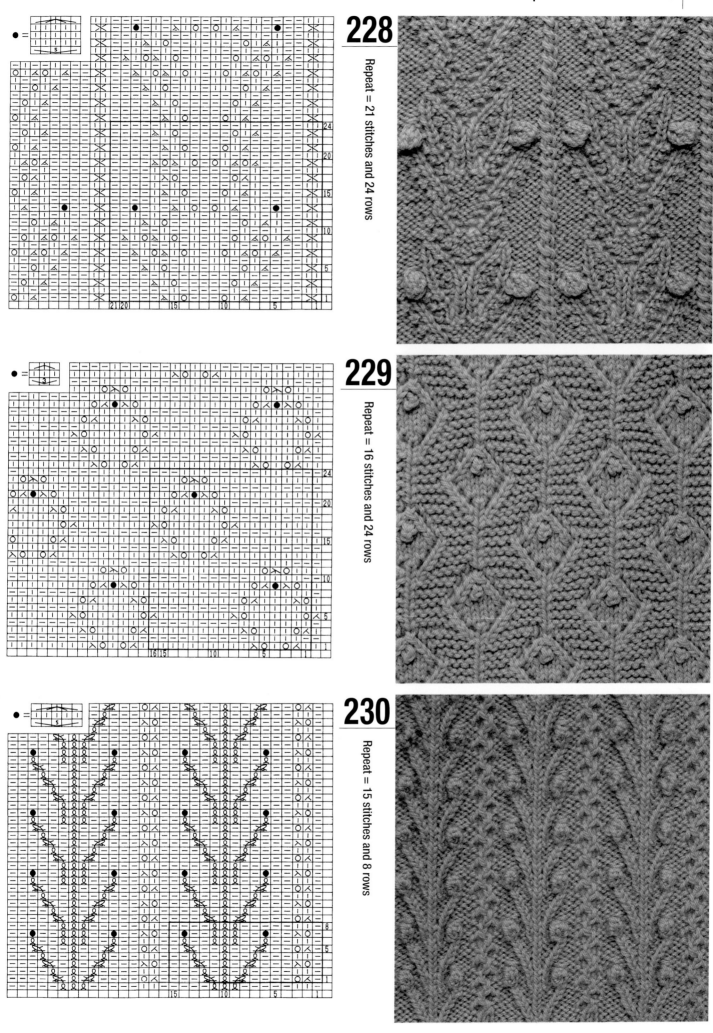

228

Repeat = 21 stitches and 24 rows

229

Repeat = 16 stitches and 24 rows

230

Repeat = 15 stitches and 8 rows

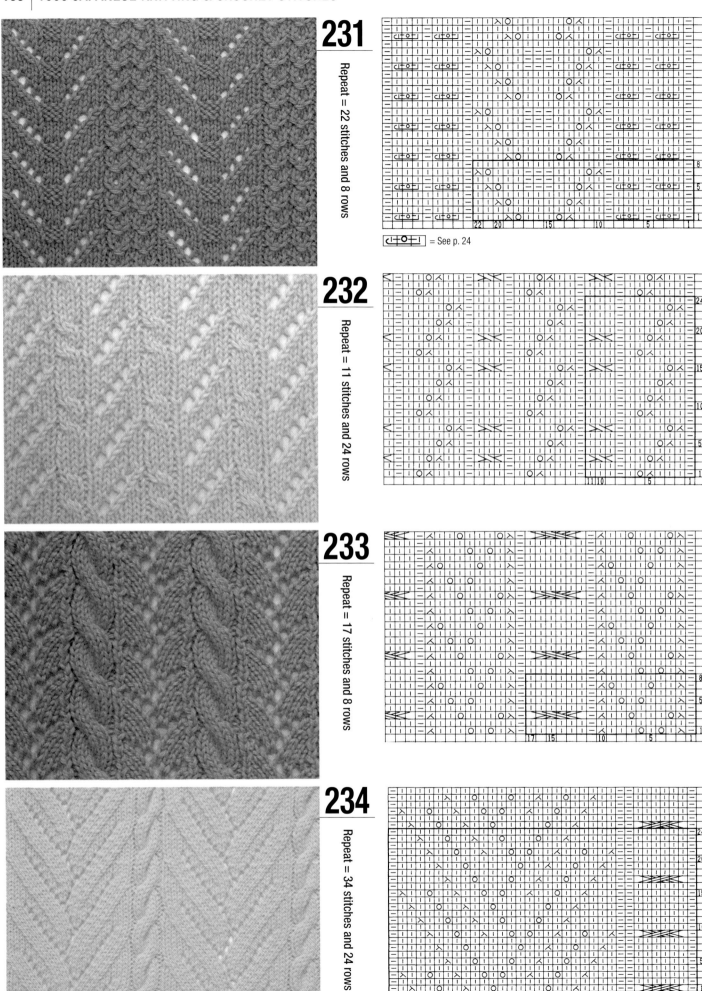

231
Repeat = 22 stitches and 8 rows

⌐⊏+O+⌐ = See p. 24

232
Repeat = 11 stitches and 24 rows

233
Repeat = 17 stitches and 8 rows

234
Repeat = 34 stitches and 24 rows

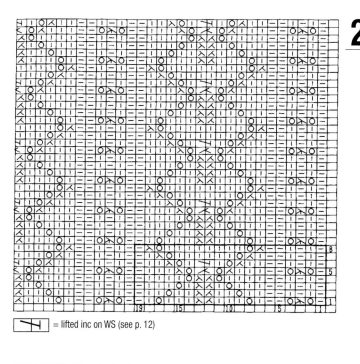

235

Repeat = 19 stitches and 8 rows

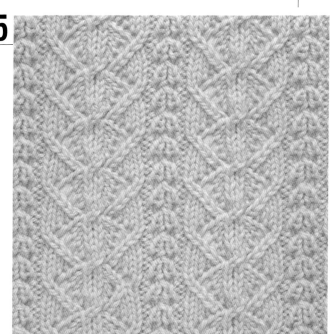

= lifted inc on WS (see p. 12)

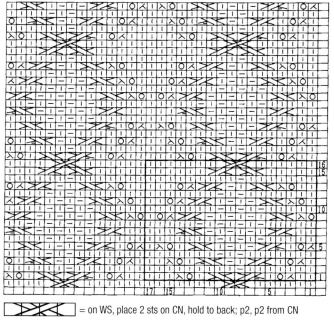

236

Repeat = 17 stitches and 16 rows

= on WS, place 2 sts on CN, hold to back; p2, p2 from CN

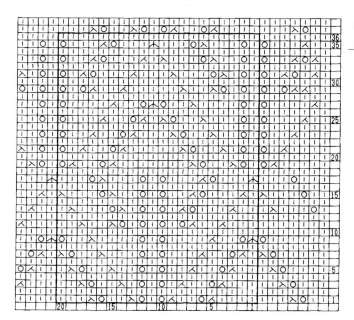

237

Repeat = 20 stitches and 36 rows

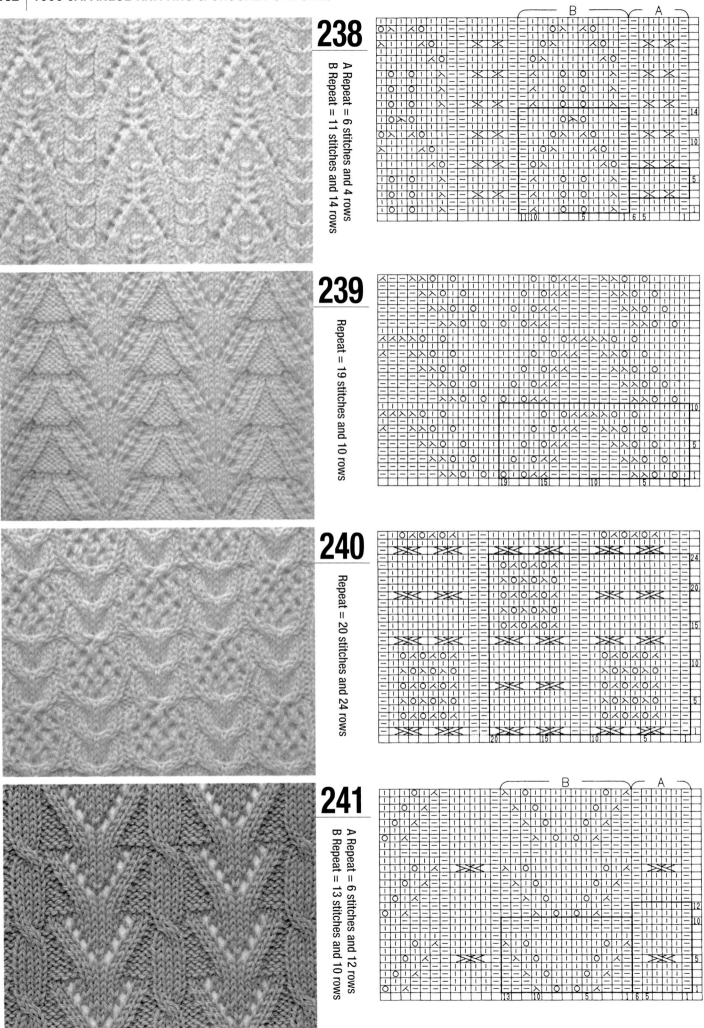

238
A Repeat = 6 stitches and 4 rows
B Repeat = 11 stitches and 14 rows

239
Repeat = 19 stitches and 10 rows

240
Repeat = 20 stitches and 24 rows

241
A Repeat = 6 stitches and 12 rows
B Repeat = 13 stitches and 10 rows

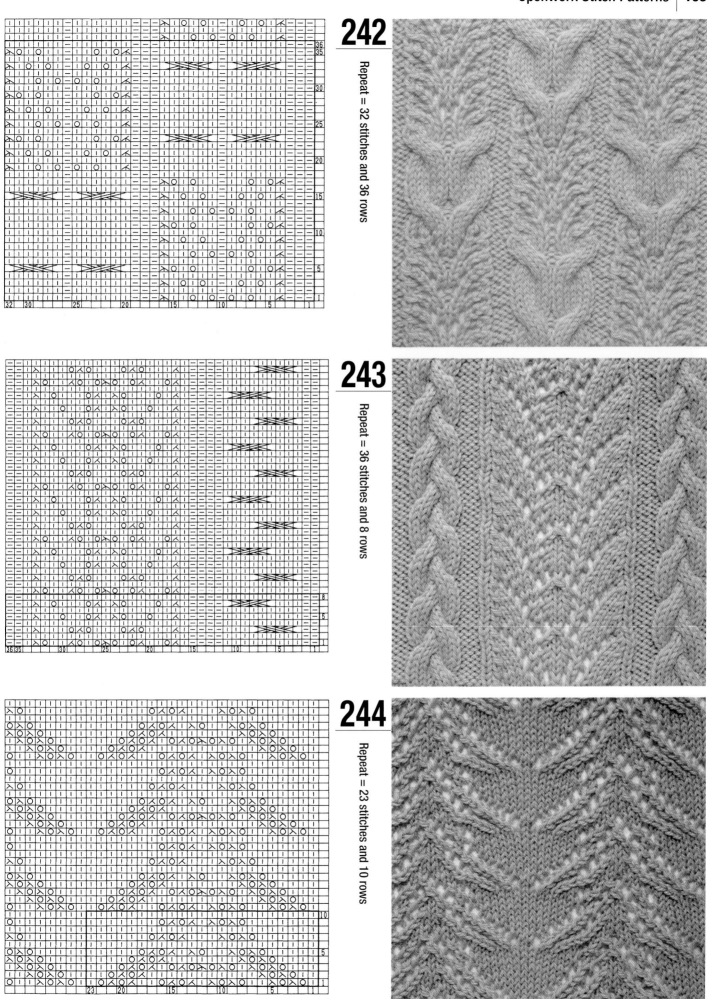

242
Repeat = 32 stitches and 36 rows

243
Repeat = 36 stitches and 8 rows

244
Repeat = 23 stitches and 10 rows

245

Repeat = 16 stitches and 8 rows

246

Repeat = 17 stitches and 8 rows

247

Repeat = 14 stitches and 6 rows

248

Repeat = 22 stitches and 8 rows

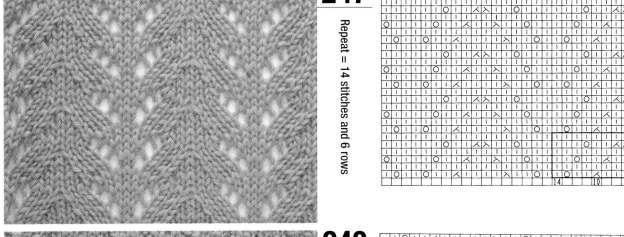

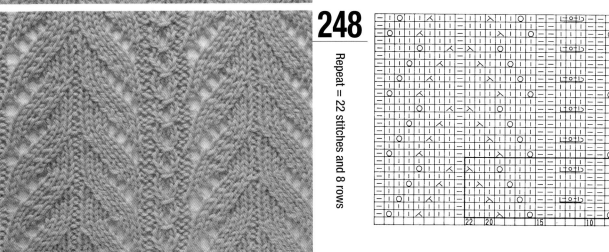

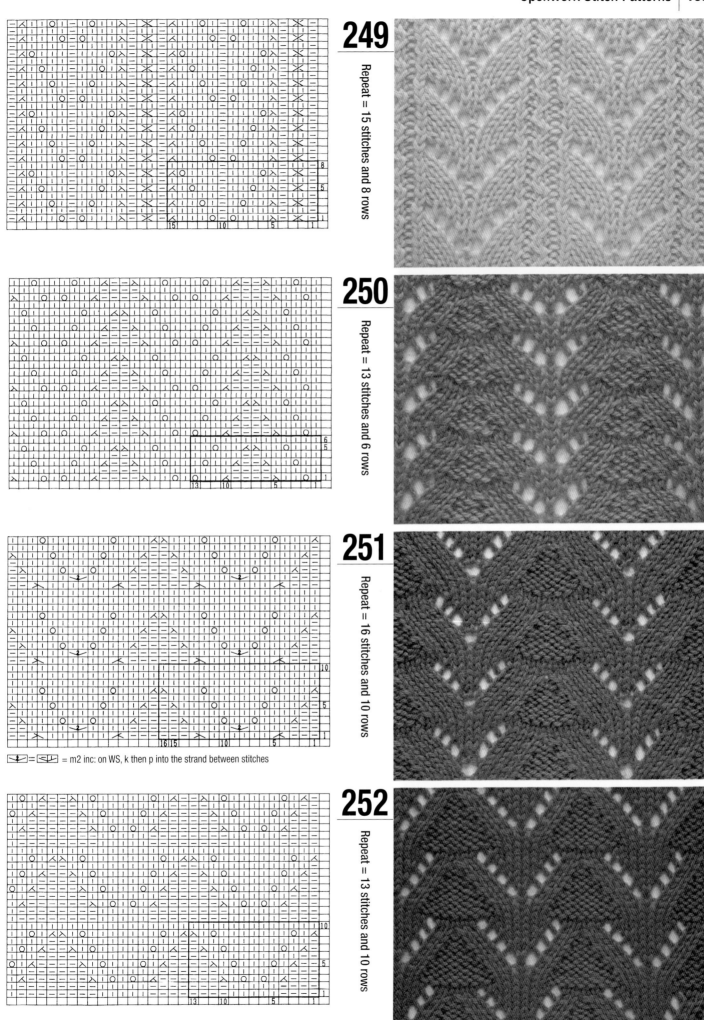

249

Repeat = 15 stitches and 8 rows

250

Repeat = 13 stitches and 6 rows

251

Repeat = 16 stitches and 10 rows

= m2 inc: on WS, k then p into the strand between stitches

252

Repeat = 13 stitches and 10 rows

253

Repeat = 33 stitches and 32 rows

254

Repeat = 16 stitches and 16 rows

255

Repeat = 28 stitches and 48 rows

• = 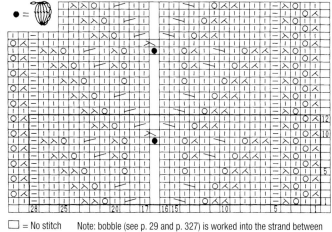 See p. 29

256

Repeat = 28 stitches and 12 rows

□ = No stitch   Note: bobble (see p. 29 and p. 327) is worked into the strand between stitches

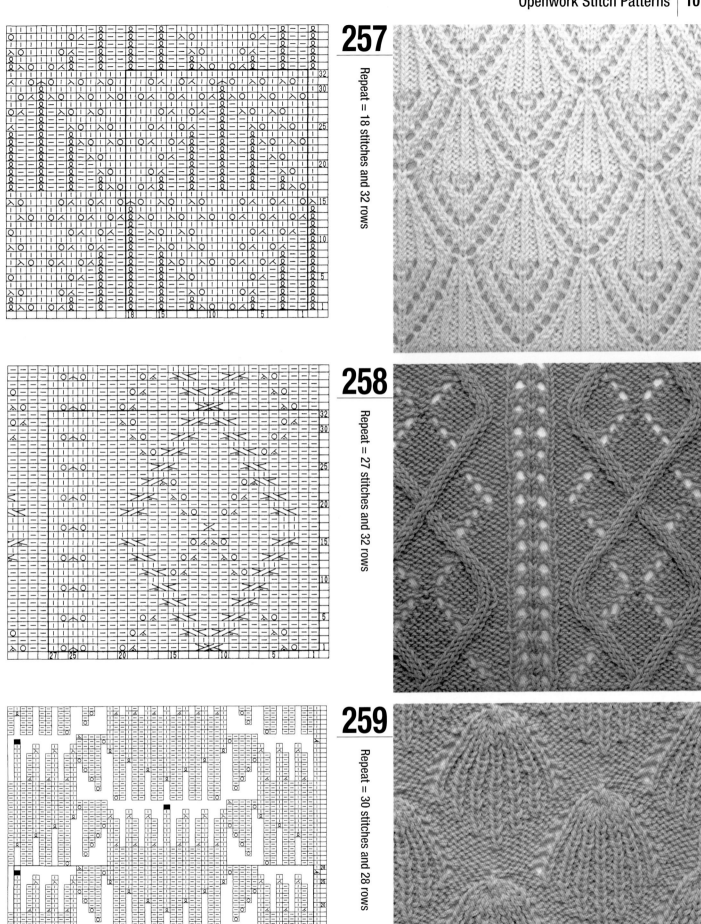

257

Repeat = 18 stitches and 32 rows

258

Repeat = 27 stitches and 32 rows

259

Repeat = 30 stitches and 28 rows

□ = No stitch   ■ = = sl 4 sts tog knitwise; k3tog; p4sso   ⧄ = m1 increase

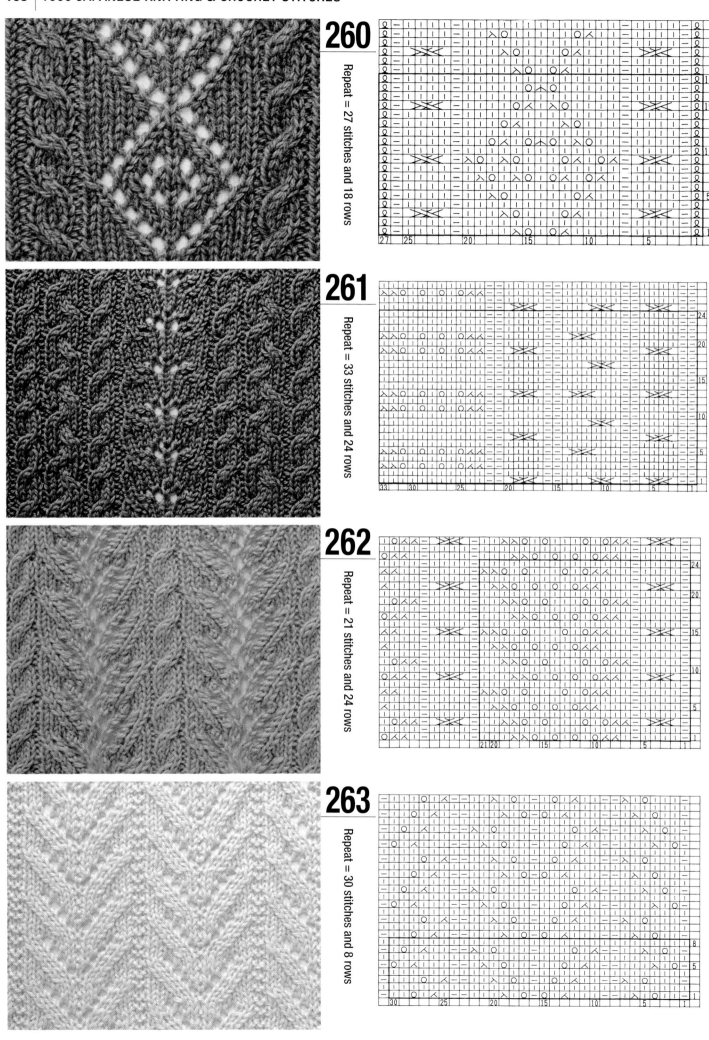

260 Repeat = 27 stitches and 18 rows

261 Repeat = 33 stitches and 24 rows

262 Repeat = 21 stitches and 24 rows

263 Repeat = 30 stitches and 8 rows

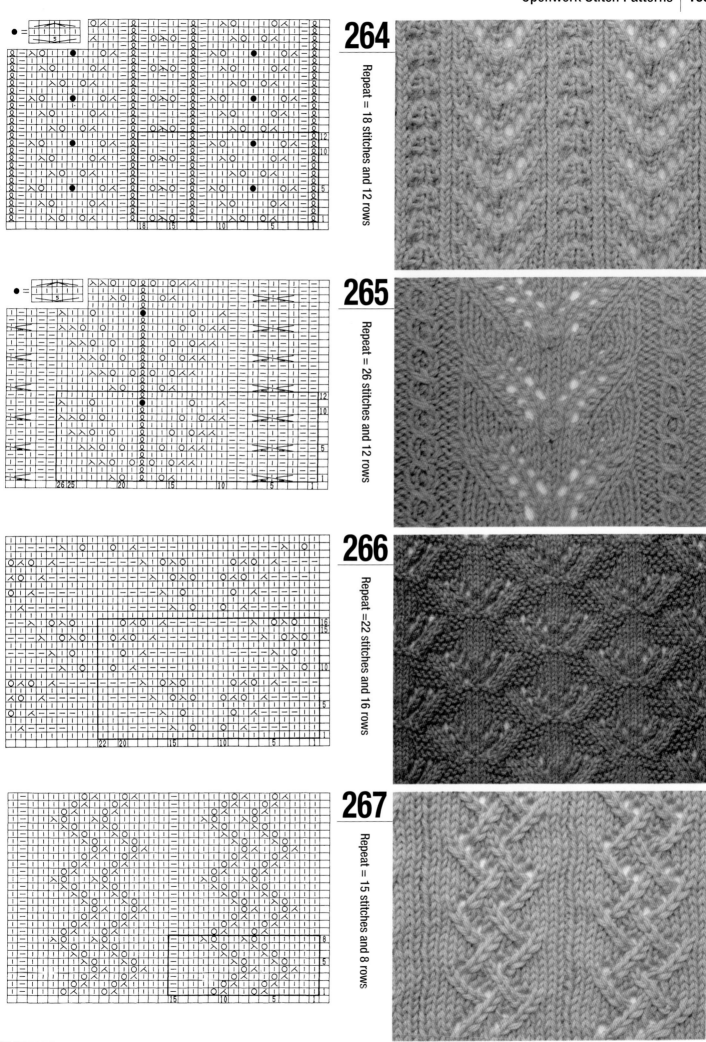

264 Repeat = 18 stitches and 12 rows

265 Repeat = 26 stitches and 12 rows

266 Repeat =22 stitches and 16 rows

267 Repeat = 15 stitches and 8 rows

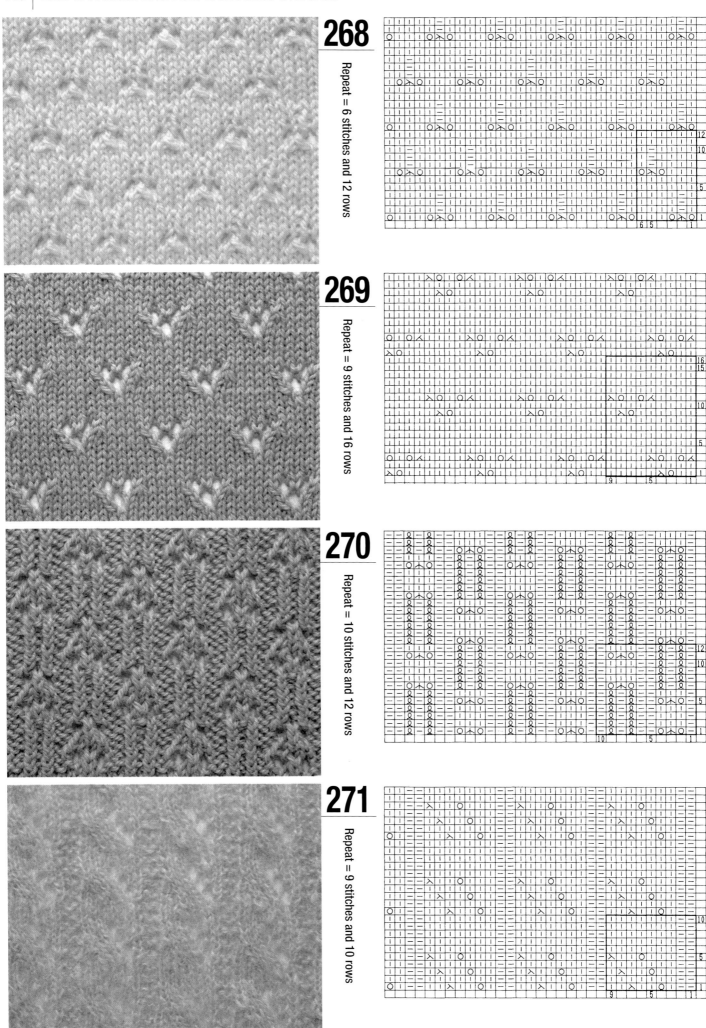

268

Repeat = 6 stitches and 12 rows

269

Repeat = 9 stitches and 16 rows

270

Repeat = 10 stitches and 12 rows

271

Repeat = 9 stitches and 10 rows

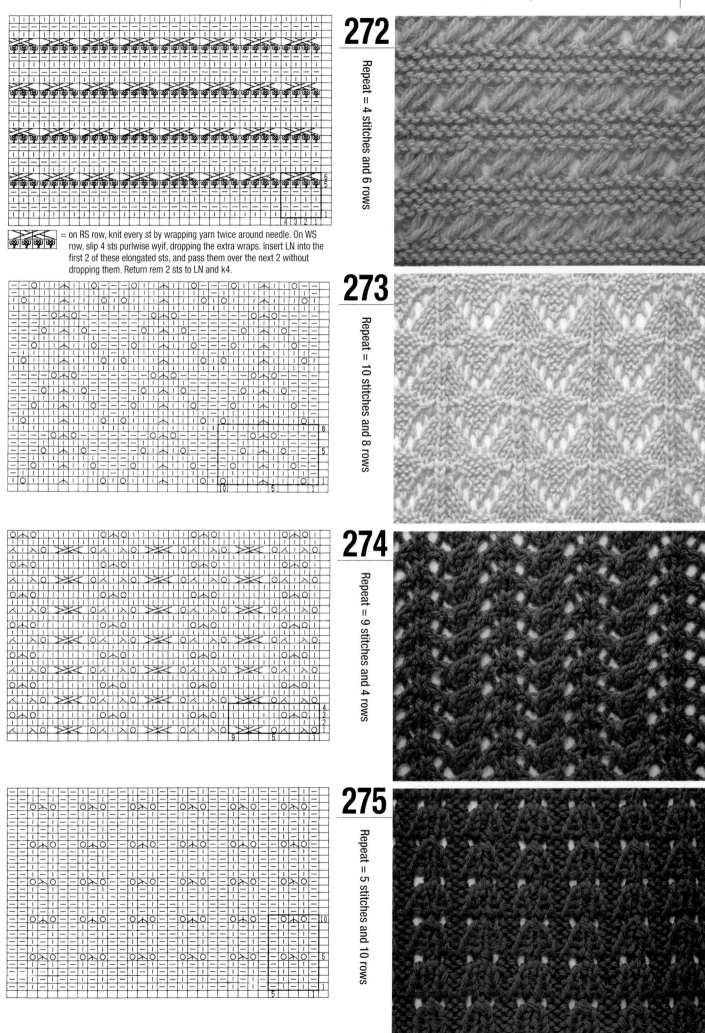

272

Repeat = 4 stitches and 6 rows

⟩⟨⟩⟨ = on RS row, knit every st by wrapping yarn twice around needle. On WS row, slip 4 sts purlwise wyif, dropping the extra wraps. Insert LN into the first 2 of these elongated sts, and pass them over the next 2 without dropping them. Return rem 2 sts to LN and k4.

273

Repeat = 10 stitches and 8 rows

274

Repeat = 9 stitches and 4 rows

275

Repeat = 5 stitches and 10 rows

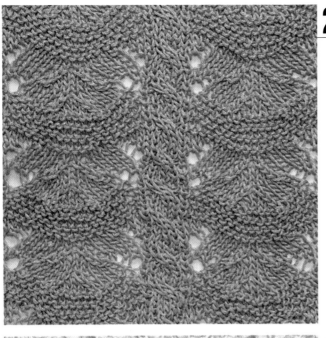

276

A Repeat = 20 stitches and 16 rows
B Repeat = 6 stitches and 6 rows

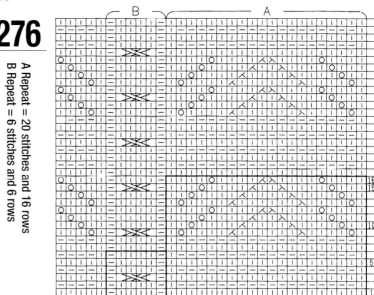

277

Repeat = 36 stitches and 16 rows

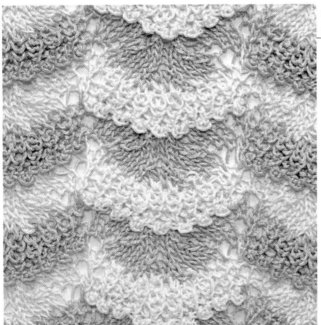

Top left inset: First, using a crochet hook, work 8 picots (p.241) as shown with a separate strand of yarn in new color. On the designated WS row, pick up through the back loop of each chain or sl st and work it together with the next st on the LN.

278

Repeat = 36 stitches and 16 rows

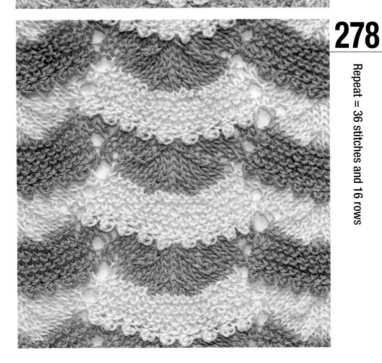

Top left inset: First, using a crochet hook, work 8 picots (p.241) as shown with a separate strand of yarn in new color. On the designated WS row, pick up through the back loop of each chain or sl st and work it together with the next st on the LN.

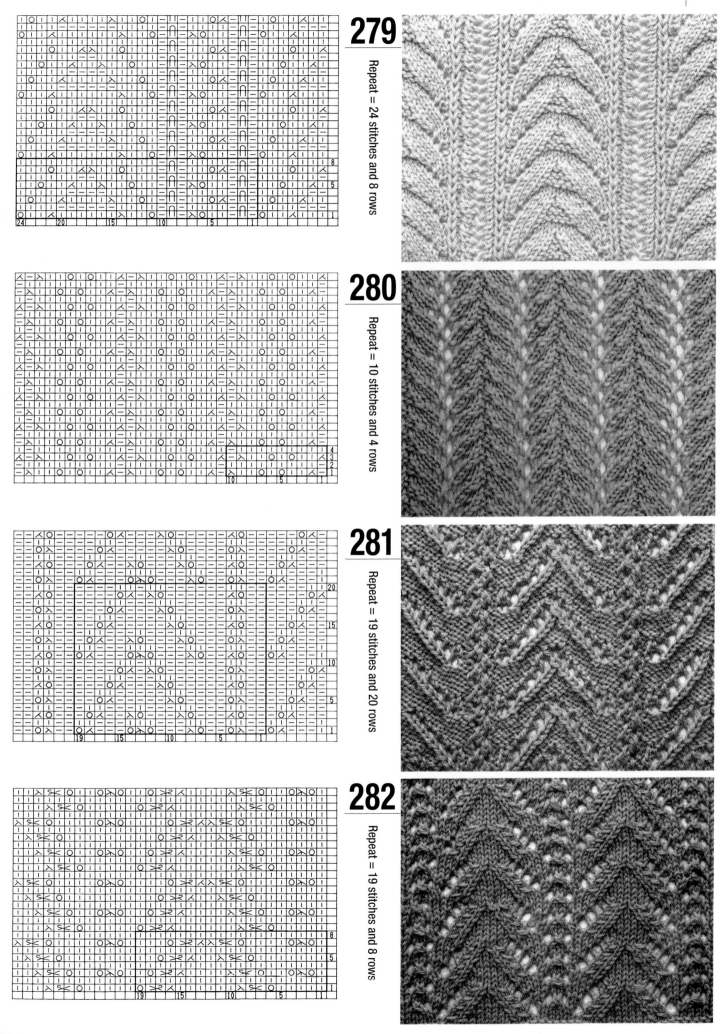

279
Repeat = 24 stitches and 8 rows

280
Repeat = 10 stitches and 4 rows

281
Repeat = 19 stitches and 20 rows

282
Repeat = 19 stitches and 8 rows

283

Repeat = 16 stitches and 4 rows

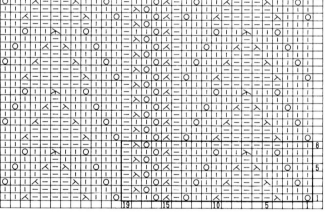

284

Repeat = 16 stitches and 8 rows

285

Repeat = 19 stitches and 8 rows

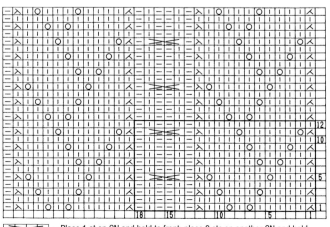

286

Repeat = 18 stitches and 12 rows

= Place 1 st on CN and hold to front; place 2 sts on another CN and hold to back; k1; p2 from back CN, k1 from front CN

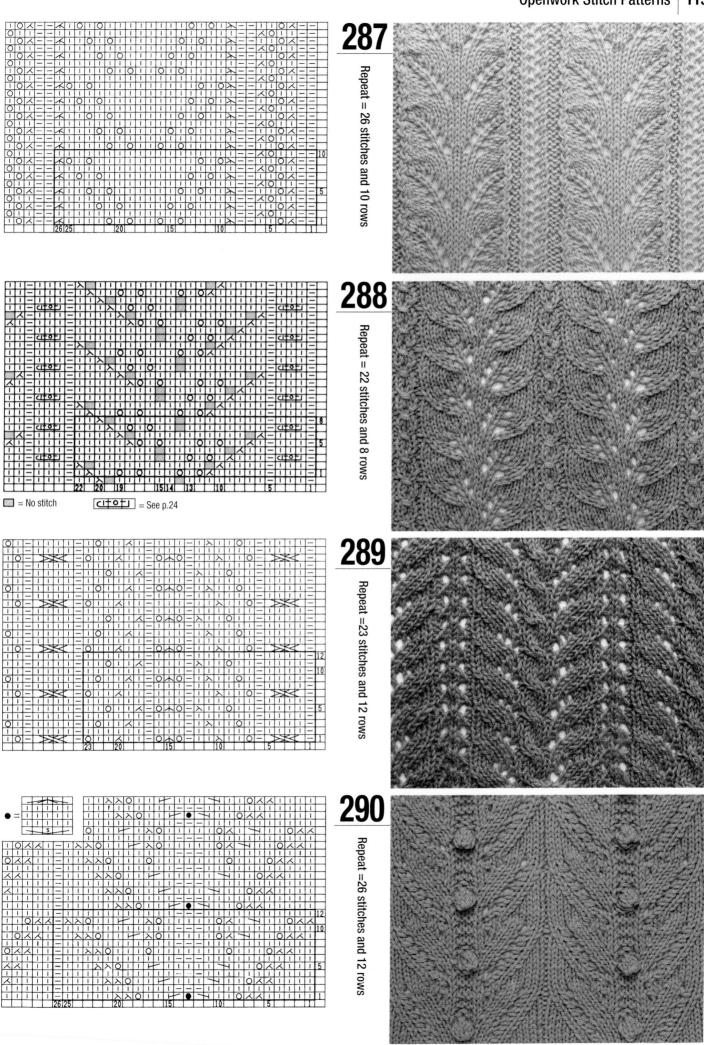

287 — Repeat = 26 stitches and 10 rows

288 — Repeat = 22 stitches and 8 rows

□ = No stitch   ⊂Ｉ┼Ｏ┼Ｊ = See p.24

289 — Repeat = 23 stitches and 12 rows

290 — Repeat = 26 stitches and 12 rows

● =

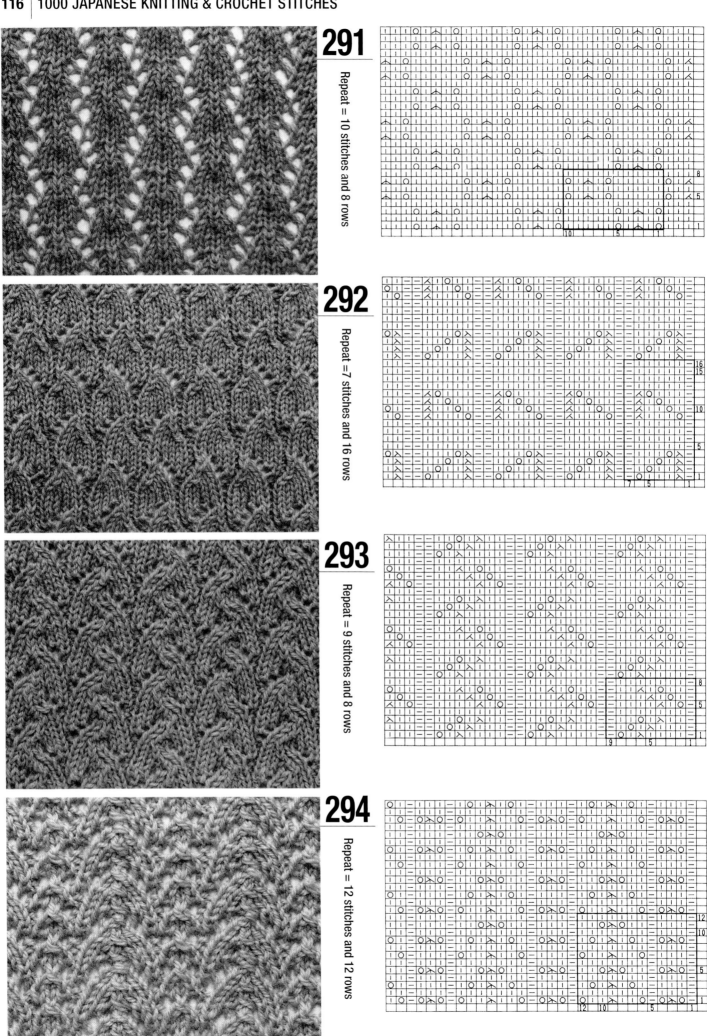

291

Repeat = 10 stitches and 8 rows

292

Repeat = 7 stitches and 16 rows

293

Repeat = 9 stitches and 8 rows

294

Repeat = 12 stitches and 12 rows

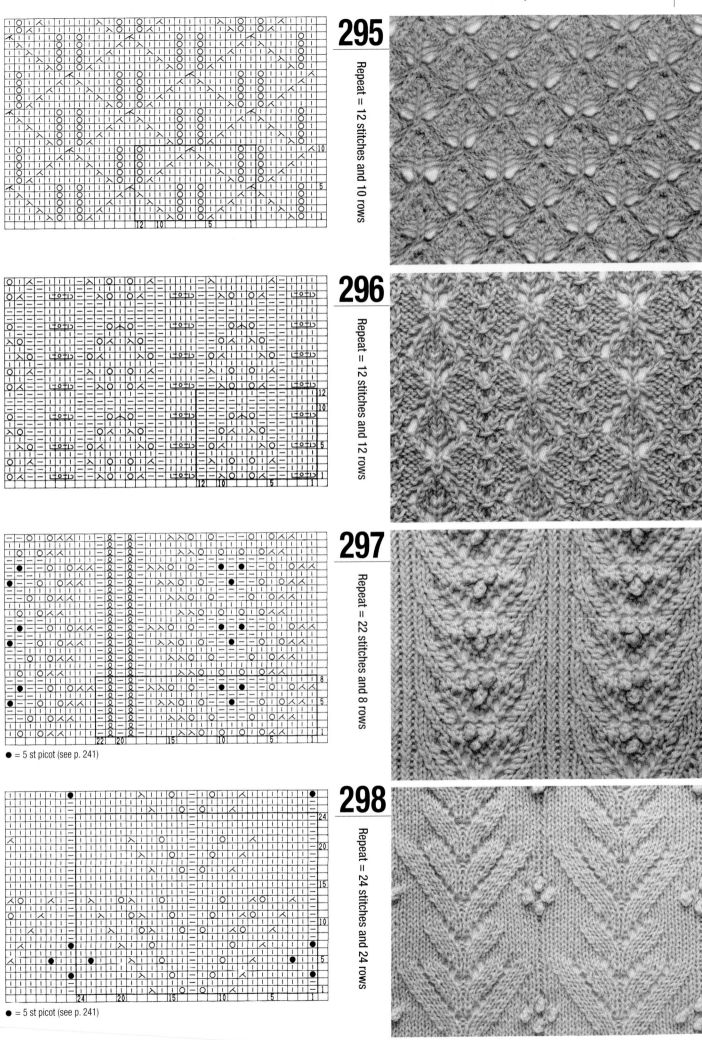

295

Repeat = 12 stitches and 10 rows

296

Repeat = 12 stitches and 12 rows

297

Repeat = 22 stitches and 8 rows

● = 5 st picot (see p. 241)

298

Repeat = 24 stitches and 24 rows

● = 5 st picot (see p. 241)

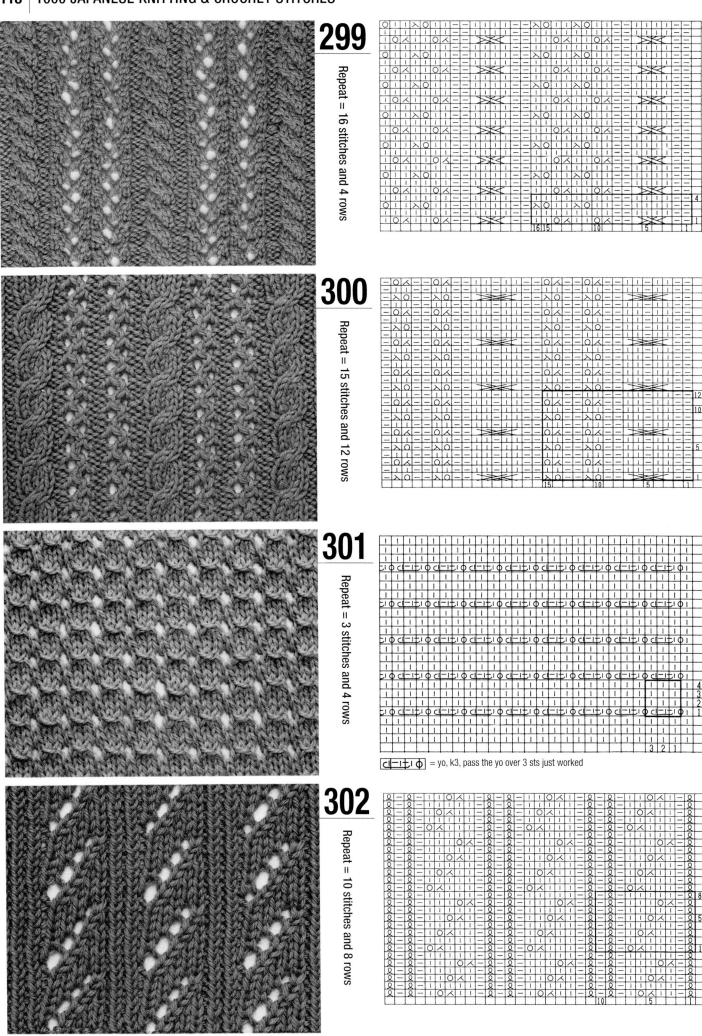

299

Repeat = 16 stitches and 4 rows

300

Repeat = 15 stitches and 12 rows

301

Repeat = 3 stitches and 4 rows

⊏⊐|⊥|⏀ = yo, k3, pass the yo over 3 sts just worked

302

Repeat = 10 stitches and 8 rows

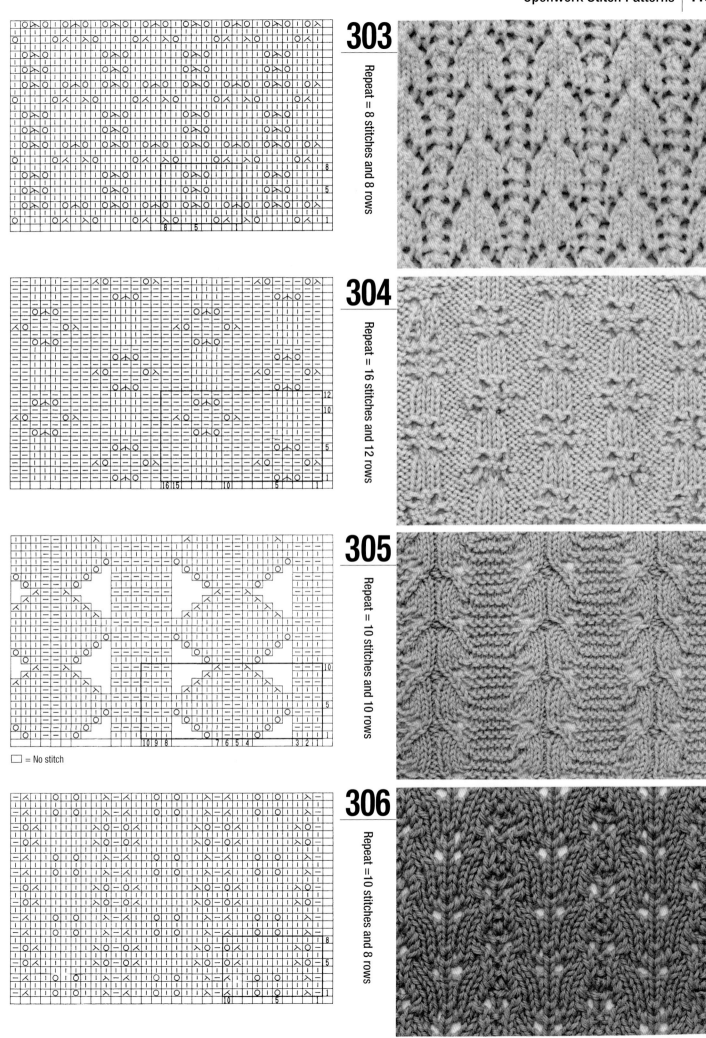

303 Repeat = 8 stitches and 8 rows

304 Repeat = 16 stitches and 12 rows

305 Repeat = 10 stitches and 10 rows

☐ = No stitch

306 Repeat =10 stitches and 8 rows

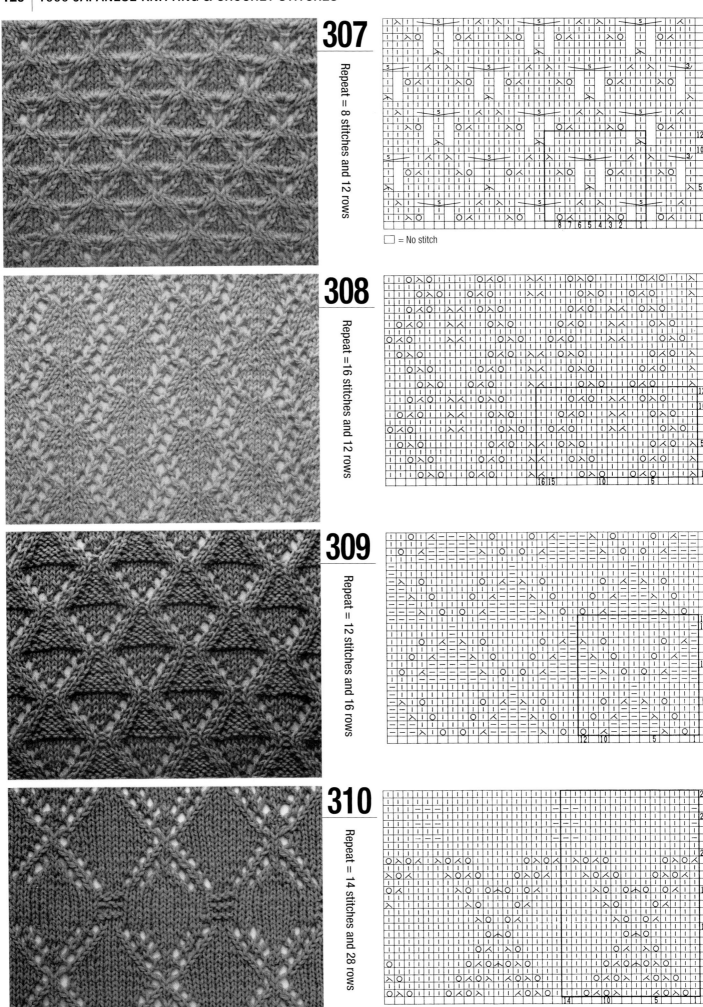

307

Repeat = 8 stitches and 12 rows

☐ = No stitch

308

Repeat = 16 stitches and 12 rows

309

Repeat = 12 stitches and 16 rows

310

Repeat = 14 stitches and 28 rows

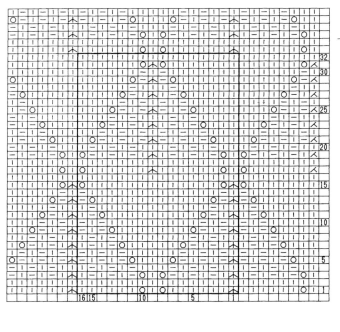

311

Repeat = 16 stitches and 32 rows

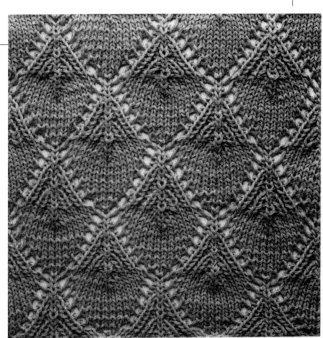

312

Repeat = 12 stitches and 20 rows

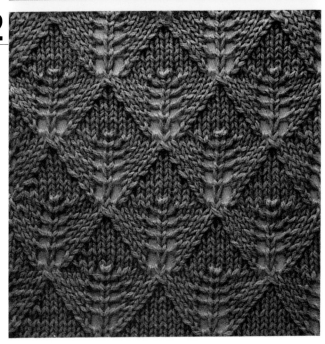

313

Repeat = 16 stitches and 20 rows

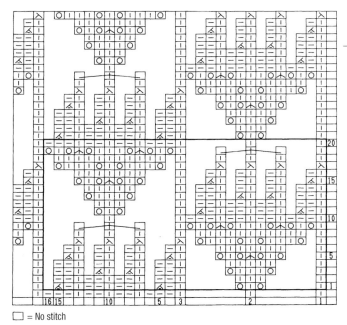

☐ = No stitch

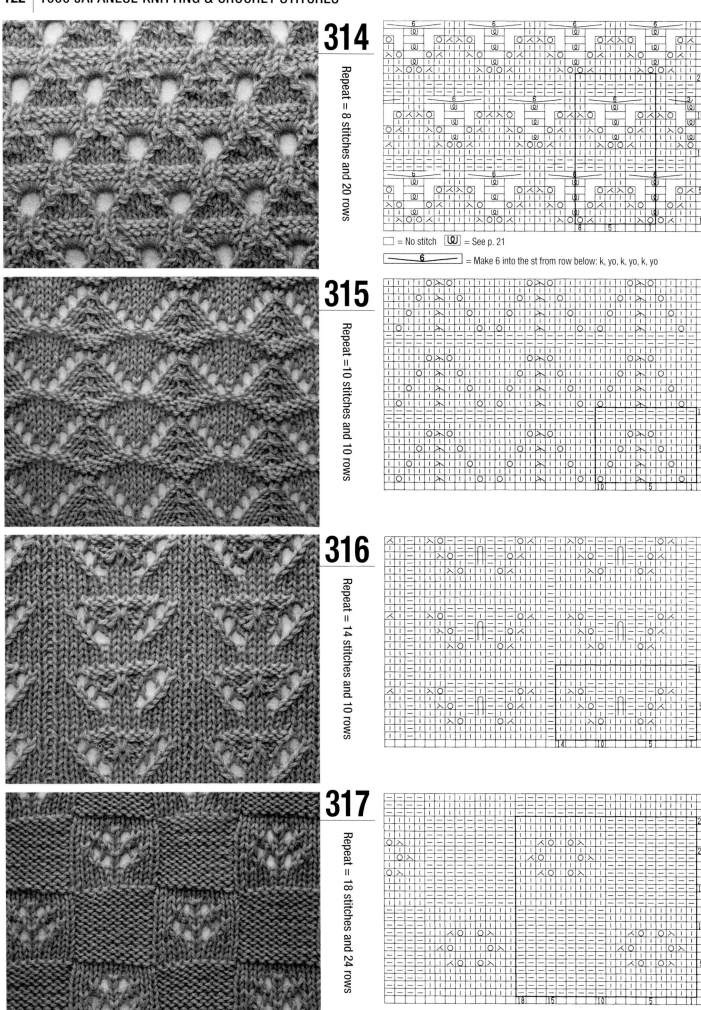

314

Repeat = 8 stitches and 20 rows

☐ = No stitch   🔟 = See p. 21

⎯⎯6⎯⎯ = Make 6 into the st from row below: k, yo, k, yo, k, yo

315

Repeat =10 stitches and 10 rows

316

Repeat = 14 stitches and 10 rows

317

Repeat = 18 stitches and 24 rows

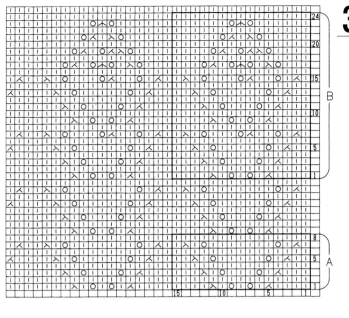

318

A Repeat = 15 stitches and 8 rows
B Repeat = 15 stitches and 24 rows

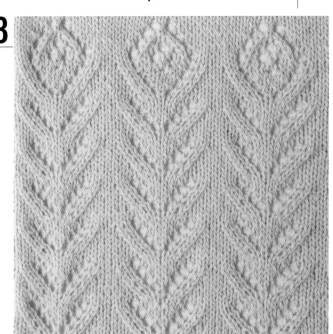

319

Repeat = 10 stitches and 16 rows

320

Repeat = 30 stitches and 36 rows

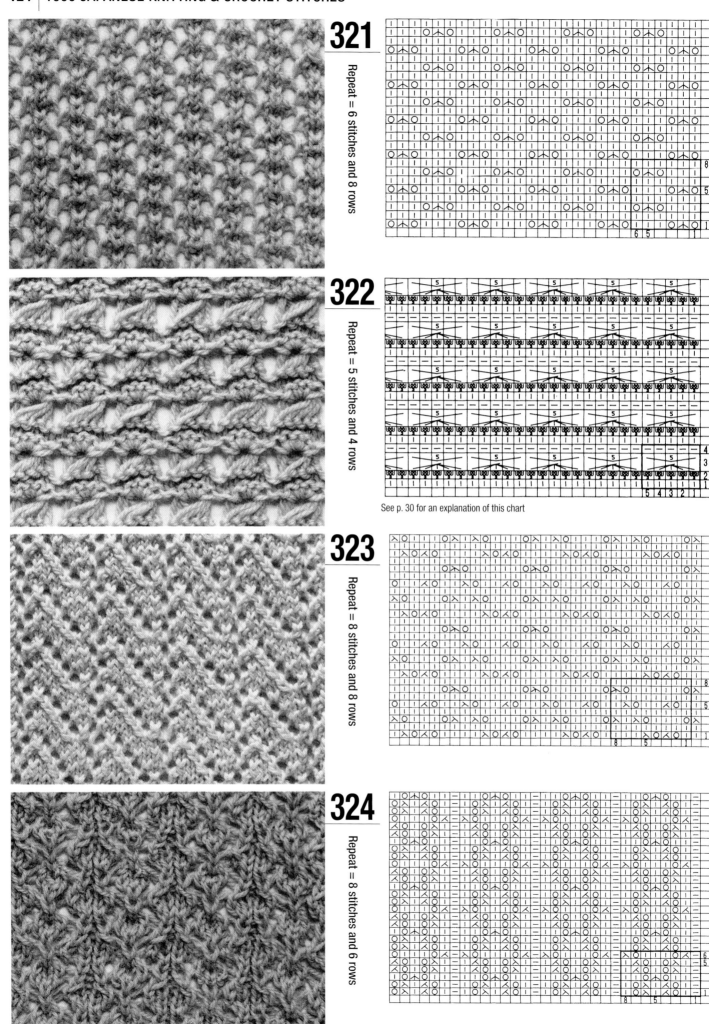

321

Repeat = 6 stitches and 8 rows

322

Repeat = 5 stitches and 4 rows

See p. 30 for an explanation of this chart

323

Repeat = 8 stitches and 8 rows

324

Repeat = 8 stitches and 6 rows

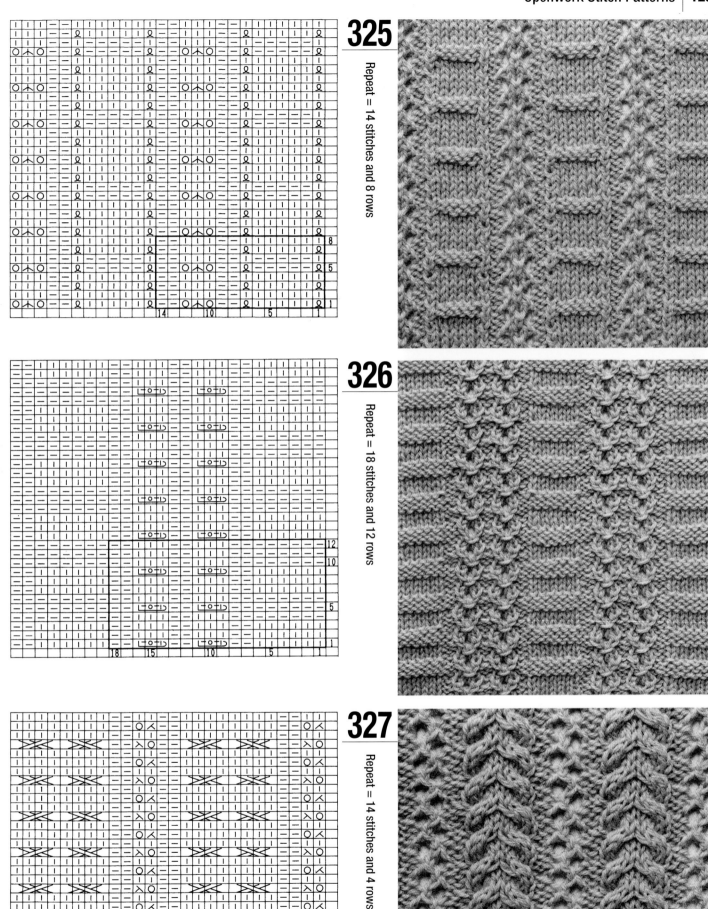

325
Repeat = 14 stitches and 8 rows

326
Repeat = 18 stitches and 12 rows

327
Repeat = 14 stitches and 4 rows

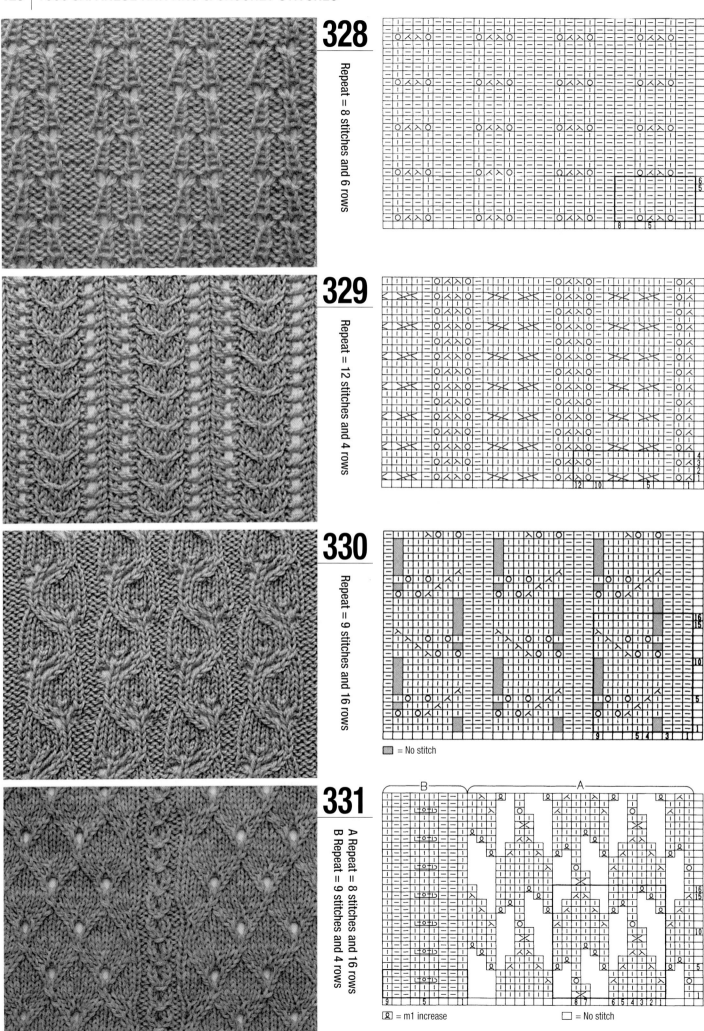

328
Repeat = 8 stitches and 6 rows

329
Repeat = 12 stitches and 4 rows

330
Repeat = 9 stitches and 16 rows

= No stitch

331
A Repeat = 8 stitches and 16 rows
B Repeat = 9 stitches and 4 rows

= m1 increase   = No stitch

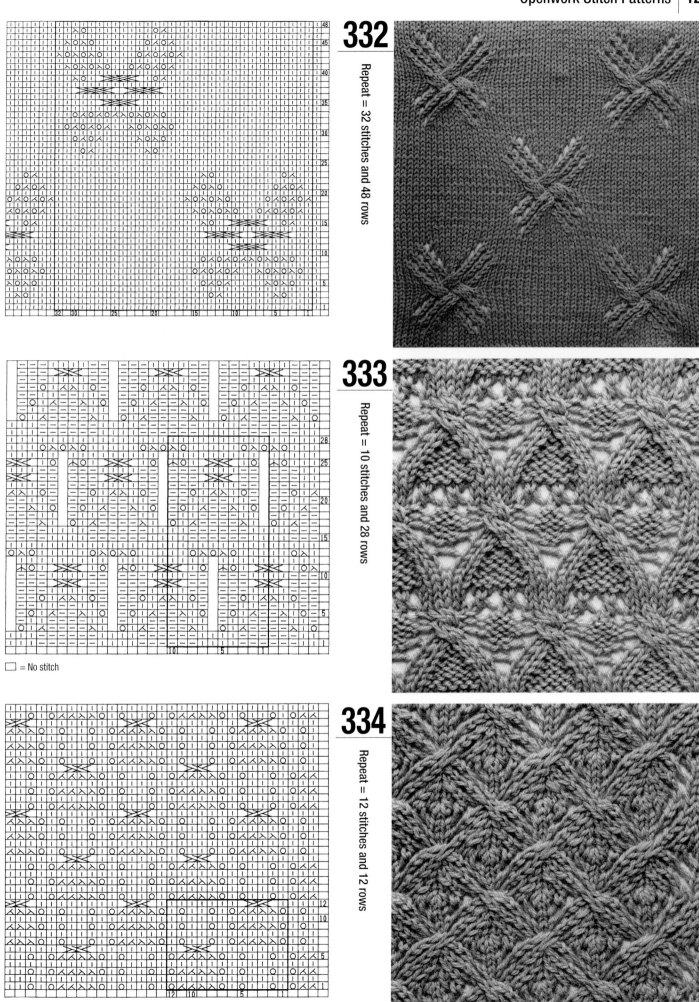

332

Repeat = 32 stitches and 48 rows

333

Repeat = 10 stitches and 28 rows

☐ = No stitch

334

Repeat = 12 stitches and 12 rows

⬚⟩⟨⬚ = on WS, place 2 sts on CN, hold to back; p2, p2 from CN

335

Repeat = 10 stitches and 24 rows

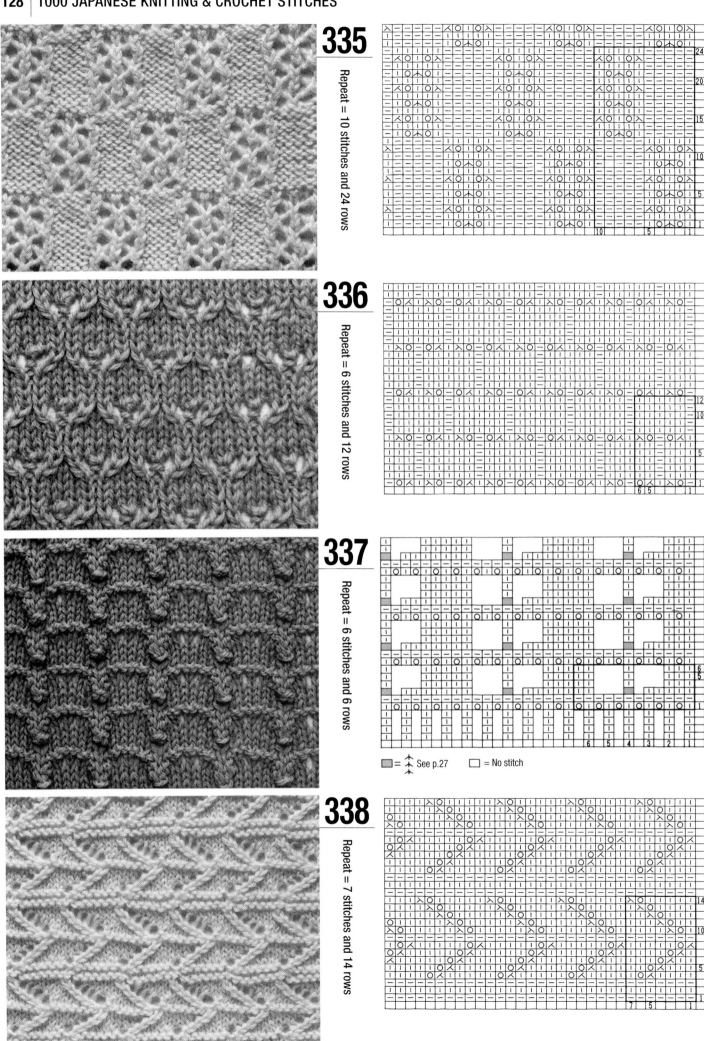

336

Repeat = 6 stitches and 12 rows

337

Repeat = 6 stitches and 6 rows

☐ = ⤧ See p.27   ☐ = No stitch

338

Repeat = 7 stitches and 14 rows

TRADITIONAL STITCH PATTERNS

Nordic, Fair Isle, and Aran stitches

Traditional stitch patterns were derived from people's everyday lives; sometimes stories or prayers are knitted into the patterns. These graphic designs are newly revised and arranged for modern knitting, while retaining the nostalgic flavor of the originals.

NOTE: Patterns 339-407 are worked entirely in stockinette. The chart symbols refer to colors, not to types of stitches. When you see a "o" in this group, it refers to a color rather than a yarnover.

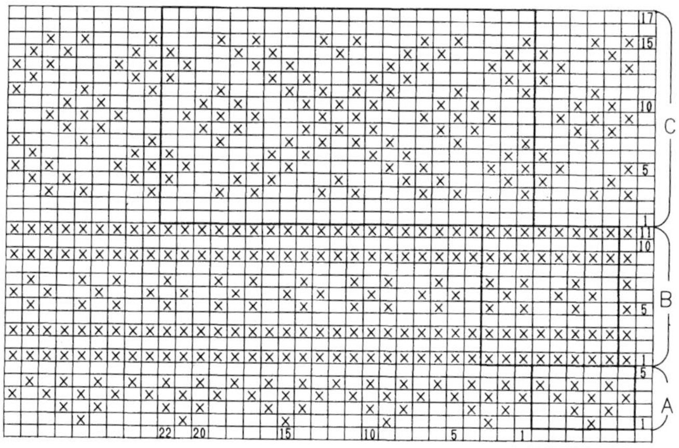

339

A Repeat = 6 stitches and 5 rows
B Repeat = 8 stitches and 11 rows
C Repeat = 22 stitches and 17 rows

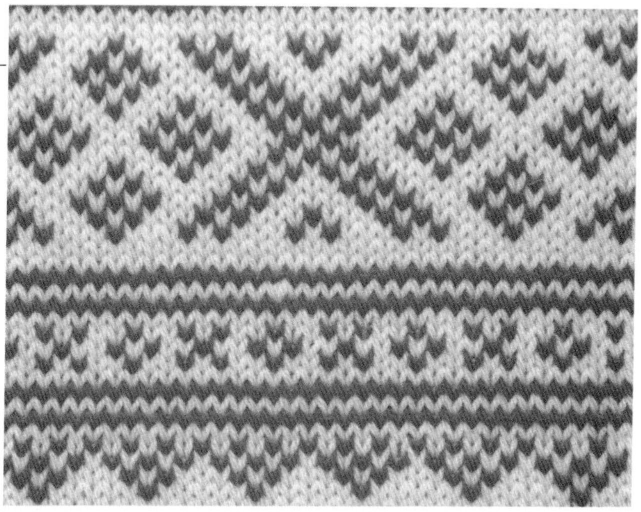

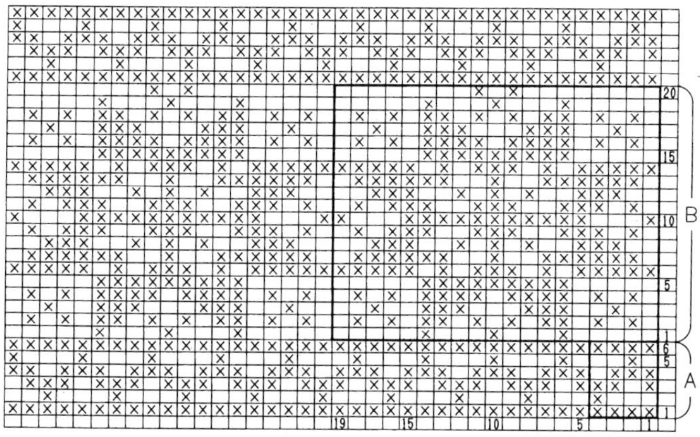

340

A Repeat = 4 stitches and 6 rows
B Repeat = 19 stitches and 20 rows

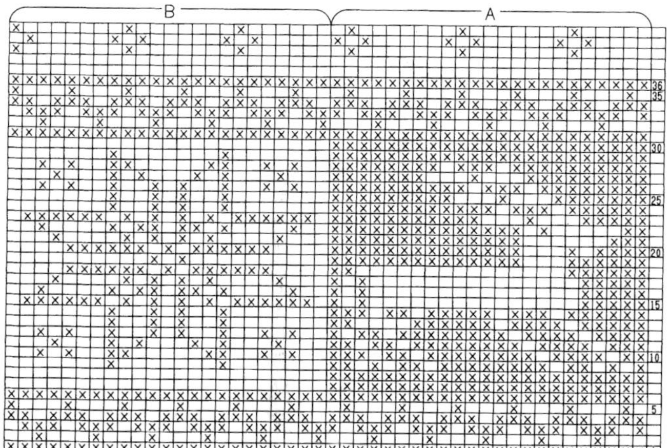

341

A & B Repeat = 23 stitches and 36 rows

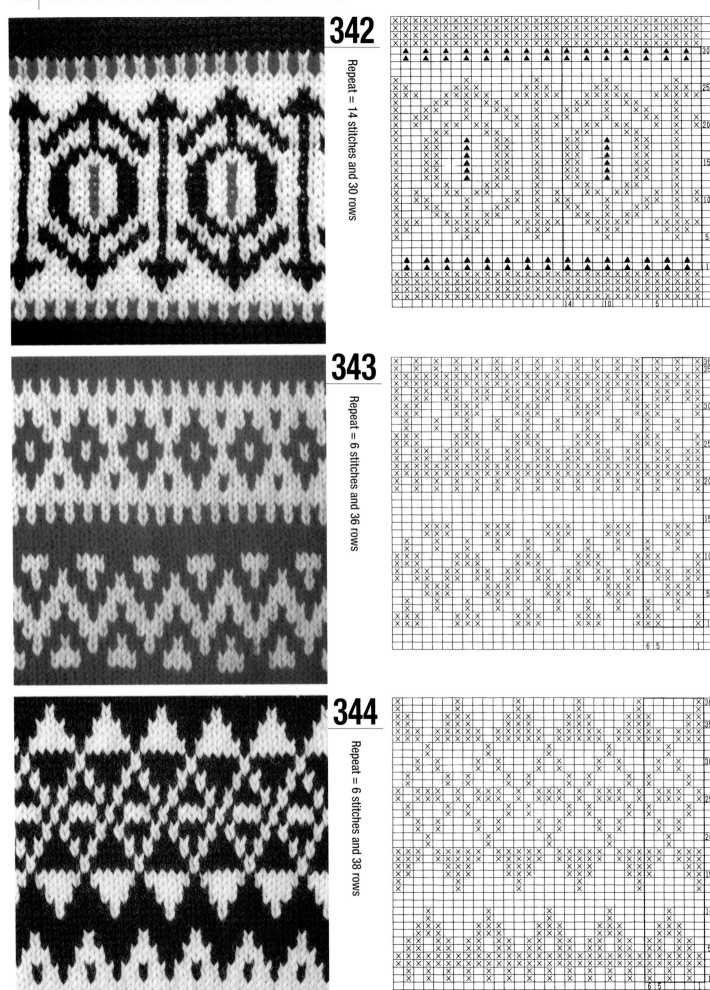

342

Repeat = 14 stitches and 30 rows

343

Repeat = 6 stitches and 36 rows

344

Repeat = 6 stitches and 38 rows

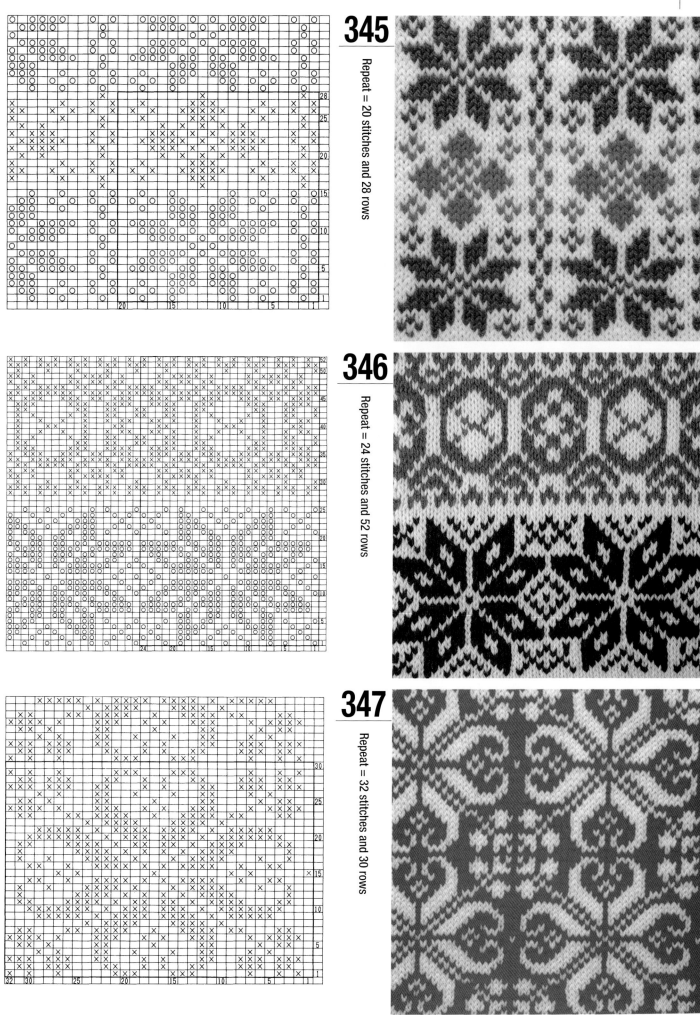

345
Repeat = 20 stitches and 28 rows

346
Repeat = 24 stitches and 52 rows

347
Repeat = 32 stitches and 30 rows

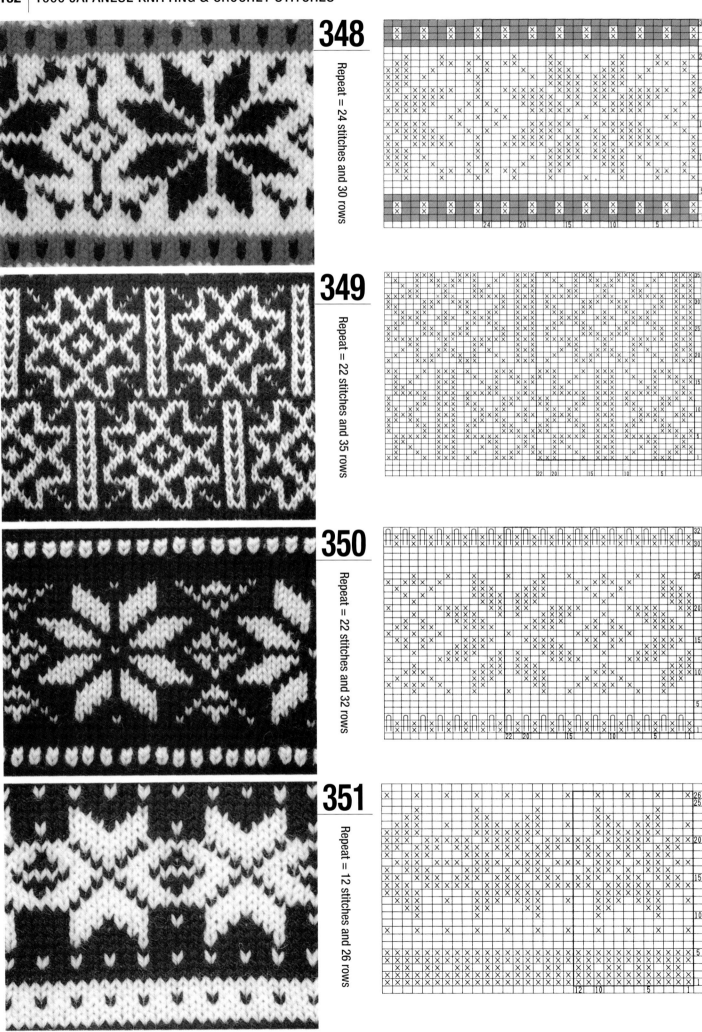

348 Repeat = 24 stitches and 30 rows

349 Repeat = 22 stitches and 35 rows

350 Repeat = 22 stitches and 32 rows

351 Repeat = 12 stitches and 26 rows

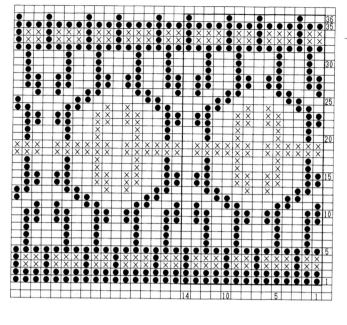

352

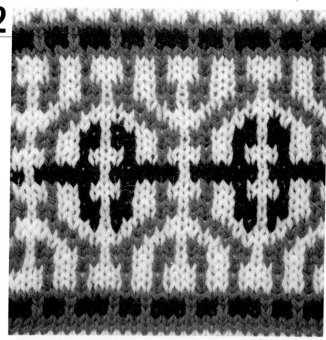

Repeat = 14 stitches and 36 rows

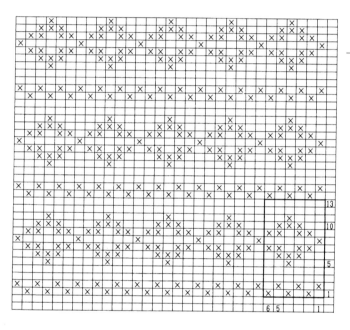

353

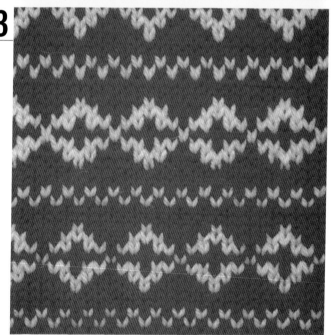

Repeat = 6 stitches and 13 rows

354

Repeat = 12 stitches and 12 rows

355

Repeat = 24 stitches and 24 rows

356

Repeat = 12 stitches and 36 rows

357

Repeat = 20 stitches and 22 rows

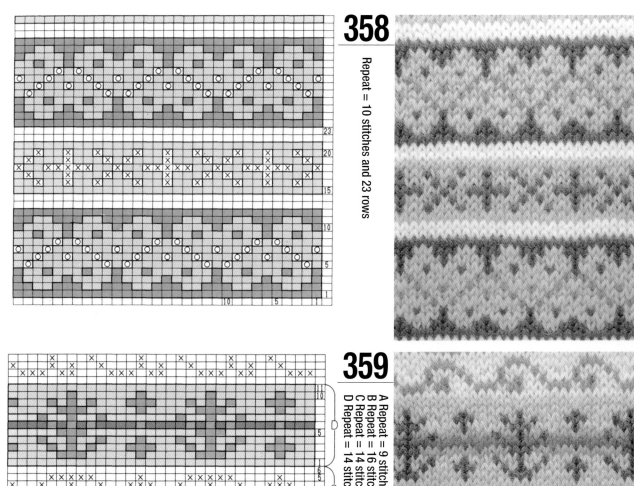

358

Repeat = 10 stitches and 23 rows

359

A Repeat = 9 stitches and 6 rows
B Repeat = 16 stitches and 11 rows
C Repeat = 14 stitches and 6 rows
D Repeat = 14 stitches and 11 rows

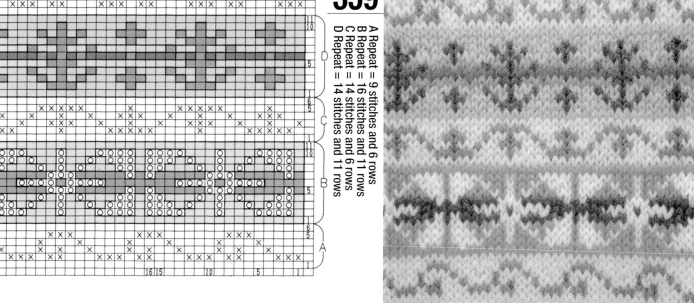

360

A Repeat = 8 stitches and 3 rows
B Repeat = 18 stitches and 19 rows

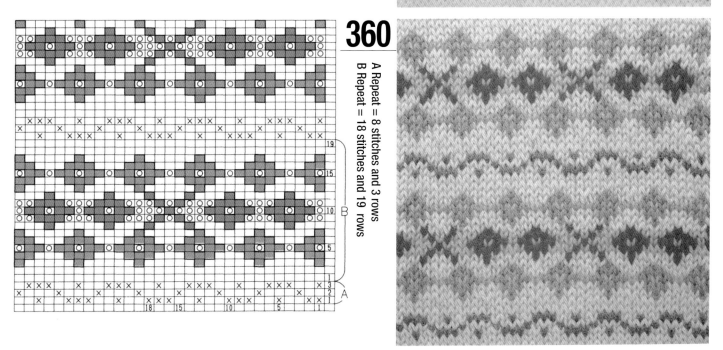

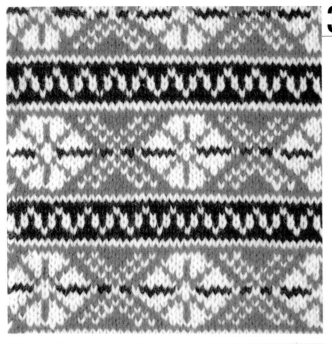

361

Repeat = 20 stitches and 21 rows

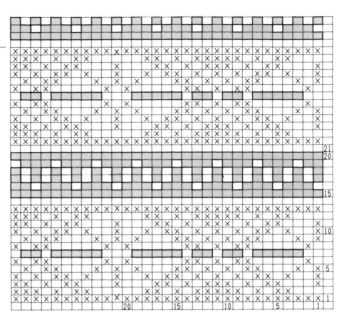

362

Repeat = 18 stitches and 24 rows

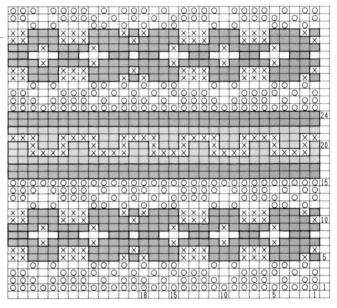

363

A Repeat = 4 stitches and 3 rows
B Repeat = 38 stitches and 29 rows

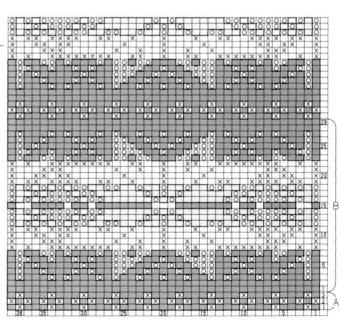

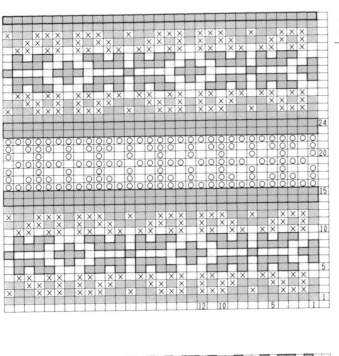

364

Repeat = 12 stitches and 24 rows

365

Repeat = 36 stitches and 36 rows

366

Repeat = 26 stitches and 42 rows

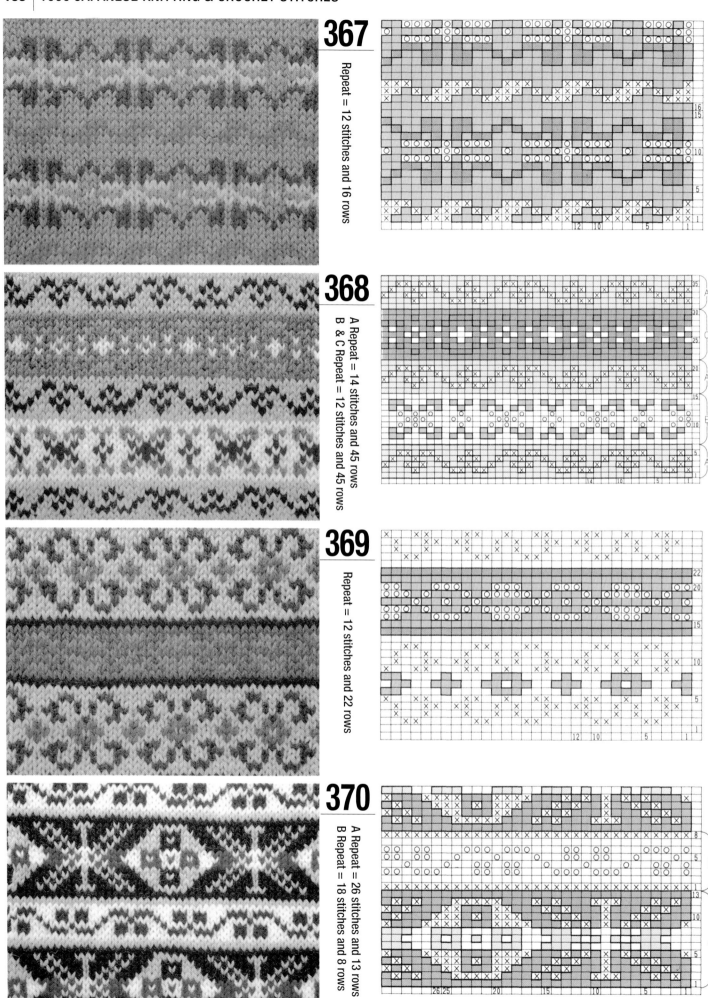

367
Repeat = 12 stitches and 16 rows

368
A Repeat = 14 stitches and 45 rows
B & C Repeat = 12 stitches and 45 rows

369
Repeat = 12 stitches and 22 rows

370
A Repeat = 26 stitches and 13 rows
B Repeat = 18 stitches and 8 rows

371

Repeat = 24 stitches and 28 rows

372

Repeat = 24 stitches and 26 rows

373

Repeat = 36 stitches and 44 rows

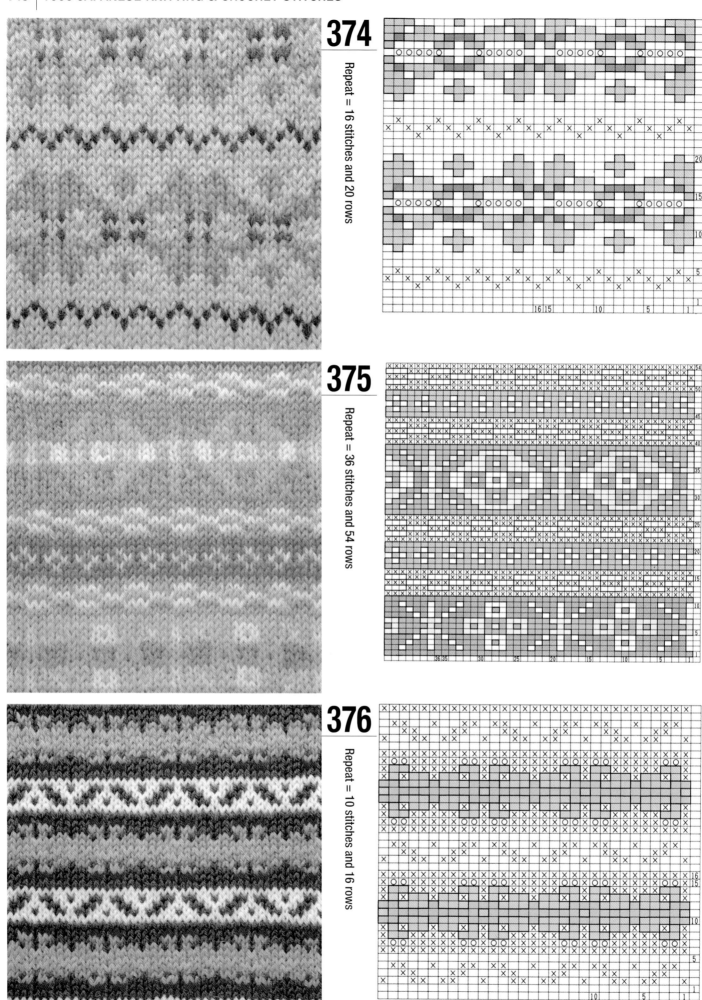

374

Repeat = 16 stitches and 20 rows

375

Repeat = 36 stitches and 54 rows

376

Repeat = 10 stitches and 16 rows

377

A Repeat = 9 stitches and 6 rows
B Repeat = 14 stitches and 15 rows
C Repeat = 9 stitches and 12 rows

378

Repeat = 28 stitches and 30 rows

379

Repeat = 20 stitches and 28 rows

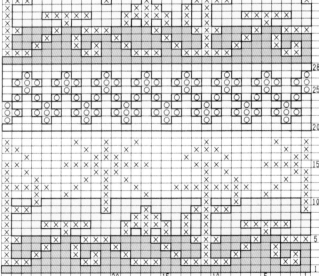

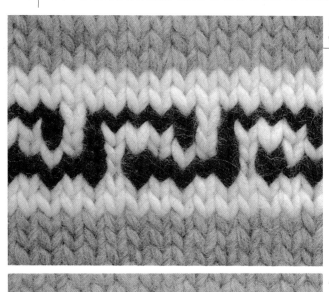

380

Repeat = 6 stitches and 8 rows

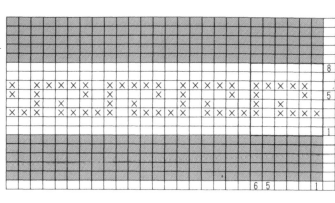

381

Repeat = 6 stitches and 12 rows

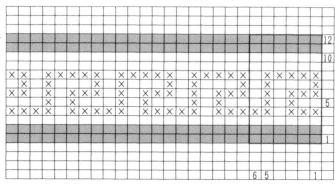

382

Repeat = 10 stitches and 11 rows

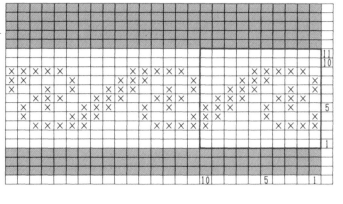

383

Repeat = 8 stitches and 19 rows

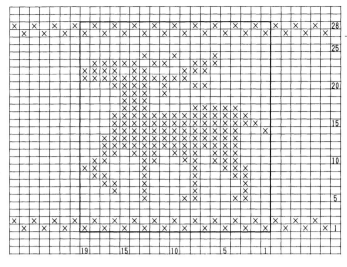

384

Repeat = 19 stitches and 28 rows

385

Repeat = 35 stitches and 23 rows

386

Repeat = 26 stitches and 12 rows

387

Repeat = 23 stitches and 20 rows

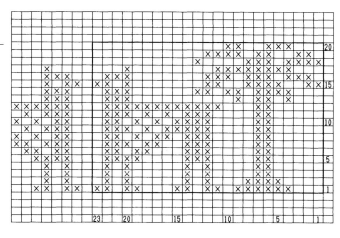

388

Repeat = 15 stitches and 18 rows

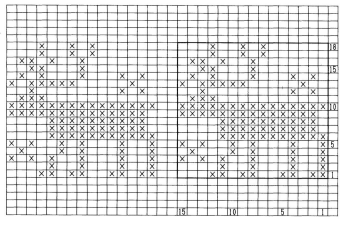

389

Repeat = 23 stitches and 18 rows

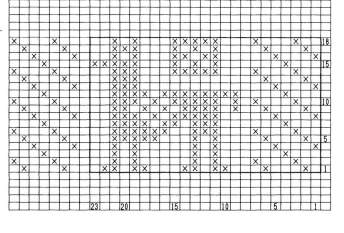

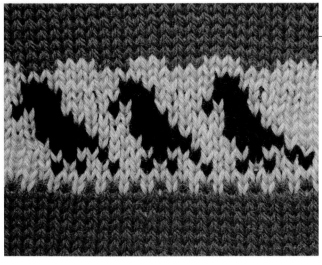

390

Repeat = 25 stitches and 14 rows

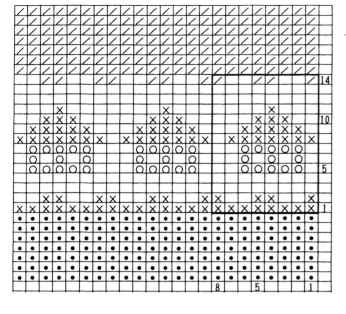

391

Repeat = 8 stitches and 14 rows

392

Repeat = 25 stitches and 15 rows

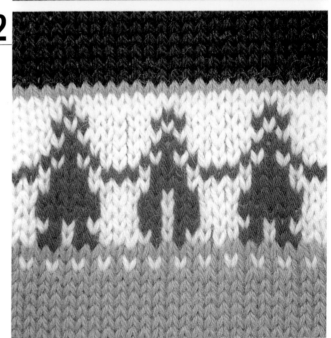

393

Repeat = 23 stitches and 26 rows

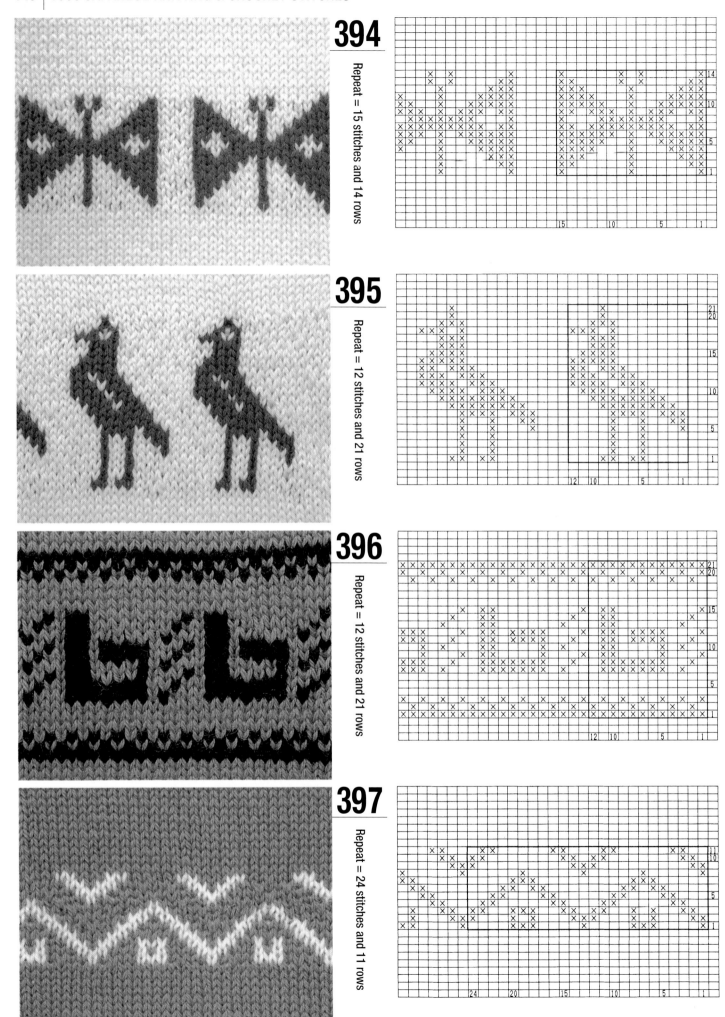

394
Repeat = 15 stitches and 14 rows

395
Repeat = 12 stitches and 21 rows

396
Repeat = 12 stitches and 21 rows

397
Repeat = 24 stitches and 11 rows

398

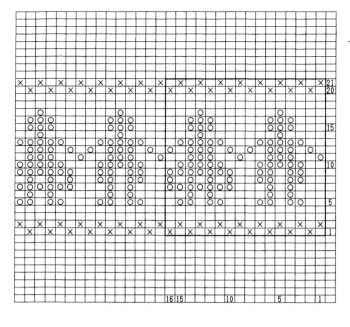

Repeat = 16 stitches and 21 rows

399

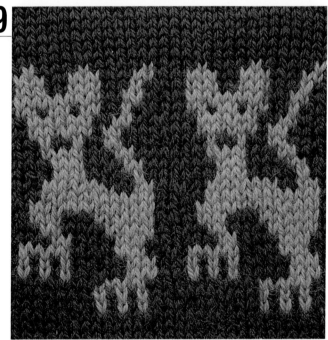

Repeat = 13 stitches and 23 rows

400

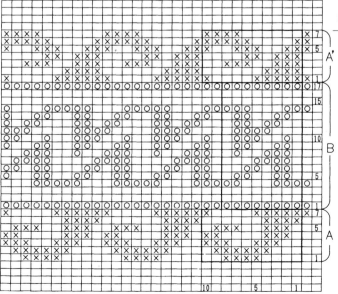

A & A' Repeat = 10 stitches and 7 rows
B Repeat = 8 stitches and 17 rows

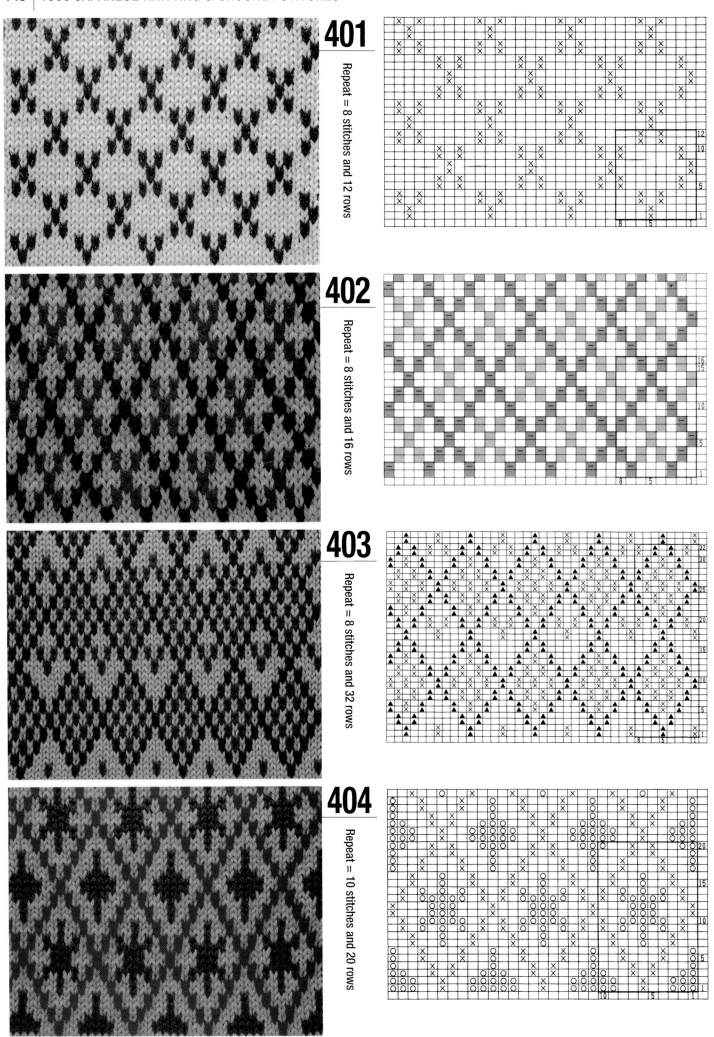

401

Repeat = 8 stitches and 12 rows

402

Repeat = 8 stitches and 16 rows

403

Repeat = 8 stitches and 32 rows

404

Repeat = 10 stitches and 20 rows

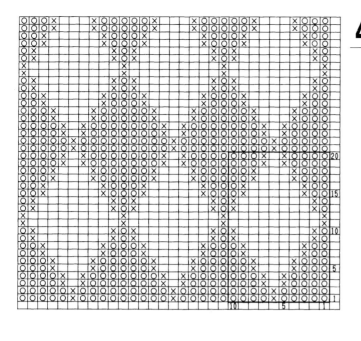

405

Repeat = 10 stitches and 20 rows

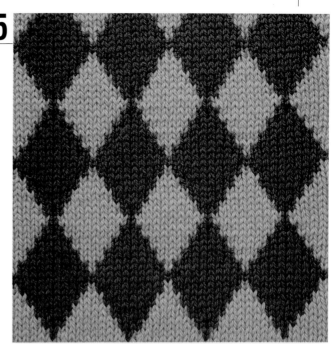

406

Repeat = 24 stitches and 20 rows

⊠ = Work these in duplicate stitch after knitting is complete

407

Repeat = 12 stitches and 12 rows

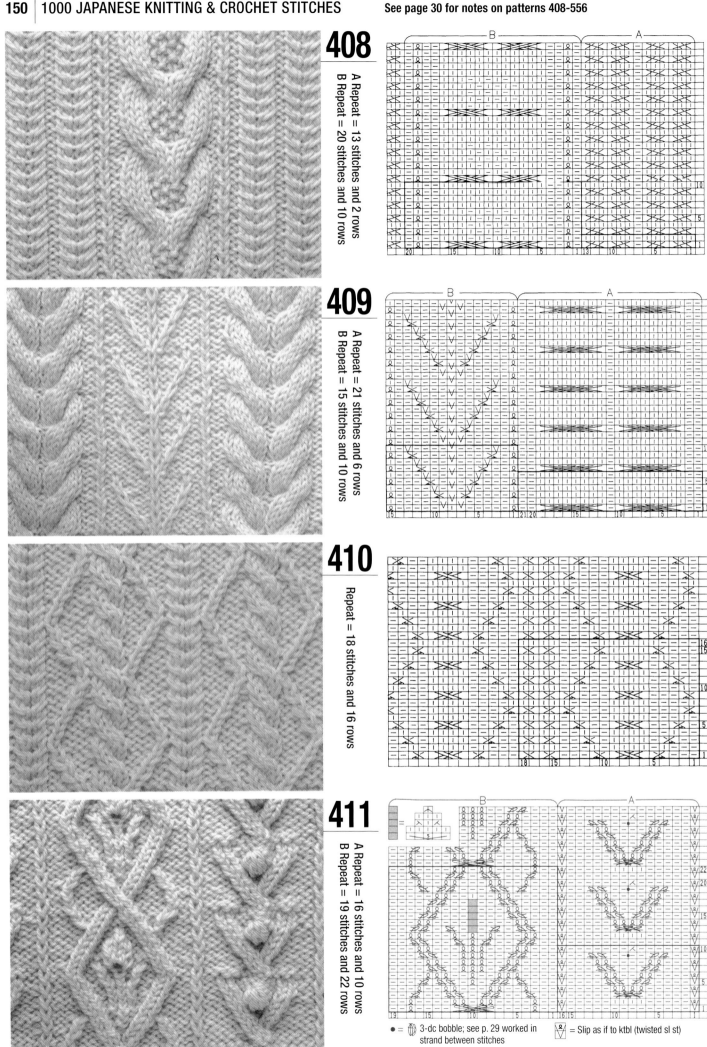

408

A Repeat = 13 stitches and 2 rows
B Repeat = 20 stitches and 10 rows

409

A Repeat = 21 stitches and 6 rows
B Repeat = 15 stitches and 10 rows

410

Repeat = 18 stitches and 16 rows

411

A Repeat = 16 stitches and 10 rows
B Repeat = 19 stitches and 22 rows

● = 3-dc bobble; see p. 29 worked in strand between stitches

= Slip as if to ktbl (twisted sl st)

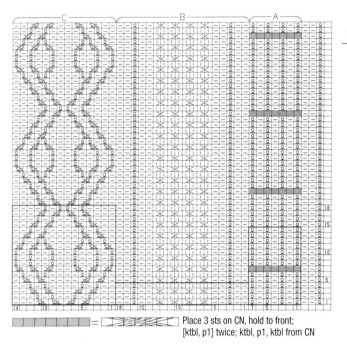

412

A Repeat = 7 stitches and 14 rows
B Repeat = 18 stitches and 4 row
C Repeat = 14 stitches and 18 rows

= Place 3 sts on CN, hold to front; [ktbl, p1] twice; ktbl, p1, ktbl from CN

413

A Repeat = 19 stitches and 24 rows
B Repeat = 23 stitches and 14 rows

First row (RS): k, yo, k, yo, k into one st. Second row (WS): turn work so RS is facing. Sl 4 sts knitwise, one at a time, from LN to RN; k1; pass the 4 sl sts, one at a time, over the k; turn work back to WS and continue

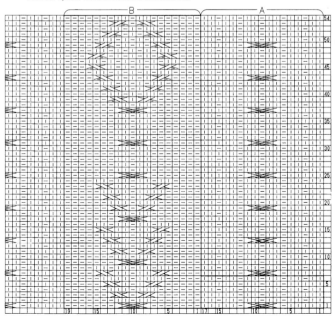

414

A Repeat = 17 stitches and 6 rows
B Repeat = 19 stitches and 54 rows

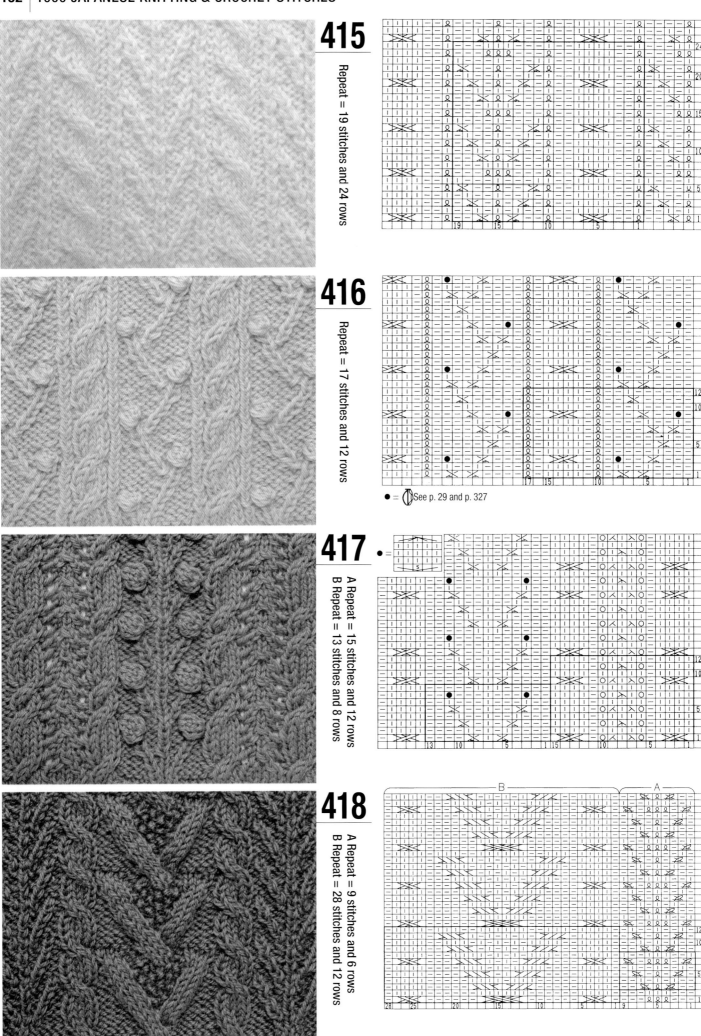

415
Repeat = 19 stitches and 24 rows

416
Repeat = 17 stitches and 12 rows

● = ⬯ See p. 29 and p. 327

417
A Repeat = 15 stitches and 12 rows
B Repeat = 13 stitches and 8 rows

418
A Repeat = 9 stitches and 6 rows
B Repeat = 28 stitches and 12 rows

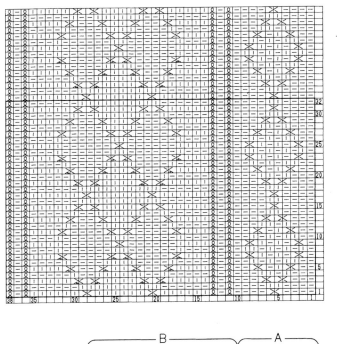

419

Repeat = 38 stitches and 32 rows

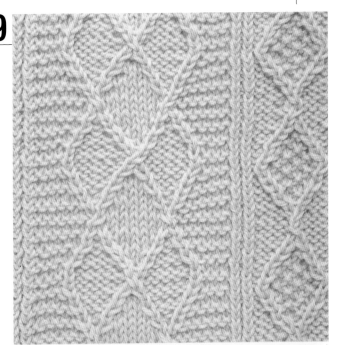

420

A Repeat = 8 stitches and 4 rows
B Repeat = 15 stitches and 18 rows

421

A Repeat = 12 stitches and 18 rows
B Repeat = 12 stitches and 4 rows
C Repeat = 23 stitches and 8 rows

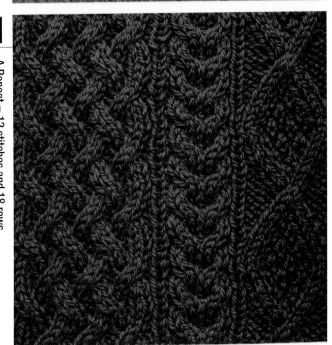

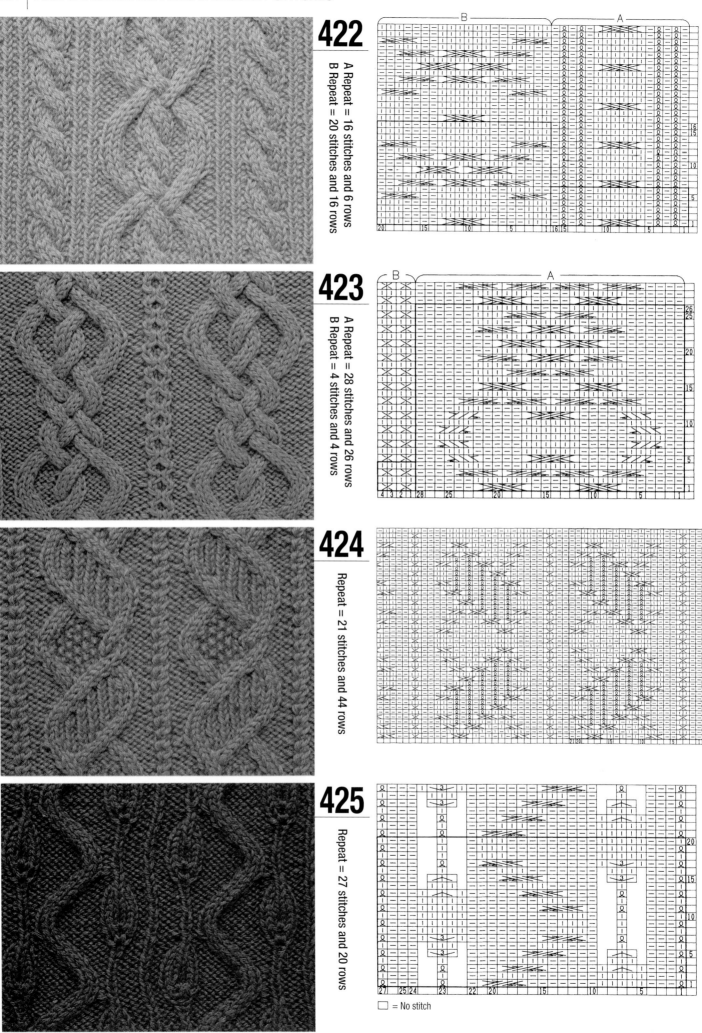

422

A Repeat = 16 stitches and 6 rows
B Repeat = 20 stitches and 16 rows

423

A Repeat = 28 stitches and 26 rows
B Repeat = 4 stitches and 4 rows

424

Repeat = 21 stitches and 44 rows

425

Repeat = 27 stitches and 20 rows

☐ = No stitch

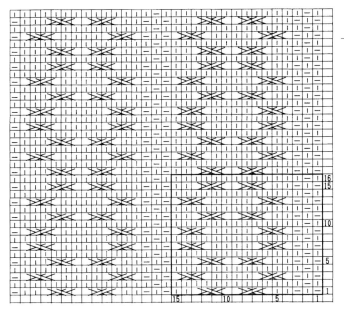

426

Repeat = 15 stitches and 16 rows

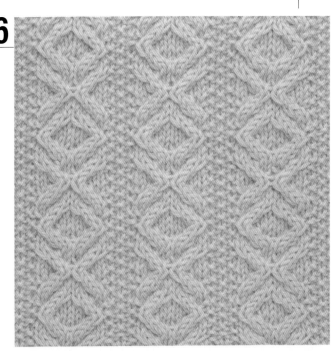

427

Repeat = 12 stitches and 24 rows

428

Repeat = 15 stitches and 18 rows

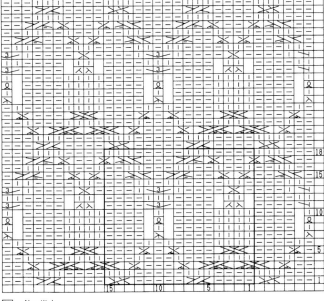

☐ = No stitch

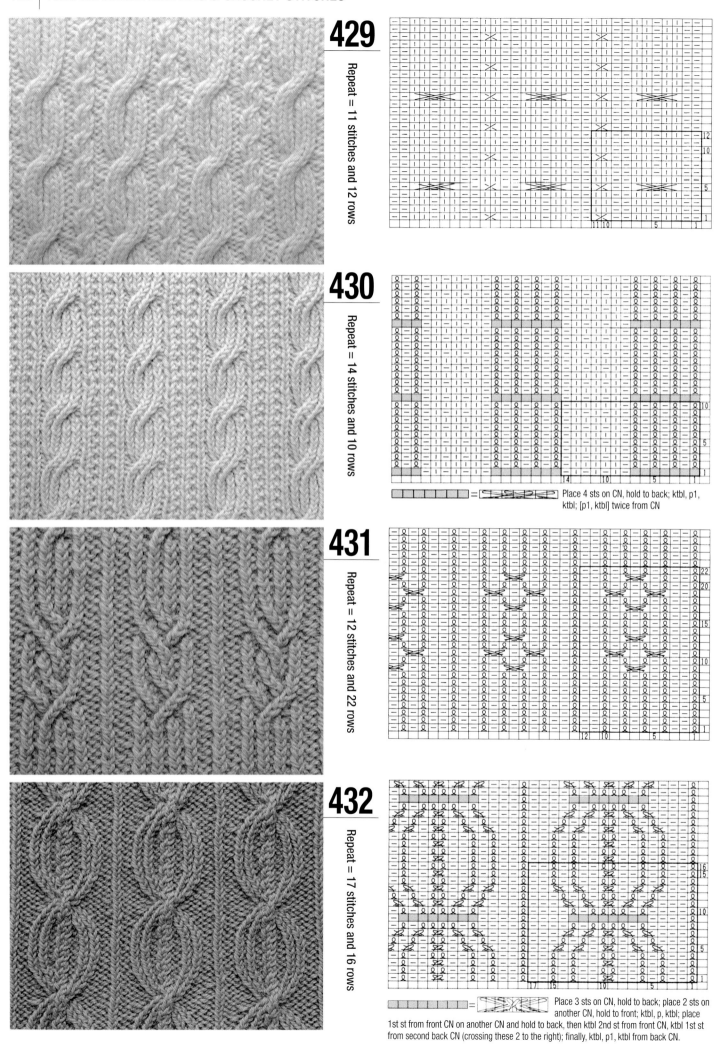

429

Repeat = 11 stitches and 12 rows

430

Repeat = 14 stitches and 10 rows

= Place 4 sts on CN, hold to back; ktbl, p1, ktbl; [p1, ktbl] twice from CN

431

Repeat = 12 stitches and 22 rows

432

Repeat = 17 stitches and 16 rows

= Place 3 sts on CN, hold to back; place 2 sts on another CN, hold to front; ktbl, p, ktbl; place 1st st from front CN on another CN and hold to back, then ktbl 2nd st from front CN, ktbl 1st st from second back CN (crossing these 2 to the right); finally, ktbl, p1, ktbl from back CN.

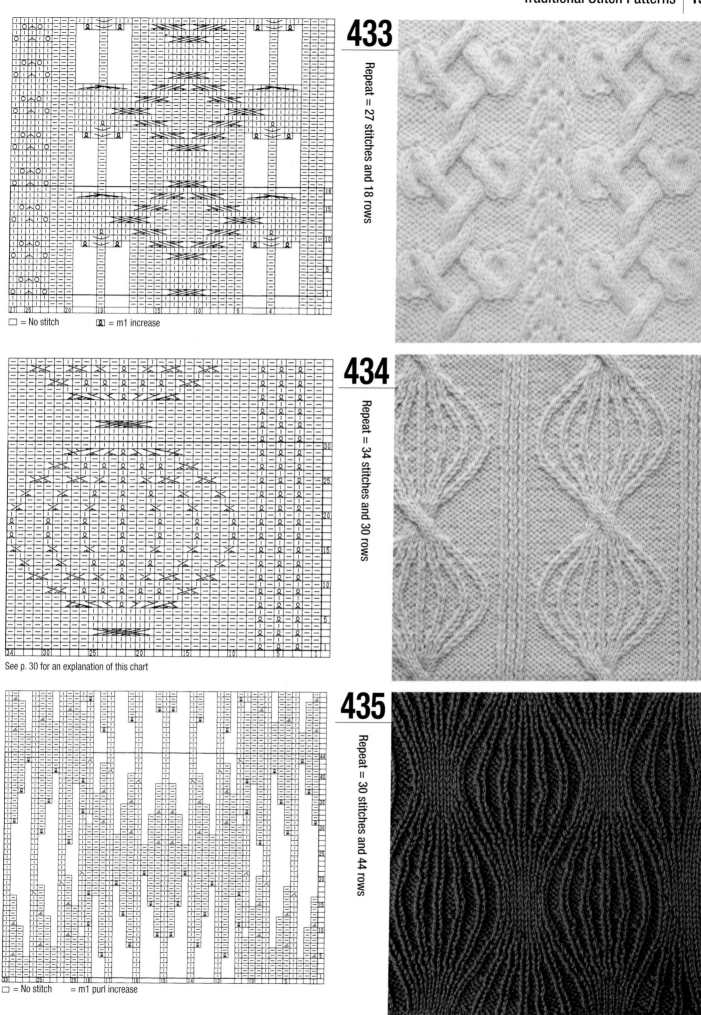

433

Repeat = 27 stitches and 18 rows

□ = No stitch 🔲 = m1 increase

434

Repeat = 34 stitches and 30 rows

See p. 30 for an explanation of this chart

435

Repeat = 30 stitches and 44 rows

□ = No stitch   = m1 purl increase

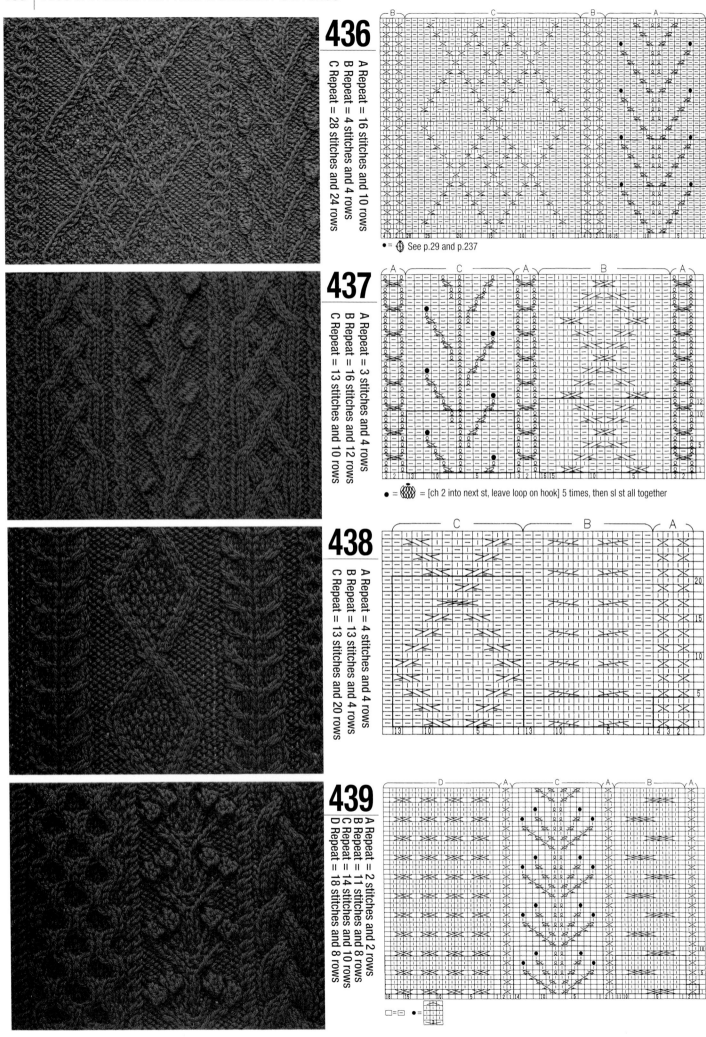

436

A Repeat = 16 stitches and 10 rows
B Repeat = 4 stitches and 4 rows
C Repeat = 28 stitches and 24 rows

● = ⊕ See p.29 and p.237

437

A Repeat = 3 stitches and 4 rows
B Repeat = 16 stitches and 12 rows
C Repeat = 13 stitches and 10 rows

● = 🕸 = [ch 2 into next st, leave loop on hook] 5 times, then sl st all together

438

A Repeat = 4 stitches and 4 rows
B Repeat = 13 stitches and 4 rows
C Repeat = 13 stitches and 20 rows

439

A Repeat = 2 stitches and 2 rows
B Repeat = 11 stitches and 8 rows
C Repeat = 14 stitches and 10 rows
D Repeat = 18 stitches and 8 rows

□ = ⊟ ● =

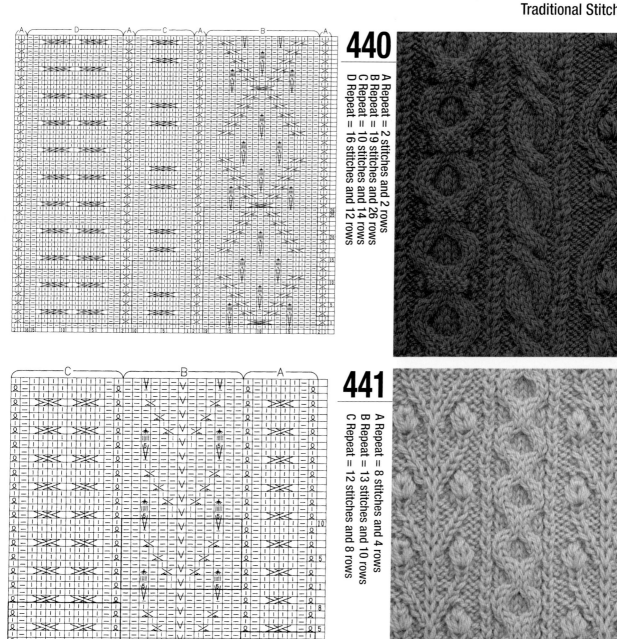

440

A Repeat = 2 stitches and 2 rows
B Repeat = 19 stitches and 26 rows
C Repeat = 10 stitches and 14 rows
D Repeat = 16 stitches and 12 rows

441

A Repeat = 8 stitches and 4 rows
B Repeat = 13 stitches and 10 rows
C Repeat = 12 stitches and 8 rows

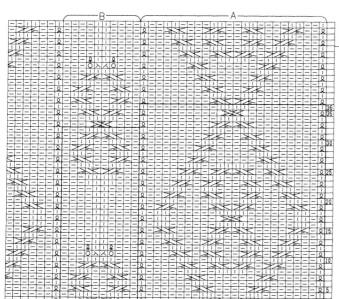

442

A Repeat = 24 stitches and 36 rows
B Repeat = 10 stitches and 32 rows

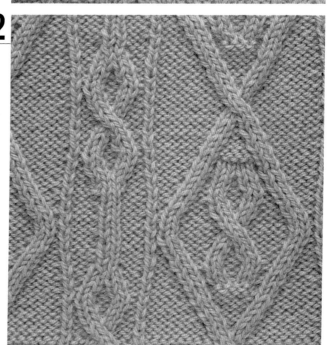

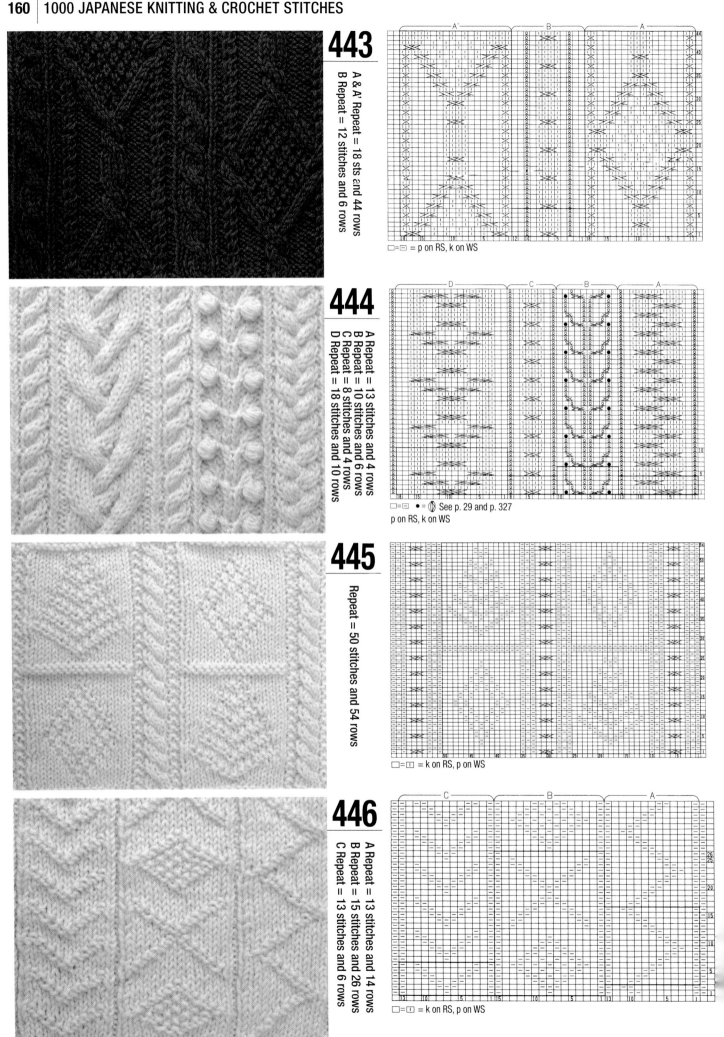

443

A & A' Repeat = 18 sts and 44 rows
B Repeat = 12 stitches and 6 rows

□=⊟ = p on RS, k on WS

444

A Repeat = 13 stitches and 4 rows
B Repeat = 10 stitches and 6 rows
C Repeat = 8 stitches and 4 rows
D Repeat = 18 stitches and 10 rows

□=⊟ ● = ◈ See p. 29 and p. 327
p on RS, k on WS

445

Repeat = 50 stitches and 54 rows

□=⊡ = k on RS, p on WS

446

A Repeat = 13 stitches and 14 rows
B Repeat = 15 stitches and 26 rows
C Repeat = 13 stitches and 6 rows

□=⊡ = k on RS, p on WS

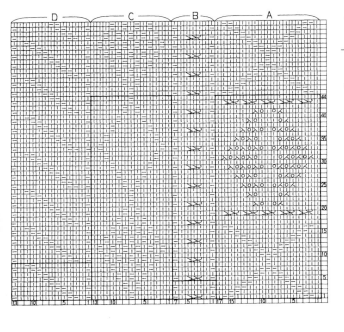

447

A Repeat = 17 stitches and 44 rows
B Repeat = 7 stitches and 4 rows
C Repeat = 13 stitches and 44 rows
D Repeat = 13 stitches and 8 rows

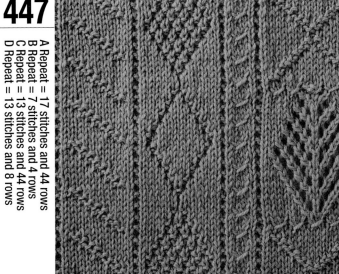

448

Repeat = 37 stitches and 48 rows

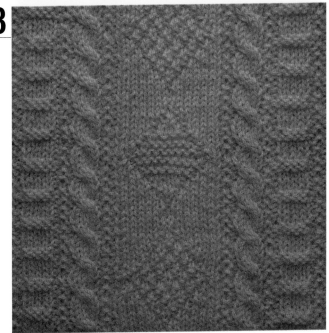

449

A Repeat = 9 stitches and 8 rows
B Repeat = 3 stitches and 6 rows
C Repeat = 6 stitches and 6 rows
D Repeat = 29 stitches and 30 rows

450

A Repeat = 2 stitches and 4 rows
B Repeat = 14 stitches and 24 rows
C Repeat = 10 stitches and 16 rows
D Repeat = 13 stitches and 16 rows

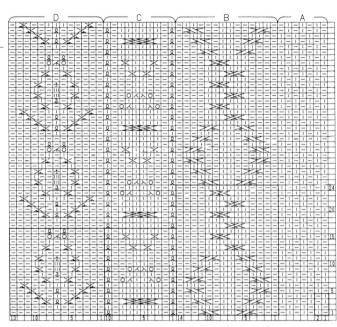

451

A Repeat = 10 stitches and 4 rows
B Repeat = 10 stitches and 12 rows
C Repeat = 16 stitches and 24 rows

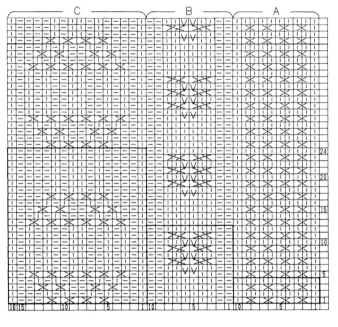

452

A Repeat = 26 stitches and 12 rows
B Repeat = 16 stitches and 16 rows

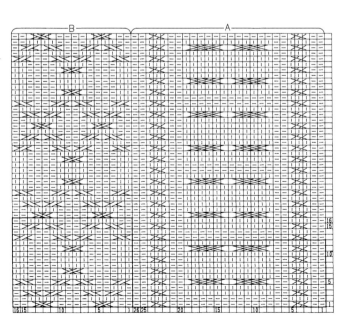

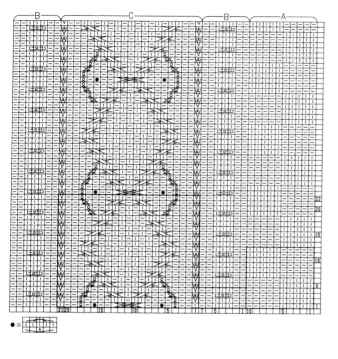

453

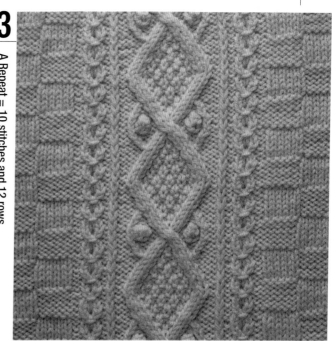

A Repeat = 10 stitches and 12 rows
B Repeat = 7 stitches and 4 rows
C Repeat = 21 stitches and 22 rows

454

Repeat = 21 stitches and 24 rows

455

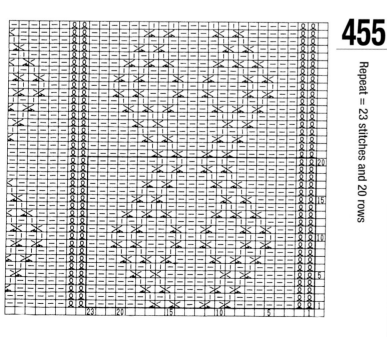

Repeat = 23 stitches and 20 rows

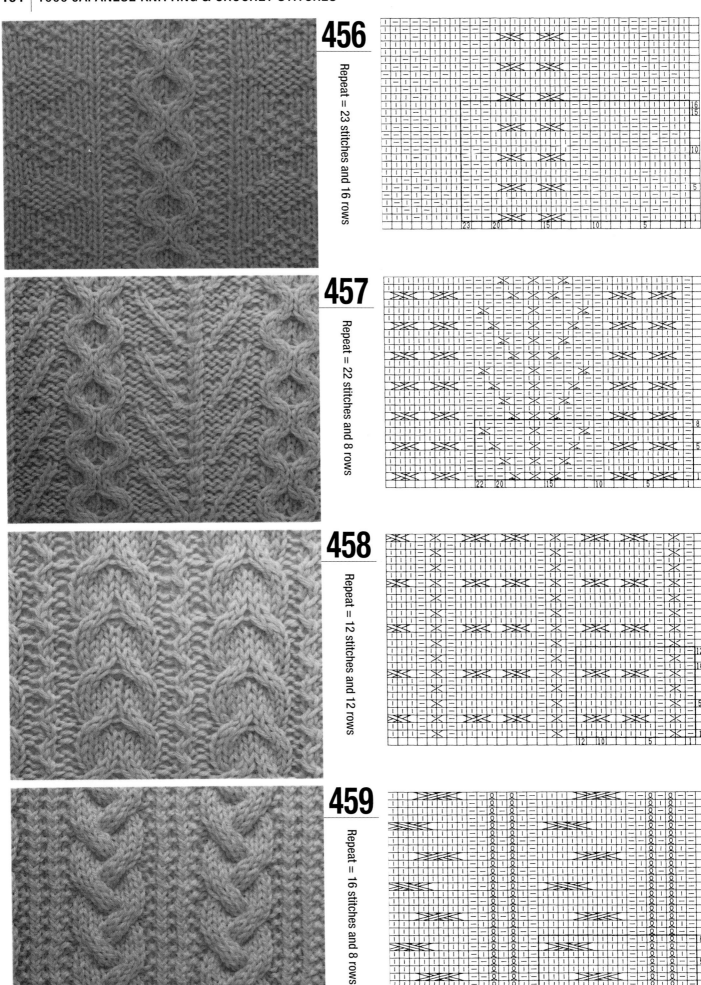

456

Repeat = 23 stitches and 16 rows

457

Repeat = 22 stitches and 8 rows

458

Repeat = 12 stitches and 12 rows

459

Repeat = 16 stitches and 8 rows

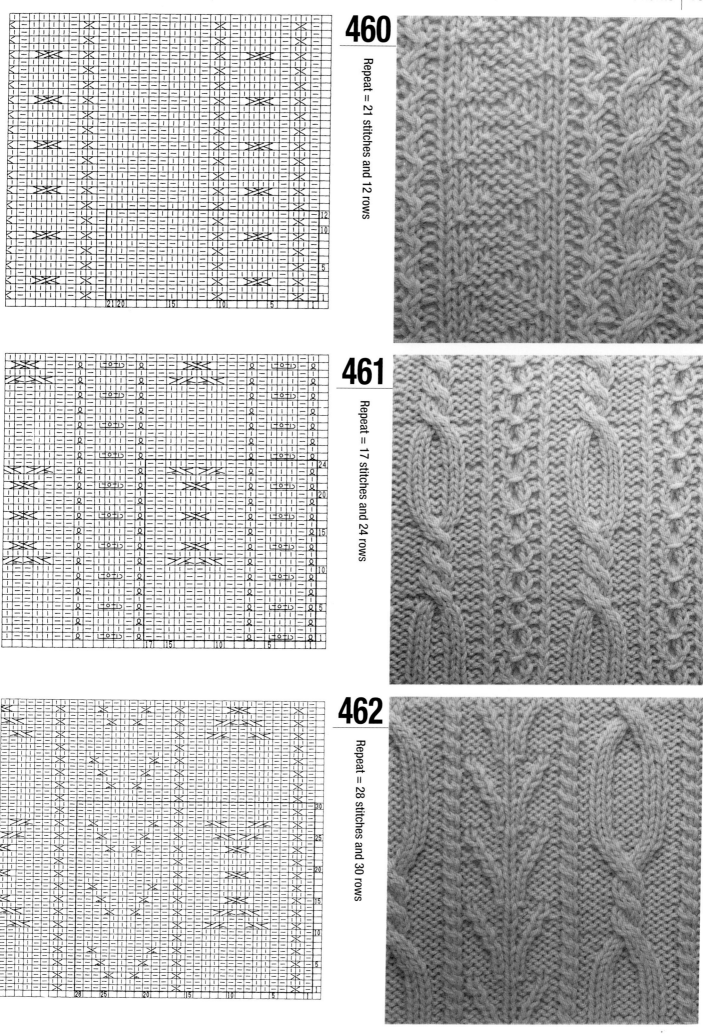

460

Repeat = 21 stitches and 12 rows

461

Repeat = 17 stitches and 24 rows

462

Repeat = 28 stitches and 30 rows

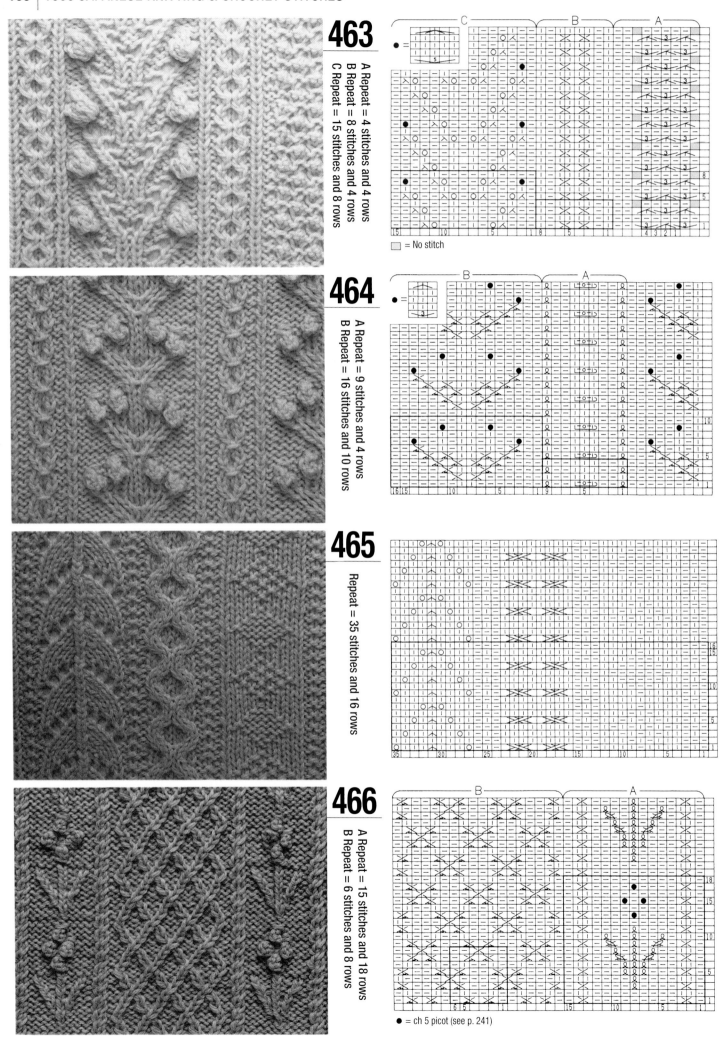

463

A Repeat = 4 stitches and 4 rows
B Repeat = 8 stitches and 4 rows
C Repeat = 15 stitches and 8 rows

= No stitch

464

A Repeat = 9 stitches and 4 rows
B Repeat = 16 stitches and 10 rows

465

Repeat = 35 stitches and 16 rows

466

A Repeat = 15 stitches and 18 rows
B Repeat = 6 stitches and 8 rows

● = ch 5 picot (see p. 241)

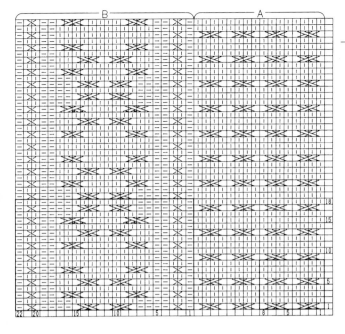

467

A Repeat = 8 stitches and 8 rows
B Repeat = 22 stitches and 18 rows

468

A Repeat = 16 stitches and 8 rows
B Repeat = 14 stitches and 26 rows
C Repeat = 15 stitches and 22 rows

469

A Repeat = 17 stitches and 22 rows
B Repeat = 12 stitches and 8 rows
C Repeat = 22 stitches and 8 rows

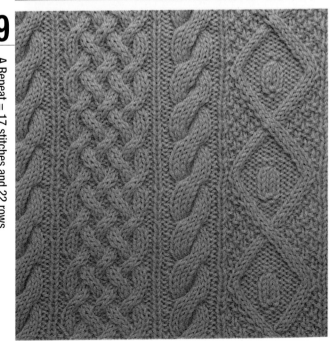

470
Repeat = 19 stitches and 10 rows

471
A Repeat = 13 stitches and 8 rows
B Repeat = 17 stitches and 12 rows

472
A Repeat = 11 stitches and 10 rows
B Repeat = 12 stitches and 4 rows

473
A Repeat = 2 stitches and 4 rows
B Repeat = 30 stitches and 8 rows

= Slip as if to ktbl (twisted sl st)

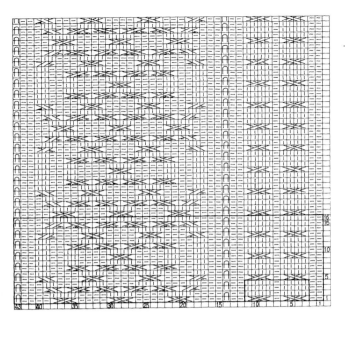

474

Repeat = 43 stitches and 16 rows

475

A Repeat = 12 stitches and 2 rows
B Repeat = 12 stitches and 4 rows
C Repeat = 24 stitches and 34 rows

476

Repeat = 21 stitches and 48 rows

● = = See p. 29

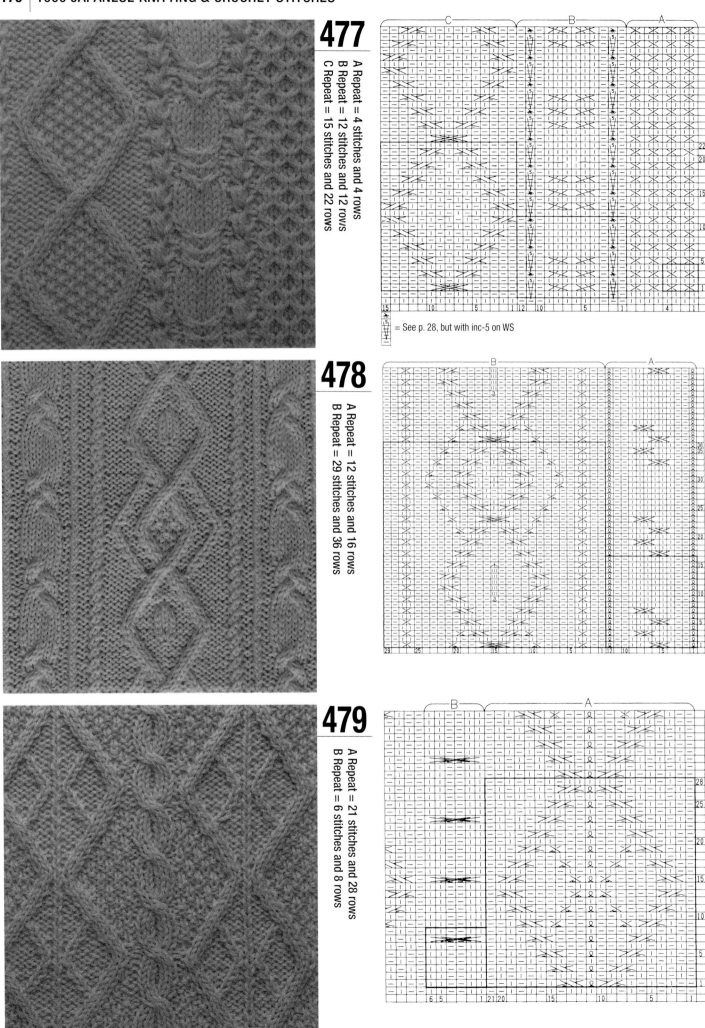

477

A Repeat = 4 stitches and 4 rows
B Repeat = 12 stitches and 12 rows
C Repeat = 15 stitches and 22 rows

= See p. 28, but with inc-5 on WS

478

A Repeat = 12 stitches and 16 rows
B Repeat = 29 stitches and 36 rows

479

A Repeat = 21 stitches and 28 rows
B Repeat = 6 stitches and 8 rows

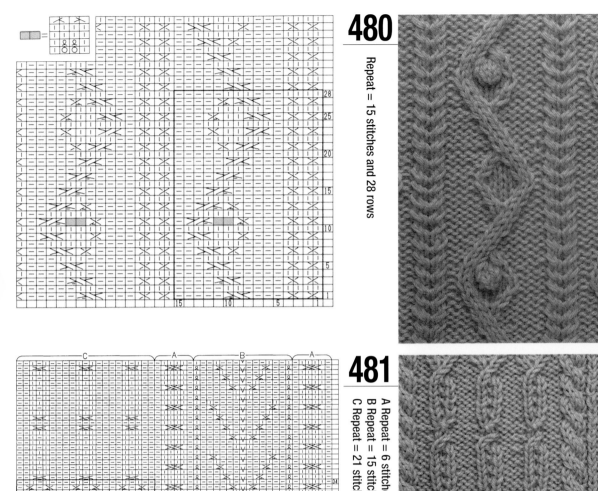

480

Repeat = 15 stitches and 28 rows

481

A Repeat = 6 stitches and 4 rows
B Repeat = 15 stitches and 10 rows
C Repeat = 21 stitches and 34 rows

482

Repeat = 22 stitches and 8 rows

483

Repeat = 11 stitches and 6 rows

484

A Repeat = 2 stitches and 4 rows
B Repeat = 10 stitches and 4 rows
C Repeat = 14 stitches and 10 rows

485

A Repeat = 2 stitches and 2 rows
B Repeat = 11 stitches and 8 rows
C Repeat = 18 stitches and 8 rows

486

Repeat = 20 stitches and 8 rows

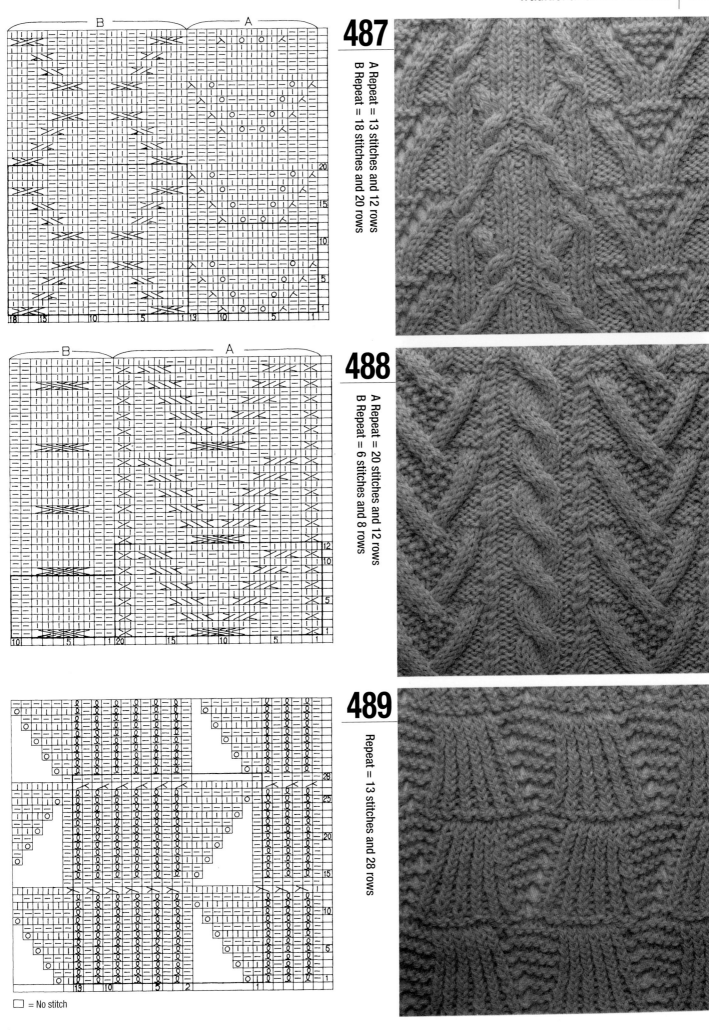

487
A Repeat = 13 stitches and 12 rows
B Repeat = 18 stitches and 20 rows

488
A Repeat = 20 stitches and 12 rows
B Repeat = 6 stitches and 8 rows

489
Repeat = 13 stitches and 28 rows

☐ = No stitch

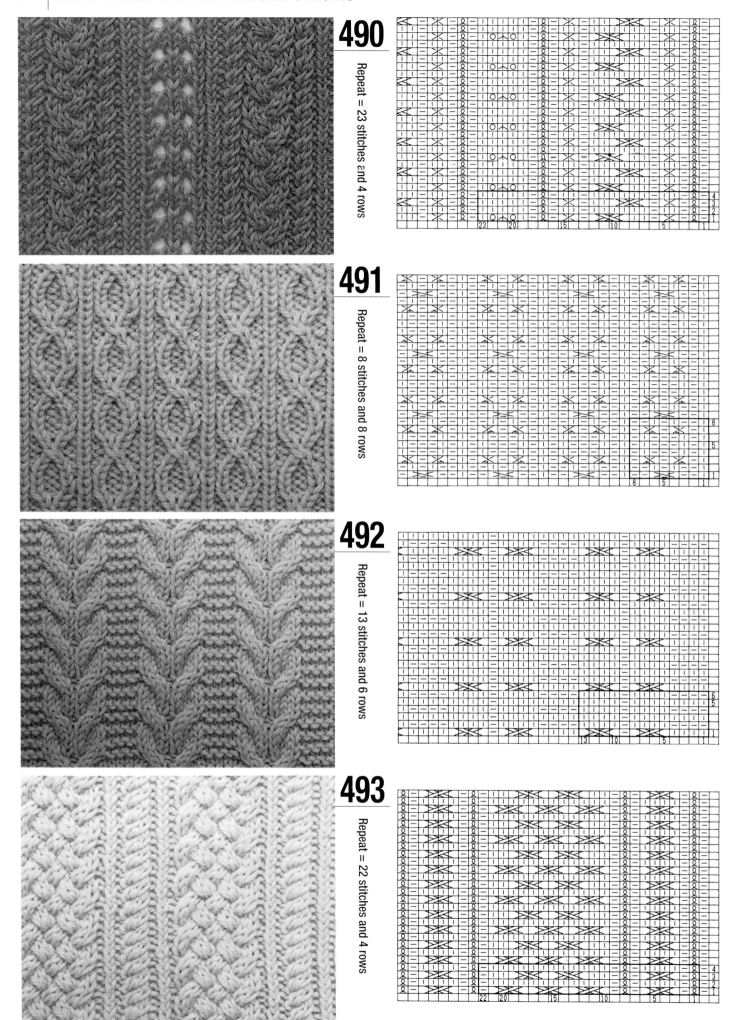

490 Repeat = 23 stitches and 4 rows

491 Repeat = 8 stitches and 8 rows

492 Repeat = 13 stitches and 6 rows

493 Repeat = 22 stitches and 4 rows

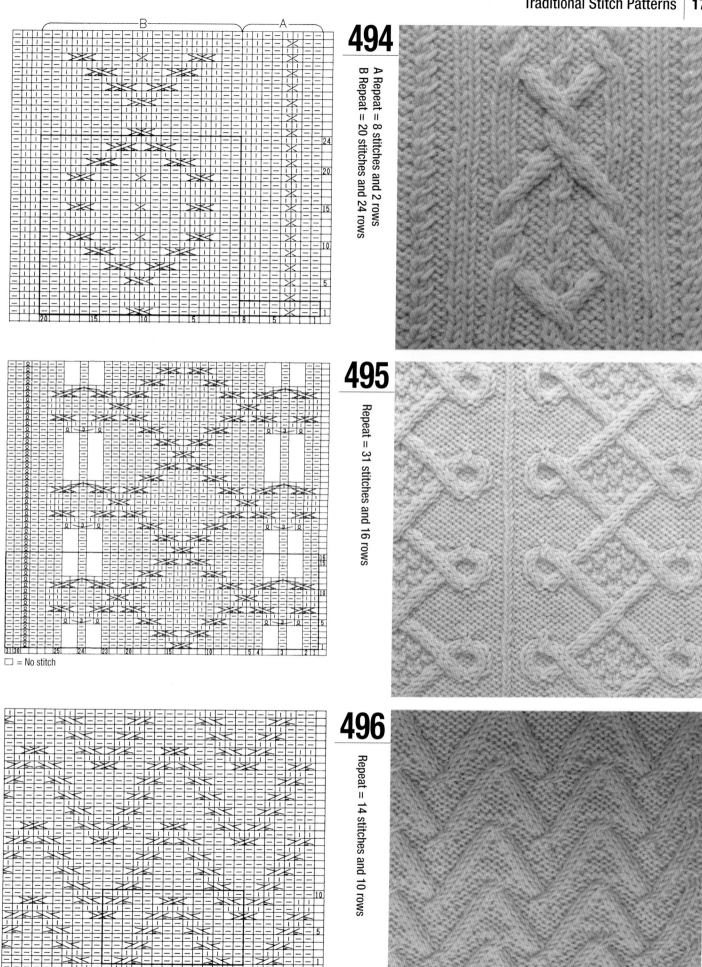

494

A Repeat = 8 stitches and 2 rows
B Repeat = 20 stitches and 24 rows

495

Repeat = 31 stitches and 16 rows

□ = No stitch

496

Repeat = 14 stitches and 10 rows

497

Repeat = 24 stitches and 20 rows

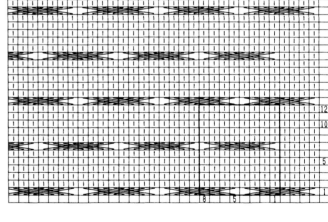

498

Repeat = 16 stitches and 12 rows

499

Repeat = 8 stitches and 12 rows

500

Repeat = 12 stitches and 12 rows

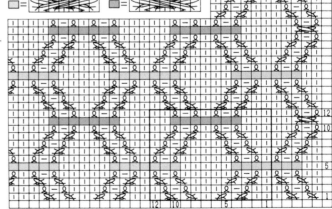

Top symbol left: Place 3 sts on CN, hold to back; place 1 st on another CN, hold to back; ktbl, p1, ktbl; p1 from second CN; ktbl, p1, ktbl from first CN

Top symbol right: Place 3 sts on CN, hold to front; place 1 st on CN, hold to back; ktbl, p1, ktbl; p1 from back CN; ktbl, p1, ktbl from front CN

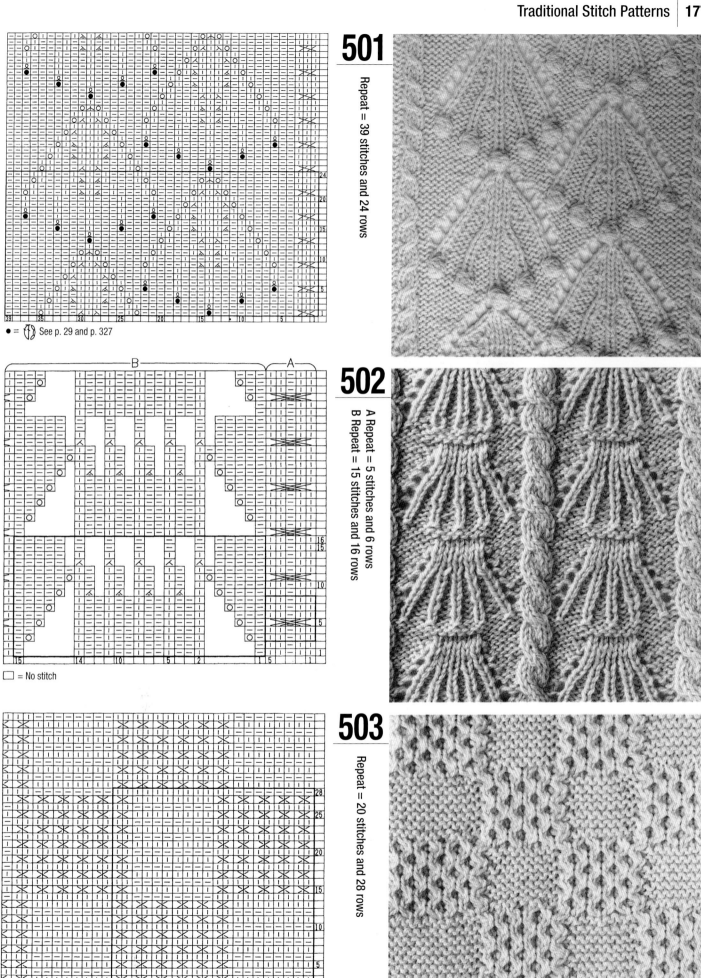

501

Repeat = 39 stitches and 24 rows

● = 🦋 See p. 29 and p. 327

☐ = No stitch

502

A Repeat = 5 stitches and 6 rows
B Repeat = 15 stitches and 16 rows

503

Repeat = 20 stitches and 28 rows

504

Repeat = 17 stitches and 24 rows

505

Repeat = 8 stitches and 12 rows

506

Repeat = 6 stitches and 16 rows

507

Repeat = 10 stitches and 14 rows

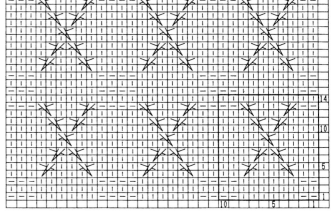

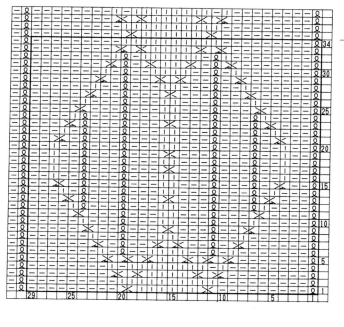

508

Repeat = 29 stitches and 34 rows

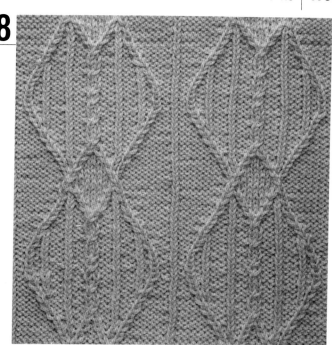

509

Repeat = 16 stitches and 40 rows

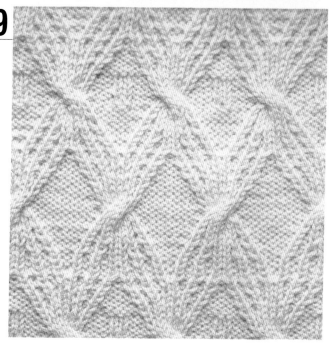

510

A Repeat = 13 stitches and 8 rows
B Repeat = 13 stitches and 20 rows

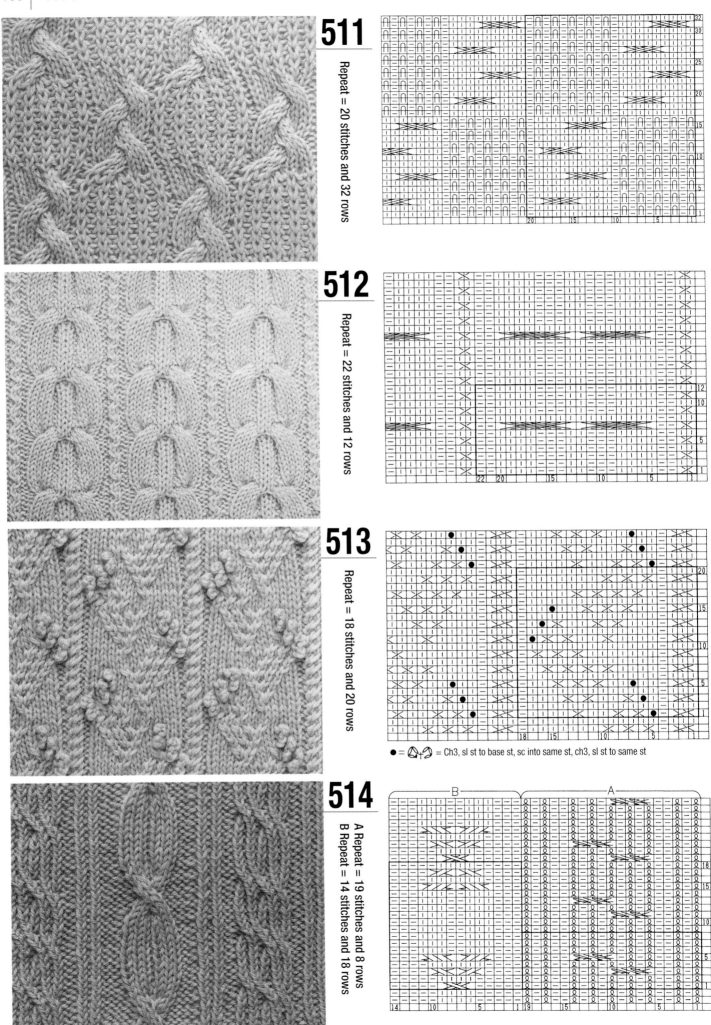

511

Repeat = 20 stitches and 32 rows

512

Repeat = 22 stitches and 12 rows

513

Repeat = 18 stitches and 20 rows

● = Ch3, sl st to base st, sc into same st, ch3, sl st to same st

514

A Repeat = 19 stitches and 8 rows
B Repeat = 14 stitches and 18 rows

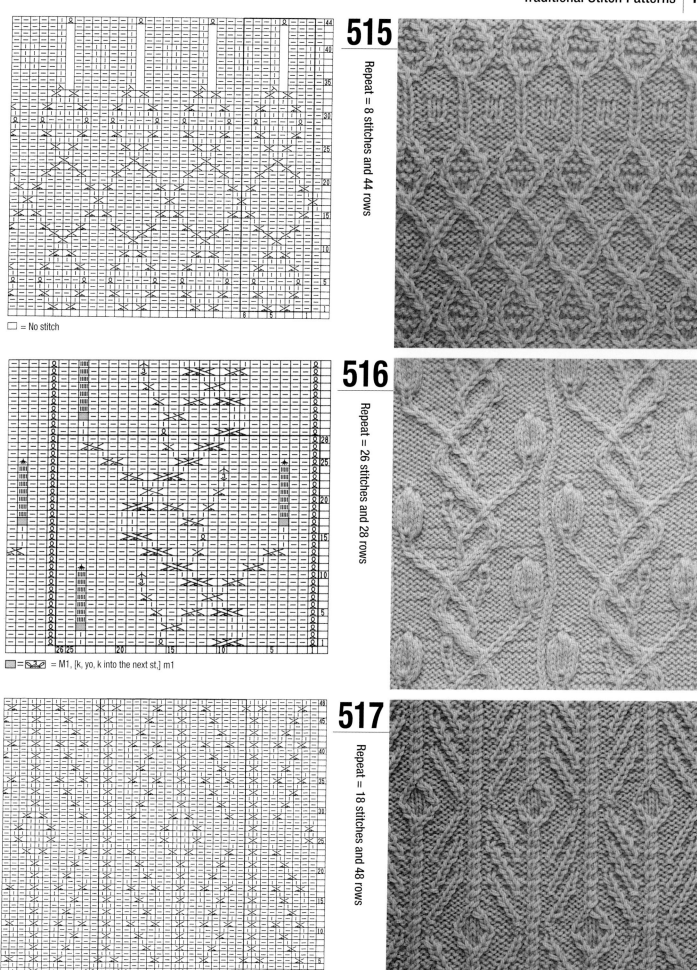

515

Repeat = 8 stitches and 44 rows

☐ = No stitch

516

Repeat = 26 stitches and 28 rows

■ = = M1, [k, yo, k into the next st,] m1

517

Repeat = 18 stitches and 48 rows

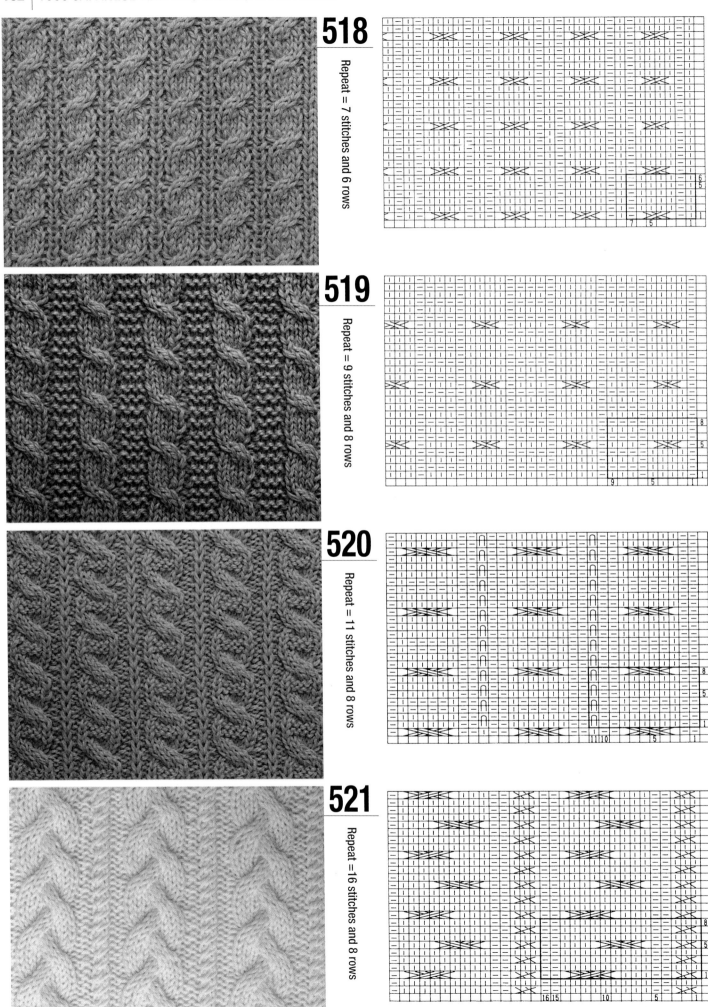

518

Repeat = 7 stitches and 6 rows

519

Repeat = 9 stitches and 8 rows

520

Repeat = 11 stitches and 8 rows

521

Repeat = 16 stitches and 8 rows

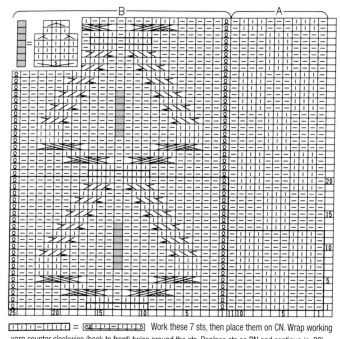

522

A Repeat = 11 stitches and 12 rows
B Repeat = 25 stitches and 20 rows

= Work these 7 sts, then place them on CN. Wrap working yarn counter clockwise (back to front) twice around the sts. Replace sts on RN and continue (p. 22).

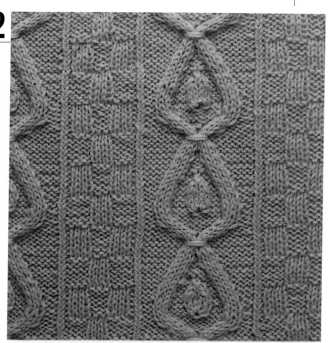

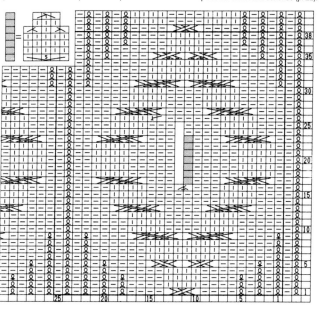

523

Repeat = 25 stitches and 38 rows

524

Repeat = 24 stitches and 32 rows

525

Repeat = 10 stitches and 12 rows

526

Repeat = 19 stitches and 20 rows

● = For bobble: k, p, k into the same st; turn and p3; turn and sl 1, k2tog, psso.

527

Repeat = 18 stitches and 8 rows

528

Repeat = 14 stitches and 4 rows

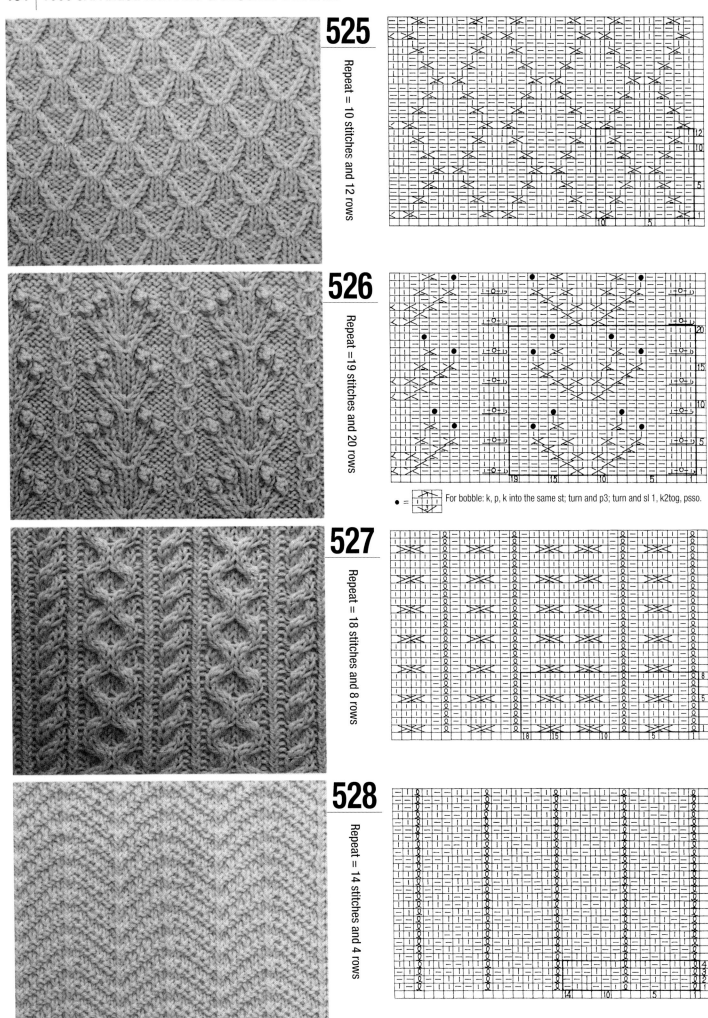

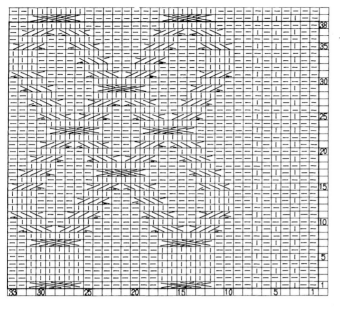

529

Repeat = 33 stitches and 38 rows

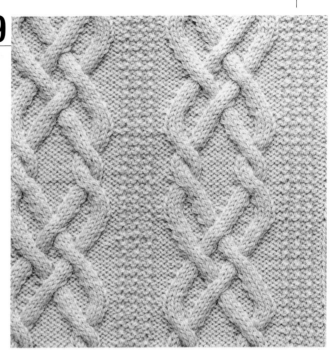

530

Repeat = 6 stitches and 24 rows

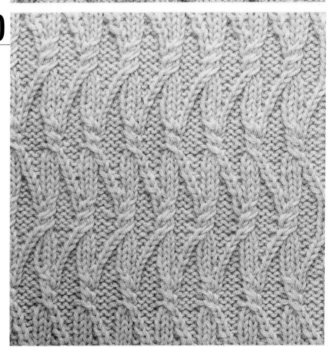

531

Repeat = 16 stitches and 14 rows

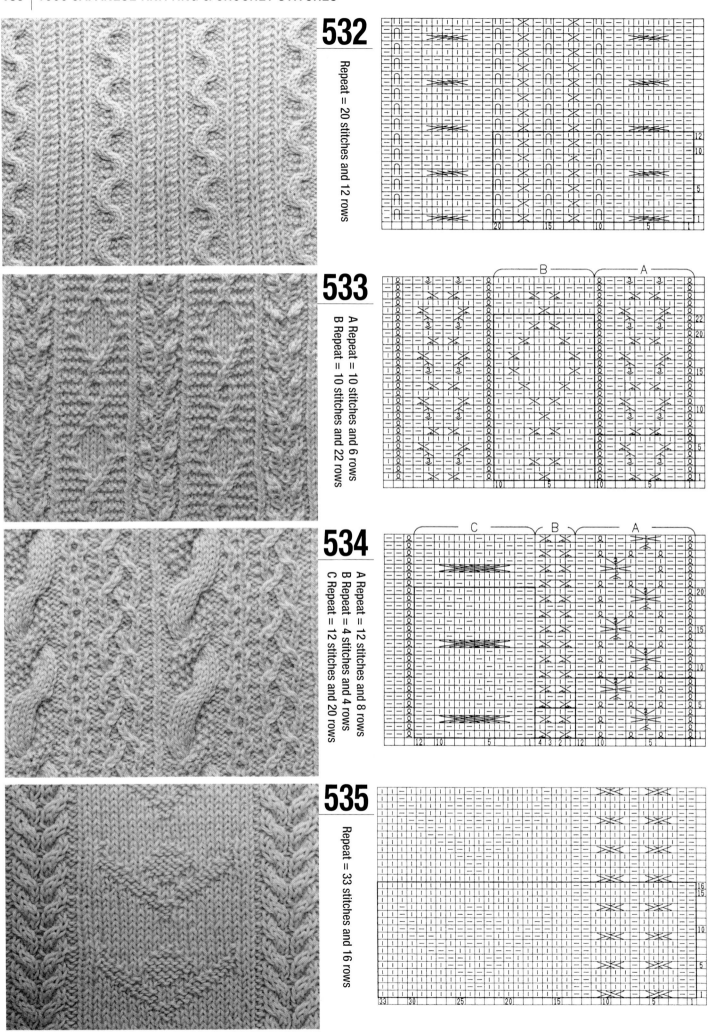

532

Repeat = 20 stitches and 12 rows

533

A Repeat = 10 stitches and 6 rows
B Repeat = 10 stitches and 22 rows

534

A Repeat = 12 stitches and 8 rows
B Repeat = 4 stitches and 4 rows
C Repeat = 12 stitches and 20 rows

535

Repeat = 33 stitches and 16 rows

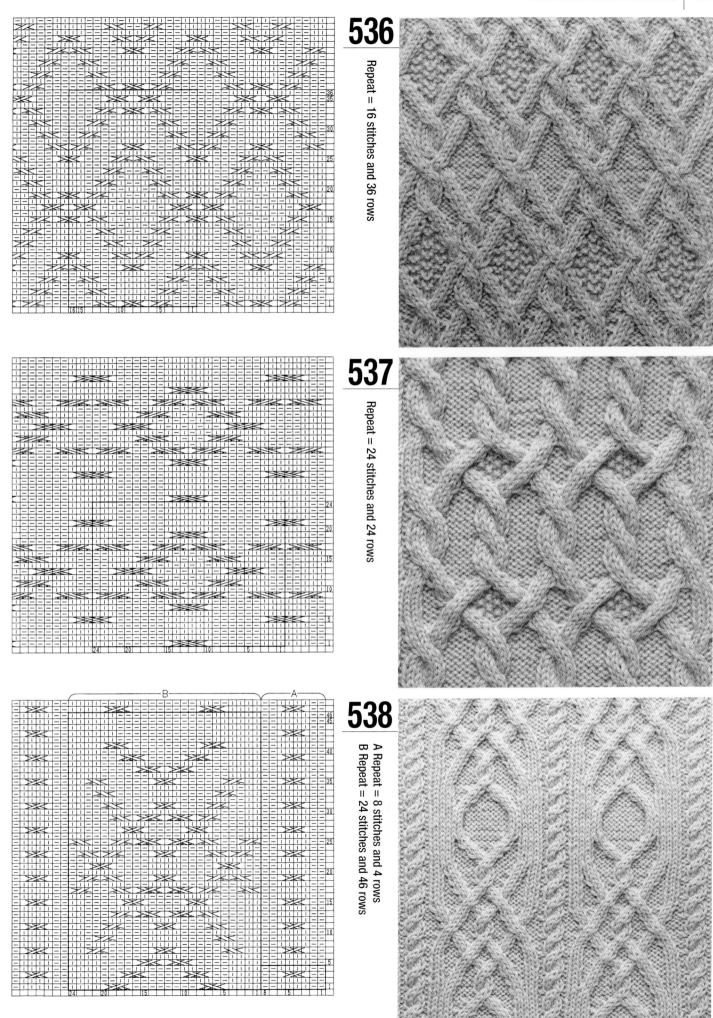

536

Repeat = 16 stitches and 36 rows

537

Repeat = 24 stitches and 24 rows

538

A Repeat = 8 stitches and 4 rows
B Repeat = 24 stitches and 46 rows

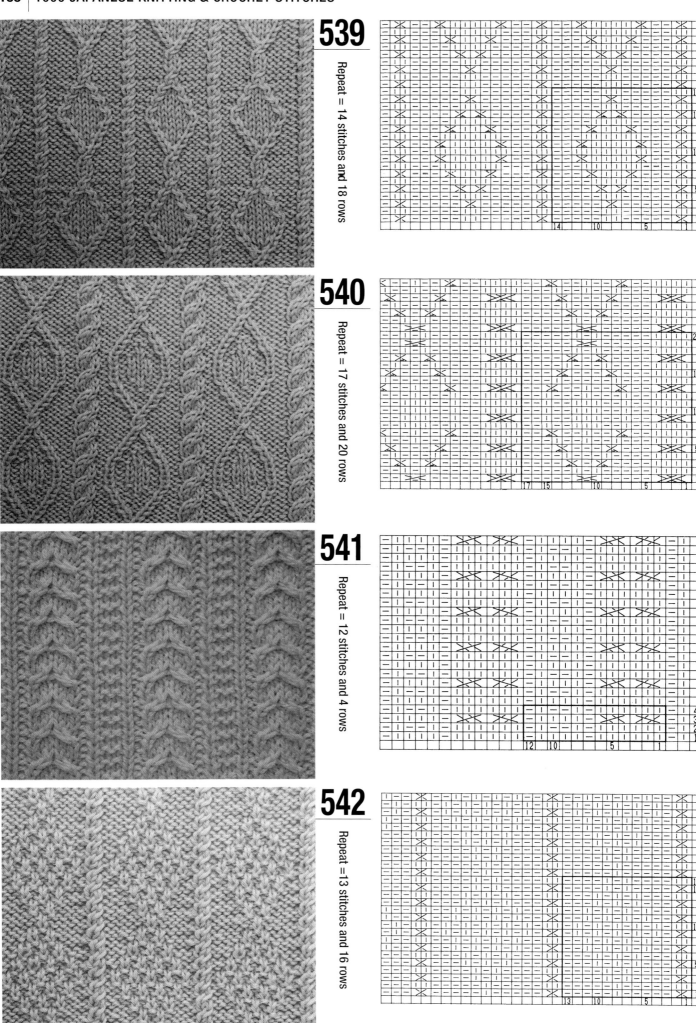

539

Repeat = 14 stitches and 18 rows

540

Repeat = 17 stitches and 20 rows

541

Repeat = 12 stitches and 4 rows

542

Repeat = 13 stitches and 16 rows

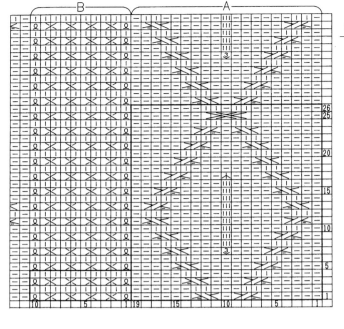

543

A Repeat = 19 stitches and 26 rows
B Repeat = 10 stitches and 4 rows

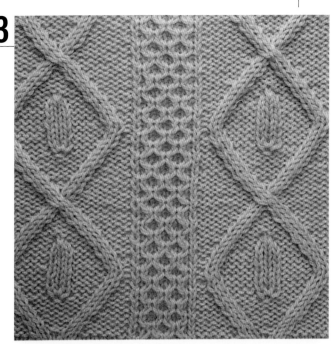

544

A Repeat = 22 stitches and 20 rows
B Repeat = 28 stitches and 24 rows

545

Repeat = 28 stitches and 32 rows

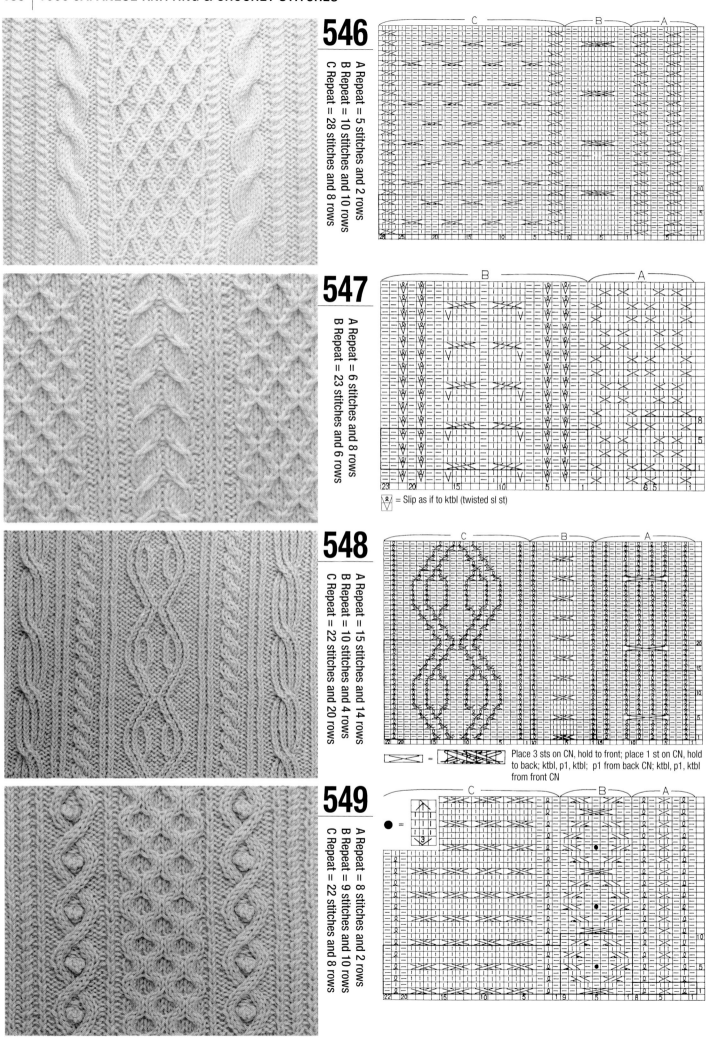

546

A Repeat = 5 stitches and 2 rows
B Repeat = 10 stitches and 10 rows
C Repeat = 28 stitches and 8 rows

547

A Repeat = 6 stitches and 8 rows
B Repeat = 23 stitches and 6 rows

$\frac{Q}{V}$ = Slip as if to ktbl (twisted sl st)

548

A Repeat = 15 stitches and 14 rows
B Repeat = 10 stitches and 4 rows
C Repeat = 22 stitches and 20 rows

= Place 3 sts on CN, hold to front; place 1 st on CN, hold to back; ktbl, p1, ktbl; p1 from back CN; ktbl, p1, ktbl from front CN

549

● =

A Repeat = 8 stitches and 2 rows
B Repeat = 9 stitches and 10 rows
C Repeat = 22 stitches and 8 rows

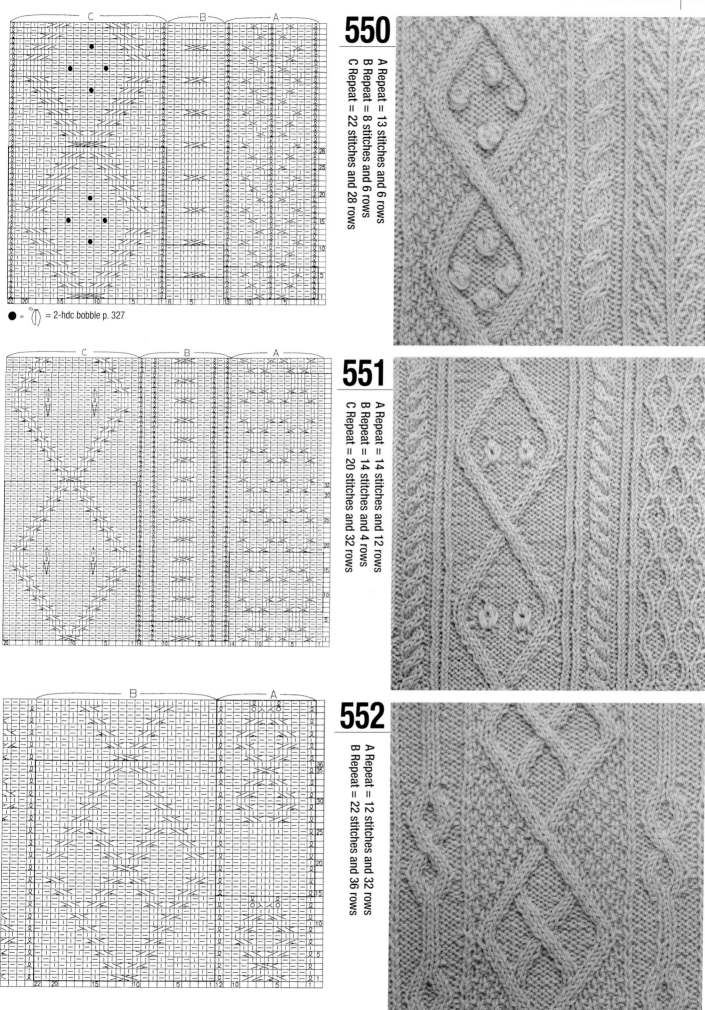

550

A Repeat = 13 stitches and 6 rows
B Repeat = 8 stitches and 6 rows
C Repeat = 22 stitches and 28 rows

● = = 2-hdc bobble p. 327

551

A Repeat = 14 stitches and 12 rows
B Repeat = 14 stitches and 4 rows
C Repeat = 20 stitches and 32 rows

552

A Repeat = 12 stitches and 32 rows
B Repeat = 22 stitches and 36 rows

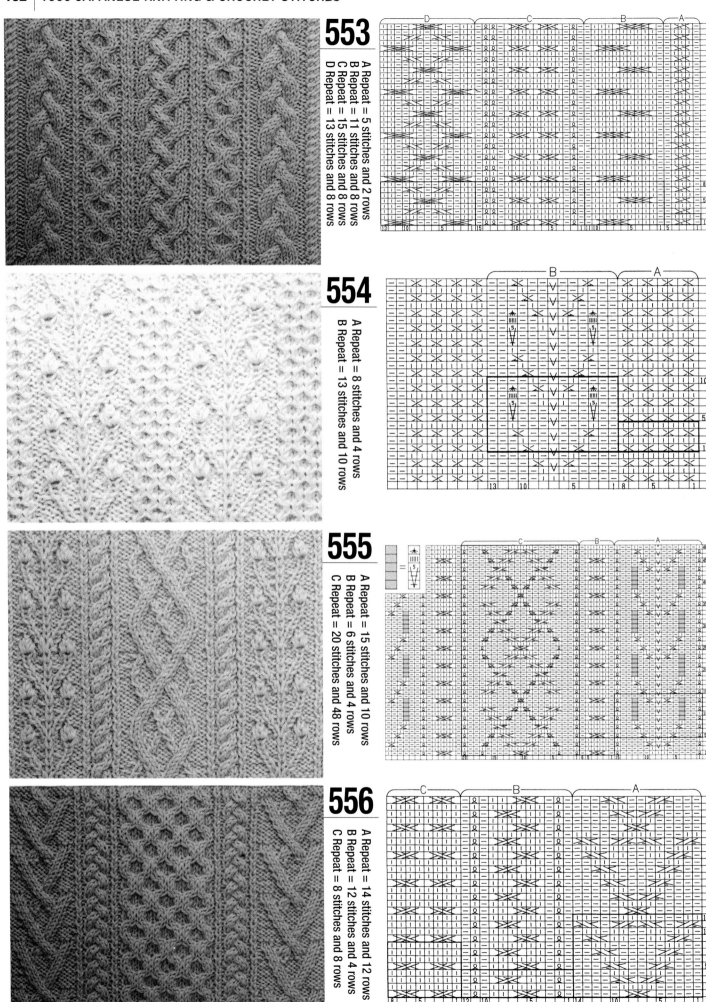

553

A Repeat = 5 stitches and 2 rows
B Repeat = 11 stitches and 8 rows
C Repeat = 15 stitches and 8 rows
D Repeat = 13 stitches and 8 rows

554

A Repeat = 8 stitches and 4 rows
B Repeat = 13 stitches and 10 rows

555

A Repeat = 15 stitches and 10 rows
B Repeat = 6 stitches and 4 rows
C Repeat = 20 stitches and 48 rows

556

A Repeat = 14 stitches and 12 rows
B Repeat = 12 stitches and 4 rows
C Repeat = 8 stitches and 8 rows

KNIT-IN COLORWORK PATTERNS ✳ Checks, colorful cables, mosaic stitches

You can play with color choices in these stitches. They can be bright and cheerful or toned down, chic or classic—there's no end to the possibilities. Crossed stitches are also included. Some patterns include textured stitches, as well as a few patterns derived from patchwork quilts.

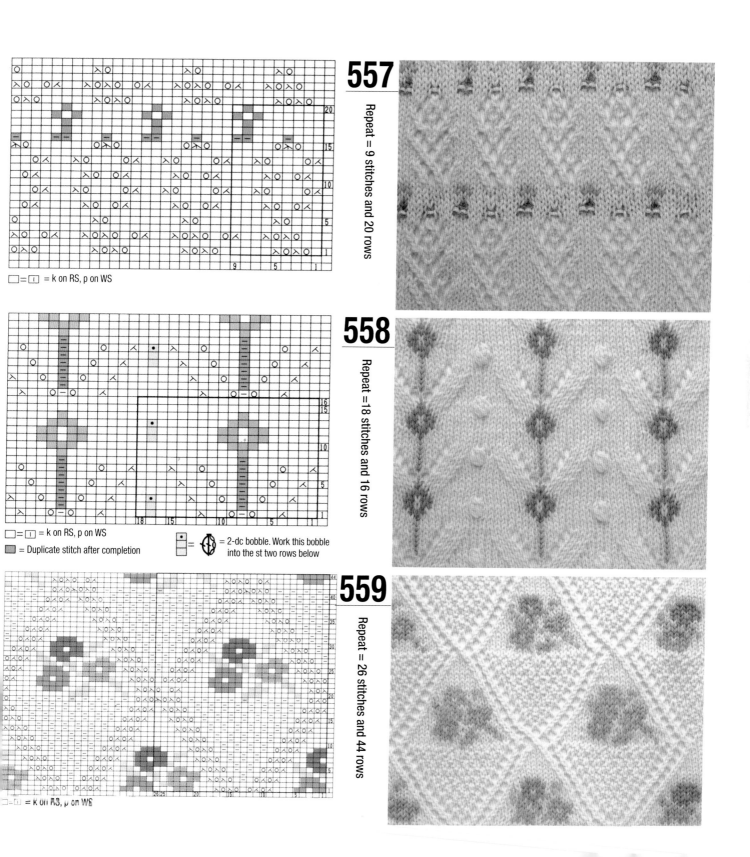

□ = 𝟙 = k on RS, p on WS

557
Repeat = 9 stitches and 20 rows

□ = 𝟙 = k on RS, p on WS

▨ = Duplicate stitch after completion

⊡ = ⬭ = 2-dc bobble. Work this bobble into the st two rows below

558
Repeat = 18 stitches and 16 rows

□ = 𝟙 = k on RS, p on WS

559
Repeat = 26 stitches and 44 rows

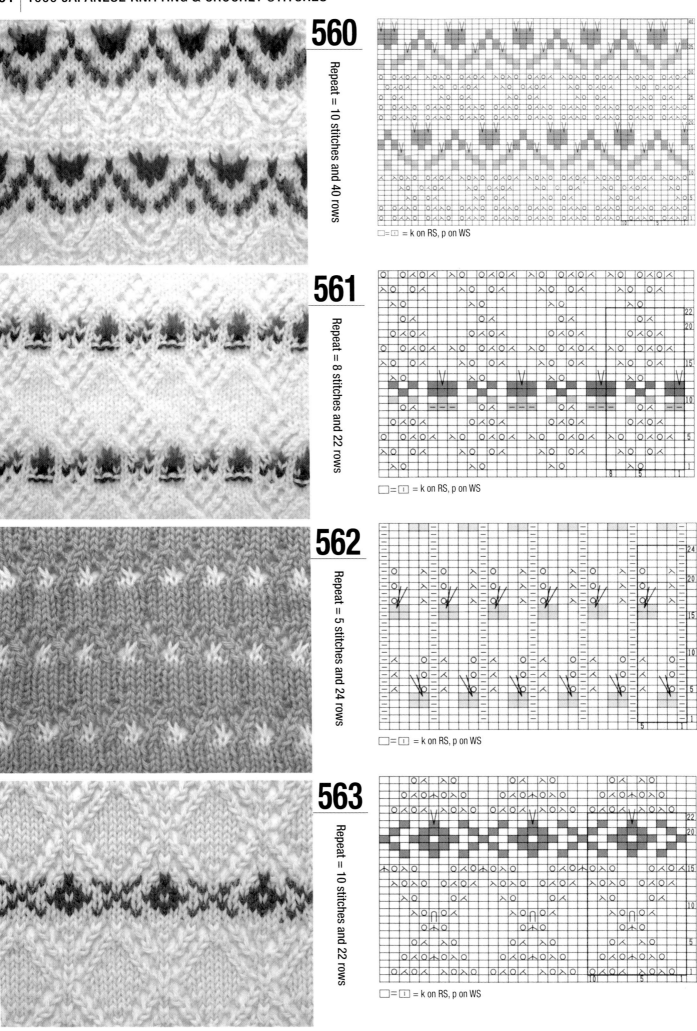

560

Repeat = 10 stitches and 40 rows

□=⊡ = k on RS, p on WS

561

Repeat = 8 stitches and 22 rows

□=⊡ = k on RS, p on WS

562

Repeat = 5 stitches and 24 rows

□=⊡ = k on RS, p on WS

563

Repeat = 10 stitches and 22 rows

□=⊡ = k on RS, p on WS

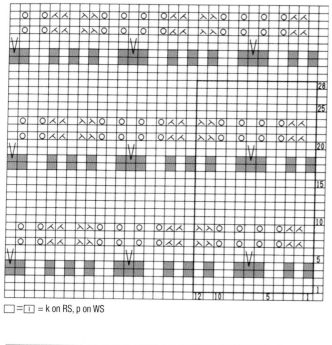

564

Repeat = 12 stitches and 28 rows

☐ = ☐ = k on RS, p on WS

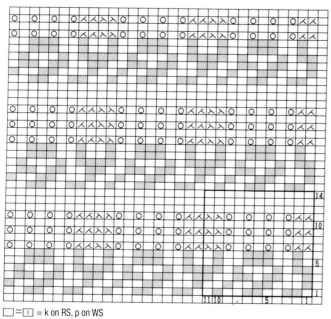

565

Repeat = 11 stitches and 14 rows

☐ = ☐ = k on RS, p on WS

566

Repeat = 10 stitches and 36 rows

☐ = ☐ = k on RS, p on WS

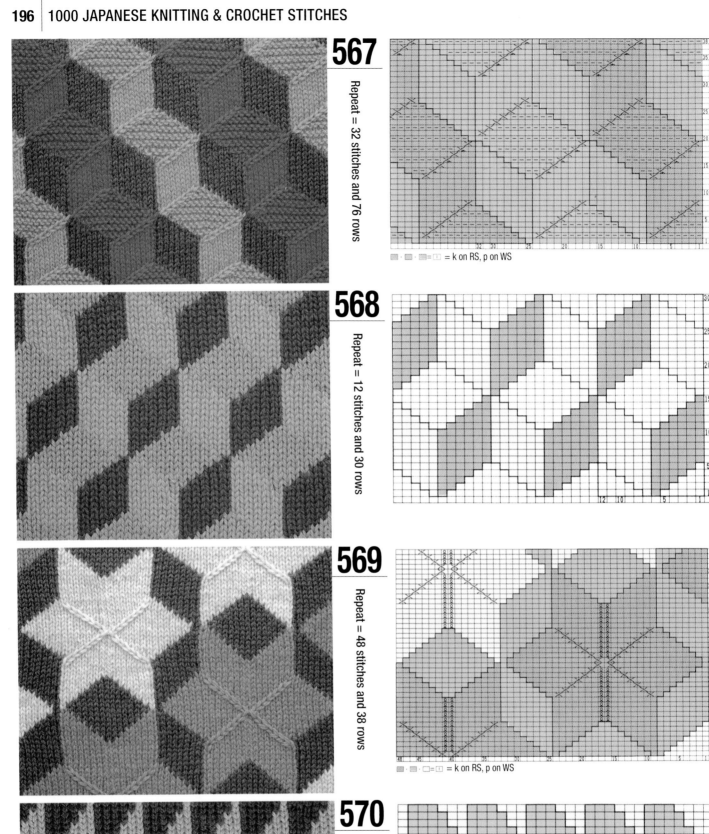

567

Repeat = 32 stitches and 76 rows

▨ · ▦ · ▦ = ⊡ = k on RS, p on WS

568

Repeat = 12 stitches and 30 rows

569

Repeat = 48 stitches and 38 rows

▨ · ▦ · □ = ⊡ = k on RS, p on WS

570

Repeat = 6 stitches and 22 rows

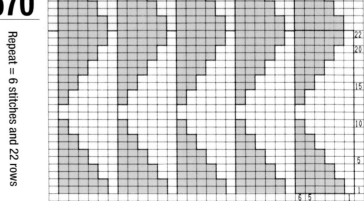

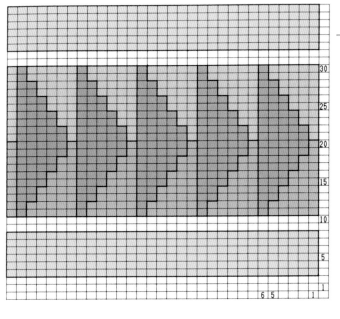

571

Repeat = 6 stitches and 30 rows

572

Repeat = 40 stitches and 60 rows

573

Repeat = 39 stitches and 53 rows

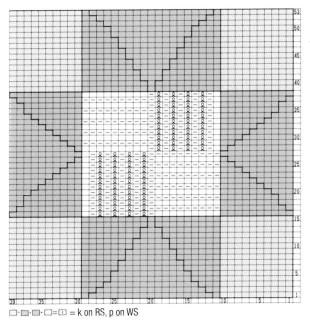

□·▦·▨·□=⬚ = k on RS, p on WS

See page 30 for notes on patterns 574-580

574

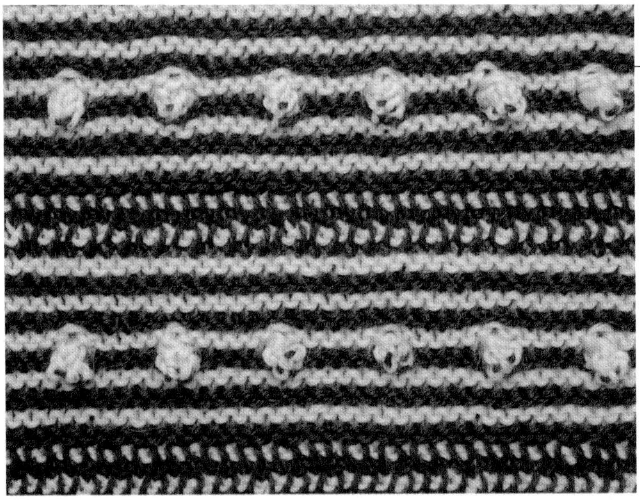

Repeat = 6 stitches and 28 rows

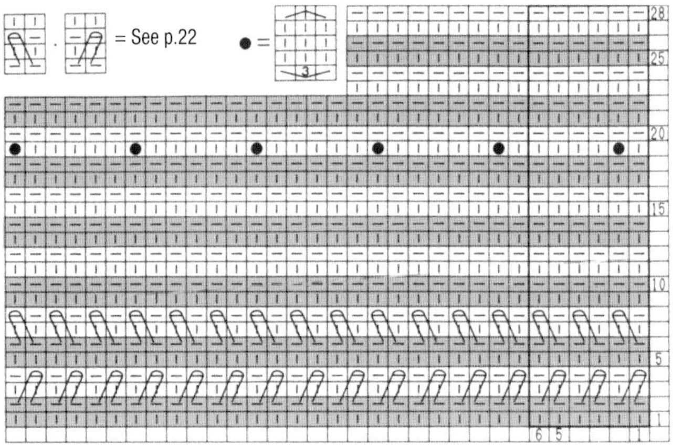

= See p.22

575

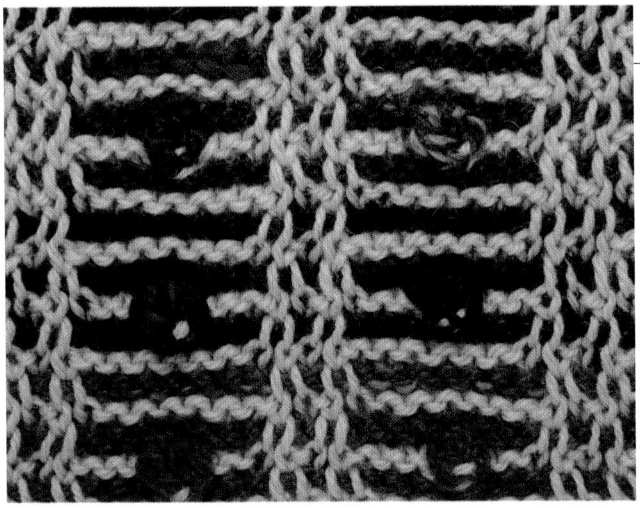

Repeat = 10 stitches and 36 rows

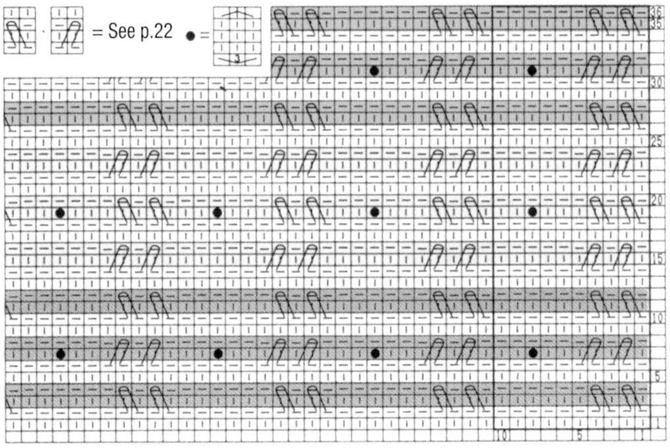

= See p.22

576

Repeat = 10 stitches and 28 rows

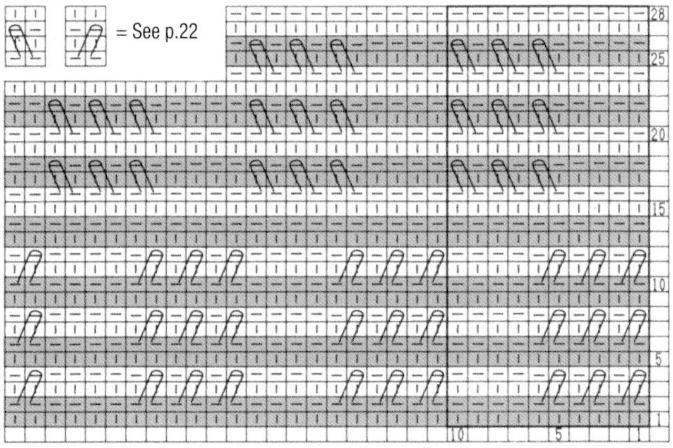

= See p.22

577

Repeat = 7 stitches and 20 rows

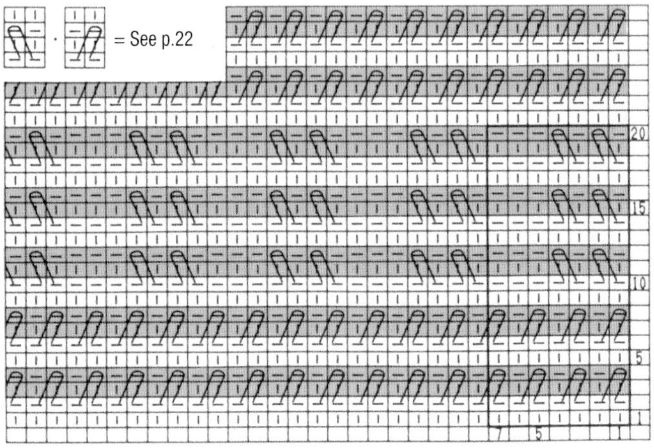

= See p.22

578

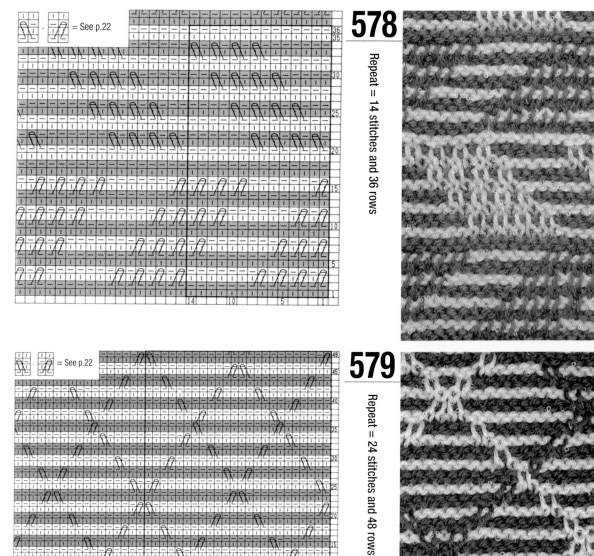

= See p.22

Repeat = 14 stitches and 36 rows

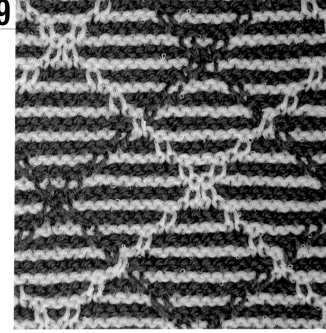

579

= See p.22

Repeat = 24 stitches and 48 rows

580

= See p. 22

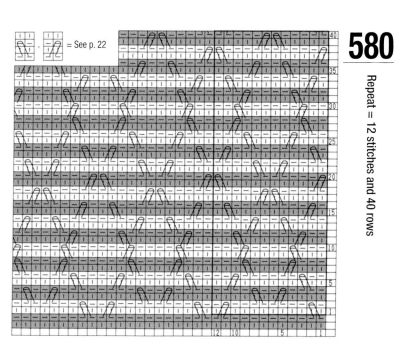

Repeat = 12 stitches and 40 rows

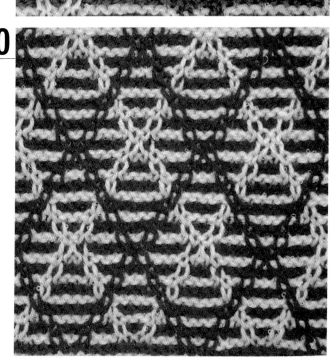

See page 30 for notes on patterns 581-615

581

Repeat = 8 stitches and 8 rows

582

Repeat = 8 stitches and 8 rows

583

Repeat = 12 stitches and 10 rows

584

Repeat = 4 stitches and 10 rows

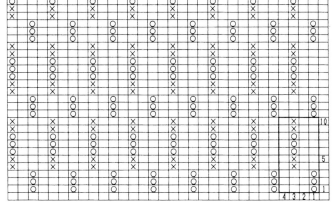

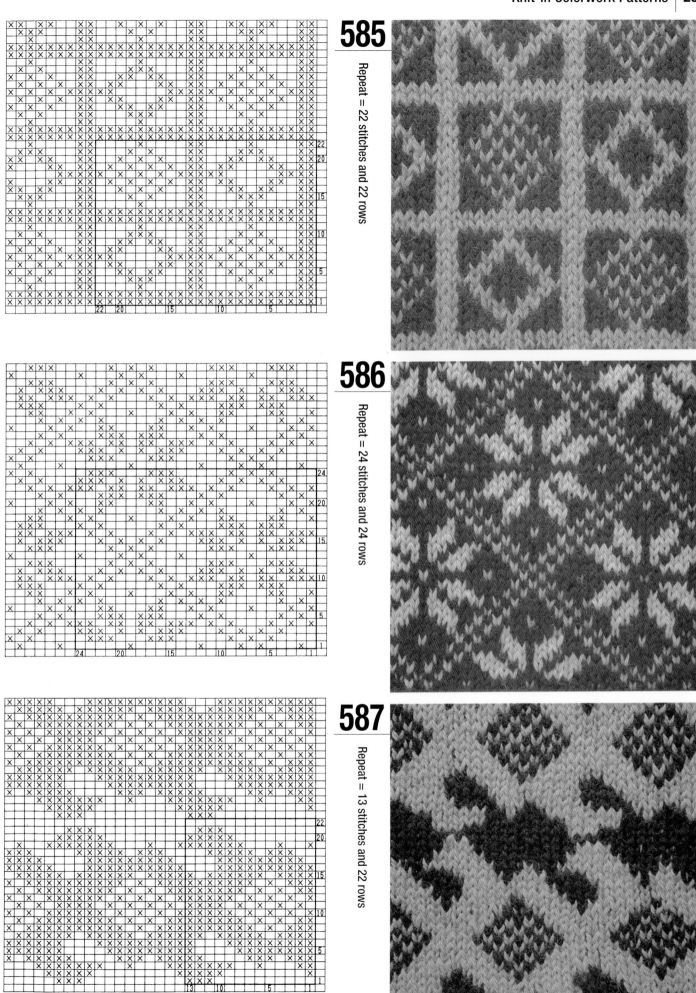

585

Repeat = 22 stitches and 22 rows

586

Repeat = 24 stitches and 24 rows

587

Repeat = 13 stitches and 22 rows

See page 30 for notes on patterns 581-615

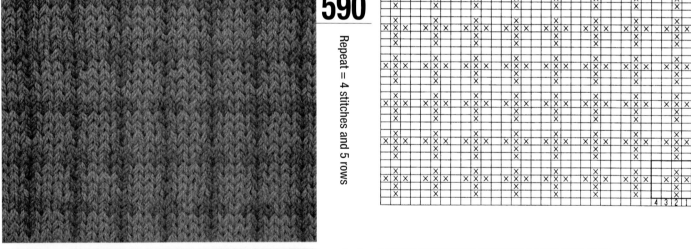

588

Repeat = 8 stitches and 12 rows

589

Repeat = 4 stitches and 12 rows

590

Repeat = 4 stitches and 5 rows

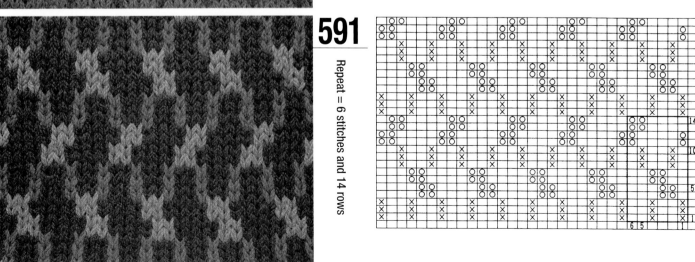

591

Repeat = 6 stitches and 14 rows

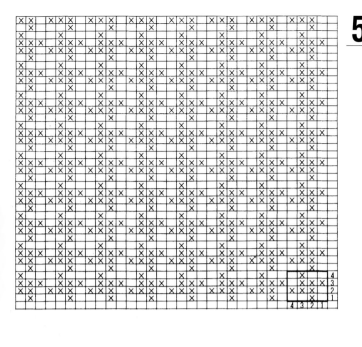

592

Repeat = 4 stitches and 4 rows

593

Repeat = 8 stitches and 8 rows

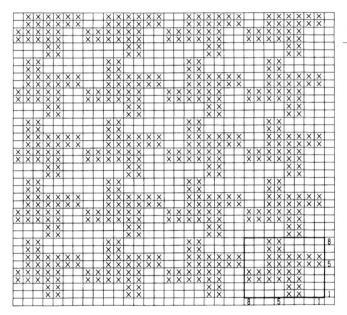

594

Repeat = 4 stitches and 8 rows

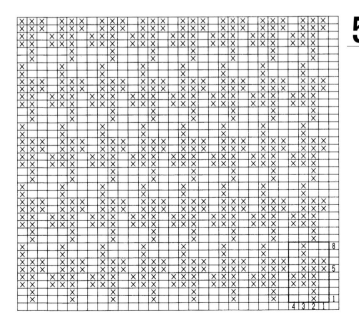

See page 30 for notes on patterns 581-615

595

Repeat = 13 stitches and 20 rows

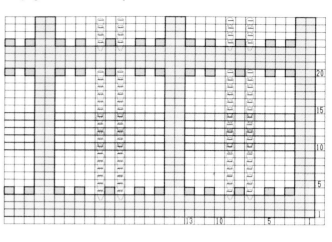

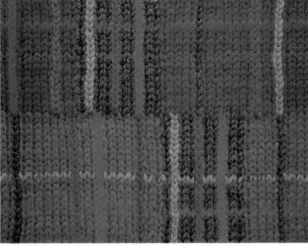

596

Repeat = 14 stitches and 15 rows

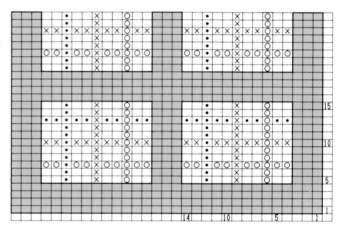

597

Repeat = 47 stitches and 41 rows

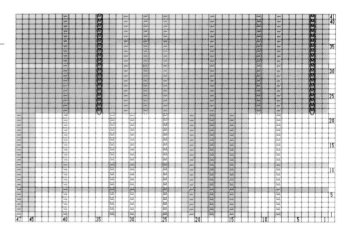

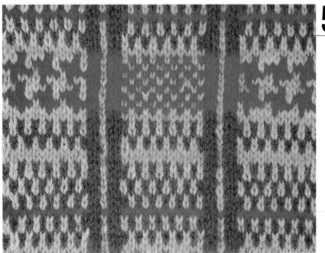

598

Repeat = 34 stitches and 27 rows

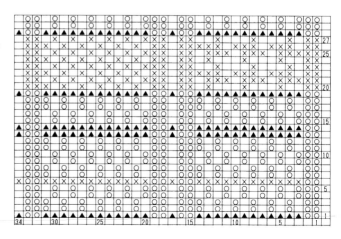

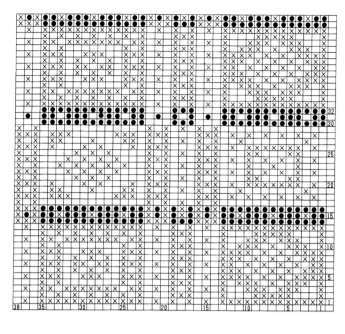

599

Repeat = 38 stitches and 32 rows

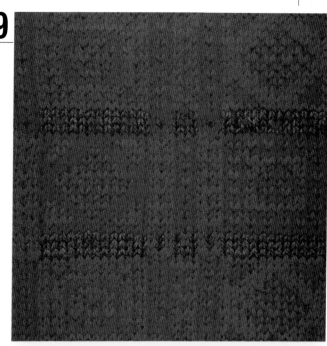

600

Repeat = 17 stitches and 28 rows

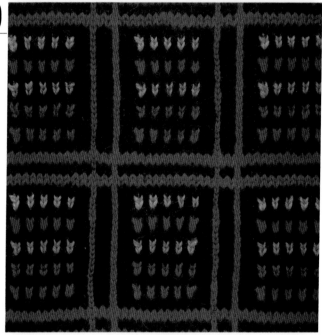

601

Repeat = 22 stitches and 30 rows

See page 30 for notes on patterns 581-615

602

Repeat = 16 stitches and 22 rows

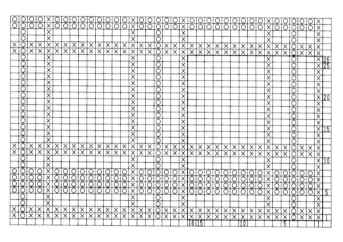

603

Repeat = 16 stitches and 26 rows

604

Repeat = 24 stitches and 20 rows

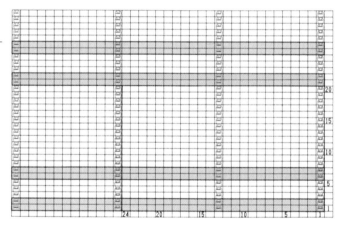

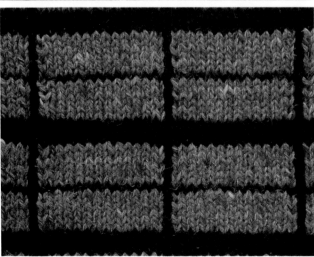

605

Repeat = 14 stitches and 17 rows

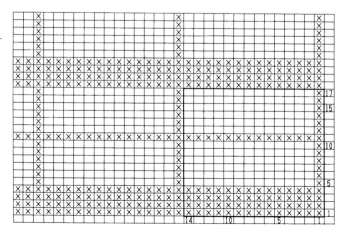

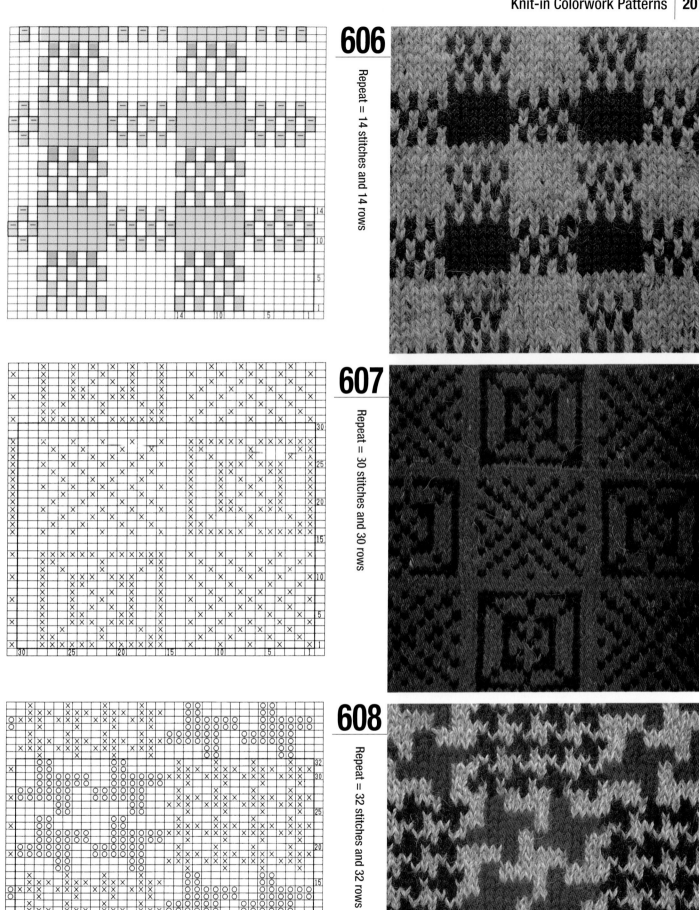

606

Repeat = 14 stitches and 14 rows

607

Repeat = 30 stitches and 30 rows

608

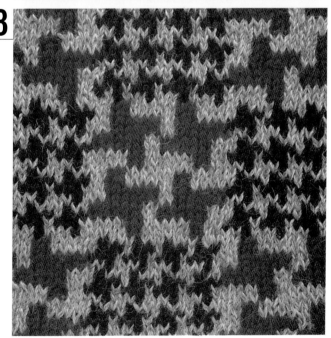

Repeat = 32 stitches and 32 rows

See page 30 for notes on patterns 581-615

609

Repeat = 21 stitches and 20 rows

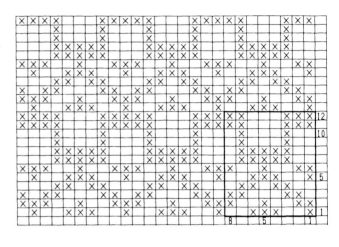

610

Repeat = 8 stitches and 12 rows

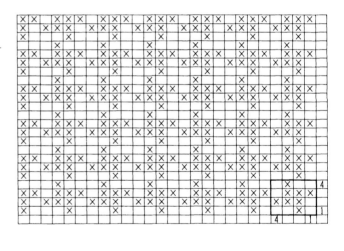

611

Repeat = 4 stitches and 4 rows

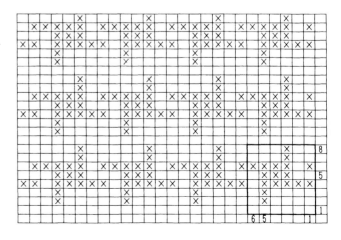

612

Repeat = 6 stitches and 8 rows

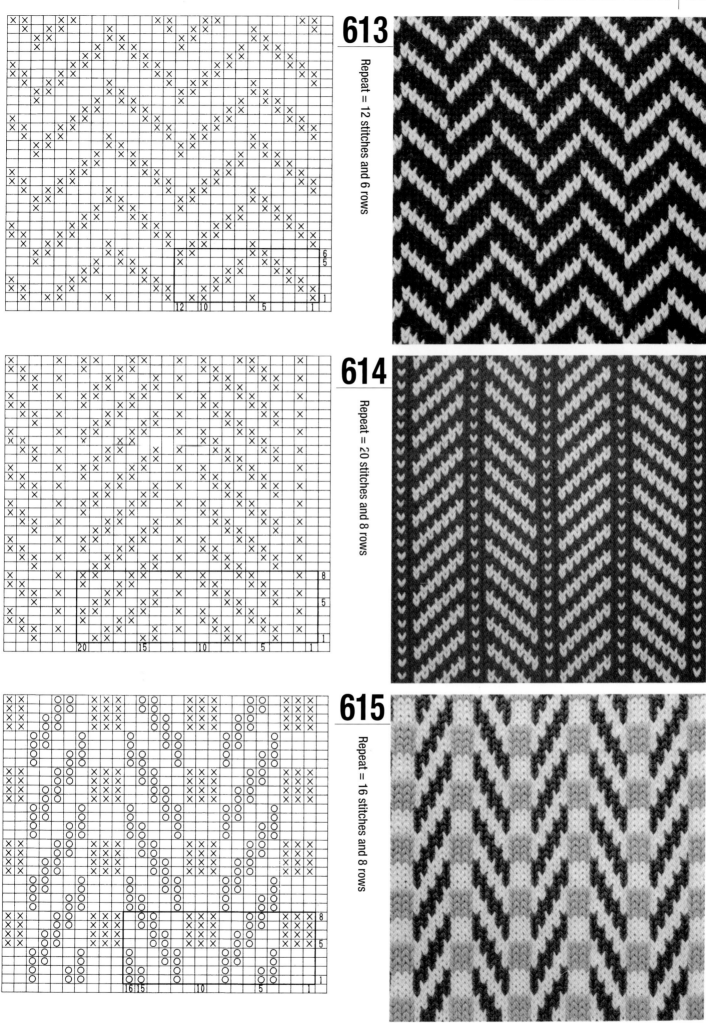

613
Repeat = 12 stitches and 6 rows

614
Repeat = 20 stitches and 8 rows

615
Repeat = 16 stitches and 8 rows

See page 30 for notes on patterns 616-631

616

Repeat = 10 stitches and 36 rows

☐ · ▦ = ⬚ = knit

617

Repeat = 18 stitches and 36 rows

☐ · ▦ = ⬚ = knit

618

Repeat = 17 stitches and 60 rows

☐ · ▦ = ⬚ = knit

619

Repeat = 16 stitches and 32 rows

☐ · ▦ = ⬚ = knit

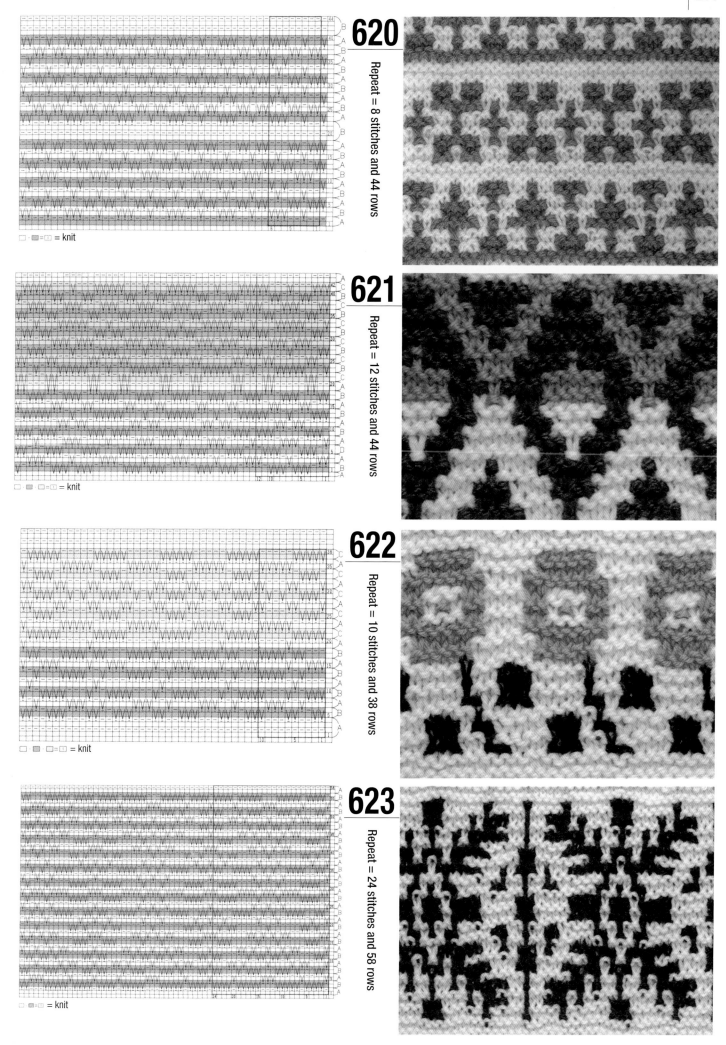

620

Repeat = 8 stitches and 44 rows

☐ · ▨ ·☐=☐ = knit

621

Repeat = 12 stitches and 44 rows

☐ · ▨ ·☐=☐ = knit

622

Repeat = 10 stitches and 38 rows

☐ · ▨ ·☐=☐ = knit

623

Repeat = 24 stitches and 58 rows

☐ · ▨ ·☐=☐ = knit

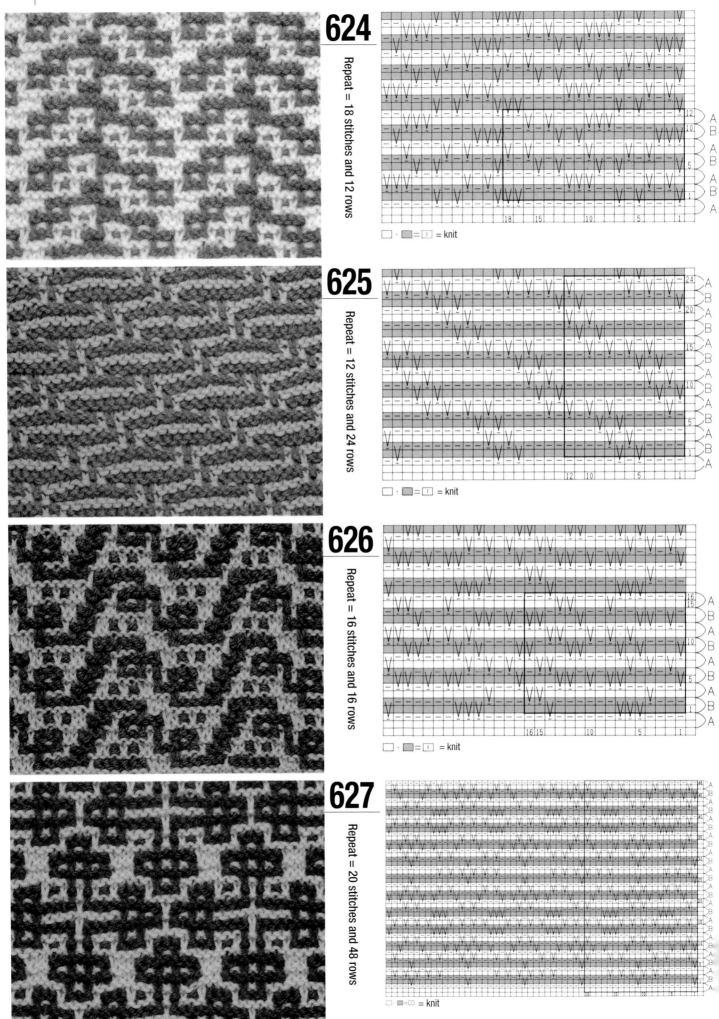

624

Repeat = 18 stitches and 12 rows

□ · ■ = □ = knit

625

Repeat = 12 stitches and 24 rows

□ · ■ = □ = knit

626

Repeat = 16 stitches and 16 rows

□ · ■ = □ = knit

627

Repeat = 20 stitches and 48 rows

□ · ■ = □ = knit

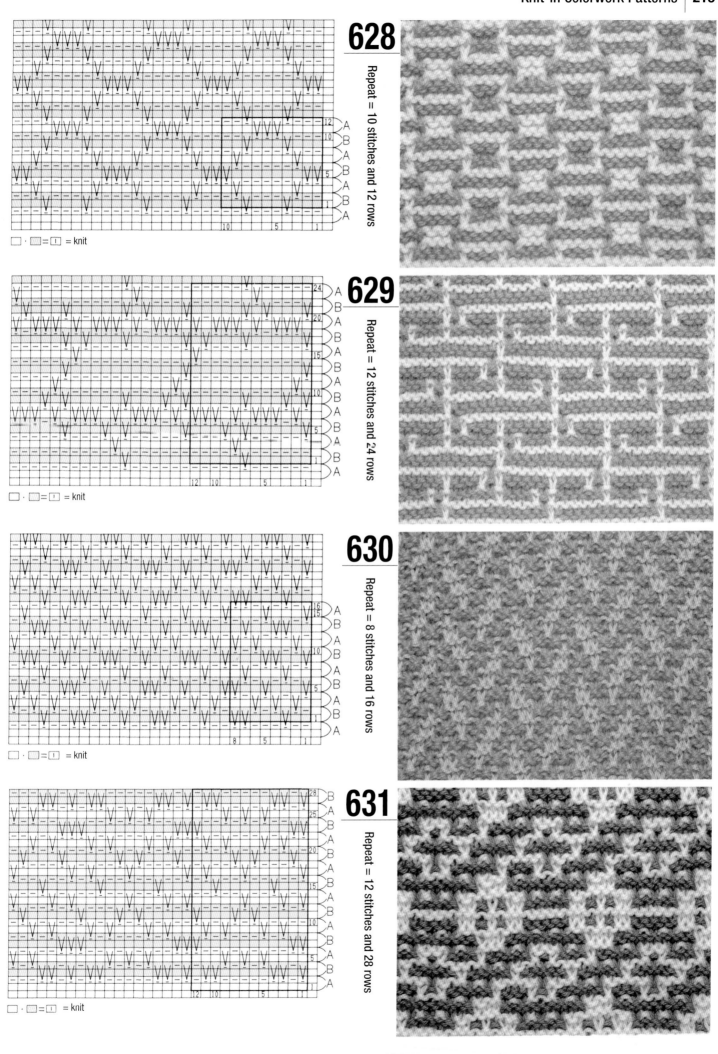

628

Repeat = 10 stitches and 12 rows

☐ · ☐ = ☐ = knit

629

Repeat = 12 stitches and 24 rows

☐ · ☐ = ☐ = knit

630

Repeat = 8 stitches and 16 rows

☐ · ☐ = ☐ = knit

631

Repeat = 12 stitches and 28 rows

☐ · ☐ = ☐ = knit

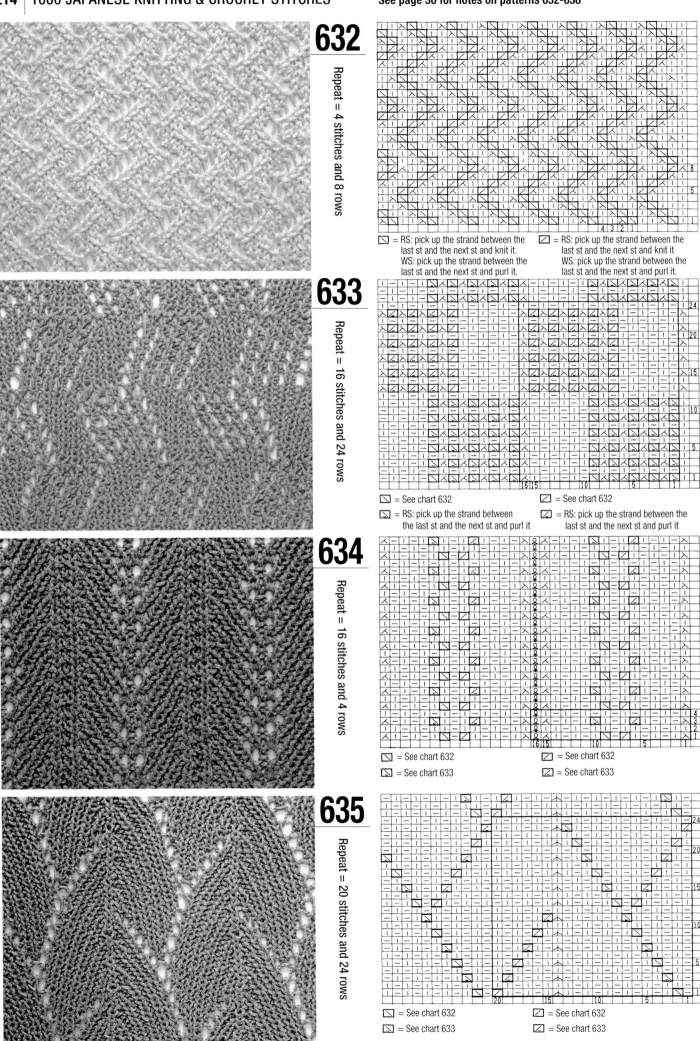

632

Repeat = 4 stitches and 8 rows

◨ = RS: pick up the strand between the last st and the next st and knit it. WS: pick up the strand between the last st and the next st and purl it.

◧ = RS: pick up the strand between the last st and the next st and knit it. WS: pick up the strand between the last st and the next st and purl it.

633

Repeat = 16 stitches and 24 rows

◨ = See chart 632

◧ = See chart 632

◨ = RS: pick up the strand between the last st and the next st and purl it

◧ = RS: pick up the strand between the last st and the next st and purl it

634

Repeat = 16 stitches and 4 rows

◨ = See chart 632

◧ = See chart 632

◨ = See chart 633

◧ = See chart 633

635

Repeat = 20 stitches and 24 rows

◨ = See chart 632

◧ = See chart 632

◨ = See chart 633

◧ = See chart 633

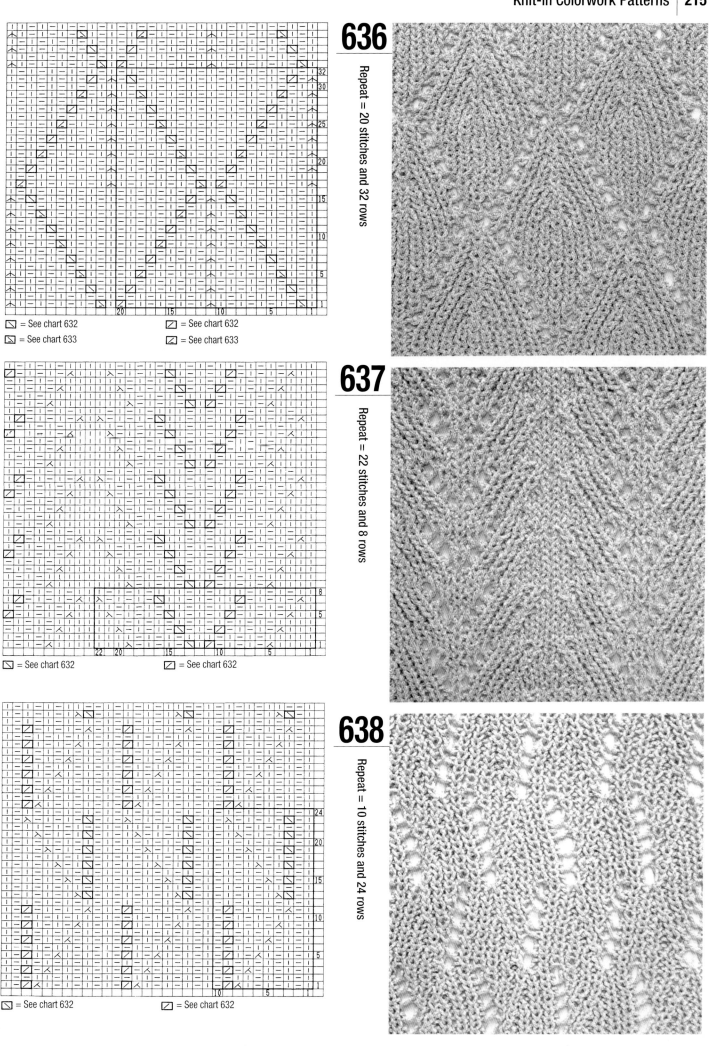

636

Repeat = 20 stitches and 32 rows

◲ = See chart 632 ◱ = See chart 632
◲ = See chart 633 ◱ = See chart 633

637

Repeat = 22 stitches and 8 rows

◲ = See chart 632 ◱ = See chart 632

638

Repeat = 10 stitches and 24 rows

◲ = See chart 632 ◱ = See chart 632

639

Repeat = 8 stitches and 20 rows

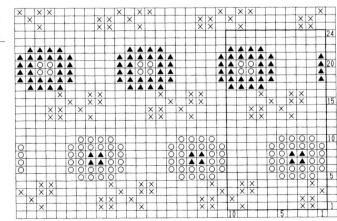

640

Repeat = 16 stitches and 24 rows

641

Repeat = 8 stitches and 12 rows

642

Repeat = 10 stitches and 24 rows

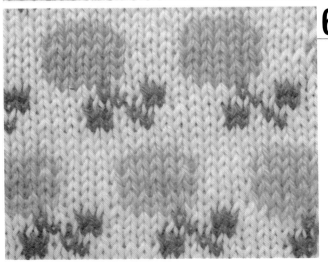

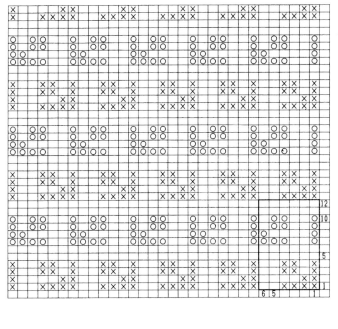

643

Repeat = 6 stitches and 12 rows

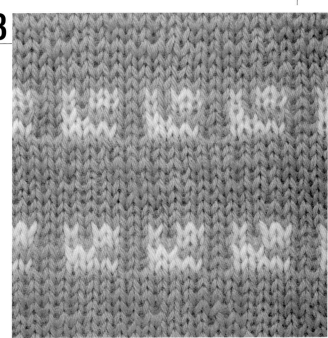

644

Repeat = 16 stitches and 18 rows

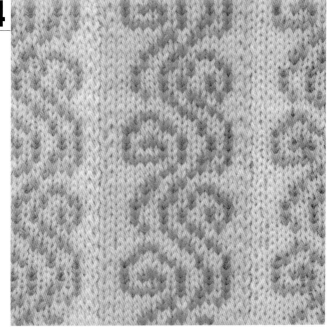

645

Repeat = 12 stitches and 28 rows

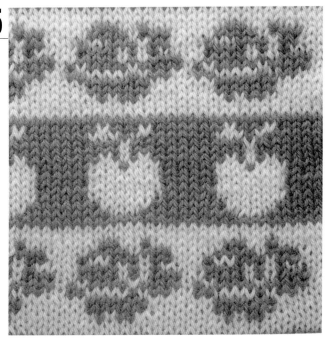

See pages 30-31 for notes on patterns 646-649

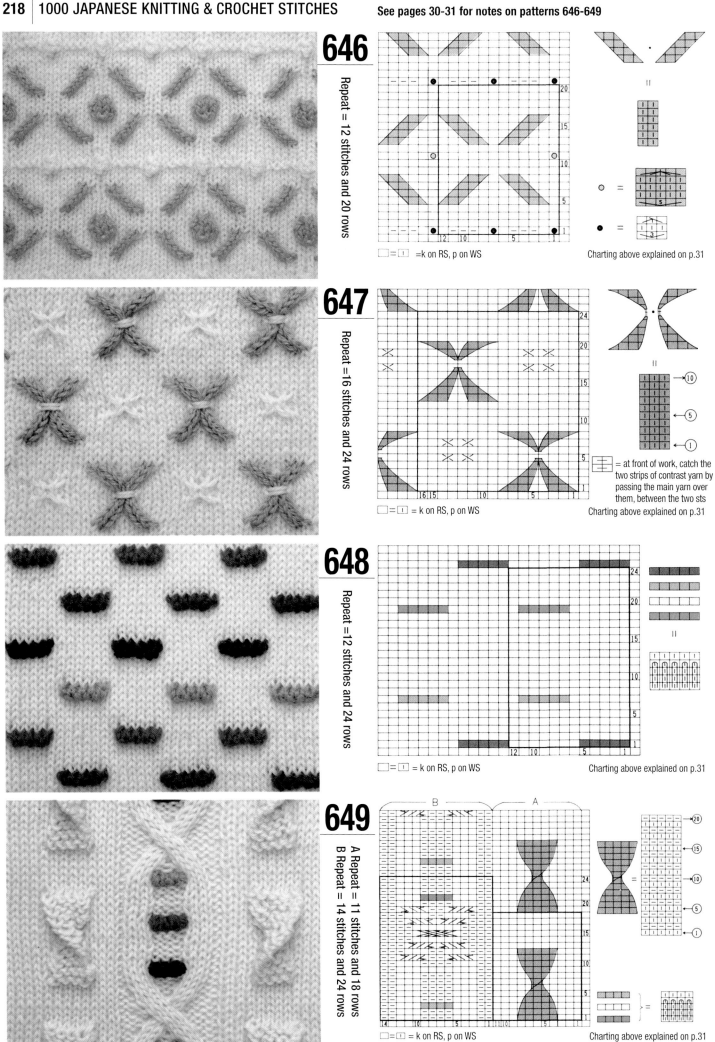

646

Repeat = 12 stitches and 20 rows

□ = [I] = k on RS, p on WS

Charting above explained on p.31

647

Repeat =16 stitches and 24 rows

□ = [I] = k on RS, p on WS

= at front of work, catch the two strips of contrast yarn by passing the main yarn over them, between the two sts

Charting above explained on p.31

648

Repeat =12 stitches and 24 rows

□ = [I] = k on RS, p on WS

Charting above explained on p.31

649

A Repeat = 11 stitches and 18 rows
B Repeat = 14 stitches and 24 rows

□ = [I] = k on RS, p on WS

Charting above explained on p.31

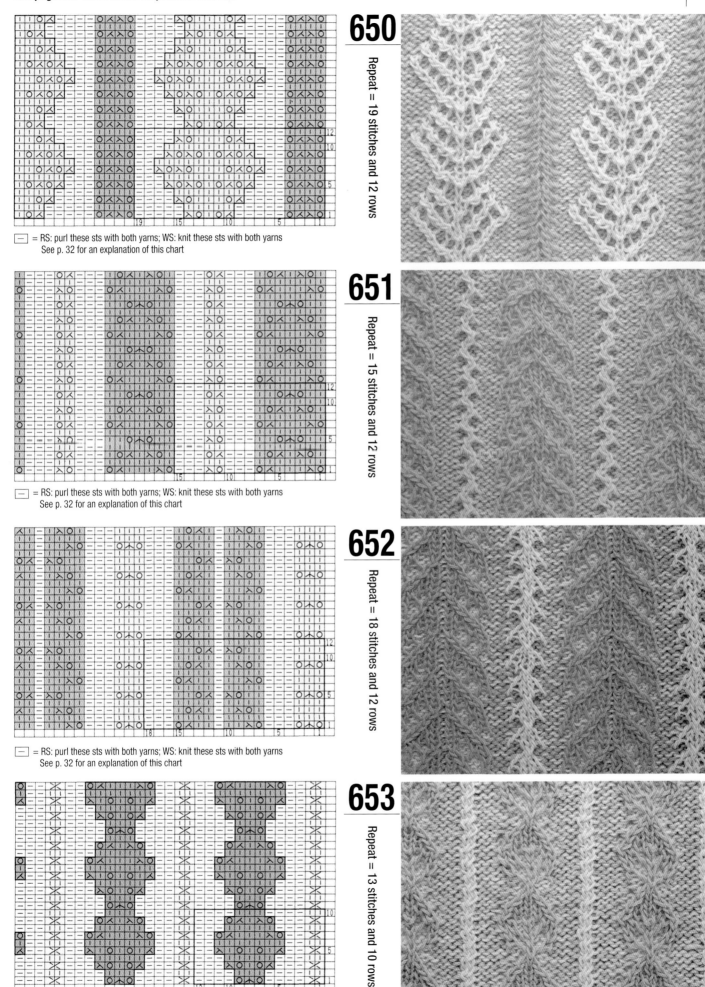

650
Repeat = 19 stitches and 12 rows

☐ = RS: purl these sts with both yarns; WS: knit these sts with both yarns
See p. 32 for an explanation of this chart

651
Repeat = 15 stitches and 12 rows

☐ = RS: purl these sts with both yarns; WS: knit these sts with both yarns
See p. 32 for an explanation of this chart

652
Repeat = 18 stitches and 12 rows

☐ = RS: purl these sts with both yarns; WS: knit these sts with both yarns
See p. 32 for an explanation of this chart

653
Repeat = 13 stitches and 10 rows

☐ = RS: purl these sts with both yarns; WS: knit these sts with both yarns
See p. 32 for an explanation of this chart

See page 32 for notes on patterns 654-661

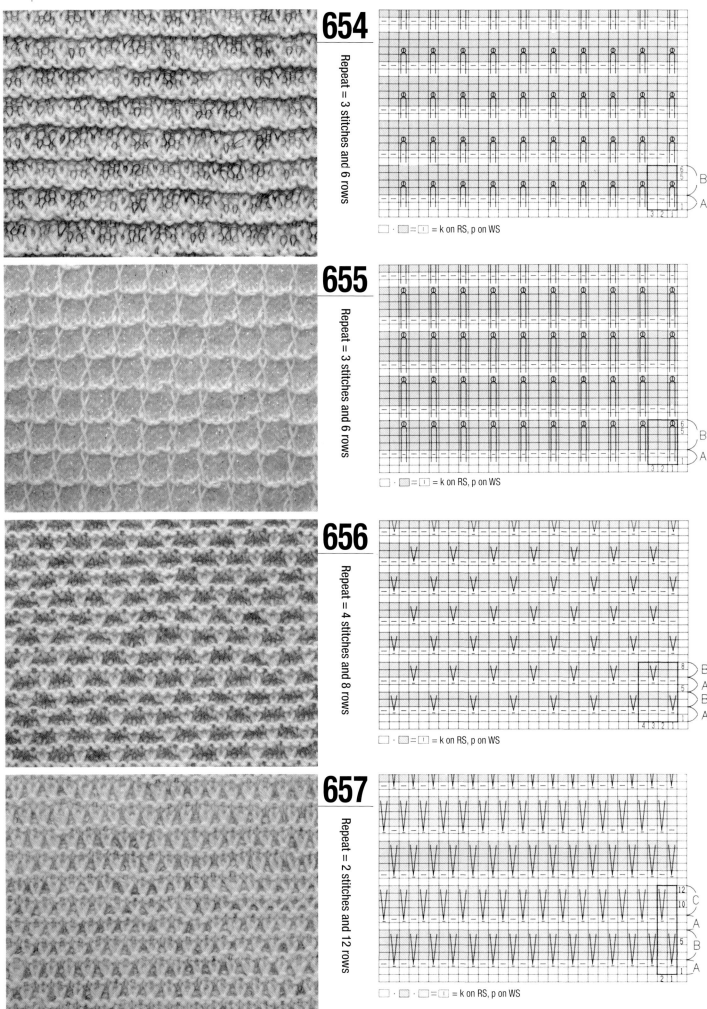

654

Repeat = 3 stitches and 6 rows

☐ · ▨ = ⊡ = k on RS, p on WS

655

Repeat = 3 stitches and 6 rows

☐ · ▨ = ⊡ = k on RS, p on WS

656

Repeat = 4 stitches and 8 rows

☐ · ▨ = ⊡ = k on RS, p on WS

657

Repeat = 2 stitches and 12 rows

☐ · ▨ · ☐ = ⊡ = k on RS, p on WS

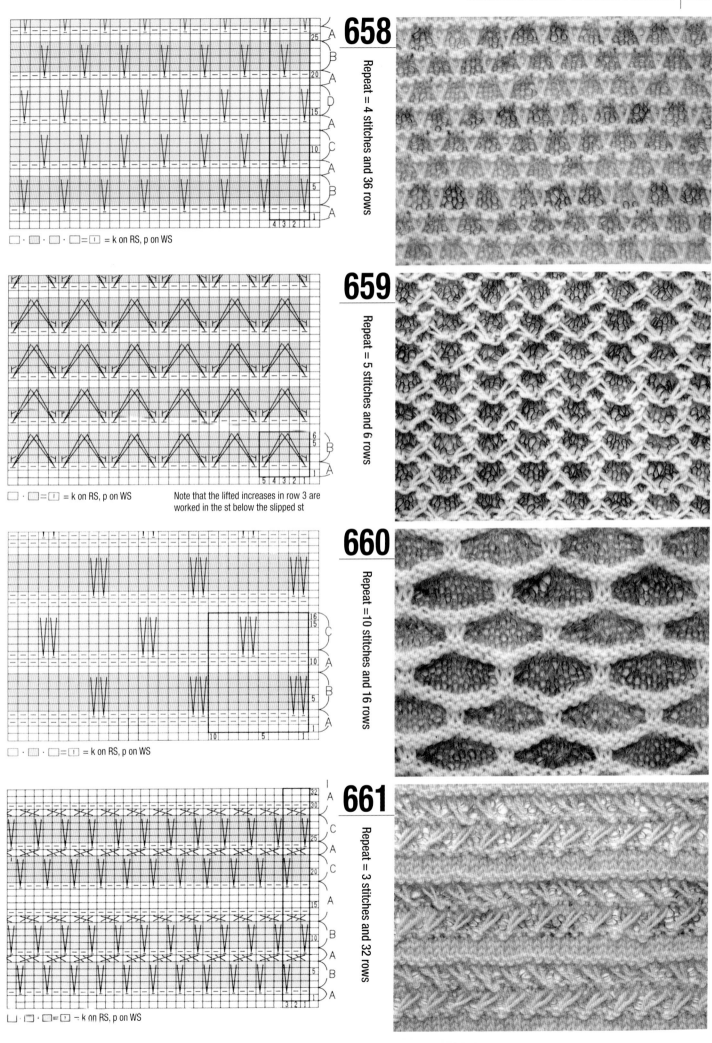

658

Repeat = 4 stitches and 36 rows

□ · □ · □ · □=□ = k on RS, p on WS

659

Repeat = 5 stitches and 6 rows

□ · □=□ = k on RS, p on WS   Note that the lifted increases in row 3 are
worked in the st below the slipped st

660

Repeat =10 stitches and 16 rows

□ · □ · □=□ = k on RS, p on WS

661

Repeat = 3 stitches and 32 rows

□ · □ · □=□ = k on RS, p on WS

See page 32 for notes on patterns 662-676

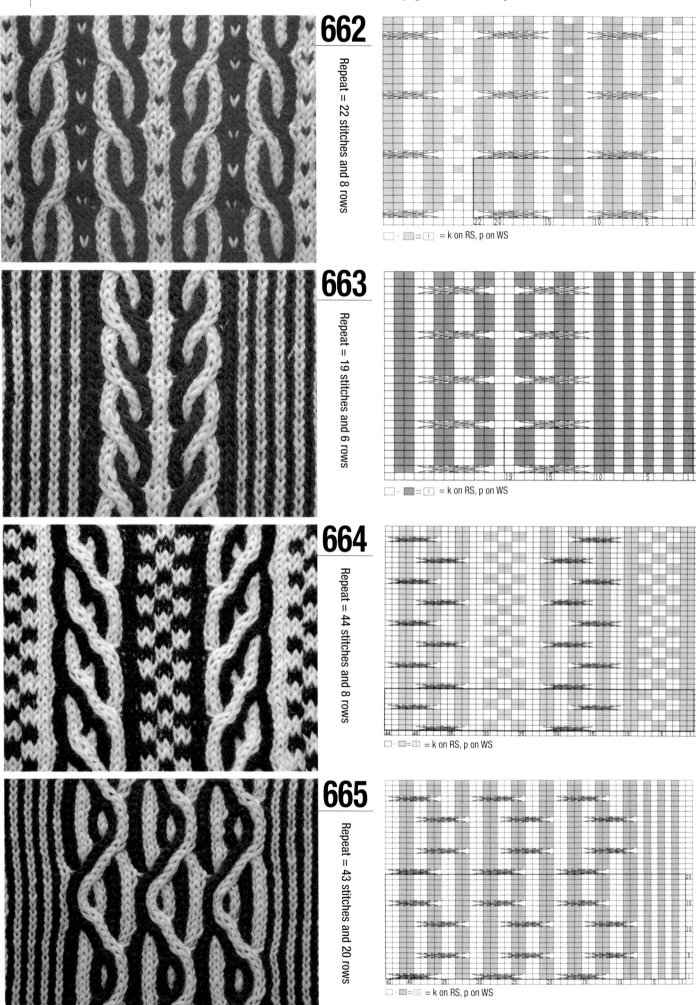

662

Repeat = 22 stitches and 8 rows

□ · ▨ = Ⅰ = k on RS, p on WS

663

Repeat = 19 stitches and 6 rows

□ · ▨ = Ⅰ = k on RS, p on WS

664

Repeat = 44 stitches and 8 rows

□ · ▨ = Ⅰ = k on RS, p on WS

665

Repeat = 43 stitches and 20 rows

□ · ▨ = Ⅰ = k on RS, p on WS

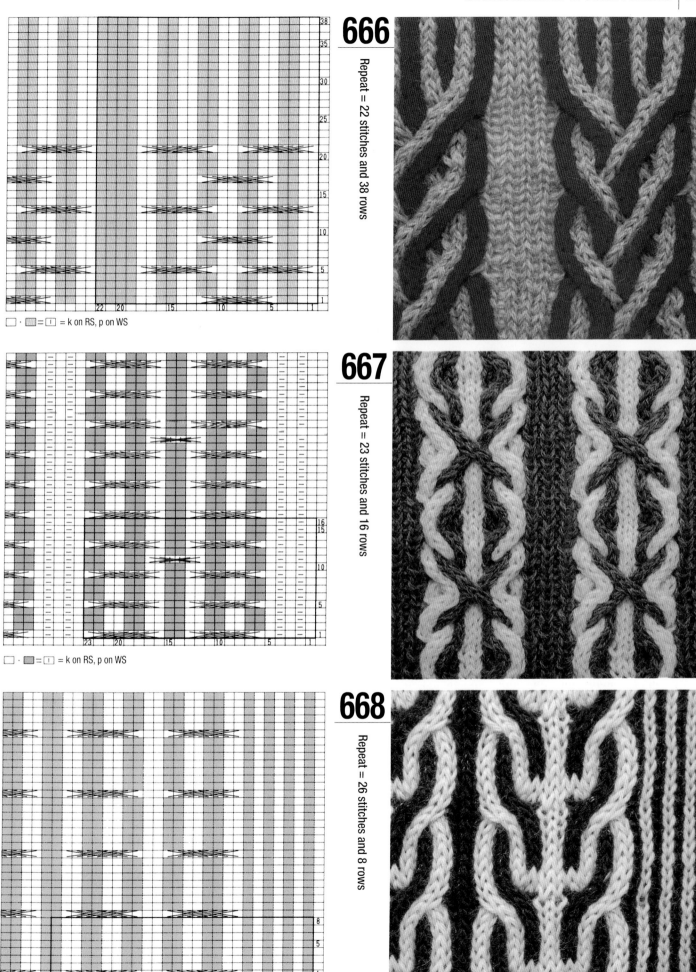

□ · □ = □ = k on RS, p on WS

666

Repeat = 22 stitches and 38 rows

□ · ■ = □ = k on RS, p on WS

667

Repeat = 23 stitches and 16 rows

□ · □ = □ = k on RS, p on WS

668

Repeat = 26 stitches and 8 rows

See page 32 for notes on patterns 662-676

669

Repeat = 32 stitches and 32 rows

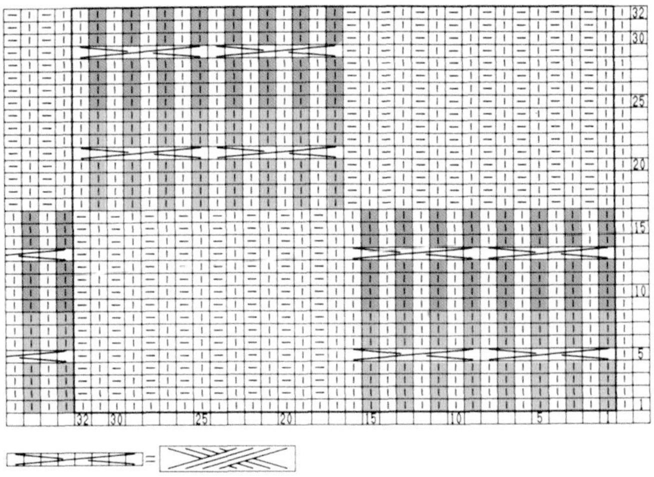

670

Repeat = 16 stitches and 8 rows

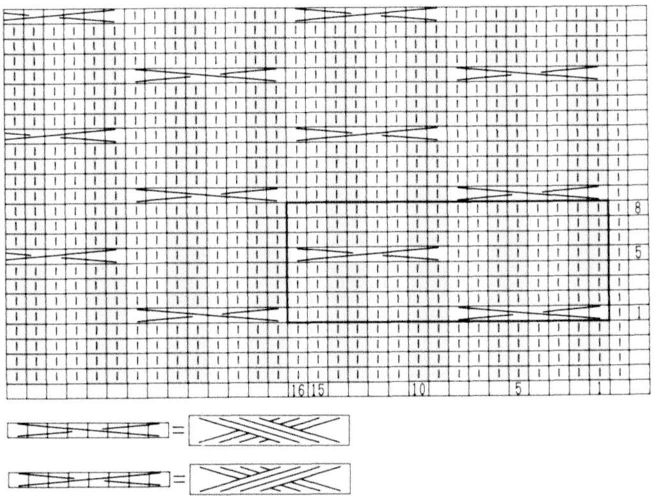

671

Repeat = 35 stitches and 12 rows

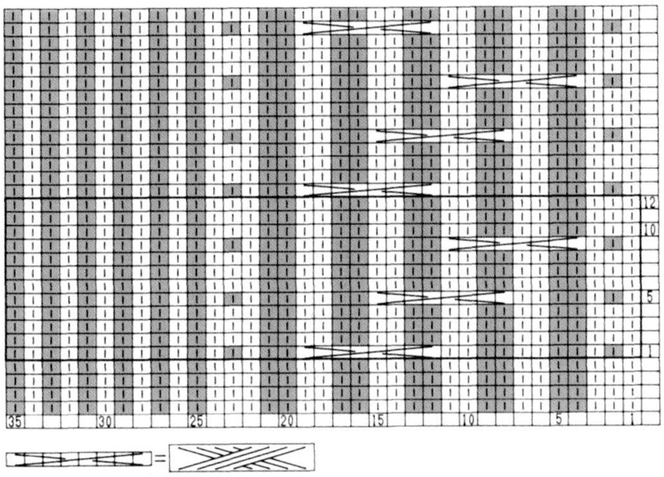

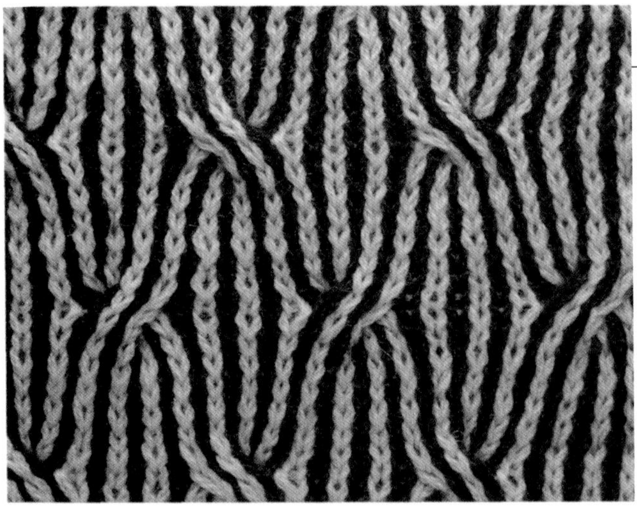

672

Repeat = 14 stitches and 16 rows

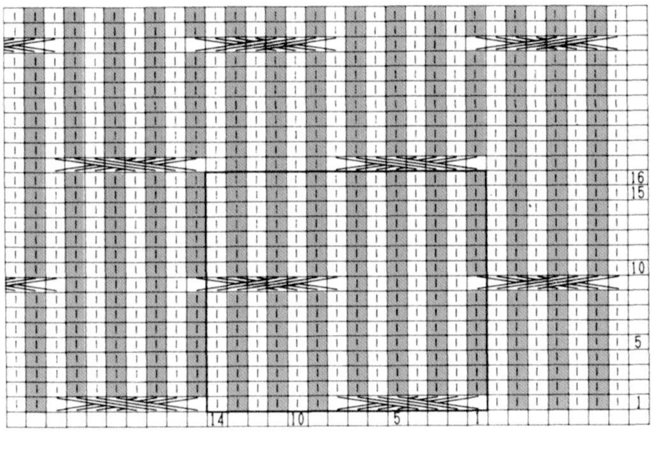

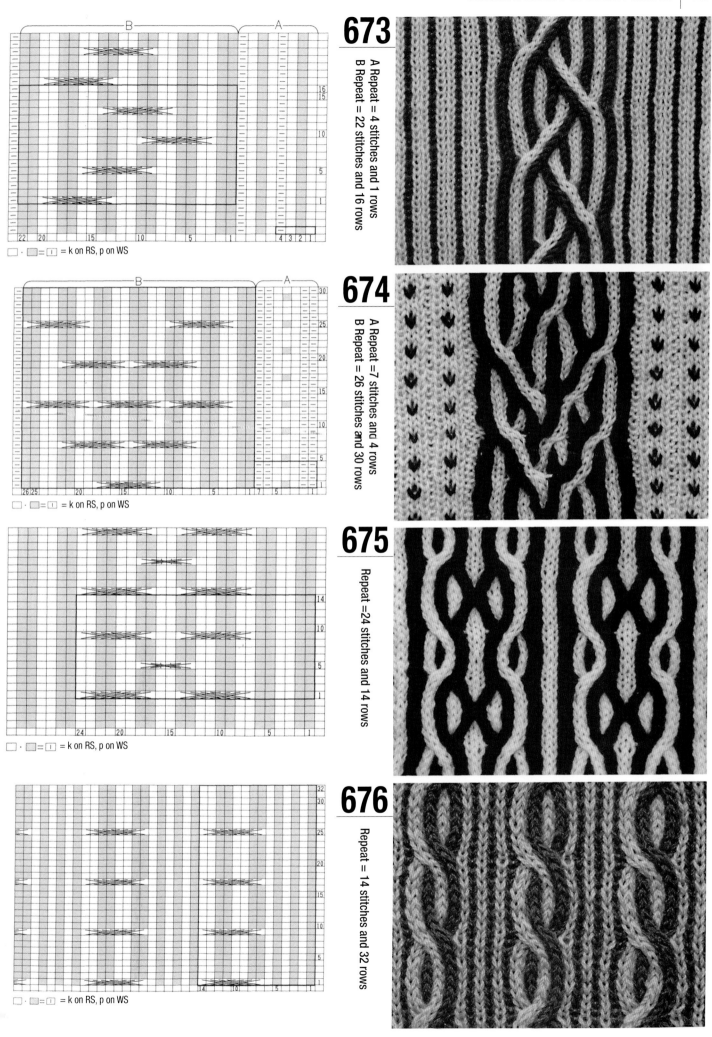

673

A Repeat = 4 stitches and 1 rows
B Repeat = 22 stitches and 16 rows

☐ · ▨ = ☐ = k on RS, p on WS

674

A Repeat = 7 stitches and 4 rows
B Repeat = 26 stitches and 30 rows

☐ · ▨ = ☐ = k on RS, p on WS

675

Repeat = 24 stitches and 14 rows

☐ · ▨ = ☐ = k on RS, p on WS

676

Repeat = 14 stitches and 32 rows

☐ · ▨ = ☐ = k on RS, p on WS

See page 32 for notes on patterns 677-684

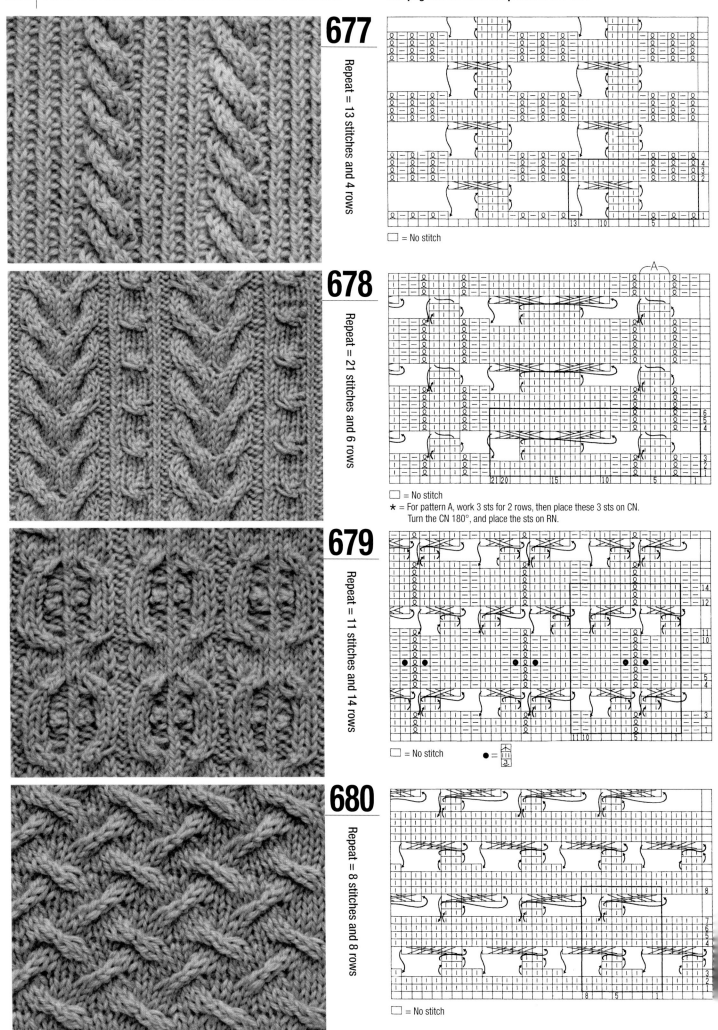

677

Repeat = 13 stitches and 4 rows

☐ = No stitch

678

Repeat = 21 stitches and 6 rows

☐ = No stitch

★ = For pattern A, work 3 sts for 2 rows, then place these 3 sts on CN.
Turn the CN 180°, and place the sts on RN.

679

Repeat = 11 stitches and 14 rows

☐ = No stitch   ● = ⬆/3

680

Repeat = 8 stitches and 8 rows

☐ = No stitch

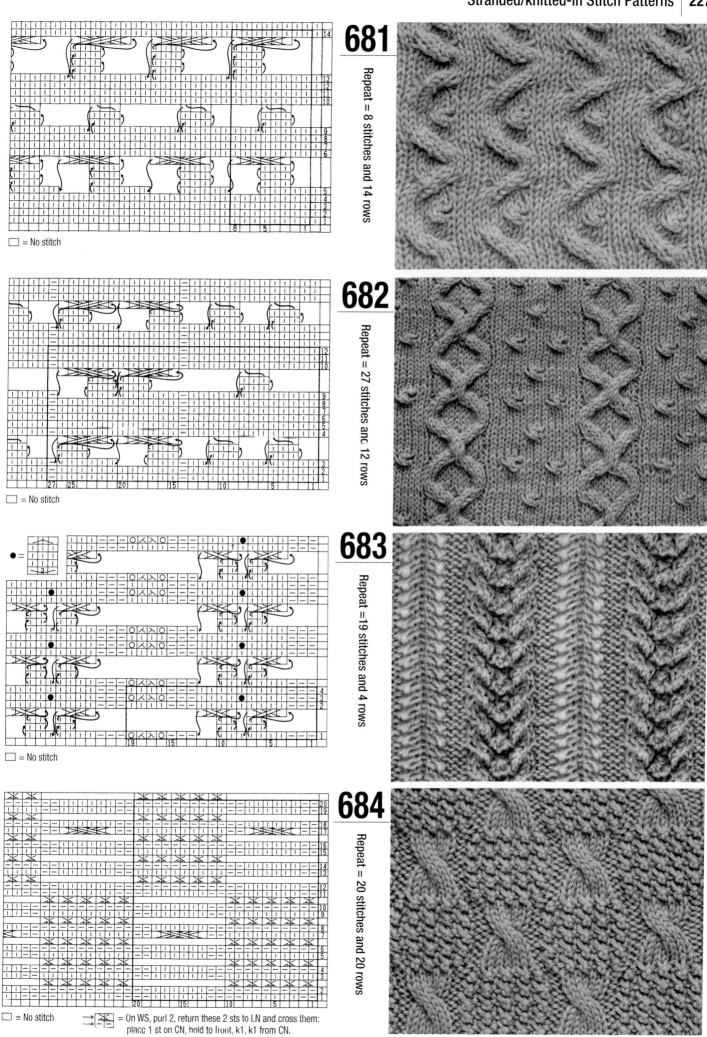

681

Repeat = 8 stitches and 14 rows

☐ = No stitch

682

Repeat = 27 stitches and 12 rows

☐ = No stitch

683

Repeat = 19 stitches and 4 rows

● =

☐ = No stitch

684

Repeat = 20 stitches and 20 rows

☐ = No stitch

→⚔ = On WS, purl 2, return these 2 sts to LN and cross them: place 1 st on CN, hold to front, k1, k1 from CN.

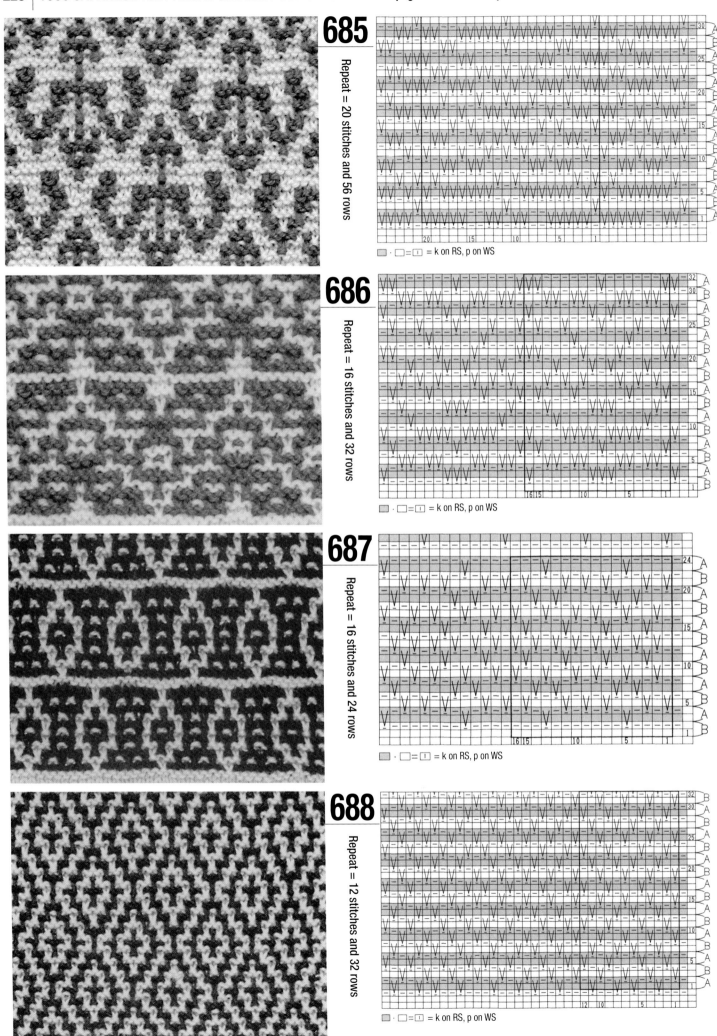

685

Repeat = 20 stitches and 56 rows

☐ · ☐ = ☐ = k on RS, p on WS

686

Repeat = 16 stitches and 32 rows

☐ · ☐ = ☐ = k on RS, p on WS

687

Repeat = 16 stitches and 24 rows

☐ · ☐ = ☐ = k on RS, p on WS

688

Repeat = 12 stitches and 32 rows

☐ · ☐ = ☐ = k on RS, p on WS

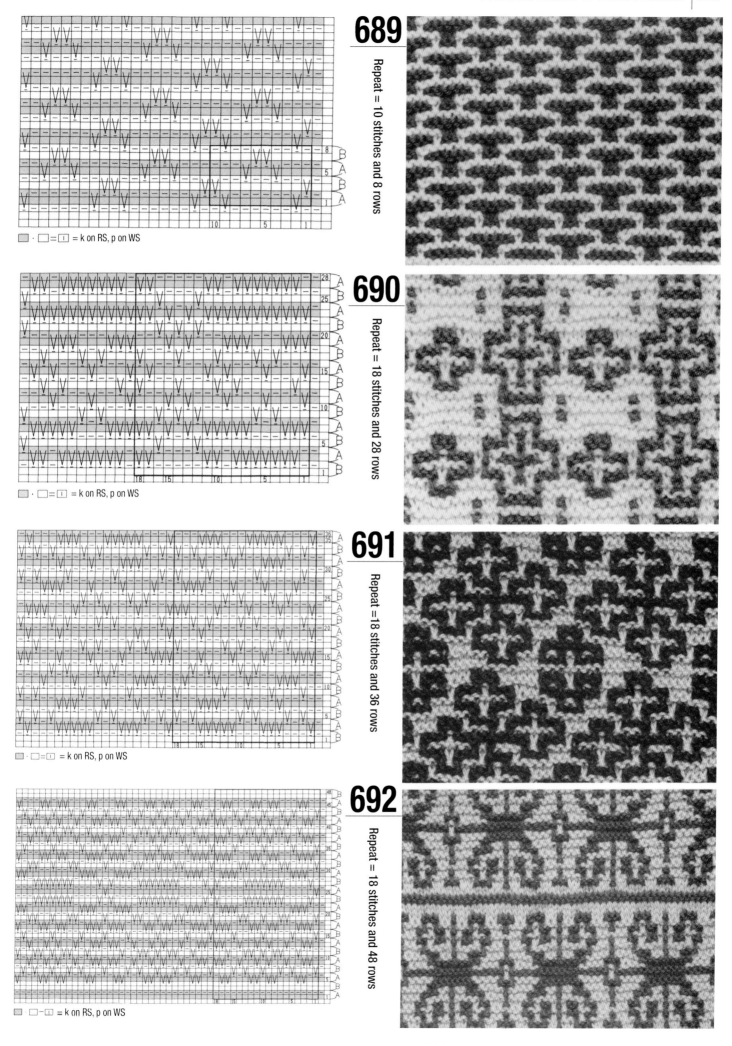

689

Repeat = 10 stitches and 8 rows

☐ · ☐ = ⊡ = k on RS, p on WS

690

Repeat = 18 stitches and 28 rows

☐ · ☐ = ⊡ = k on RS, p on WS

691

Repeat = 18 stitches and 36 rows

☐ · ☐ = ⊡ = k on RS, p on WS

692

Repeat = 18 stitches and 48 rows

☐ ☐ - ⊡ = k on RS, p on WS

693

Repeat = 12 stitches and 16 rows

▨ · ☐ = ☐ = k on RS, p on WS

694

Repeat = 8 stitches and 16 rows

▨ · ☐ = ☐ = k on RS, p on WS

695

Repeat = 8 stitches and 16 rows

▨ · ☐ = ☐ = k on RS, p on WS

696

Repeat = 12 stitches and 16 rows

▨ · ☐ = ☐ = k on RS, p on WS

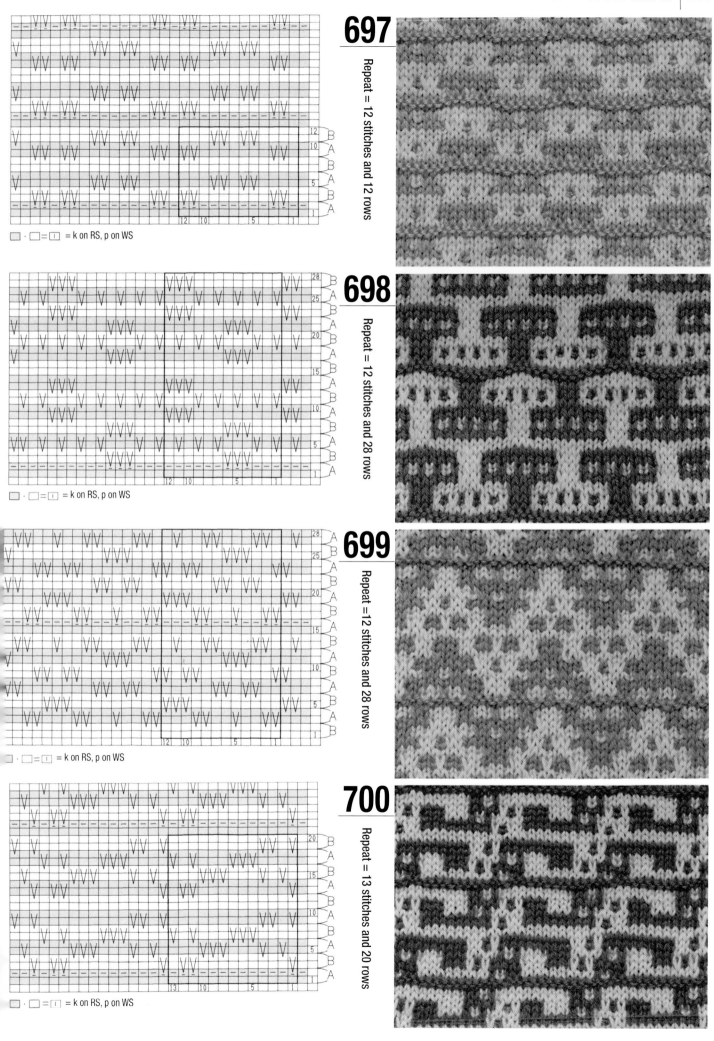

697

Repeat = 12 stitches and 12 rows

☐ · ☐ = ☐ = k on RS, p on WS

698

Repeat = 12 stitches and 28 rows

☐ · ☐ = ☐ = k on RS, p on WS

699

Repeat = 12 stitches and 28 rows

☐ · ☐ = ☐ = k on RS, p on WS

700

Repeat = 13 stitches and 20 rows

☐ · ☐ = ☐ = k on RS, p on WS

CROCHET SYMBOLS AND METHODS

Japanese crochet symbols have been standardized in the JIS (Japan Industrial Standards). The symbols in these charts are shown with the front of the work (as it will be worn or used) facing the crocheter. Except for certain stitches, no distinction is made between the right side and the wrong side of the work. When working rows back and forth, alternating right and wrong sides, the same stitch symbols are used. Thus, the front of the main pattern is normally the front side of the completed work.

Note these chart conventions:

The stitch repeat count, indicated by a bracket at the bottom, is based on the number of chains made to begin, not including the turning chain(s) for the first row or extra sts needed to balance the pattern at each side. Take this into account when working multiple repeats.

The direction in which the row is worked is indicated by an arrow.

Rows with numbers make up the row repeat. Keep in mind that there may be setup rows that aren't included in a repeat; setup rows aren't numbered.

Abbreviations used in this section (Note: American terms used throughout)

Ch	Chain	Sl	Slip stitch
Yo	Yarn over hook	Trc	Triple crochet
Sc	Single crochet	Dec	Decrease
Hdc	Half double crochet	Inc	Increase
Dc	Double crochet		

BASIC STITCHES

◯ CHAIN (CH)

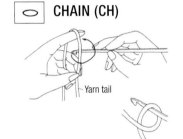

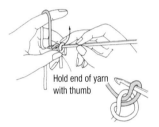

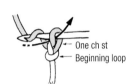

❶ Holding yarn in left hand, bring hook behind yarn, then up and around as shown, to make a loop on the hook.

❷ Bring hook behind working yarn and yarn over hook. Draw the yarn through the loop.

❸ Bring the hook behind the yarn again, in the direction of the arrow, so that yarn passes over hook from back to front.

❹ Draw yarn through the loop. One chain completed.

＋ ✕ SINGLE CROCHET (SC)

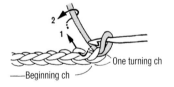

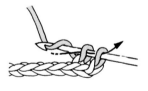

❶ Ch 1 for a turning chain. Insert hook into back of second ch from hook.

❷ Yarn over hook and draw up a loop.

❸ Yarn over hook again and draw through both loops on hook.

❹ One sc completed. Insert hook into back of next ch to continue.

⬭ SLIP STITCH (SL)

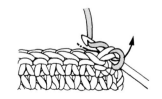

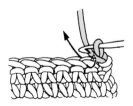

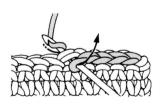

❶ Without making a turning ch, insert hook from front to back under both loops of the st in the row below.

❷ Yarn over hook and draw through all loops.

❸ Insert hook from front to back under both loops of the next st.

❹ Yarn over hook and draw through all loops. Continue.

DOUBLE CROCHET (DC)

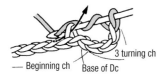   

❶ Make 3 turning ch, yarn over hook, and insert hook into back of 2nd base ch (not counting the 3 turning ch; 5th ch from hook). Draw up a loop.

❷ Yarn over hook and draw through 2 loops. At this point, the st is an incomplete dc.

❸ Yarn over hook and draw through 2 remaining loops.

❹ Yarn over hook, insert hook into back of next ch and continue.

HALF DOUBLE CROCHET (HDC)

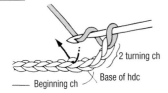   

❶ Make 2 turning ch, yarn over hook, and insert hook into back of 2nd base ch (not counting the 2 turning ch; 4th ch from hook). Draw up a loop.

❷ Yarn over hook and draw through all loops.

❸ One hdc complete. Yarn over hook, insert hook into back of next ch, and continue.

❹ The turning ch counts as stitch 1. Illustration shows 4 hdc completed.

TRIPLE CROCHET (TR)

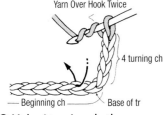   

❶ Make 4 turning ch, then yarn over hook twice. Insert hook into back of 2nd base ch (not counting the 4 turning ch, 6th ch from hook).

❷ Yarn over hook and draw up a loop, then yarn over hook and draw through 2 loops.

❸ Yarn over hook and draw through 2 loops again. At this point, the st is an incomplete tr.

❹ Yarn over hook and draw through last 2 loops.

Puff or Cluster Stitches

3-HDC PUFF

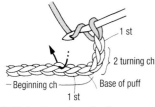  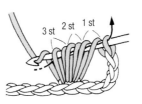 

❶ Make 2 turning ch plus one more ch (3 ch total). Yarn over hook. Insert hook into back of 3rd base ch (not counting 2 turning ch plus 1 ch, 6th ch from hook) and draw up a loop.

❷ In the same way, [yarn over hook, draw up a loop] twice more: total of three incomplete hdcs.

❸ Yarn over hook, draw through all loops.

❹ One 3-hdc puff completed. Continue in pattern.

3-DC PUFF

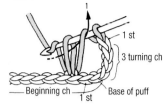

❶ Make 3 turning ch plus one more ch (4 ch total), yarn over hook. Insert hook into back of 3rd base ch (not counting 3 turning ch plus 1 ch; 7th ch from hook). Draw up a loop. Yarn over hook and draw through 2 loops.

❷ IIn the same way, [yarn over hook, draw up a loop, yarn over hook and draw through 2 loops] twice more: total of three incomplete dc..

❸ Yarn over hook, draw through all loops.

❹ One 3-hc puff completed. Continue in pattern.

3-TR PUFF

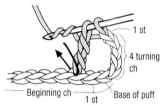

❶ Make 4 turning ch plus 1 more ch (5 ch total), yarn over hook twice. Insert hook into back of 2nd base ch (not counting 4 turning ch plus 1 ch, 8th ch from hook). Yarn over hook and draw up a loop, then [yarn over hook and draw through 2 loops] twice.

❷ In the same way, [yarn over hook, draw up a loop, yarn over hook and draw through 2 loops, yarn over hook and draw through 2 loops] twice more: total of three incomplete tr.

❸ Yarn over hook and draw through all loops. Continue in pattern.

VARIATION ON 3-HDC PUFF

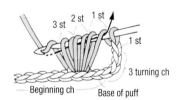

❶ Work 3 incomplete hdcs as described above. Yarn over hook, draw through 6 loops – all but the last loop, leaving 2 loops on hook.

❷ Yarn over hook, draw through last 2 loops.

❸ Two 3-hdc variations complete. This variation tightens the top of the stitch.

3-HDC PUFF WITHOUT TURNING CHAINS

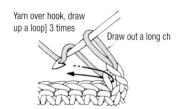

❶ From the base ch, draw up a long loop about 2 chains tall. Work 3 incomplete hdc into the same st.

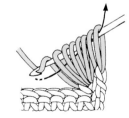

❷ Yarn over hook, draw through all 7 loops.

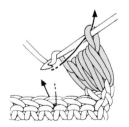

❸ Yarn over hook, draw through last loop. Work one sc into previous row to complete.

❹ Repeat steps 1 – 3.

THE DIFFERENCE BETWEEN • AND

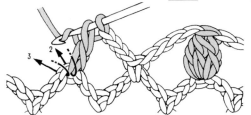

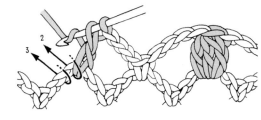

When symbols are connected at the bottom:

Work all the sts into a single st in the row below. If that st is a ch, work all sts into two of the three loops of the ch.

When symbols are separated at the bottom:

Work the sts over the entire ch, not through a single st.

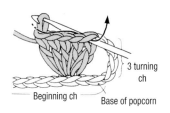 5-DC POPCORN ST

❶ Work 5 dc into one stitch, completing each one. Remove hook and insert it into the top of the first dc, then the remaining loop. Yarn over hook and draw through all loops.

❷ Chain 1 to close. 5-dc popcorn complete.

❸ Two repeats of 5-dc popcorn.

Crossed Stitches

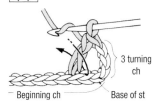 CROSSED DC

❶ Work 1 dc. Yarn over hook and insert hook, from the front, one st to the right of the just-completed st.

❷ Work the next dc around the first: draw up a loop, yarn over hook and draw through 2 loops.

❸ Yarn over hook and draw through 2 remaining loops.

❹ Completed crossed st.

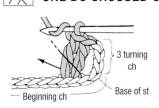 ONE DC CROSSED OVER TWO

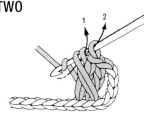

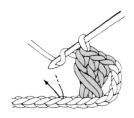

❶ Work 2 dc into the next 2 sts, then yarn over hook and insert hook, from the front, one st to the right of the just-completed sts.

❷ Work a dc around the first two: draw up a loop, [yarn over hook and draw through 2 loops] twice.

❸ Completed crossed dc, with 2 sts wrapped by the third.

TWO DC CROSSED OVER ONE

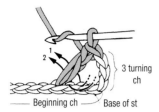

❶ Work 1 dc in the third base ch. Then yarn over hook, insert hook into the first base ch, work a dc around the first.

❷ Work a second dc around the first, completing it by drawing the yarn through as shown.

❸ Completed crossed dc, with 1 st wrapped by the second and third.

VARIATION ON CROSSED DC (CROSSING TO RIGHT)

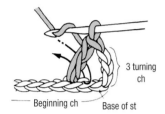

❶ Work 1 dc. Yarn over hook and insert hook, passing behind the completed st, one st to the right of the just-completed st.

❷ Working behind the completed dc, draw up a loop, yarn over hook and draw through 2 loops.

VARIATION ON CROSSED DC (CROSSING TO LEFT)

❶ Work 1 dc. Yarn over hook and insert hook, passing in front of the completed st, one st to the right of the just-completed st.

❷ Working in front of the completed st, draw up a loop, yarn over hook and draw through 2 loops.

VARIATION ON 1 DC CROSSED OVER 3 (CROSSING TO RIGHT)

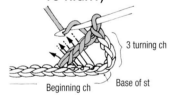

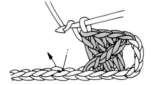

❶ Work 1 dc in the fourth base ch. Then yarn over hook and insert hook, passing behind the completed st, into the first base ch, work a dc behind the first. Repeat twice more.

❷ Completed 1 dc crossed over 3 right. Yarn over hook and insert hook into 2nd ch from completed st.

VARIATION ON 1 DC CROSSED OVER 3 (CROSSING TO LEFT)

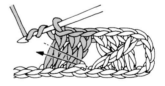

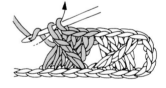

❸ Work 3 dc into the next 3 base ch. Yarn over hook and insert hook, passing in front of the completed sts, one st to the right of the just-completed sts.

❹ Working in front of the completed st, draw up a loop, yarn over hook and draw through 2 loops. Completed 1 dc crossed over 3 left.

"X" STITCH

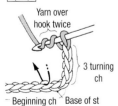

❶ Make 3 standing ch, then yarn over hook twice. Insert hook into back of 3rd base ch (not counting the 3 standing ch, 6th ch from hook), and draw up a loop.

❷ Yarn over hook and draw through 2 loops. Leave 3 loops on hook.

❸ Skip 2 ch, yarn over hook, insert hook and draw up a loop.

❹ [Yarn over hook and draw through 2 loops] 3 times = joined dc.

❺ Ch 2, yarn over hook and insert hook into top of joined dc and draw up a loop.

❻ [Yarn over hook and draw through 2 loops] twice.

"Y" STITCH

❶ Make 4 turning ch, then yarn over hook twice. Insert hook into back of 3rd base ch (not counting the 4 turning ch, 7th ch from hook), draw up a loop and work one tr.

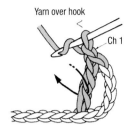

❷ Yarn over hook and ch 1, then yarn over and insert hook into 2 strands of the lower diagonal bar of tr, draw up a loop.

❸ [Yarn over and draw through 2 loops] twice.

❹ Completed Y stitch. Skip 2 ch and continue.

Decreases

SC DECREASE (SC2TOG)

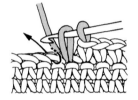

❶ Insert hook in next st and draw up a loop.

❷ Insert hook in following st and draw up a loop. Yarn over and draw through all 3 loops.

❸ Completed sc2tog.

SC DOUBLE DECREASE (SC3TOG)

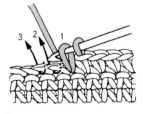

❶ [Insert hook in next st and draw up a loop] three times.

❷ Yarn over hook and draw through all 4 loops.

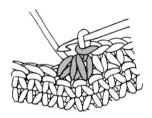

❸ Completed sc3tog.

HDC DECREASE (HDC2TOG)

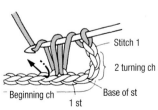

❶ [Yarn over, insert hook in next st and draw up a loop] twice.

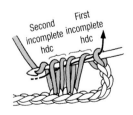

❷ Yarn over and draw through all 5 loops.

❸ One hdc2tog completed.

HDC DOUBLE DECREASE (HDC3TOG)

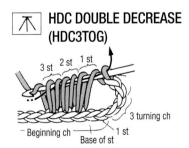

❶ Work as hdctog but draw up loops from 3 sts.

⚛ DC DECREASE (DC2TOG)

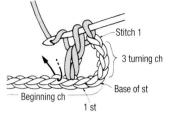  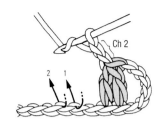

❶ Yarn over, insert hook in next st and draw up a loop, yarn over and draw through 2 loops (incomplete dc).

❷ Work another incomplete dc in the next st. Yarn over and draw through all 3 loops on hook.

❸ Completed dc2tog. Ch 2 and continue.

⚛ DC DOUBLE DECREASE (DC3TOG)

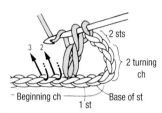 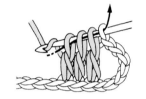 

❶ Yarn over, then work 3 incomplete dcs into the next 3 sts.

❷ Yarn over and draw through all 4 loops on hook.

❸ Completed dc3tog. Ch 3 and continue.

Increases

𝕍 HDC INCREASE (HDC INC)

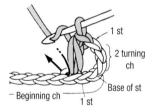 

❶ Yarn over, insert hook in st 1 and draw up a loop, yarn over and draw through all 3 loops on hook. Yarn over, insert hook in the same st and draw up a loop.

❷ Yarn over hook and draw through all 3 loops on hook.

𝕍 HDC DOUBLE INCREASE (HDC INC 2)

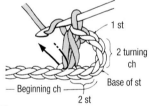 

❶ Work one hdc, then two more into the same st.

❷ Yarn over and draw through last 3 loops on hook.

𝕍 DC INCREASE (DC INC)

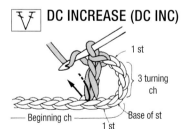 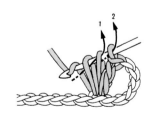 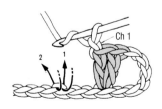

❶ Yarn over, insert hook in st and draw up a loop, [yarn over and draw through 2 loops] twice.

❷ Yarn over, insert hook in same st and work another dc.

❸ [Yarn over and draw through 2 loops] twice. Completed dc inc .

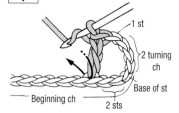 DC DOUBLE INCREASE (DC INC 2)

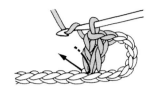 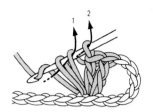

① Yarn over, insert hook in st and draw up a loop, [yarn over and draw through 2 loops] twice. Work a second dc in same st.

② Yarn over, insert hook in same st and draw up a loop.

③ [Yarn over and draw through 2 loops] twice. Completed dc inc 2.

5 DC IN SAME ST

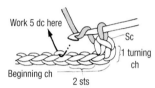  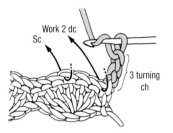 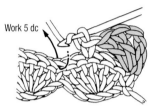

① Work sc in the first ch. Skip 2 ch or st, then work 5 dc in next ch.

② Skip 2 ch or st, then sc in next ch or st. Repeat.

③ On 2nd row, make 3 turning ch, then work 2dc in sc of previous row. Skip 2 ch or st and sc into the center dc of previous row.

④ After the sc, work 5 dc into the sc of previous row.

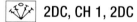 2DC, CH 1, 2DC

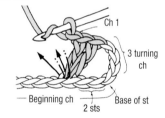  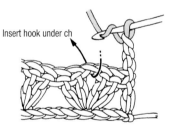 

① As illustrated, work 2 dc into the first st, ch 1, work 2 dc into the same st.

② Completed st. Yarn over, skip 4 ch and insert hook to continue.

③ On 2nd row, make 3 turning ch, yarn over and insert hook under ch of previous row. Work 2dc, ch 1, 2dc here.

④ First repeat of 2nd row complete. Continue as established.

Post Stitches

 FRONT POST SINGLE CROCHET (FPSC)

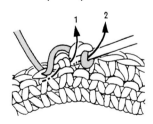 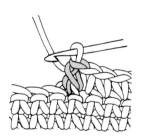

① Insert hook from front to back to front, around leg (post) of st indicated.

② Yarn over and draw up a loop, yarn over and draw through both loops.

③ Completed FPsc. Top of st in previous row shows on back of work.

た BACK POST SINGLE CROCHET (BPSC)

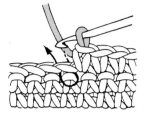 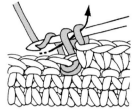 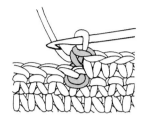

❶ Insert hook from back to front to back around leg (post) of st indicated.

❷ Yarn over and draw up a loop. Yarn over and draw through both loops.

❸ Completed BPsc. Top of st in previous row shows on front.

ぢ FRONT POST HALF DOUBLE CROCHET (FPHDC)

 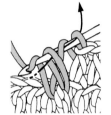 

❶ Yarn over, insert hook from front to back to front around leg (post) of st indicated; draw up a loop.

❷ Yarn over and draw through all 3 loops on hook.

❸ Completed FPhdc.

ち BACK POST HALF DOUBLE CROCHET (BPHDC)

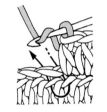  

❶ Yarn over, insert hook from back to front to back around leg (post) of st indicated.

❷ Yarn over and draw through all 3 loops on hook.

❸ Completed BPhdc.

づ FRONT POST DOUBLE CROCHET (FPDC)

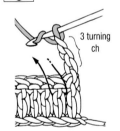  

❶ Ch 3 to begin. Yarn over, insert hook from front to back to front around leg (post) of st indicated; draw up a loop.

❷ [Yarn over and draw through 2 loops] twice.

❸ Completed FPdc.

つ BACK POST DOUBLE CROCHET

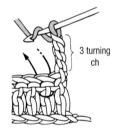  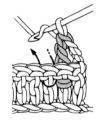

❶ Ch 3 to begin. Yarn over, insert hook from back to front to back around leg (post) of st indicated.

❷ [Yarn over and draw through 2 loops] twice.

❸ Completed BPdc.

て FRONT POST TRIPLE CROCHET PUFF

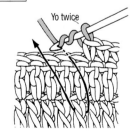 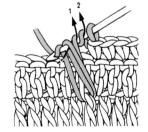 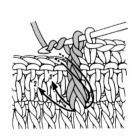 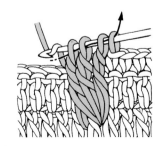

❶ Yarn over twice, insert hook from front to back to front around leg (post) of st indicated; draw up a loop.

❷ [Yarn over and draw through 2 loops] twice, leaving 2 loops on hook.

❸ Repeat steps 1 and 2 twice more in the same st: 4 loops on hook.

❹ Yarn over and draw through all 4 loops.

FRONT POST TRIPLE CROCHET CROSSED OVER 2DC

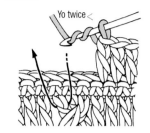

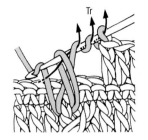

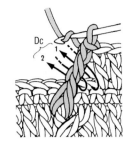

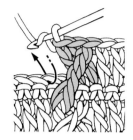

❶ Yarn over twice, insert hook from front to back to front around leg (post) of st indicated (3 st from hook); draw up a loop.

❷ [Yarn over and draw through 2 loops] three times.

❸ Yarn over and insert hook into first st from hook as shown by the arrow (behind the post st), and work a dc. Work another dc into the next st.

❹ Completed st. Skip 1 st and continue.

Picots

 OPEN 3-ST PICOT

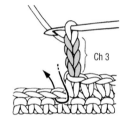

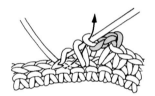

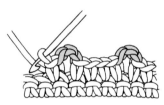

❶ Ch 3, then insert hook into next st.

❷ Yarn over, draw up a loop, then yarn over and draw through both loops.

❸ Completed picot.

❹ Place picots as shown in chart, or wherever you want them.

CH 3 PICOT WITH SL

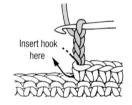

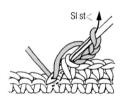

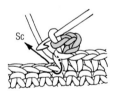

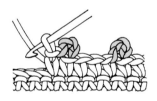

❶ Ch 3, then insert hook in front loop of base st and left strand of same st.

❷ Yarn over and draw through all 3 loops (sl st).

❸ Completed picot. Work sc into next st.

❹ Work picots in the same way at indicated intervals.

Variety stitches

 SOLOMON'S KNOT STITCH

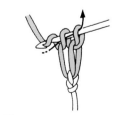

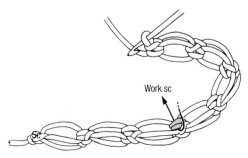

❶ Ch 2, then pull to lengthen the last ch to the length desired (about 2 or 3 ch length); yarn over and draw through loop.

❷ Insert hook under the strand leading to the new loop (not the long ch); yarn over and draw up a loop.

❸ Yarn over again and draw through both loops. One st completed.

❹ To work next row, work sc into sc of 4th loop from hook.

WRAPPING WITH CARRIED YARN (CHARTED IN CONTRAST COLOR)

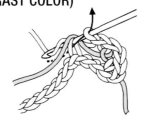
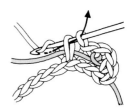

❶ Ch 1, then place carried yarn on top of hook, front to back. Ch 1 with main yarn, catching carried yarn.

❷ Ch 1 with main yarn.

❸ Insert hook into 3rd st, lay carried yarn over hook back to front, yarn over with main yarn, and draw up a loop, catching carried yarn.

❹ Yarn over and draw through 2 loops of main yarn.

PUFF WITH CARRIED YARN

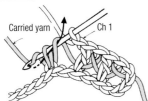
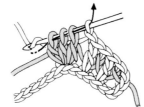
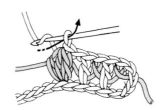
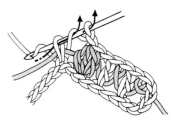

❶ Ch 1 with main yarn, skip 1 st and insert hook into 2nd st and work incomplete dc with carried yarn.

❷ Work 2 more incomplete dc with carried yarn into the same st. Yarn over with main yarn, draw through all 4 loops on hook.

❸ Ch 1 with main yarn.

❹ Lay carried yarn over hook, then work dc with main yarn.

 CROSSED LOOPS

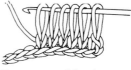

❶ Ch 1, then work sc into next st, drawing up the loop longer than usual to elongate it.

❷ Insert hook into next st and draw up a loop, ch 1 and elongate the loop as in step 1.

❸ Repeat step 2 for the number of sts needed.

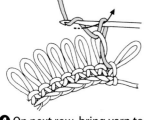
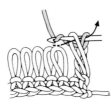
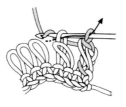
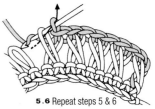

5.6 Repeat steps 5 & 6

❹ On next row, bring yarn to front, remove first loop from hook, draw up a loop from second loop and ch 1.

❺ Insert hook into first st from the front (crossing over st 2) and sl st through both loops on hook.

❻ Remove hook from 3rd loop, insert hook into 4th loop and sl st through both loops on hook. Insert hook into 3rd loop.

❼ Repeat steps 5 and 6, crossing right-hand loop over left-hand loop and sl st to join.

 **JOINED LOOPS**

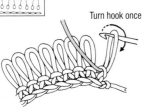
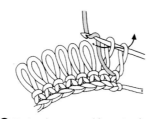
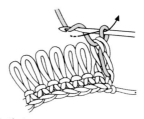
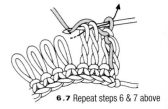

Turn hook once

6.7 Repeat steps 6 & 7 above

❶ Work steps 1 to 3 of the crossed loops, above, for the number of sts needed. Step 4: insert hook into loop from behind, then swivel hook 180 degrees in the direction of the arrow to twist the loop.

❷ Twist the second loop in the same way, bring yarn to front and sl st the two loops together.

❸ Ch 1.

❹ Continue in the same way, twisting each loop, then joining two loops with sl st.

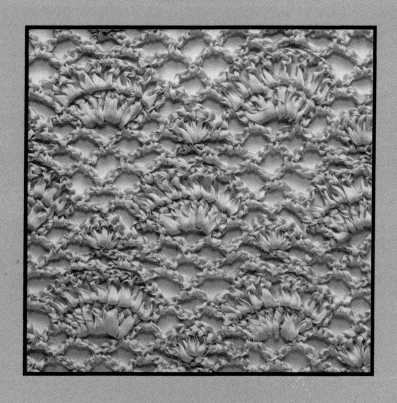

GRID, PINEAPPLE AND FAN PATTERNS

This group of stitches is based on double crochet. The stitches form grids,
or curved lines that look like pine tree branches or fans.
The variations of these basic stitches are interesting to work.

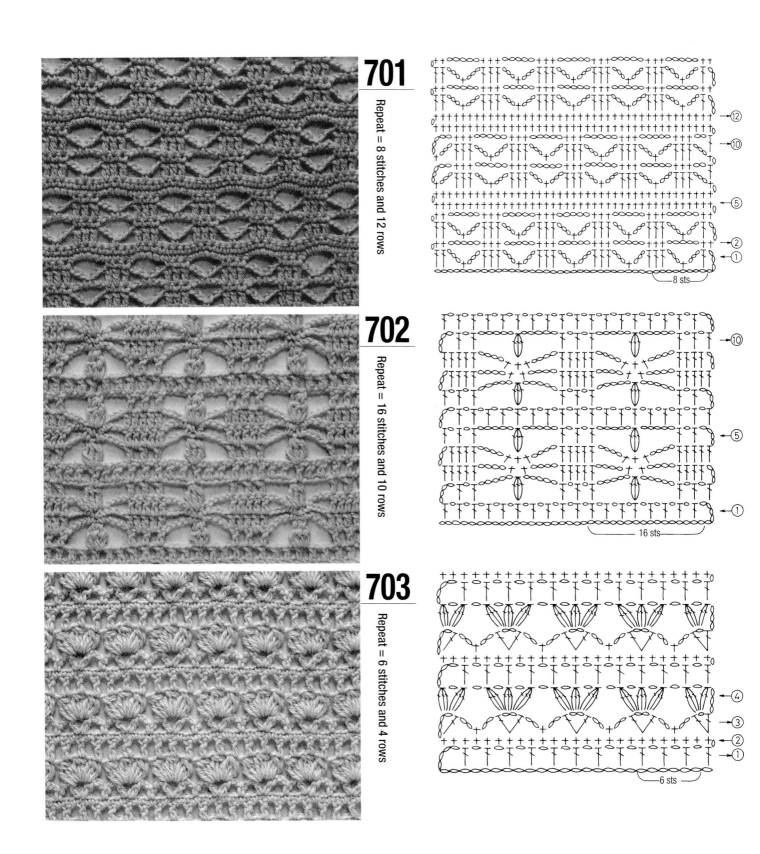

701 Repeat = 8 stitches and 12 rows

702 Repeat = 16 stitches and 10 rows

703 Repeat = 6 stitches and 4 rows

704

Repeat = 12 stitches and 10 rows

705

Repeat = 24 stitches and 12 rows

706

Repeat = 24 stitches and 8 rows

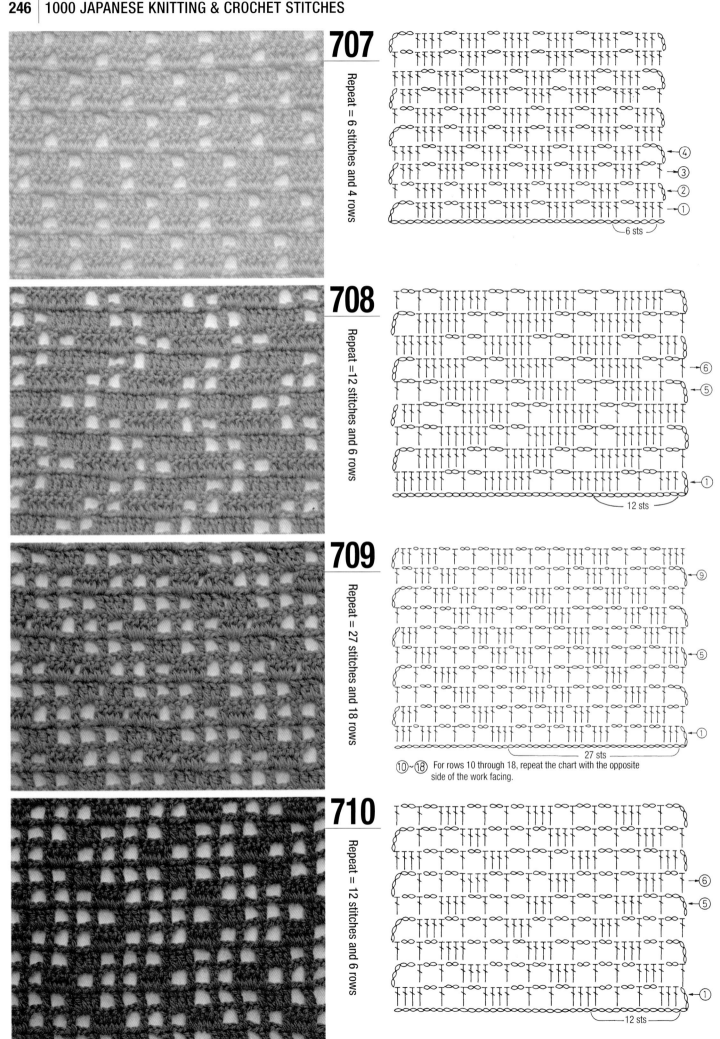

707

Repeat = 6 stitches and 4 rows

6 sts

708

Repeat = 12 stitches and 6 rows

12 sts

709

Repeat = 27 stitches and 18 rows

27 sts

⑩~⑱ For rows 10 through 18, repeat the chart with the opposite side of the work facing.

710

Repeat = 12 stitches and 6 rows

12 sts

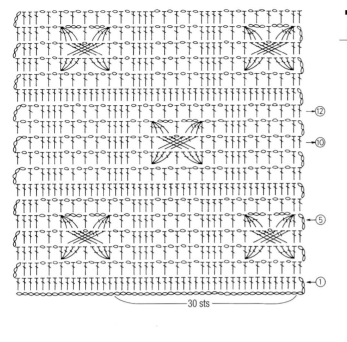

711

Repeat = 30 stitches and 12 rows

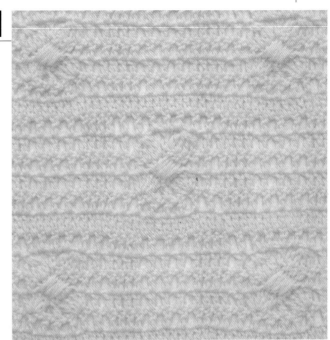

30 sts

712

Repeat = 14 stitches and 8 rows

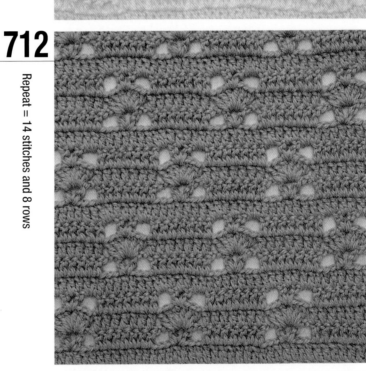

14 sts

713

Repeat = 12 stitches and 4 rows

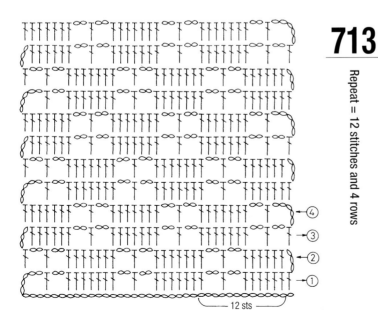

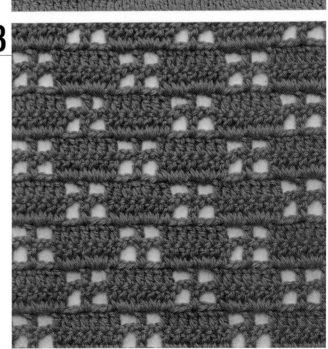

12 sts

714

Repeat = 4 stitches and 2 rows

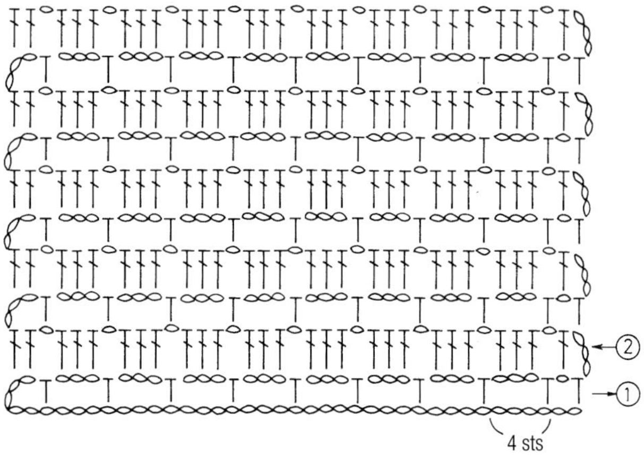

4 sts

715

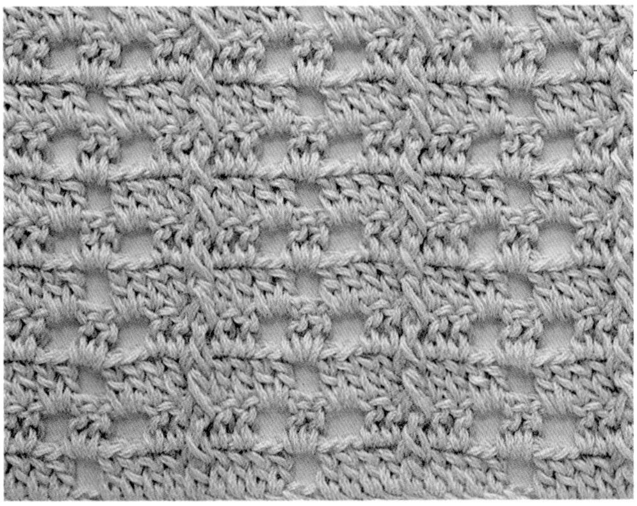

Repeat = 11 stitches and 2 rows

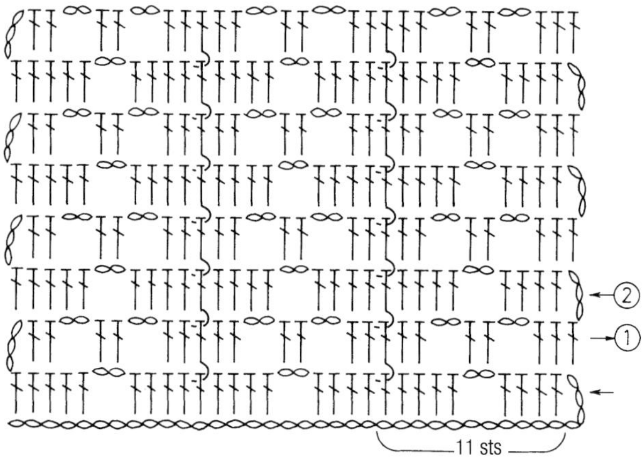

11 sts

716

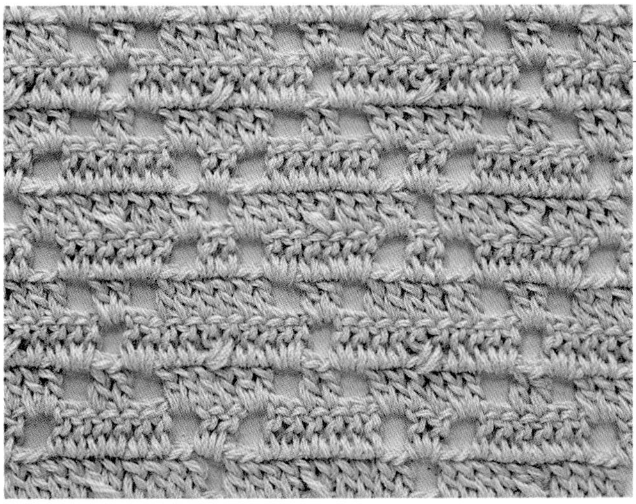

Repeat = 12 stitches and 6 rows

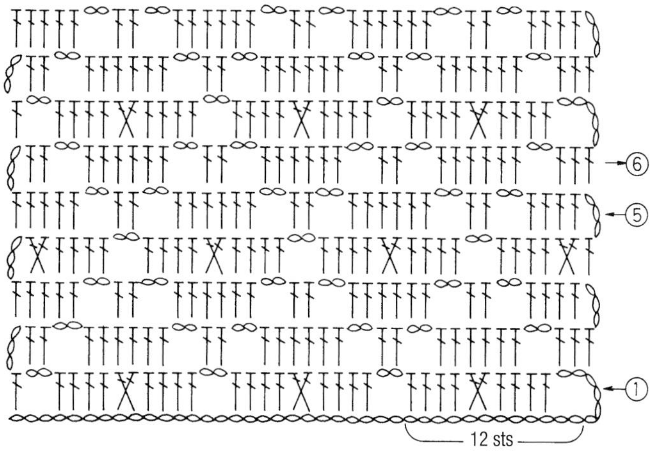

12 sts

717

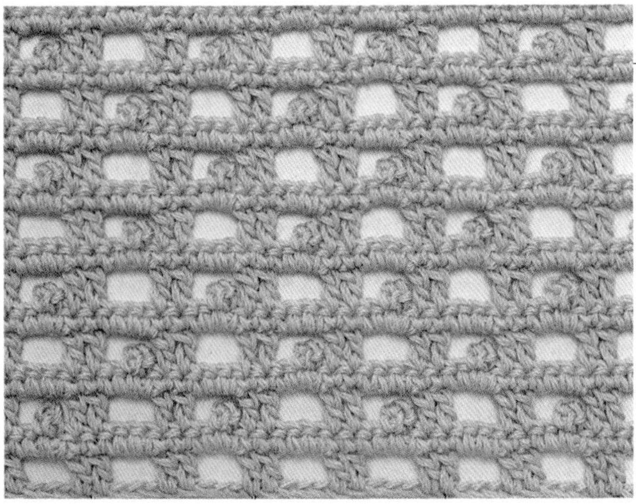

Repeat = 10 stitches and 4 rows

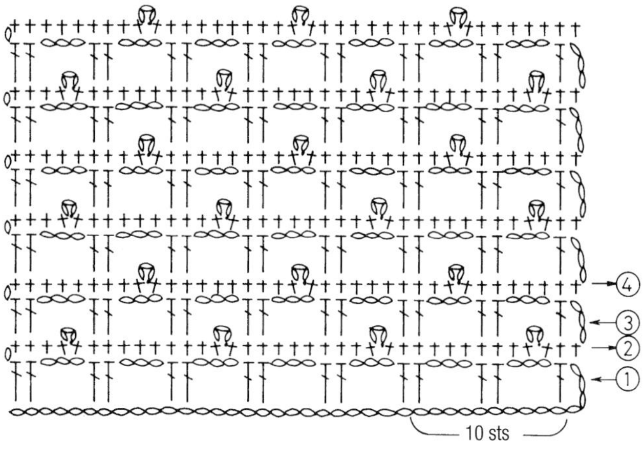

10 sts

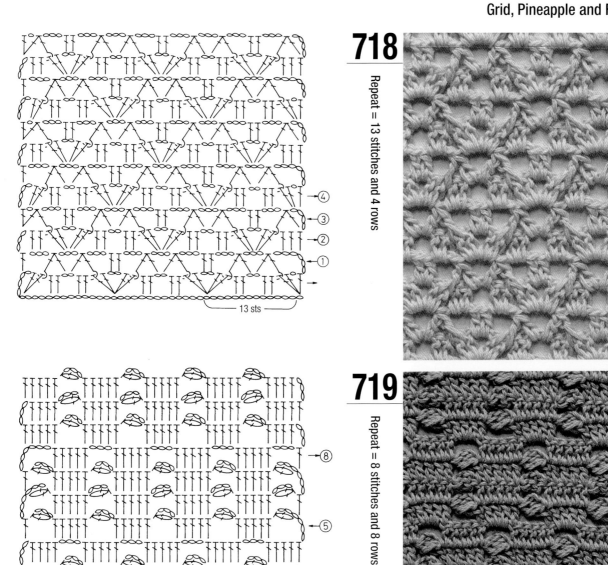

718

Repeat = 13 stitches and 4 rows

13 sts

719

Repeat = 8 stitches and 8 rows

8 sts

720

Repeat = 14 stitches and 12 rows

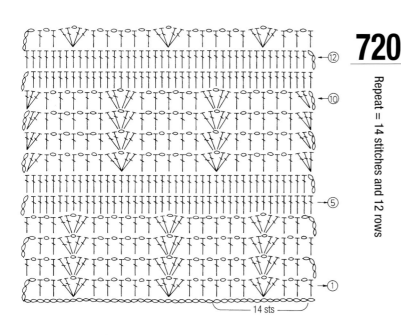

14 sts

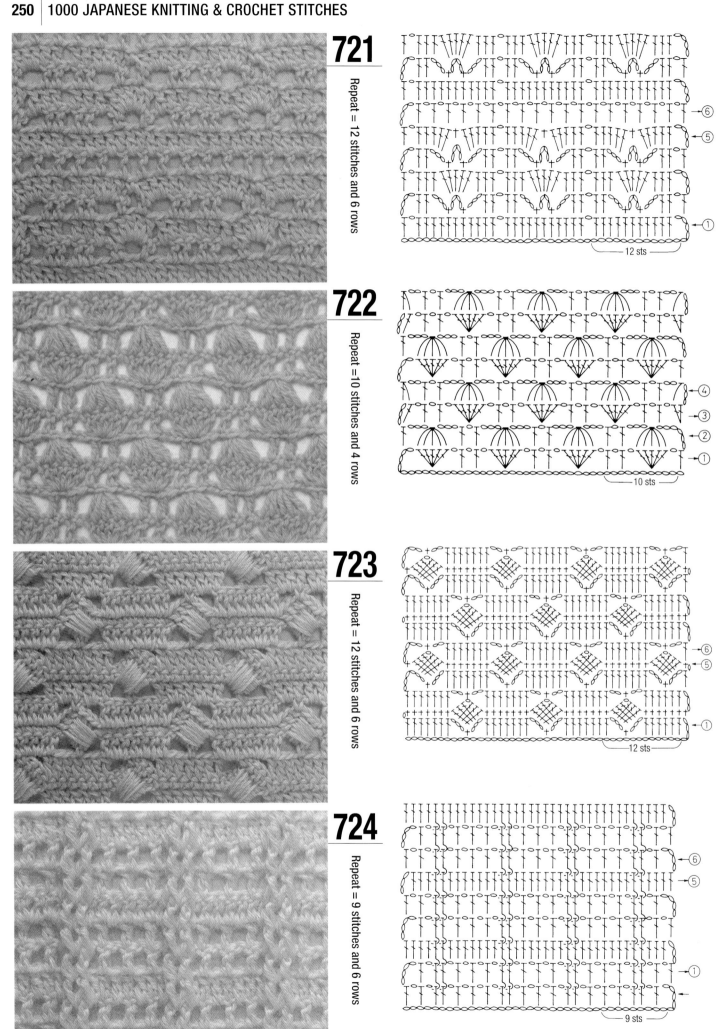

721
Repeat = 12 stitches and 6 rows

722
Repeat = 10 stitches and 4 rows

723
Repeat = 12 stitches and 6 rows

724
Repeat = 9 stitches and 6 rows

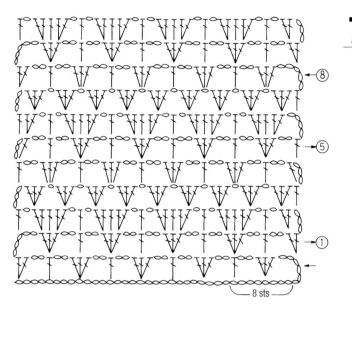

725

Repeat = 8 stitches and 8 rows

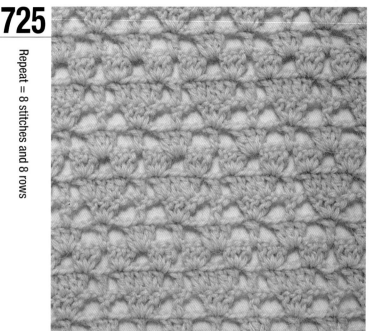

— 8 sts —

726

Repeat = 6 stitches and 4 rows

— 6 sts —

727

Repeat = 8 stitches and 2 rows

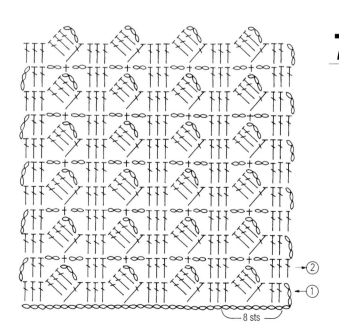

— 8 sts —

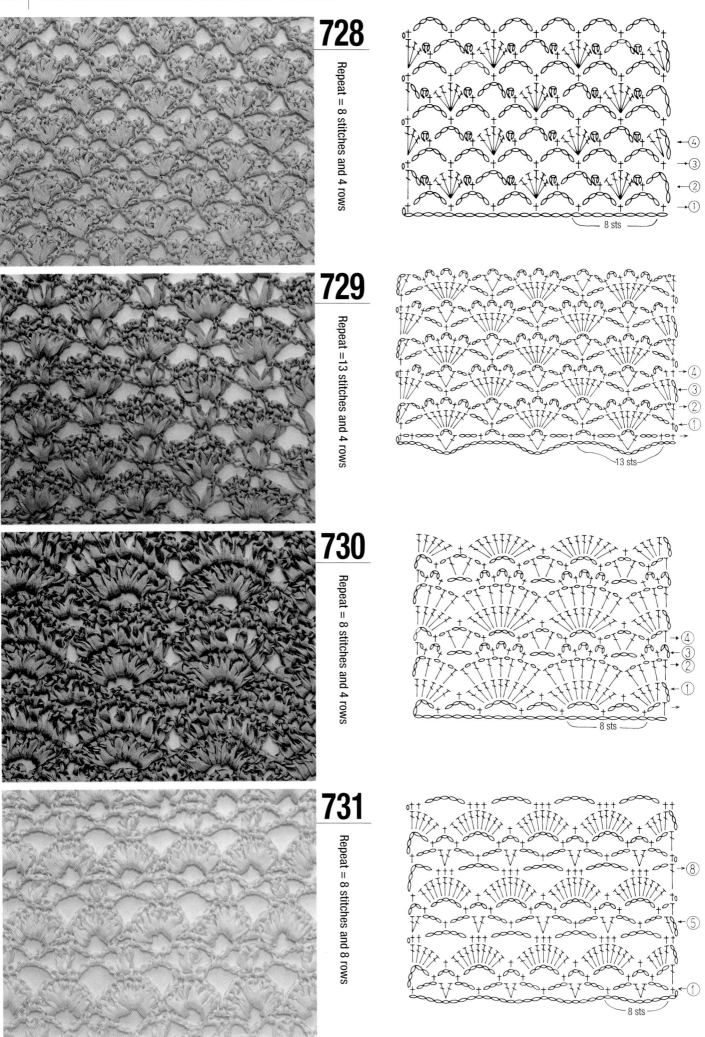

728

Repeat = 8 stitches and 4 rows

729

Repeat = 13 stitches and 4 rows

730

Repeat = 8 stitches and 4 rows

731

Repeat = 8 stitches and 8 rows

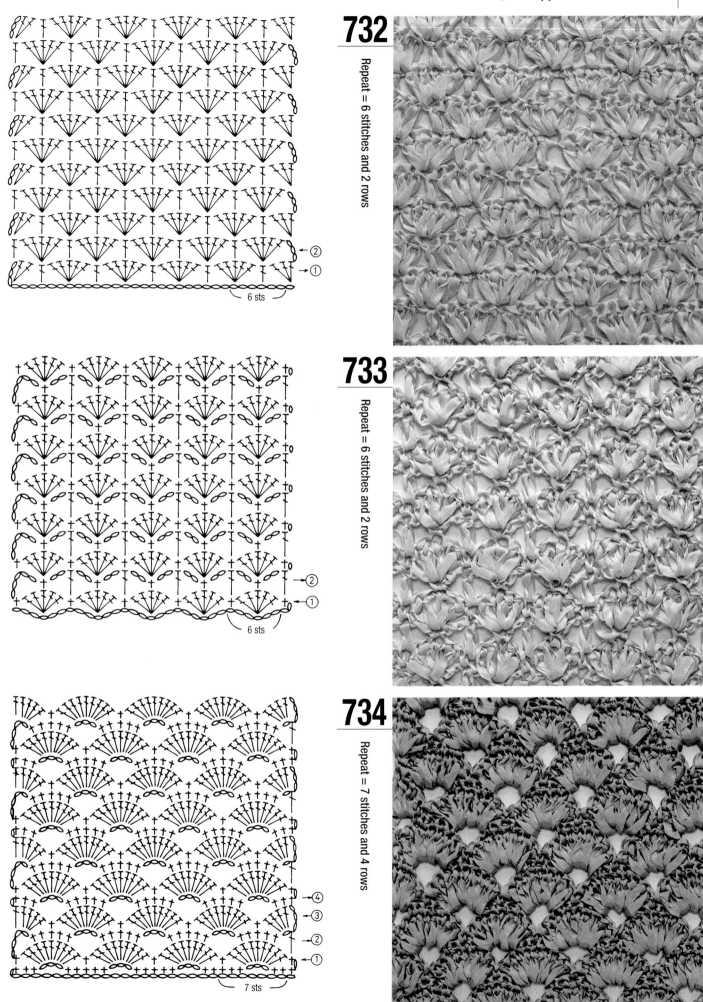

732

Repeat = 6 stitches and 2 rows

6 sts

733

Repeat = 6 stitches and 2 rows

6 sts

734

Repeat = 7 stitches and 4 rows

7 sts

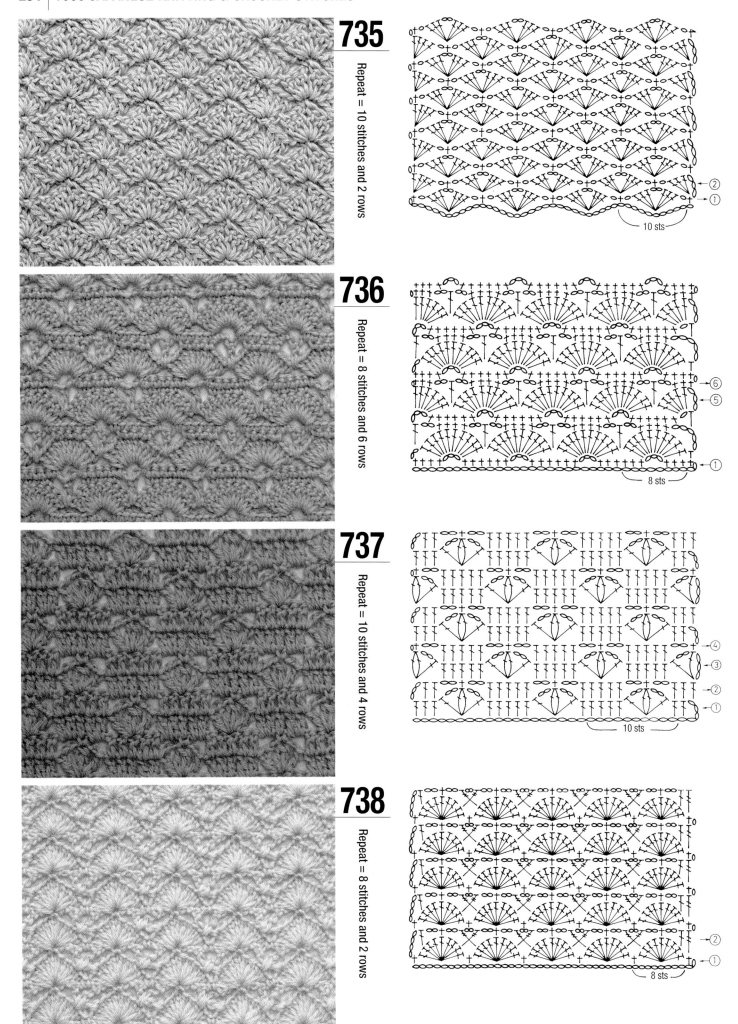

735

Repeat = 10 stitches and 2 rows

10 sts

736

Repeat = 8 stitches and 6 rows

8 sts

737

Repeat = 10 stitches and 4 rows

10 sts

738

Repeat = 8 stitches and 2 rows

8 sts

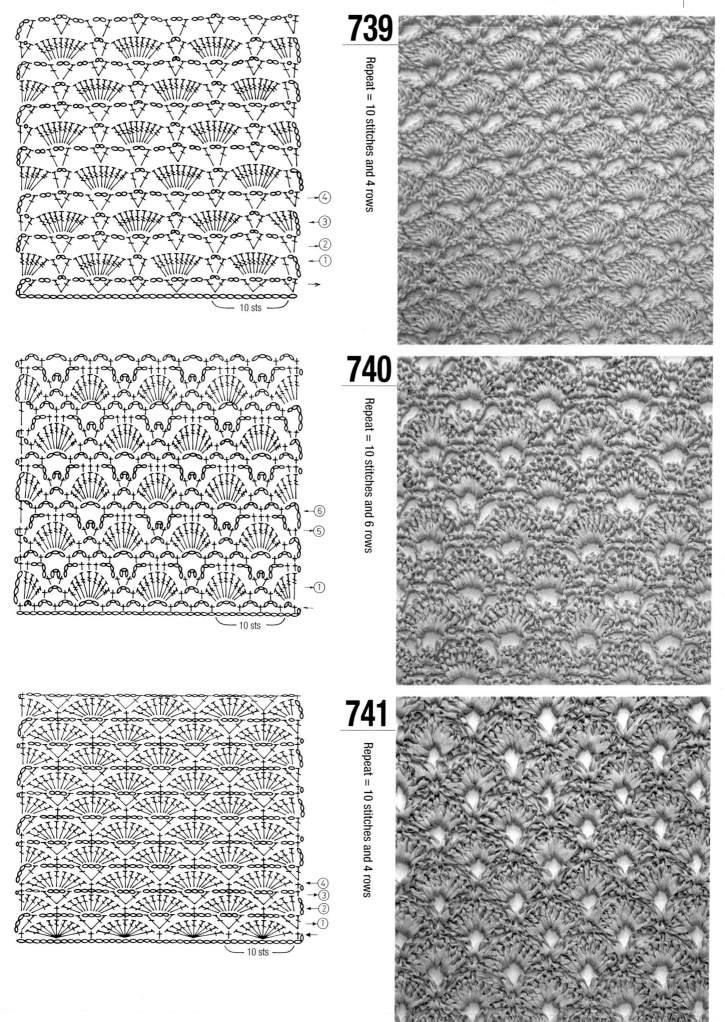

739

Repeat = 10 stitches and 4 rows

10 sts

740

Repeat = 10 stitches and 6 rows

10 sts

741

Repeat = 10 stitches and 4 rows

10 sts

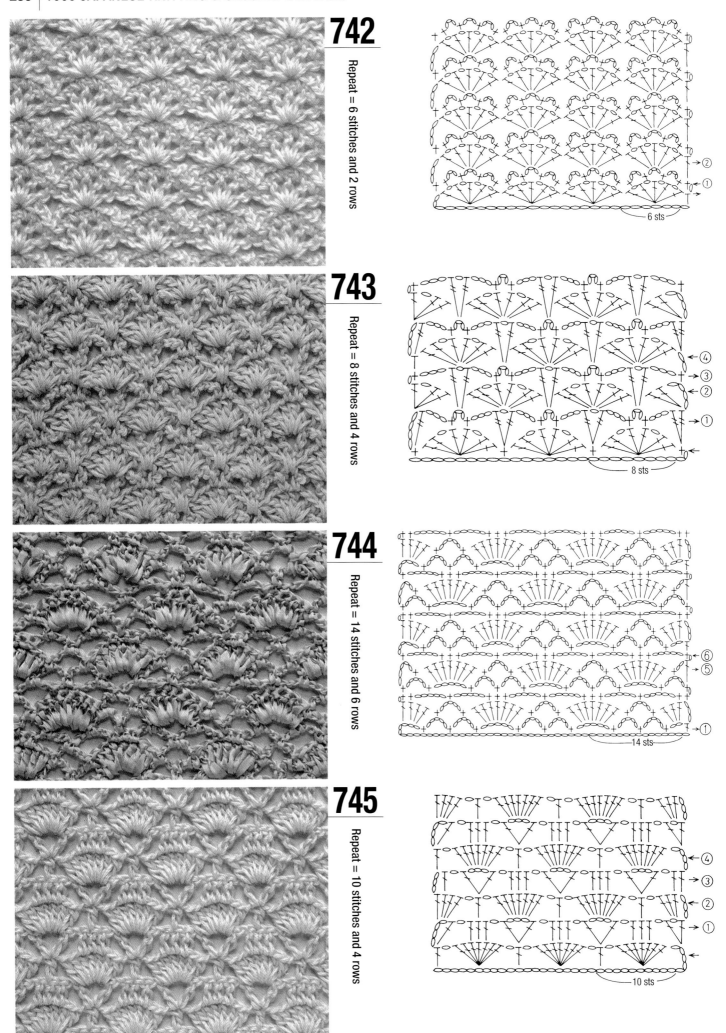

742

Repeat = 6 stitches and 2 rows

6 sts

743

Repeat = 8 stitches and 4 rows

8 sts

744

Repeat = 14 stitches and 6 rows

14 sts

745

Repeat = 10 stitches and 4 rows

10 sts

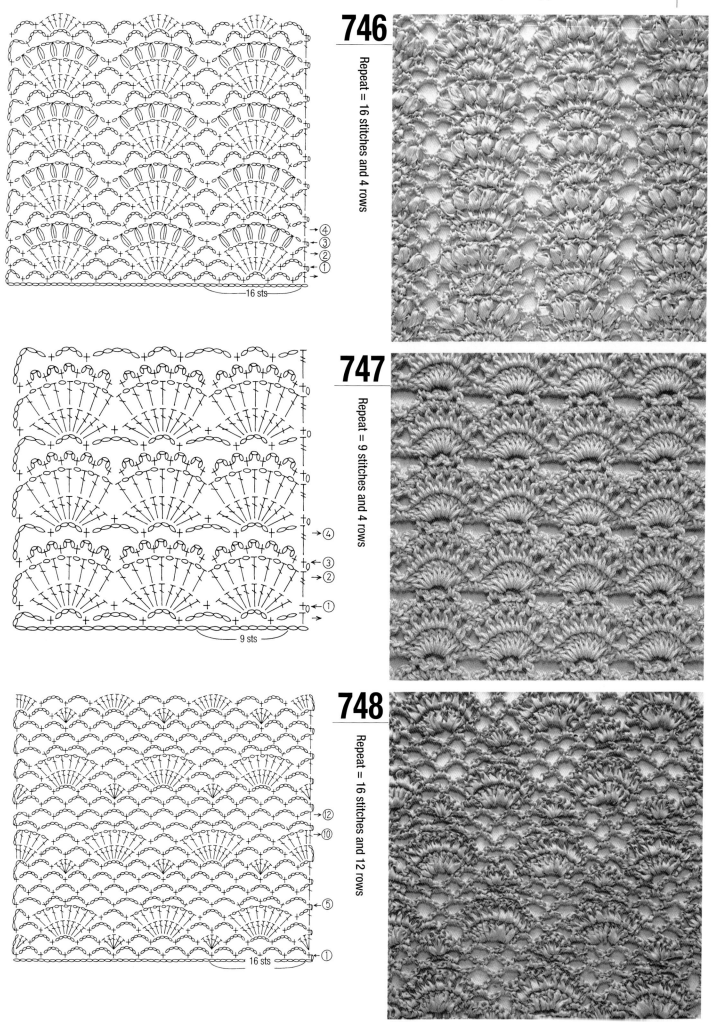

746
Repeat = 16 stitches and 4 rows

16 sts

747
Repeat = 9 stitches and 4 rows

9 sts

748
Repeat = 16 stitches and 12 rows

16 sts

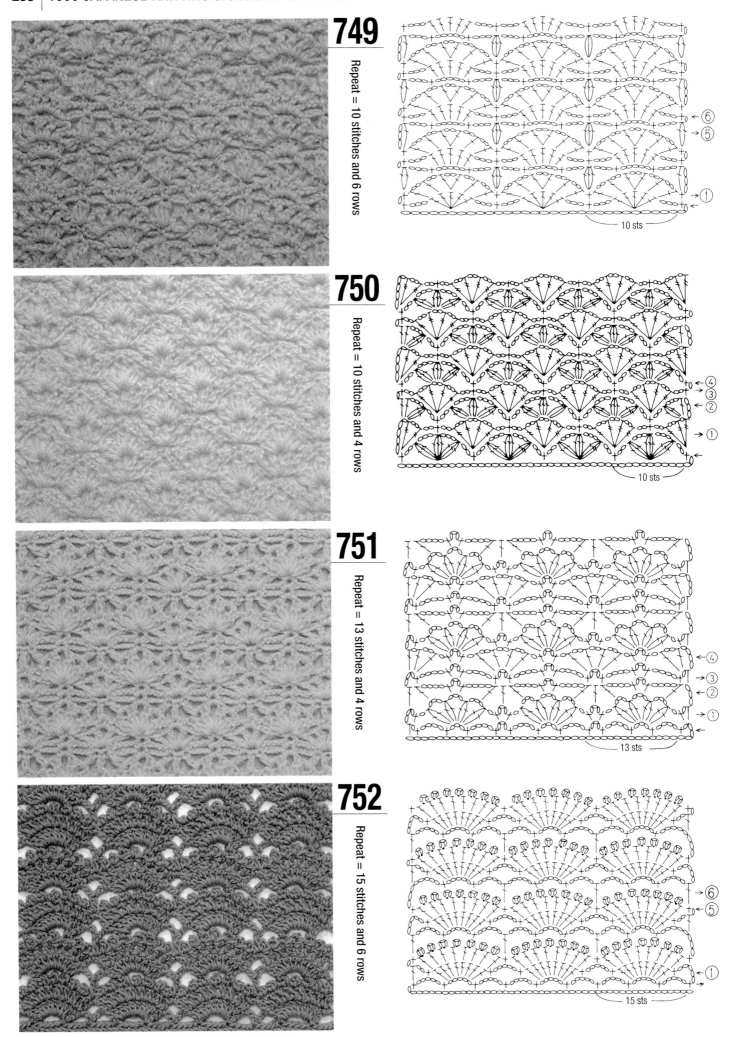

749

Repeat = 10 stitches and 6 rows

10 sts

750

Repeat = 10 stitches and 4 rows

10 sts

751

Repeat = 13 stitches and 4 rows

13 sts

752

Repeat = 15 stitches and 6 rows

15 sts

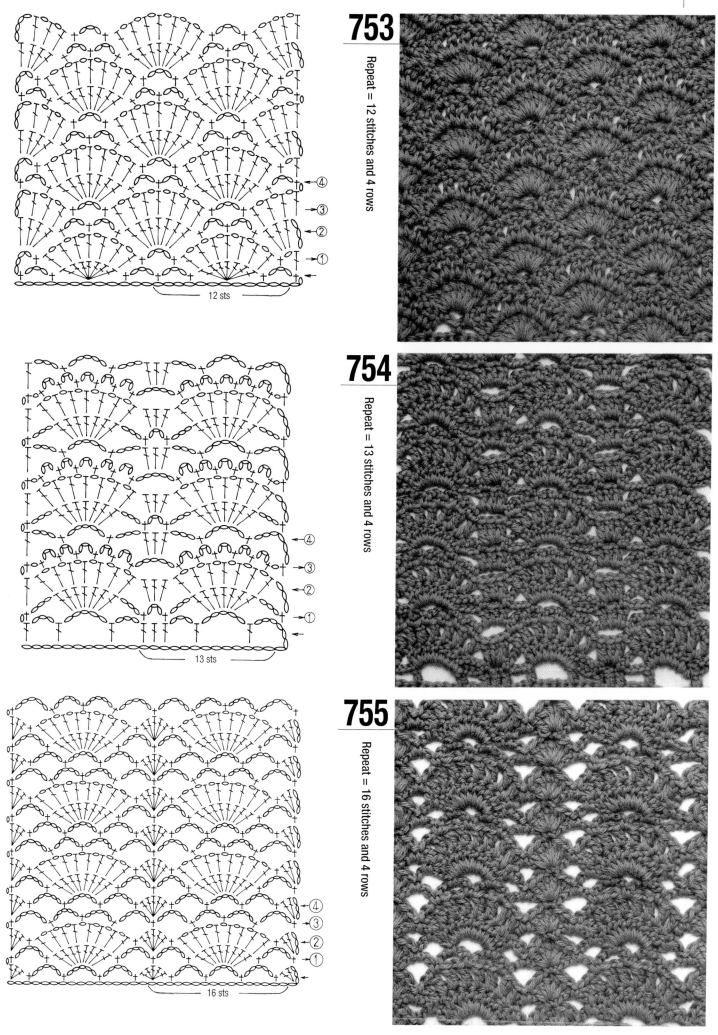

753

Repeat = 12 stitches and 4 rows

12 sts

754

Repeat = 13 stitches and 4 rows

13 sts

755

Repeat = 16 stitches and 4 rows

16 sts

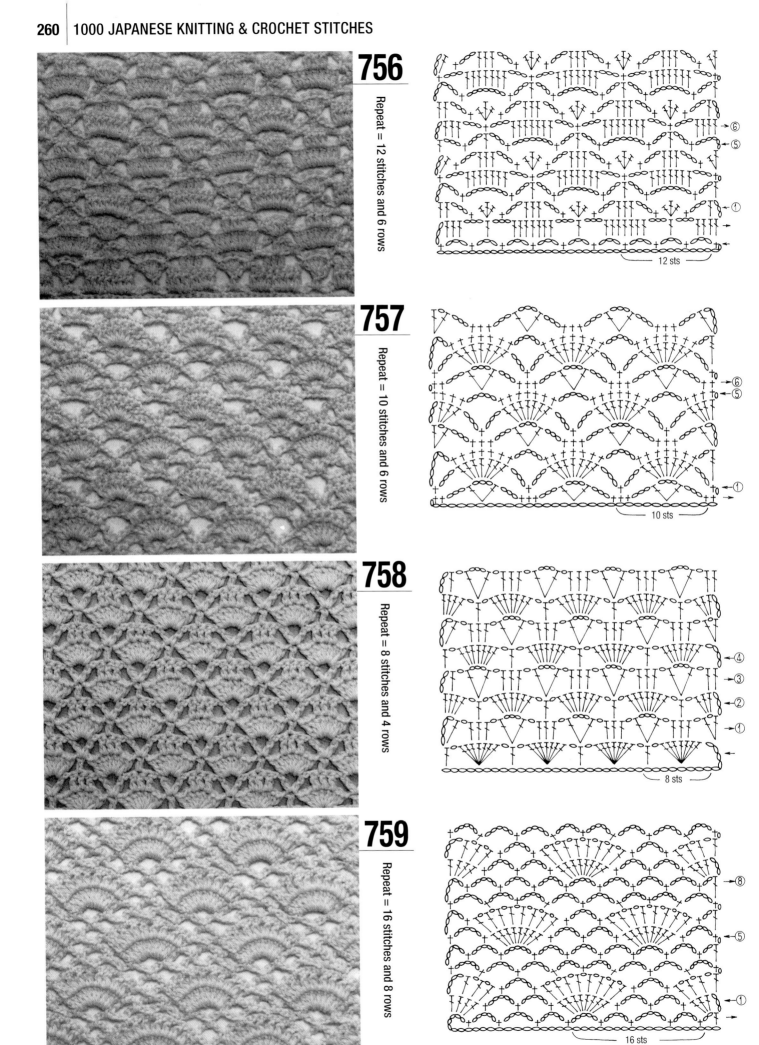

756

Repeat = 12 stitches and 6 rows

757

Repeat = 10 stitches and 6 rows

758

Repeat = 8 stitches and 4 rows

759

Repeat = 16 stitches and 8 rows

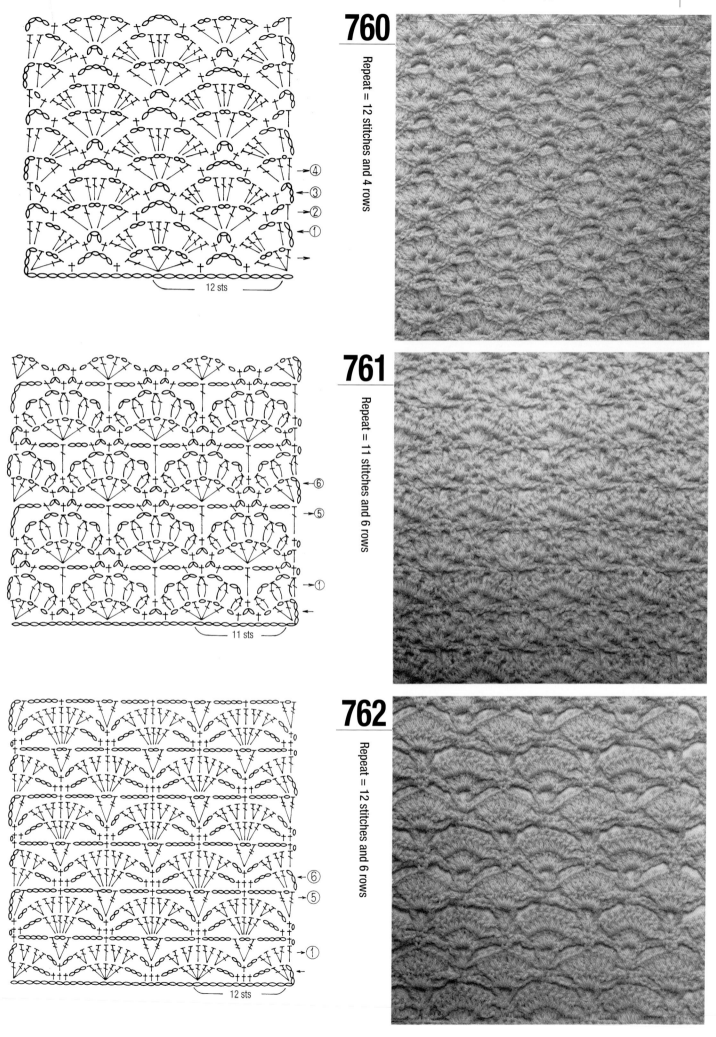

760

Repeat = 12 stitches and 4 rows

12 sts

761

Repeat = 11 stitches and 6 rows

11 sts

762

Repeat = 12 stitches and 6 rows

12 sts

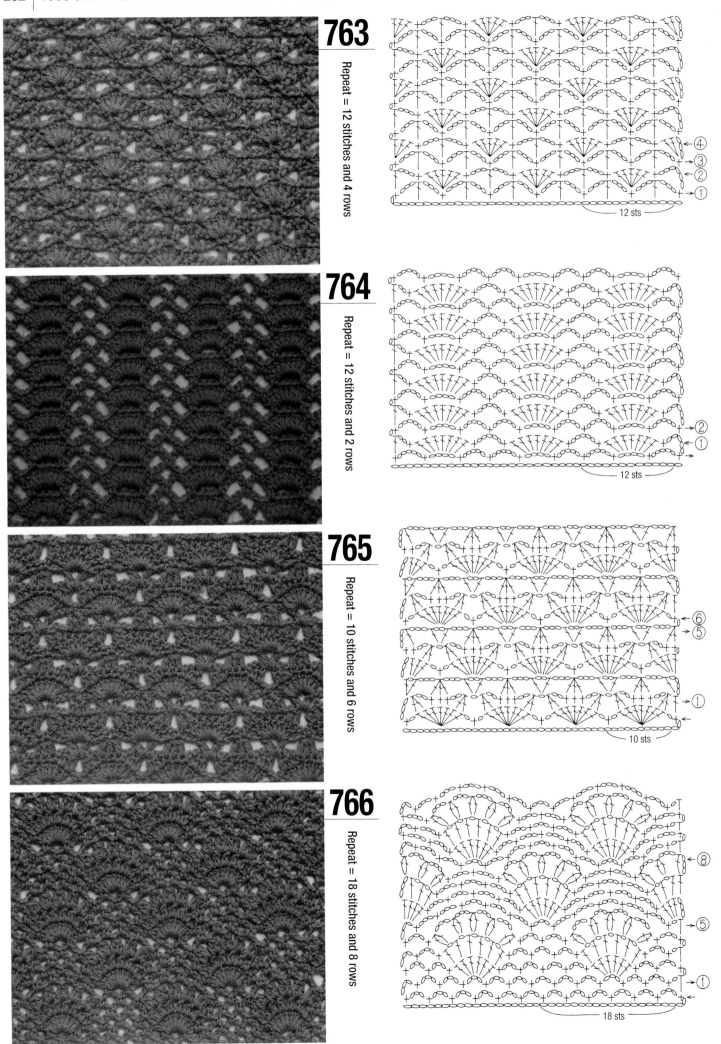

763

Repeat = 12 stitches and 4 rows

12 sts

764

Repeat = 12 stitches and 2 rows

12 sts

765

Repeat = 10 stitches and 6 rows

10 sts

766

Repeat = 18 stitches and 8 rows

18 sts

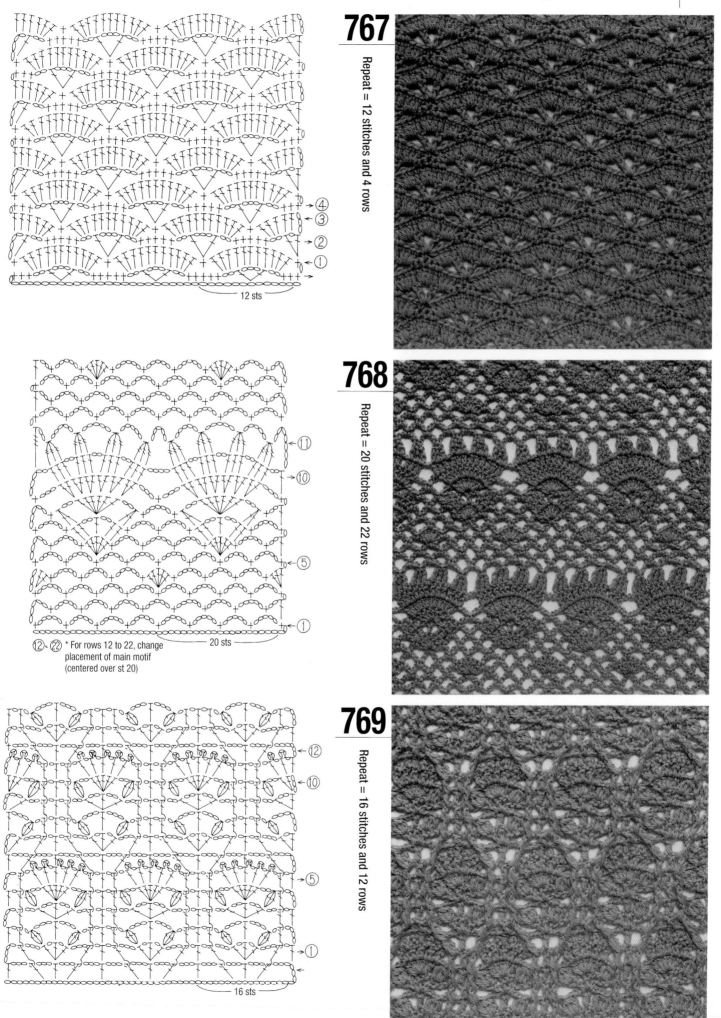

767

Repeat = 12 stitches and 4 rows

12 sts

768

Repeat = 20 stitches and 22 rows

20 sts

⑫~㉒ * For rows 12 to 22, change
placement of main motif
(centered over st 20)

769

Repeat = 16 stitches and 12 rows

16 sts

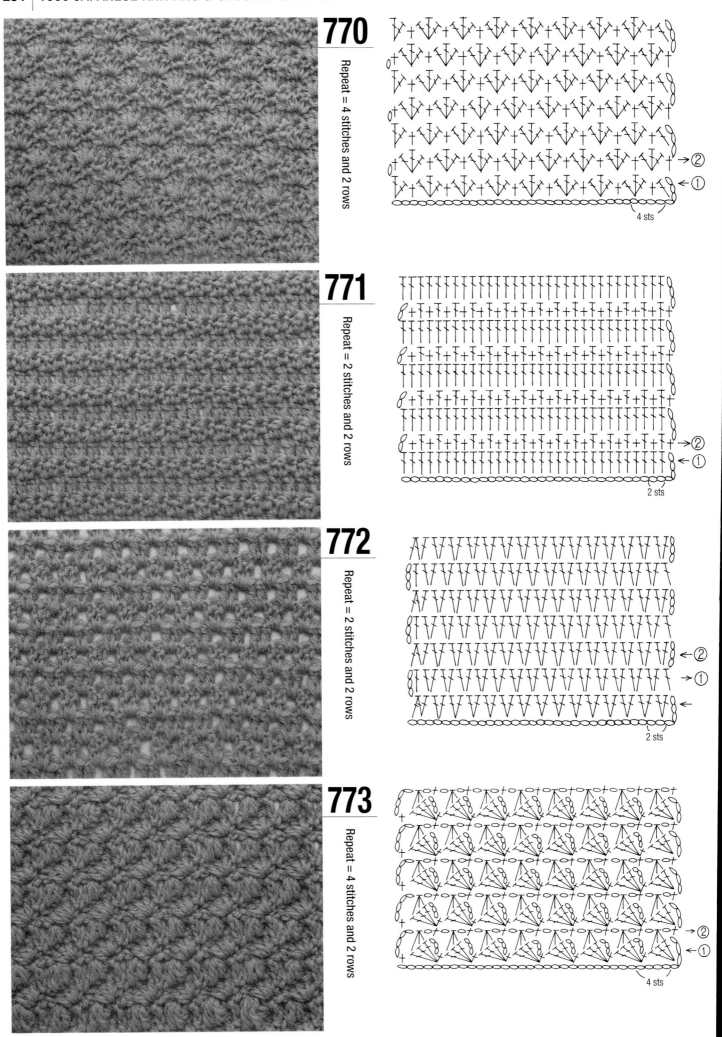

770

Repeat = 4 stitches and 2 rows

771

Repeat = 2 stitches and 2 rows

772

Repeat = 2 stitches and 2 rows

773

Repeat = 4 stitches and 2 rows

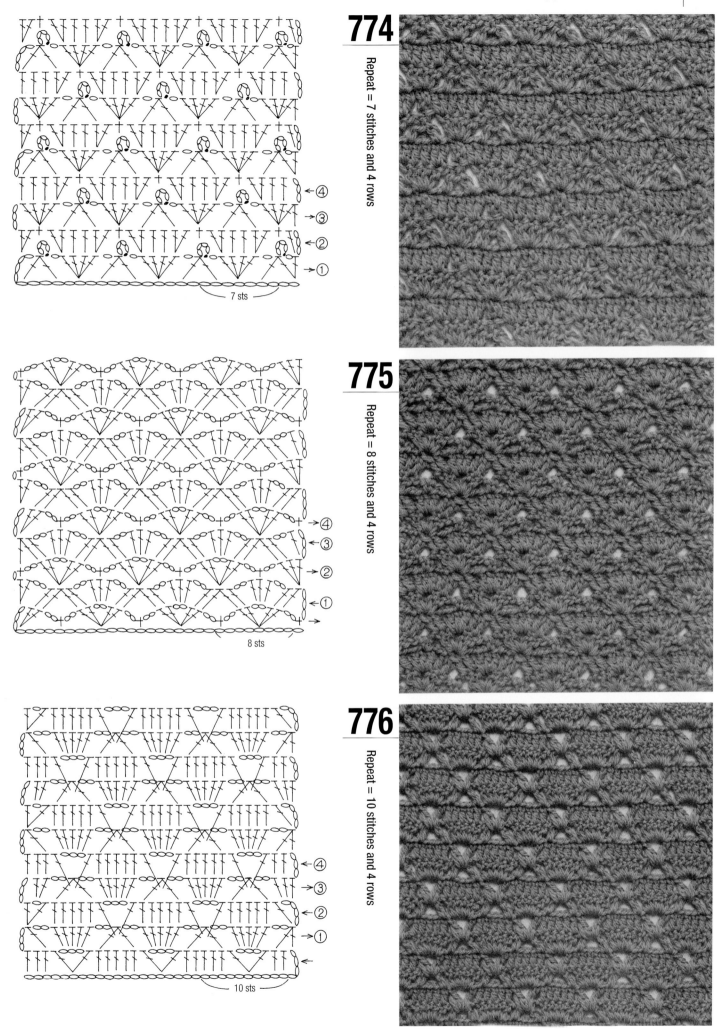

774

Repeat = 7 stitches and 4 rows

7 sts

775

Repeat = 8 stitches and 4 rows

8 sts

776

Repeat = 10 stitches and 4 rows

10 sts

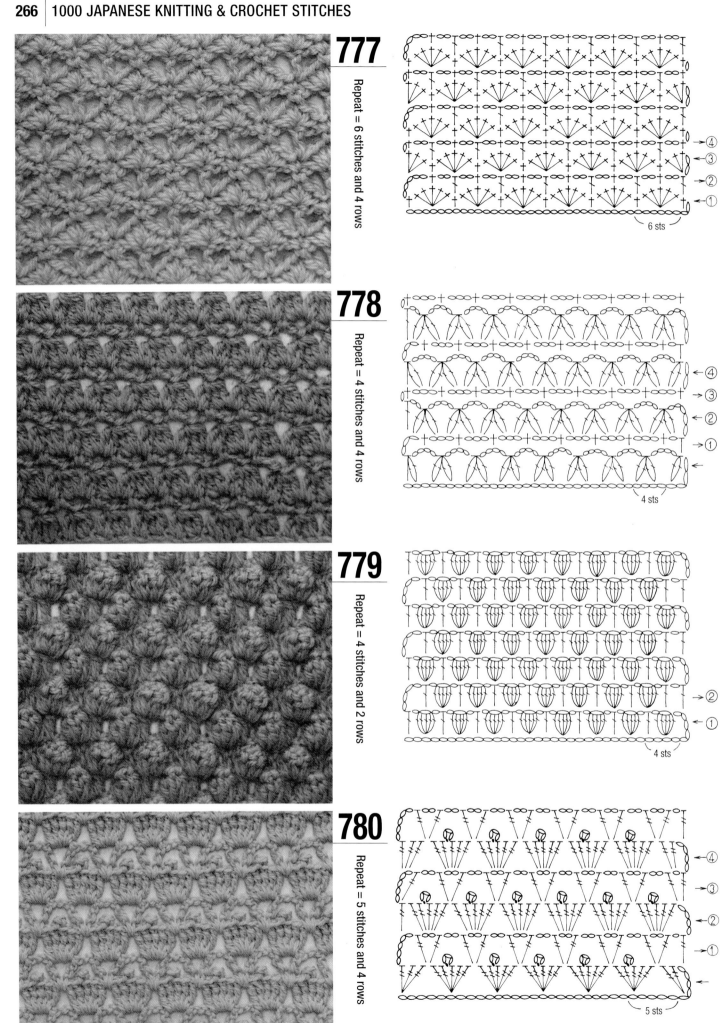

777

Repeat = 6 stitches and 4 rows

6 sts

778

Repeat = 4 stitches and 4 rows

4 sts

779

Repeat = 4 stitches and 2 rows

4 sts

780

Repeat = 5 stitches and 4 rows

5 sts

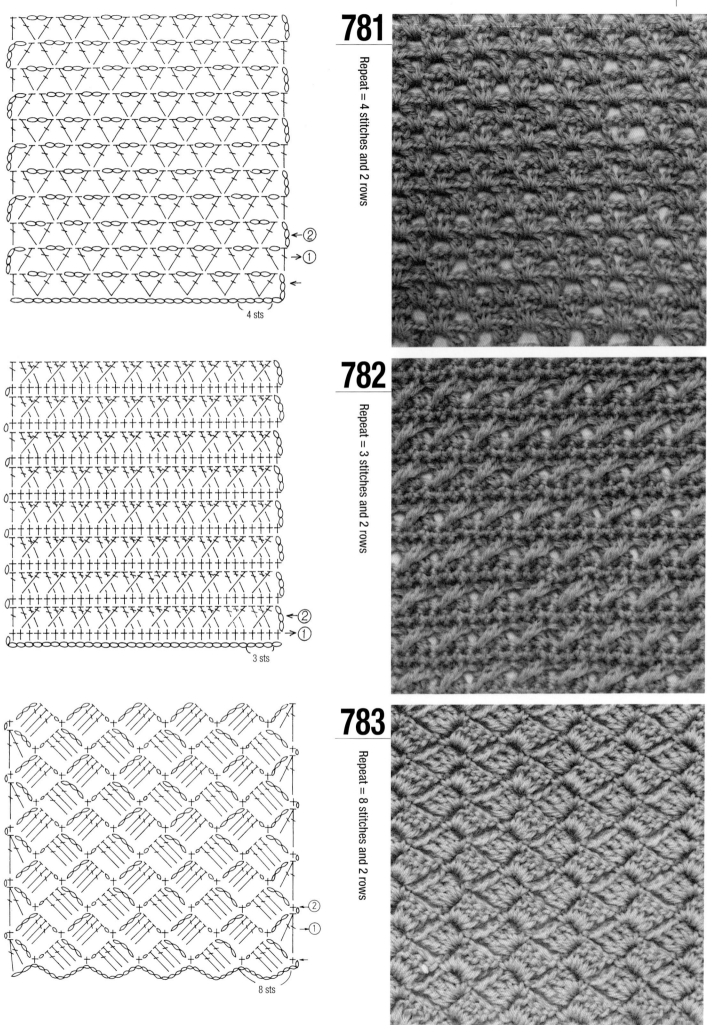

781

Repeat = 4 stitches and 2 rows

4 sts

782

Repeat = 3 stitches and 2 rows

3 sts

783

Repeat = 8 stitches and 2 rows

8 sts

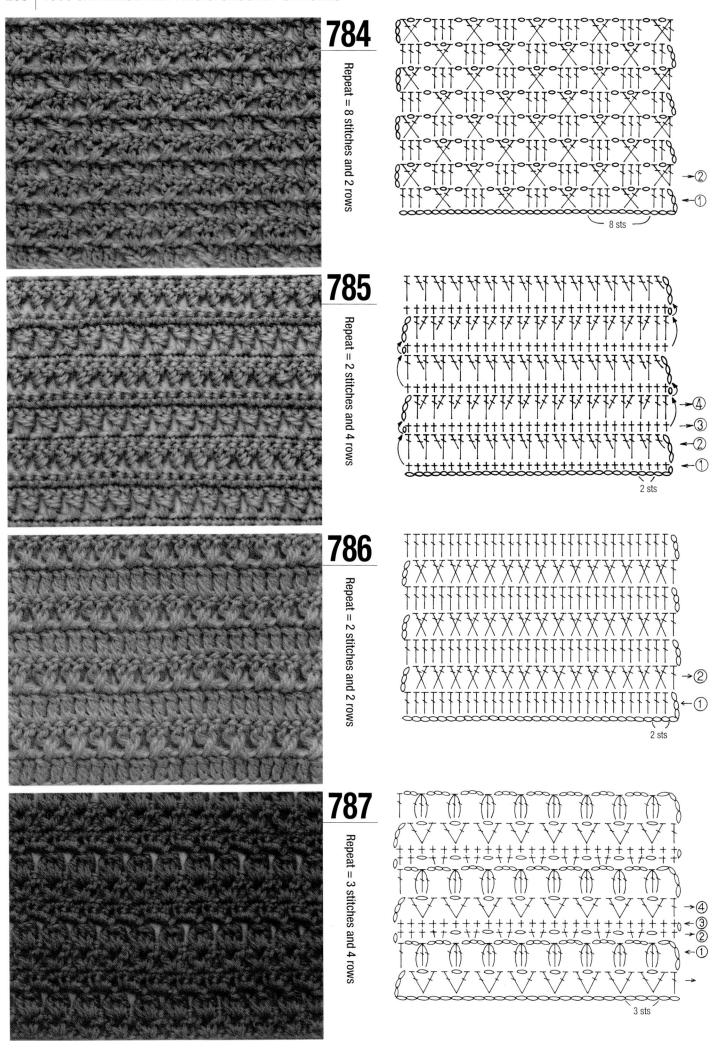

784

Repeat = 8 stitches and 2 rows

8 sts

785

Repeat = 2 stitches and 4 rows

2 sts

786

Repeat = 2 stitches and 2 rows

2 sts

787

Repeat = 3 stitches and 4 rows

3 sts

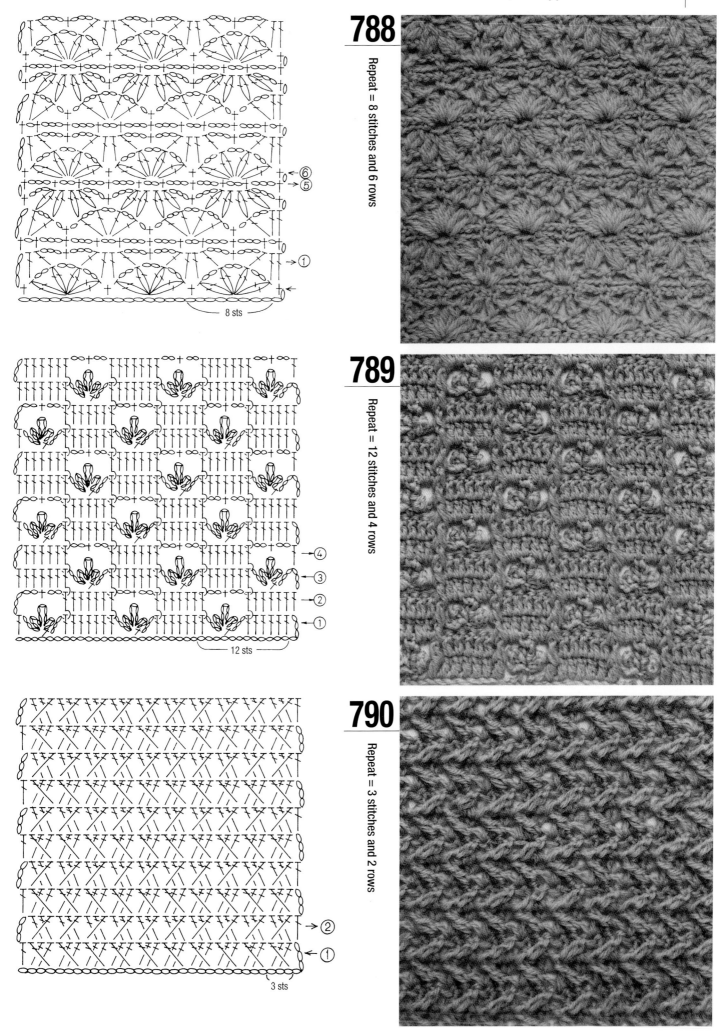

788

Repeat = 8 stitches and 6 rows

8 sts

789

Repeat = 12 stitches and 4 rows

12 sts

790

Repeat = 3 stitches and 2 rows

3 sts

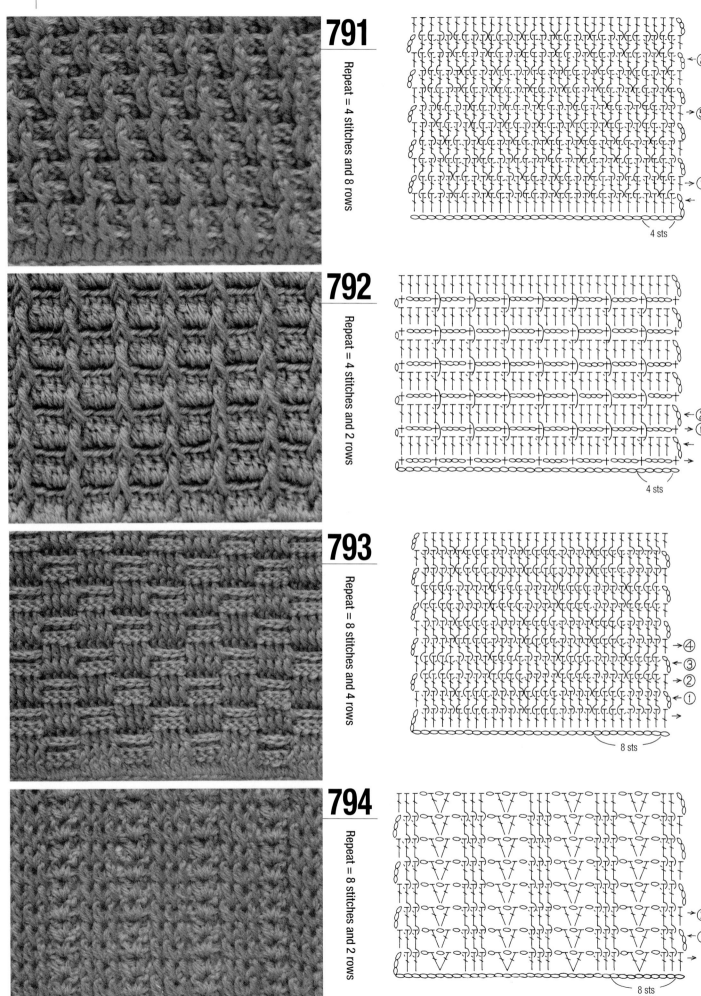

791

Repeat = 4 stitches and 8 rows

792

Repeat = 4 stitches and 2 rows

793

Repeat = 8 stitches and 4 rows

794

Repeat = 8 stitches and 2 rows

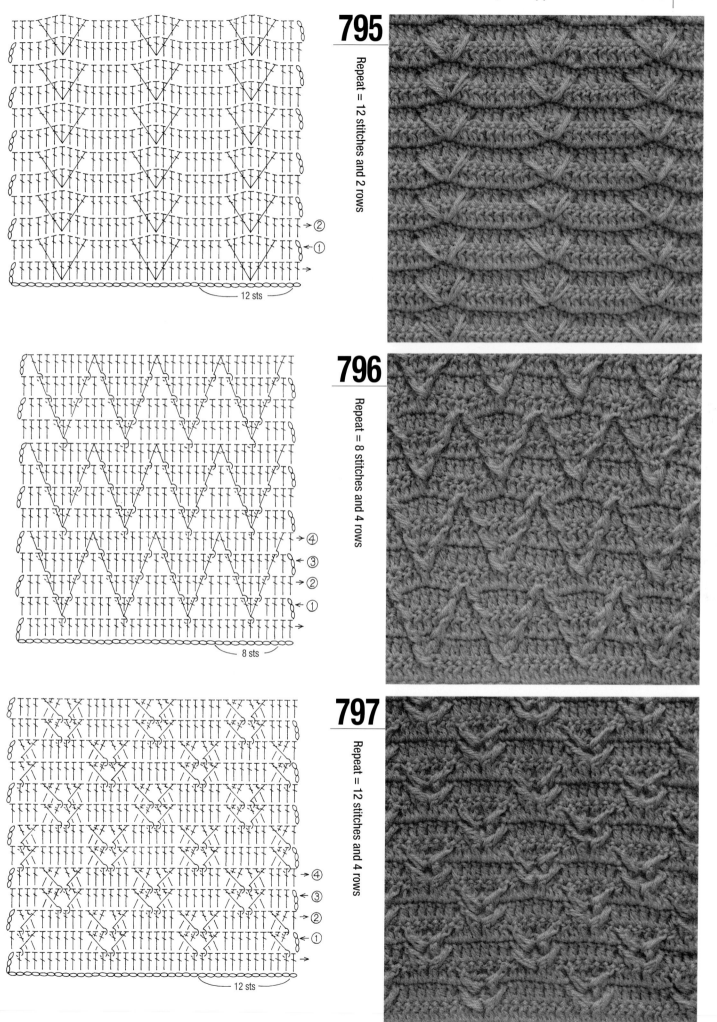

795

Repeat = 12 stitches and 2 rows

12 sts

796

Repeat = 8 stitches and 4 rows

8 sts

797

Repeat = 12 stitches and 4 rows

12 sts

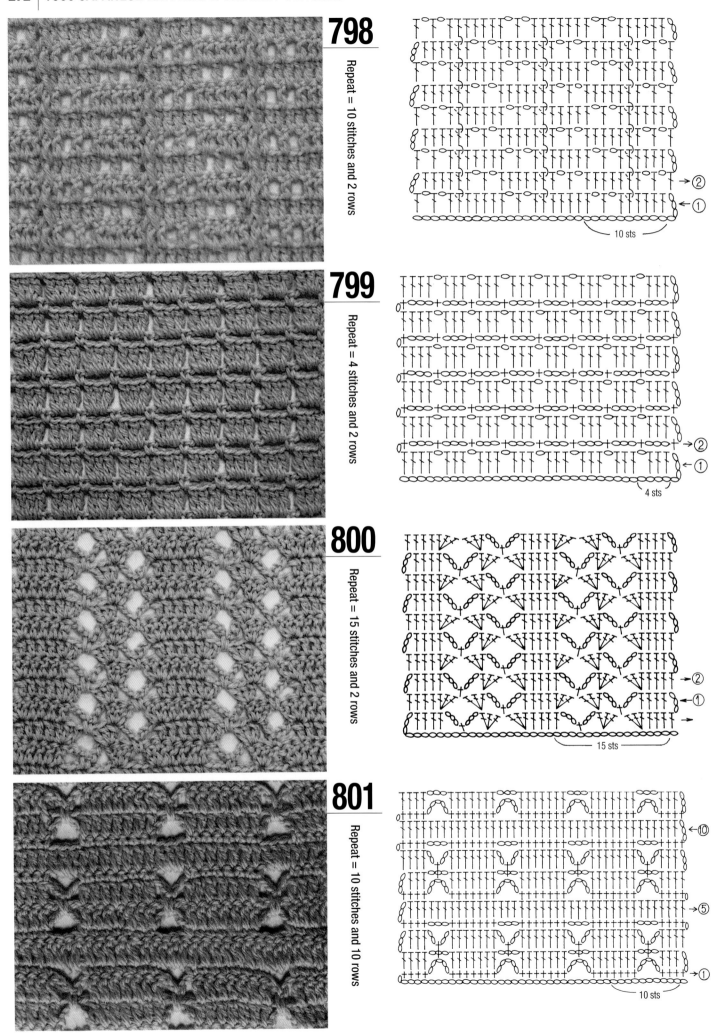

798

Repeat = 10 stitches and 2 rows

10 sts

799

Repeat = 4 stitches and 2 rows

4 sts

800

Repeat = 15 stitches and 2 rows

15 sts

801

Repeat = 10 stitches and 10 rows

10 sts

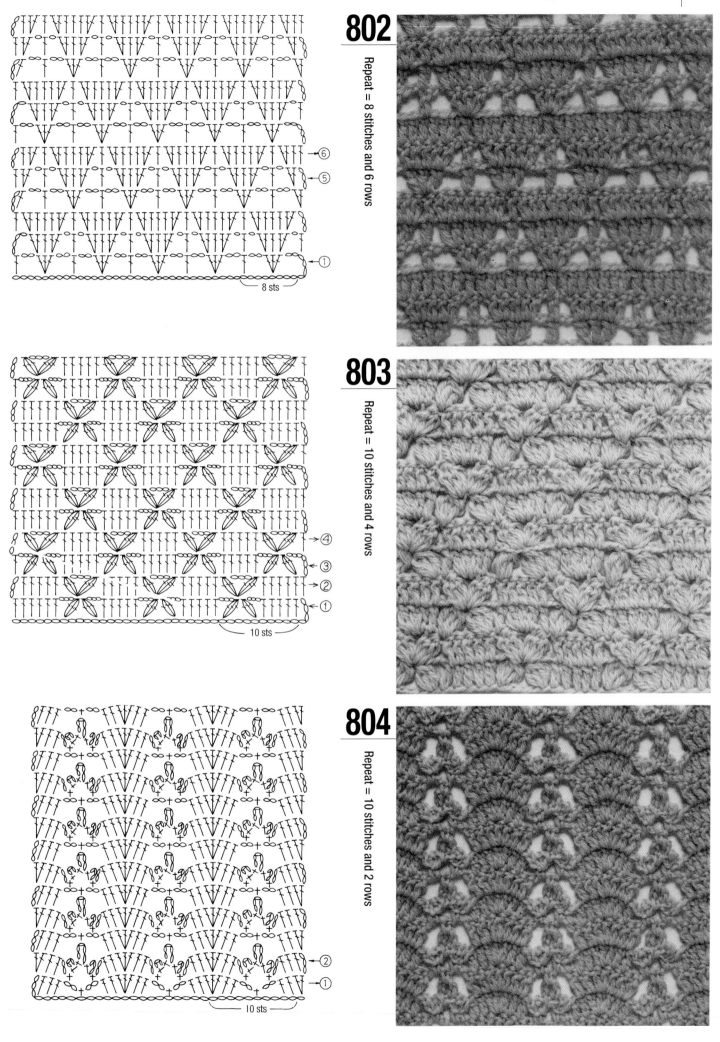

802

Repeat = 8 stitches and 6 rows

8 sts

803

Repeat = 10 stitches and 4 rows

10 sts

804

Repeat = 10 stitches and 2 rows

10 sts

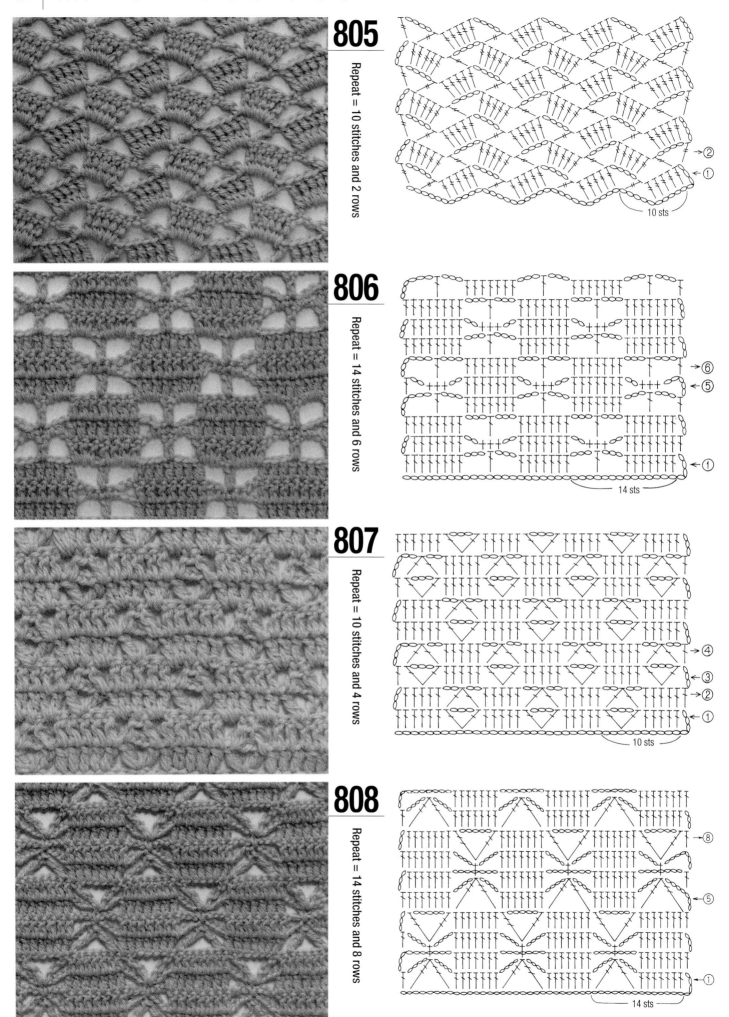

805

Repeat = 10 stitches and 2 rows

806

Repeat = 14 stitches and 6 rows

807

Repeat = 10 stitches and 4 rows

808

Repeat = 14 stitches and 8 rows

COLOR CHANGING STITCHES

You can make very interesting patterns when you strand one color with another, or change colors by row. Some stitches seem to float on the surface of the fabric, some are reversible, and all have a special character that's enjoyable to create.

The materials you use have a big influence on the fabric you make.

Pay careful attention to whether a stitch in a new color lies in front or in back of the previous stitch–the stitch that lies in front will have an *unbroken* line.

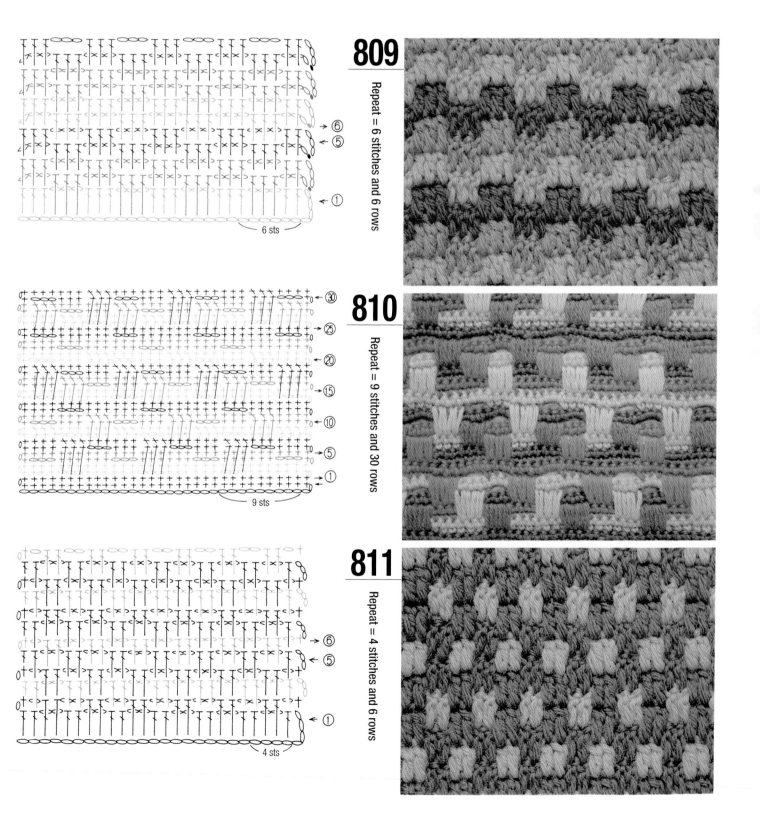

809
Repeat = 6 stitches and 6 rows
6 sts

810
Repeat = 9 stitches and 30 rows
9 sts

811
Repeat = 4 stitches and 6 rows
4 sts

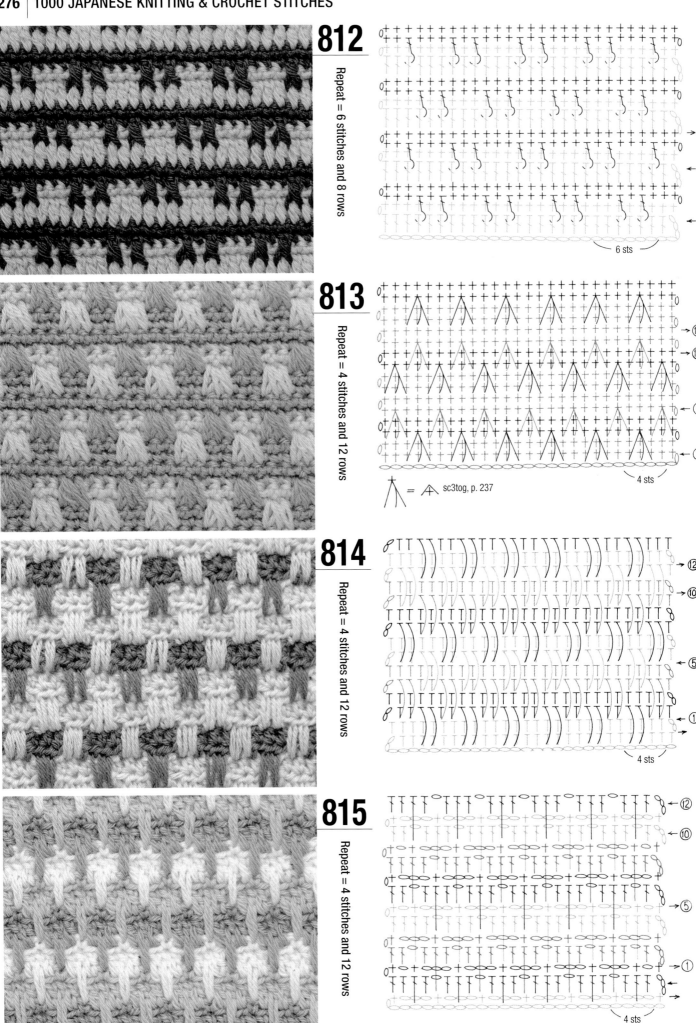

812

Repeat = 6 stitches and 8 rows

6 sts

813

Repeat = 4 stitches and 12 rows

= sc3tog, p. 237

4 sts

814

Repeat = 4 stitches and 12 rows

4 sts

815

Repeat = 4 stitches and 12 rows

4 sts

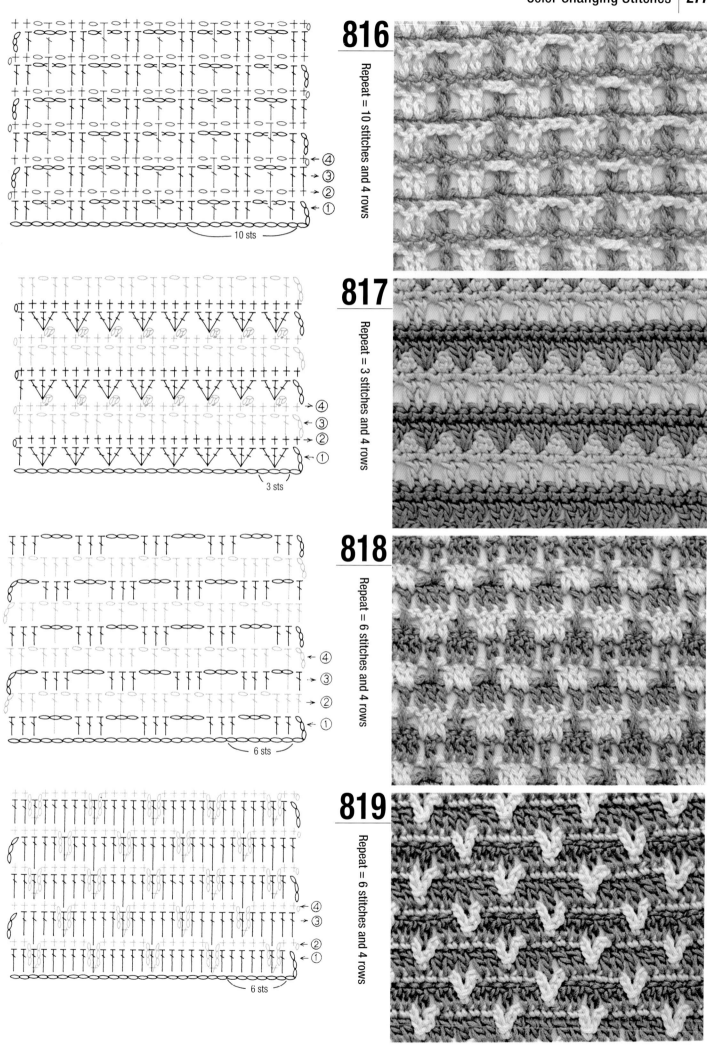

816

Repeat = 10 stitches and 4 rows

← ④
← ③
← ②
← ①

10 sts

817

Repeat = 3 stitches and 4 rows

→ ④
→ ③
→ ②
← ①

3 sts

818

Repeat = 6 stitches and 4 rows

← ④
← ③
→ ②
← ①

6 sts

819

Repeat = 6 stitches and 4 rows

← ④
← ③
→ ②
← ①

6 sts

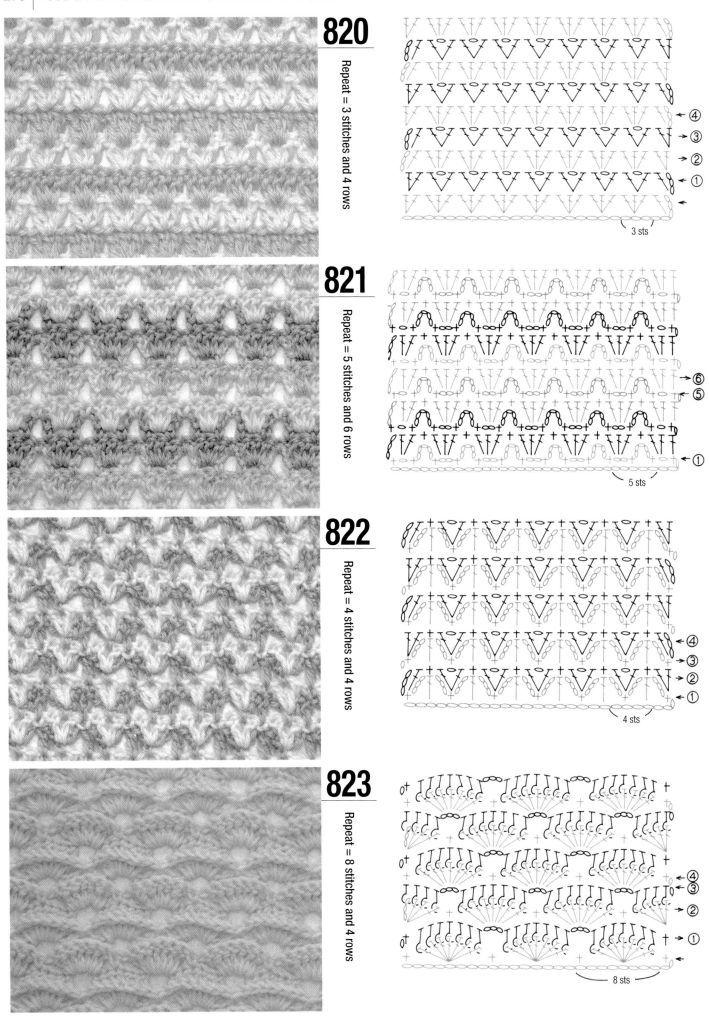

820

Repeat = 3 stitches and 4 rows

3 sts

821

Repeat = 5 stitches and 6 rows

5 sts

822

Repeat = 4 stitches and 4 rows

4 sts

823

Repeat = 8 stitches and 4 rows

8 sts

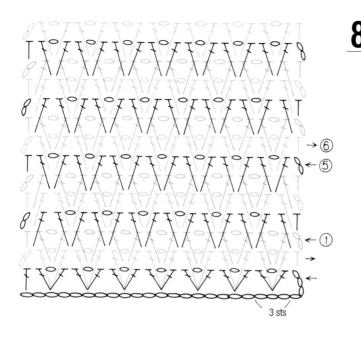

824

Repeat = 3 stitches and 6 rows

→ ⑥
← ⑤
← ①
←
←

3 sts

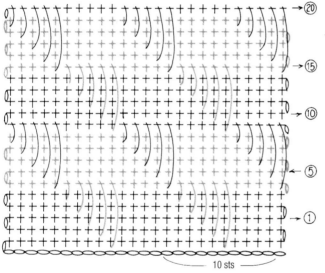

825

Repeat = 10 stitches and 12 rows

→ ⑳
→ ⑮
→ ⑩
← ⑤
→ ①

10 sts

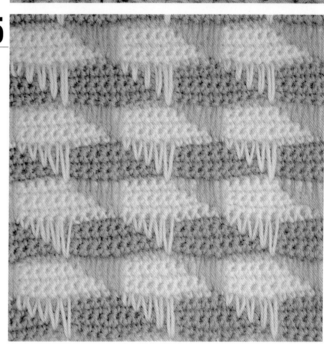

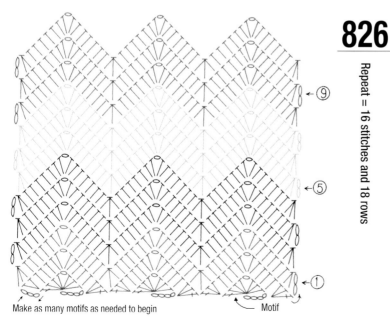

826

Repeat = 16 stitches and 18 rows

← ⑨
← ⑤
← ①

Make as many motifs as needed to begin

Motif

⑩ - ⑱ For rows 10 through 18, repeat the chart with the opposite side of the work facing.

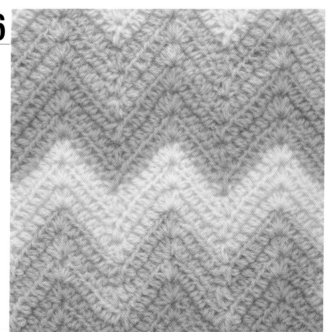

827

Repeat = 3 stitches and 2 rows

This group of stitches (827 to 834) use the technique of carrying and wrapping a contrasting strand of yarn, illustrated on p. 242. The carried/wrapped yarn is shown in a contrast color.

828

Repeat = 8 stitches and 4 rows

See explanation on p. 242

829

Repeat = 6 stitches and 2 rows

830

Repeat = 6 stitches and 2 rows

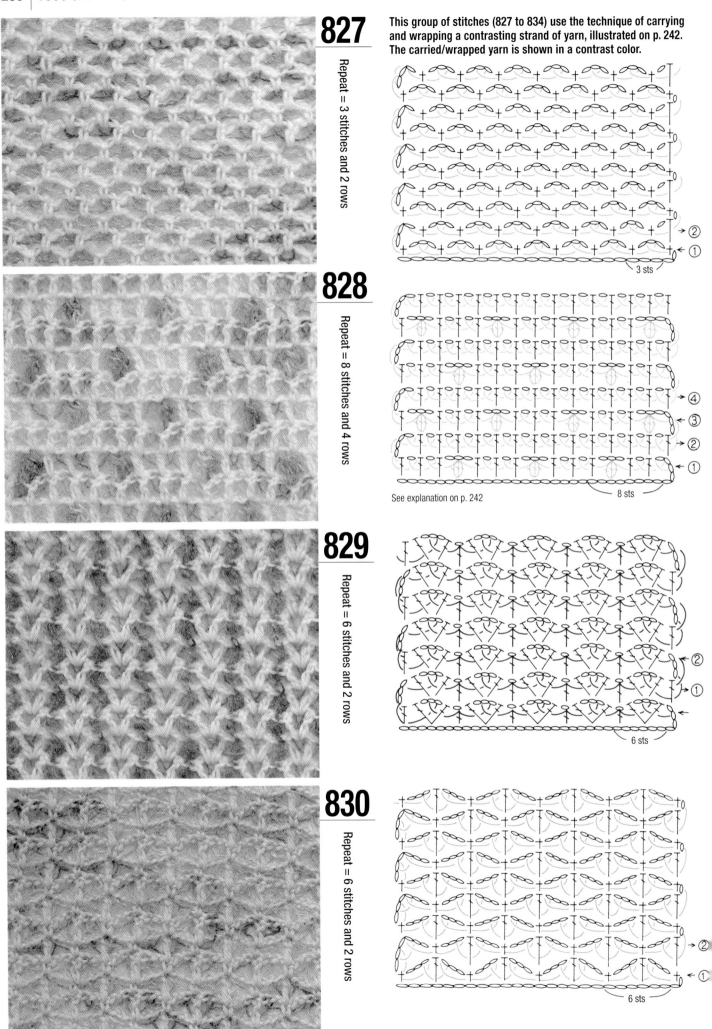

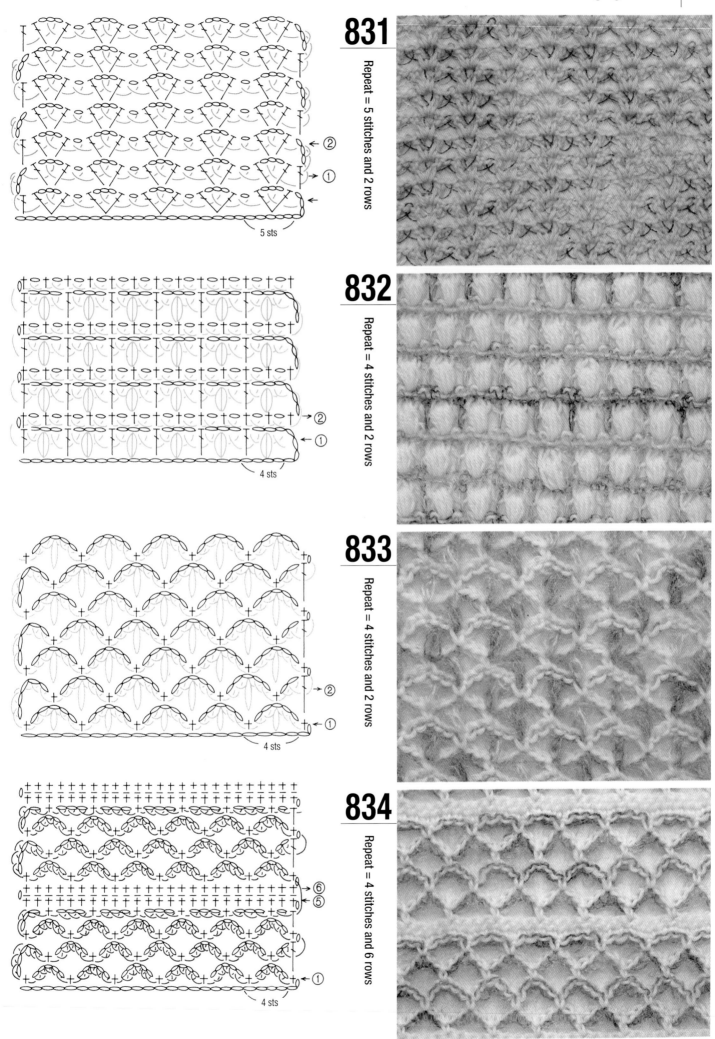

831

Repeat = 5 stitches and 2 rows

5 sts

832

Repeat = 4 stitches and 2 rows

4 sts

833

Repeat = 4 stitches and 2 rows

4 sts

834

Repeat = 4 stitches and 6 rows

4 sts

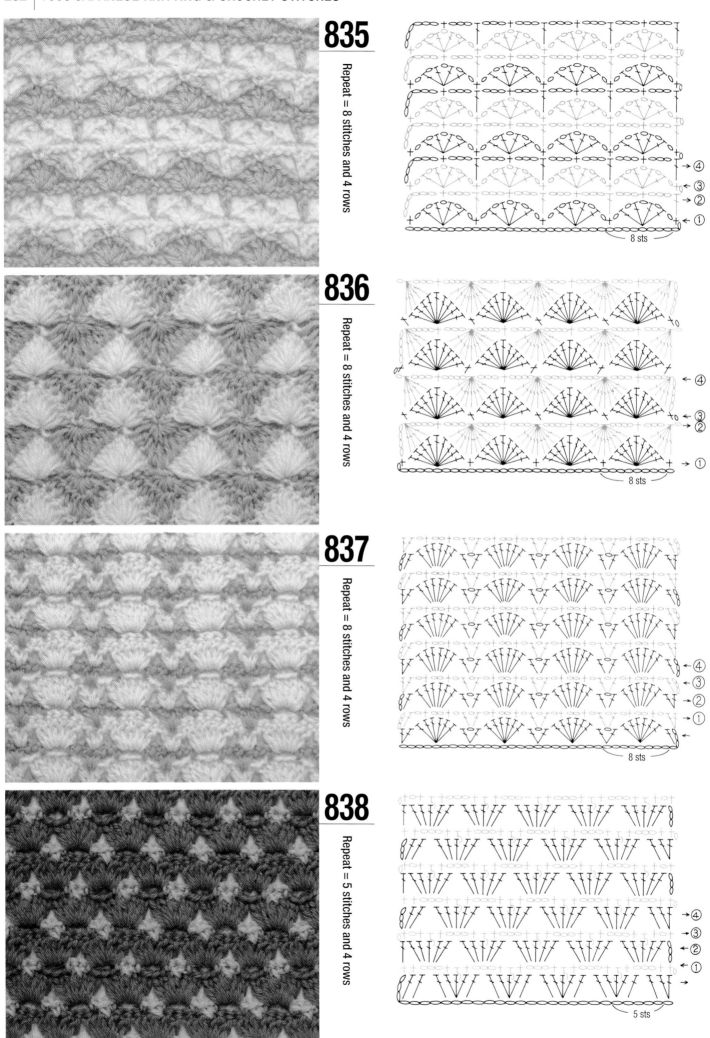

835

Repeat = 8 stitches and 4 rows

836

Repeat = 8 stitches and 4 rows

837

Repeat = 8 stitches and 4 rows

838

Repeat = 5 stitches and 4 rows

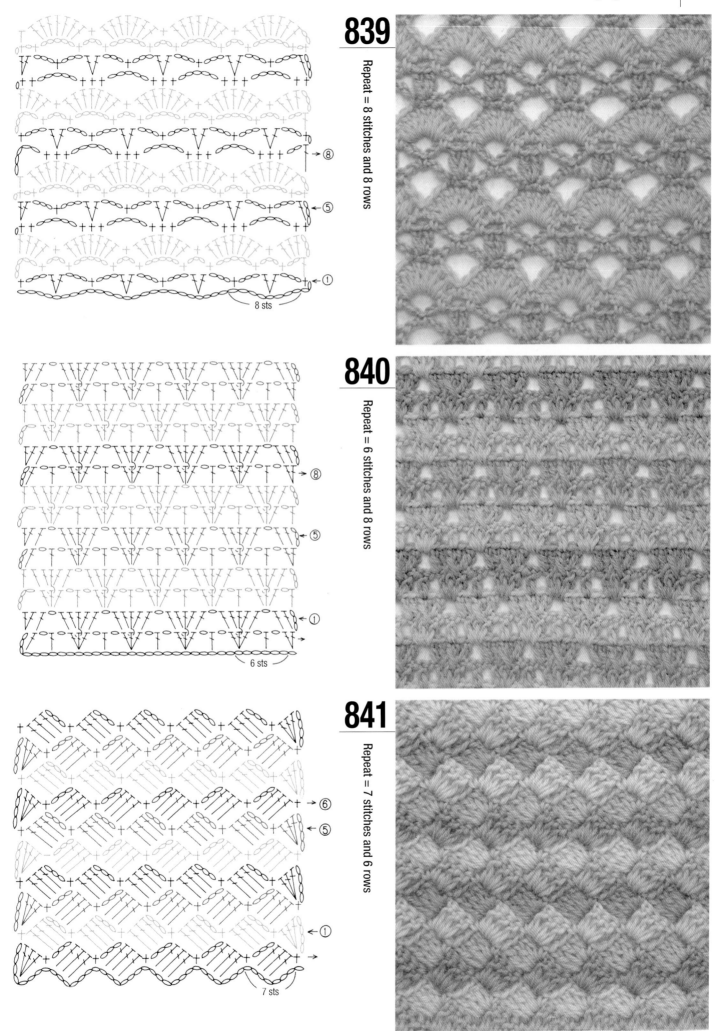

839

Repeat = 8 stitches and 8 rows

8 sts

840

Repeat = 6 stitches and 8 rows

6 sts

841

Repeat = 7 stitches and 6 rows

7 sts

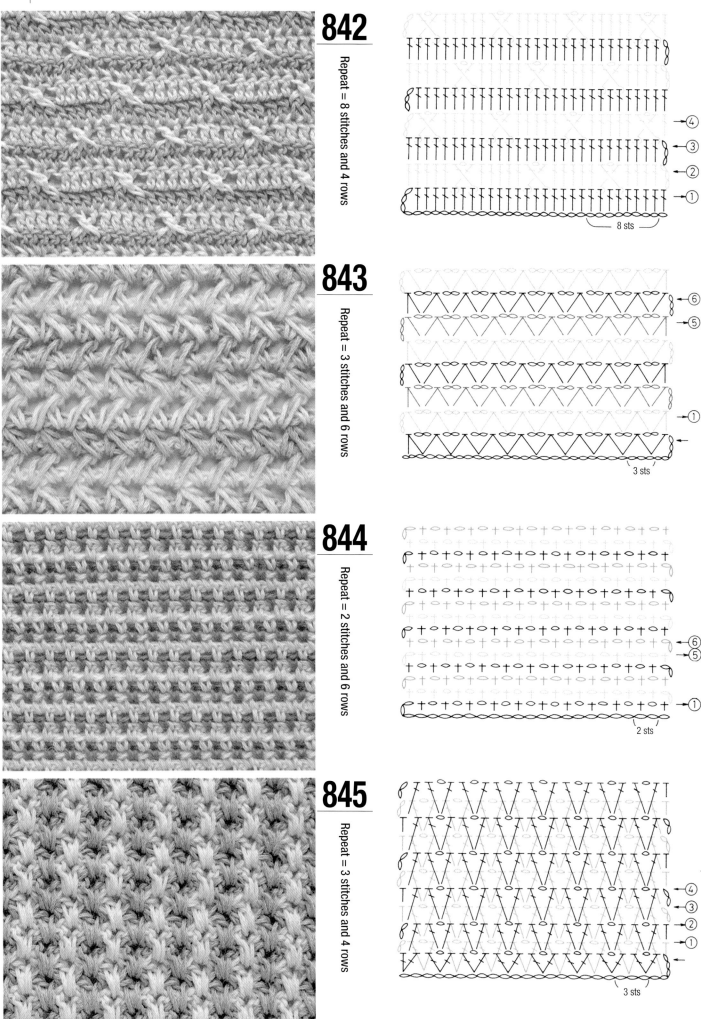

842

Repeat = 8 stitches and 4 rows

8 sts

843

Repeat = 3 stitches and 6 rows

3 sts

844

Repeat = 2 stitches and 6 rows

2 sts

845

Repeat = 3 stitches and 4 rows

3 sts

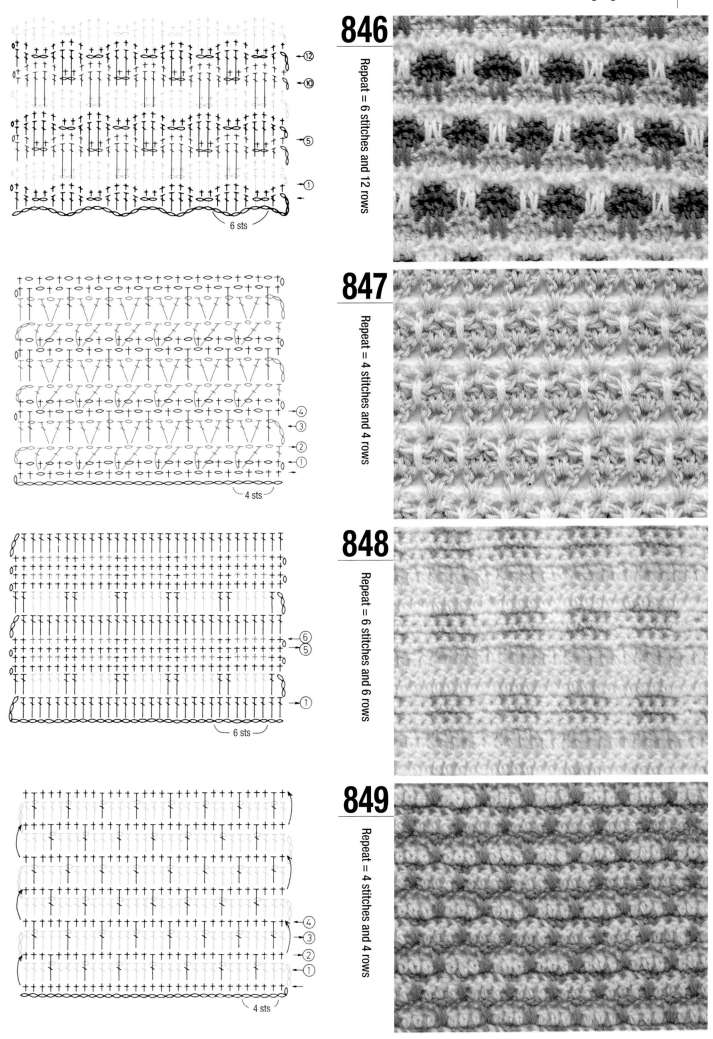

846

Repeat = 6 stitches and 12 rows

6 sts

847

Repeat = 4 stitches and 4 rows

4 sts

848

Repeat = 6 stitches and 6 rows

6 sts

849

Repeat = 4 stitches and 4 rows

4 sts

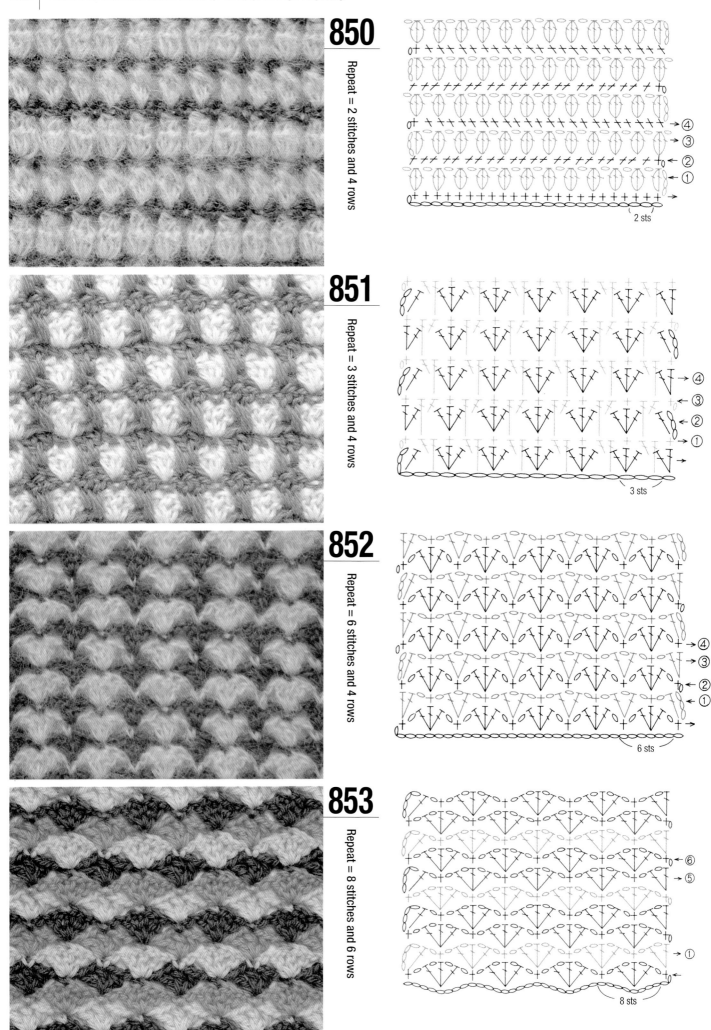

850

Repeat = 2 stitches and 4 rows

851

Repeat = 3 stitches and 4 rows

852

Repeat = 6 stitches and 4 rows

853

Repeat = 8 stitches and 6 rows

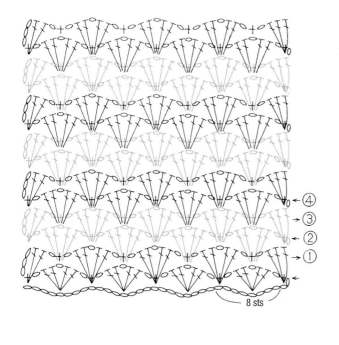

854

Repeat = 8 stitches and 4 rows

8 sts

④
③
②

855

Repeat = 8 stitches and 8 rows

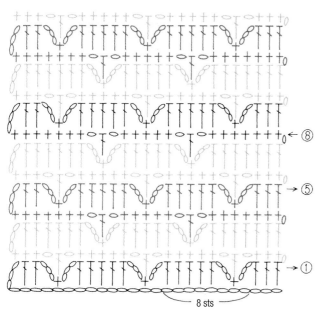

⑧
⑤
①

8 sts

856

Repeat = 6 stitches and 4 rows

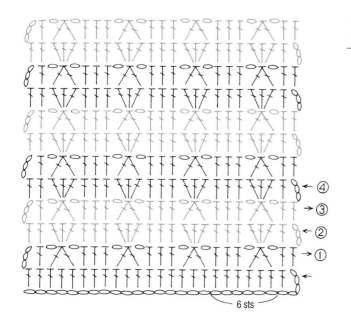

④
③
②
①

6 sts

See page 32 for notes on patterns 857, 859-865

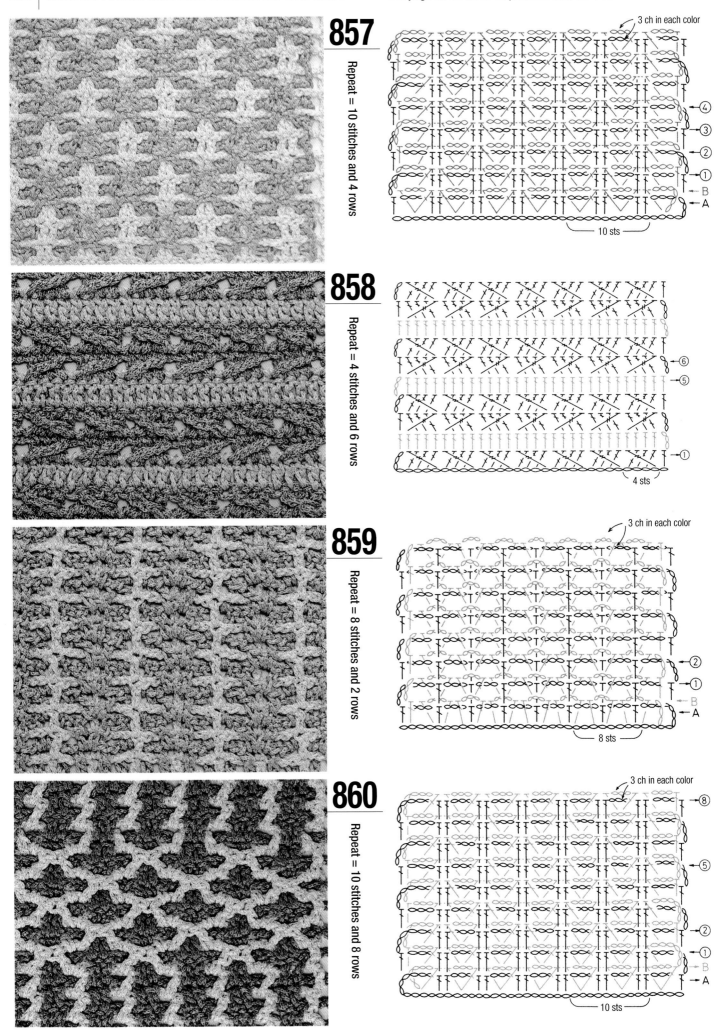

857
Repeat = 10 stitches and 4 rows

858
Repeat = 4 stitches and 6 rows

859
Repeat = 8 stitches and 2 rows

860
Repeat = 10 stitches and 8 rows

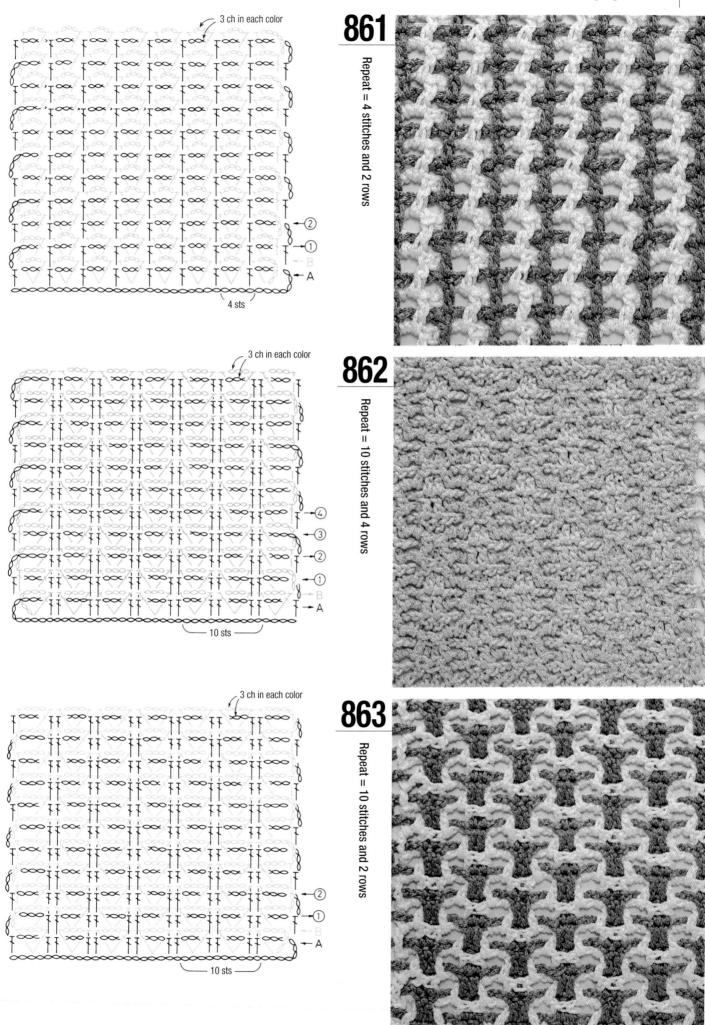

3 ch in each color

861

Repeat = 4 stitches and 2 rows

② →
① →
B →
A →

4 sts

3 ch in each color

862

Repeat = 10 stitches and 4 rows

④ →
③ →
② →
① →
B →
A →

10 sts

3 ch in each color

863

Repeat = 10 stitches and 2 rows

② →
① →
B →
A →

10 sts

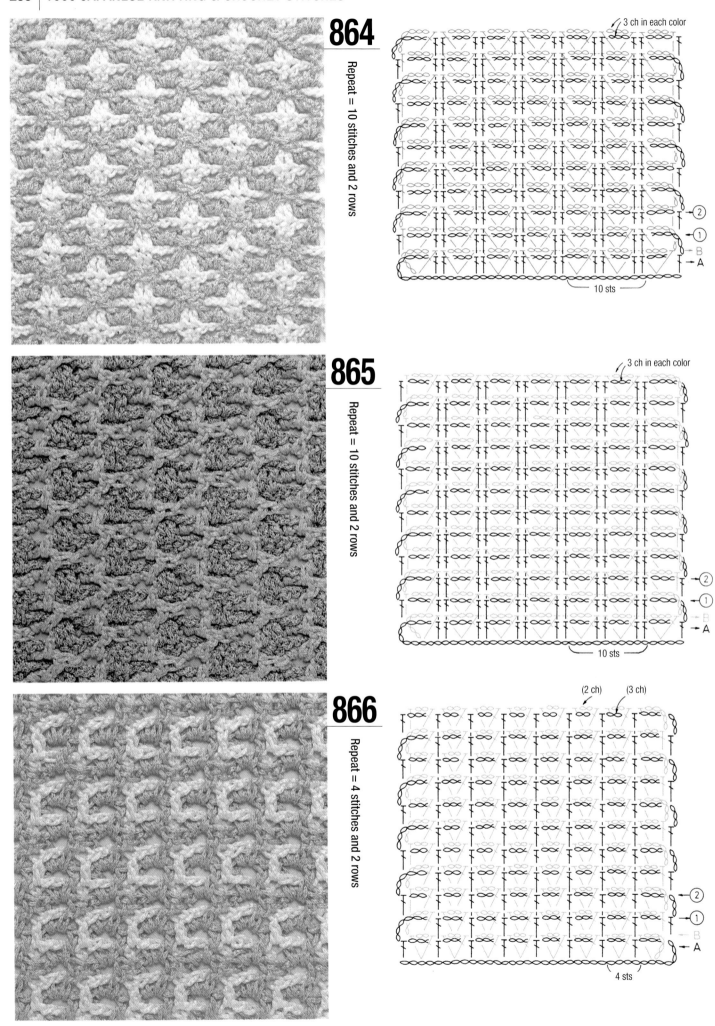

864

Repeat = 10 stitches and 2 rows

3 ch in each color

10 sts

865

Repeat = 10 stitches and 2 rows

3 ch in each color

10 sts

866

Repeat = 4 stitches and 2 rows

(2 ch)　(3 ch)

4 sts

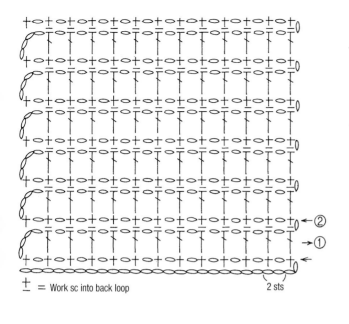

± = Work sc into back loop

2 sts

867

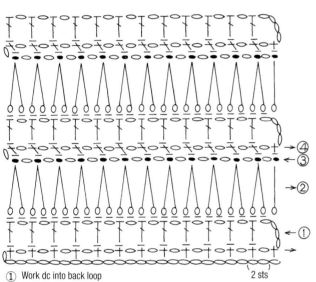

① Work dc into back loop
② Work into front loop
③ Twist each stitch before working 2 together
④ Work into front loop

2 sts

868

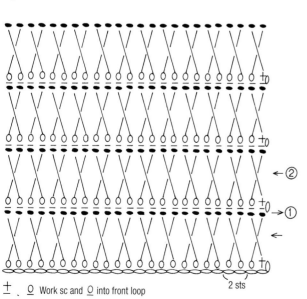

± , ọ Work sc and ọ into front loop

2 sts

868、869 see p 242

869

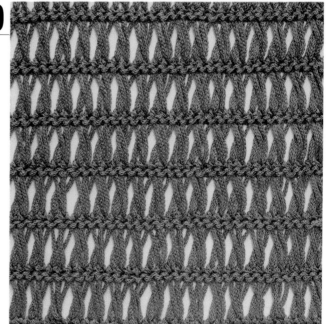

SHELL AND NET PATTERNS

"Shell" patterns take their name from the shape of the stitch. Net stitches take many forms, including the gorgeous pineapple stitch. The many ways to use dc and ch give a special flavor to these patterns.

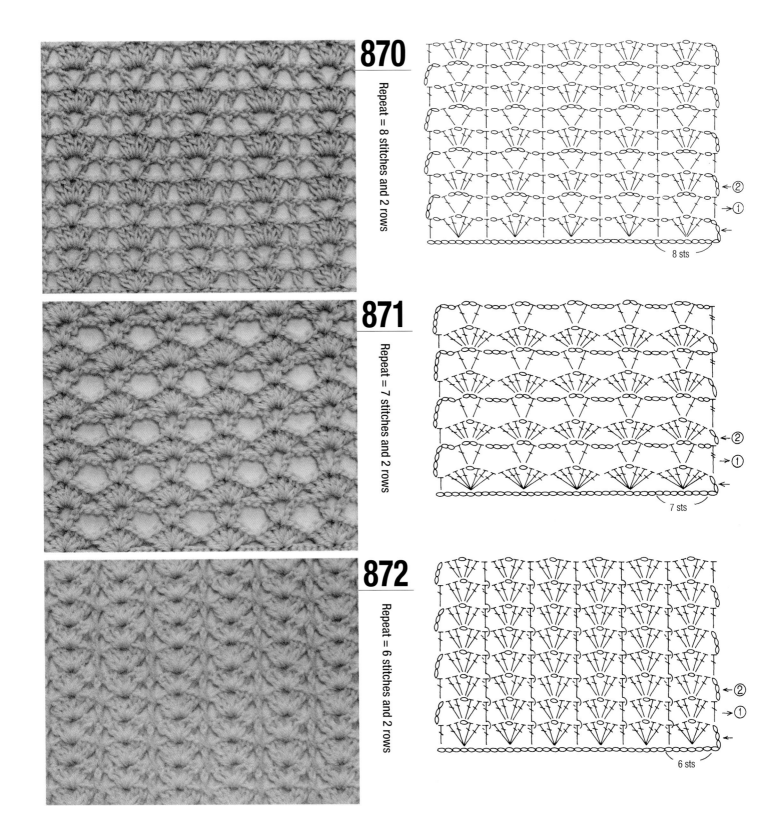

870

Repeat = 8 stitches and 2 rows

8 sts

871

Repeat = 7 stitches and 2 rows

7 sts

872

Repeat = 6 stitches and 2 rows

6 sts

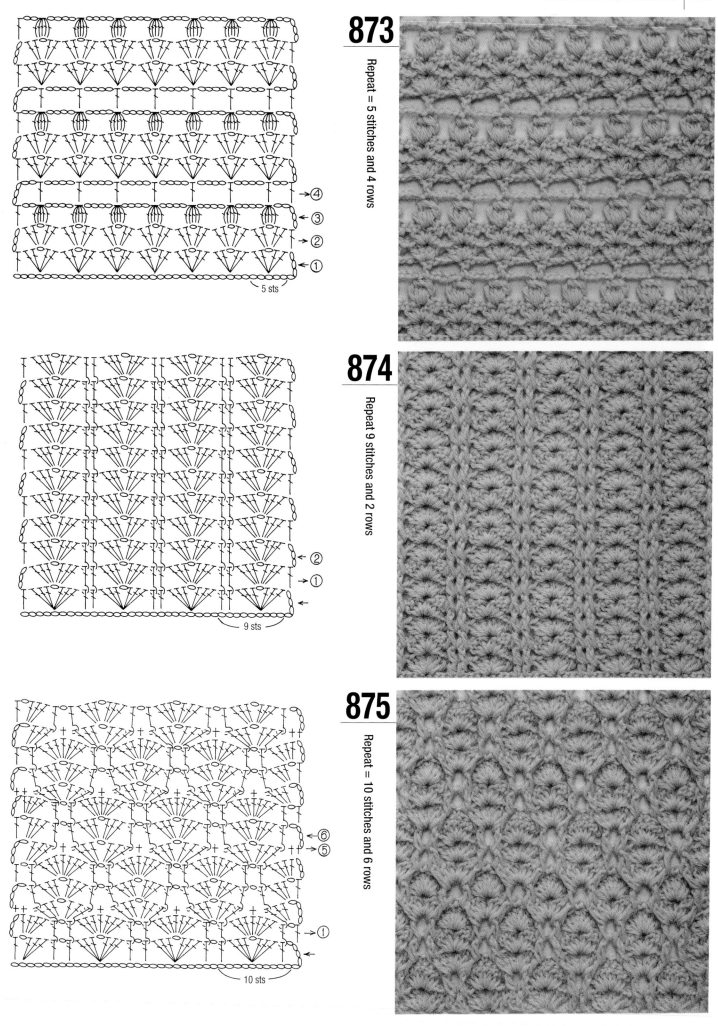

873

Repeat = 5 stitches and 4 rows

5 sts

874

Repeat 9 stitches and 2 rows

9 sts

875

Repeat = 10 stitches and 6 rows

10 sts

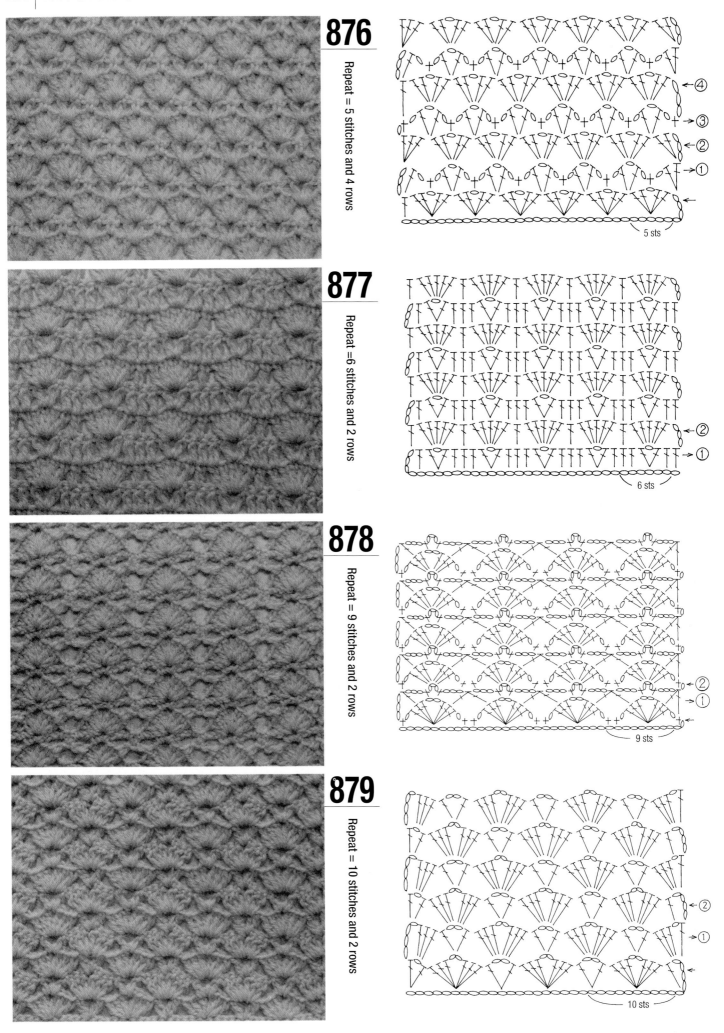

876

Repeat = 5 stitches and 4 rows

877

Repeat = 6 stitches and 2 rows

878

Repeat = 9 stitches and 2 rows

879

Repeat = 10 stitches and 2 rows

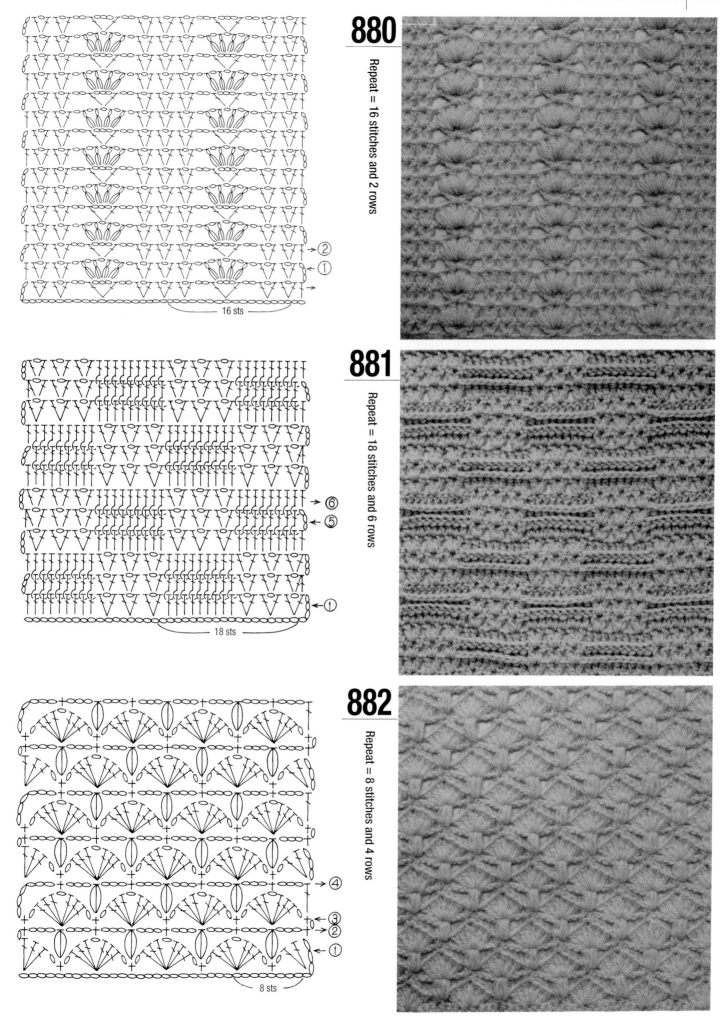

880

Repeat = 16 stitches and 2 rows

16 sts

881

Repeat = 18 stitches and 6 rows

18 sts

882

Repeat = 8 stitches and 4 rows

8 sts

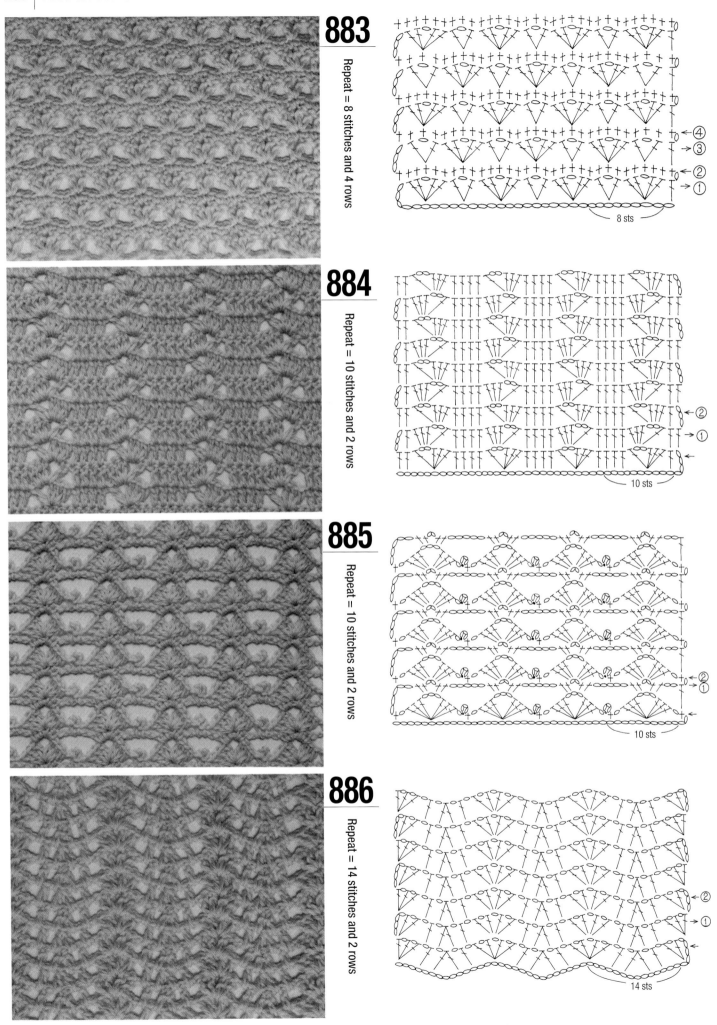

883

Repeat = 8 stitches and 4 rows

8 sts

884

Repeat = 10 stitches and 2 rows

10 sts

885

Repeat = 10 stitches and 2 rows

10 sts

886

Repeat = 14 stitches and 2 rows

14 sts

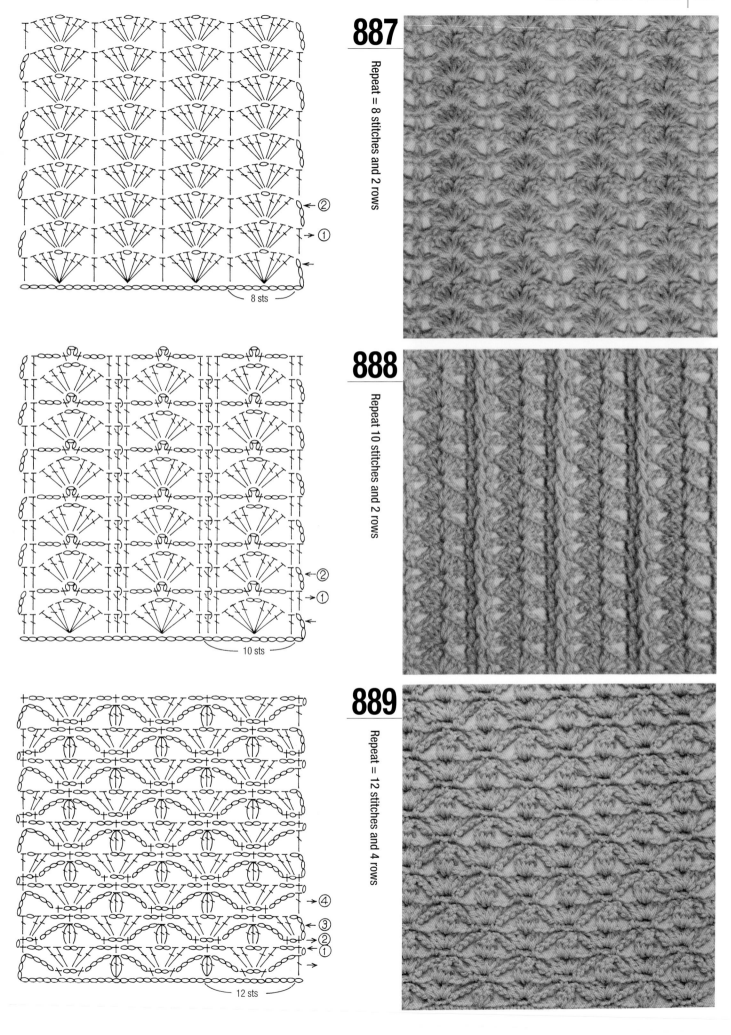

887

Repeat = 8 stitches and 2 rows

8 sts

888

Repeat 10 stitches and 2 rows

10 sts

889

Repeat = 12 stitches and 4 rows

12 sts

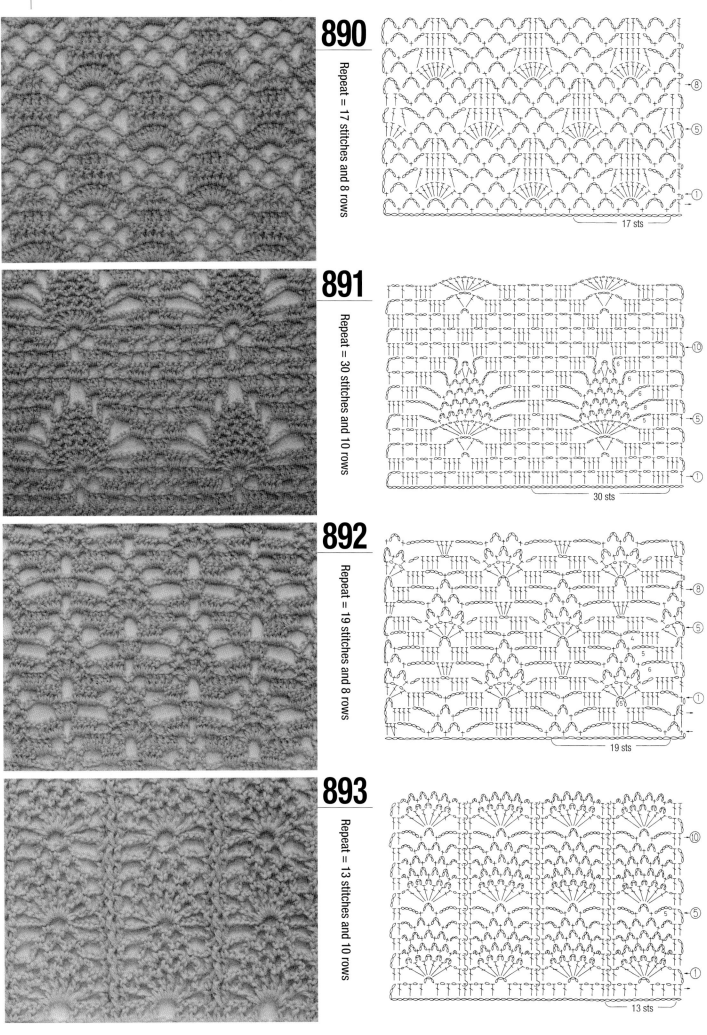

890
Repeat = 17 stitches and 8 rows

17 sts

891
Repeat = 30 stitches and 10 rows

30 sts

892
Repeat = 19 stitches and 8 rows

19 sts

893
Repeat = 13 stitches and 10 rows

13 sts

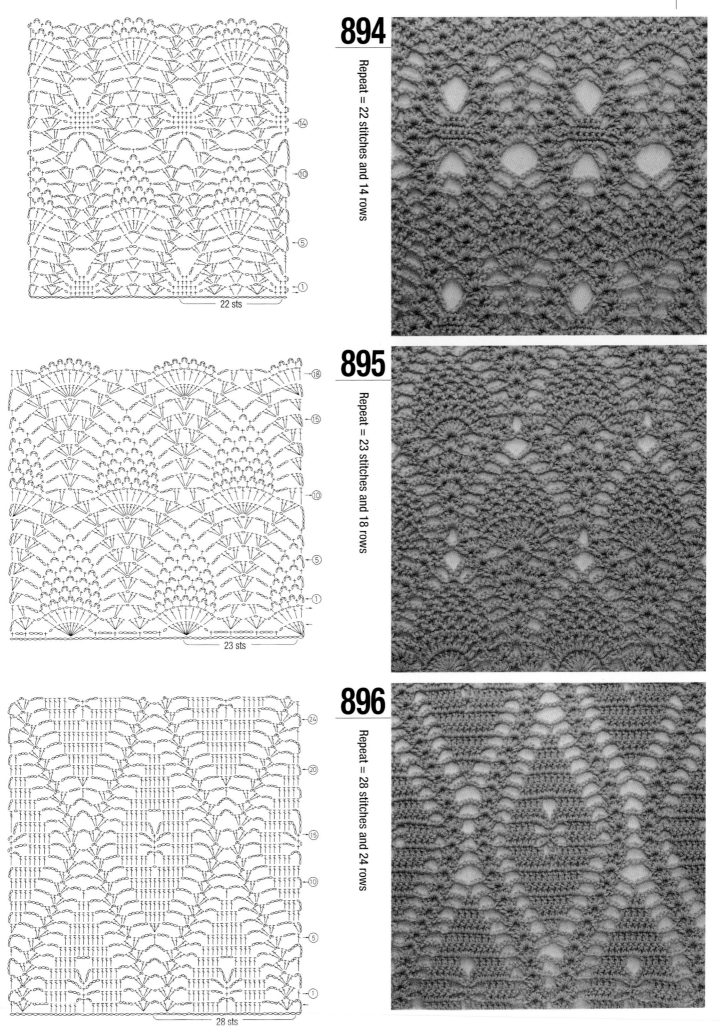

894

Repeat = 22 stitches and 14 rows

22 sts

895

Repeat = 23 stitches and 18 rows

23 sts

896

Repeat = 28 stitches and 24 rows

28 sts

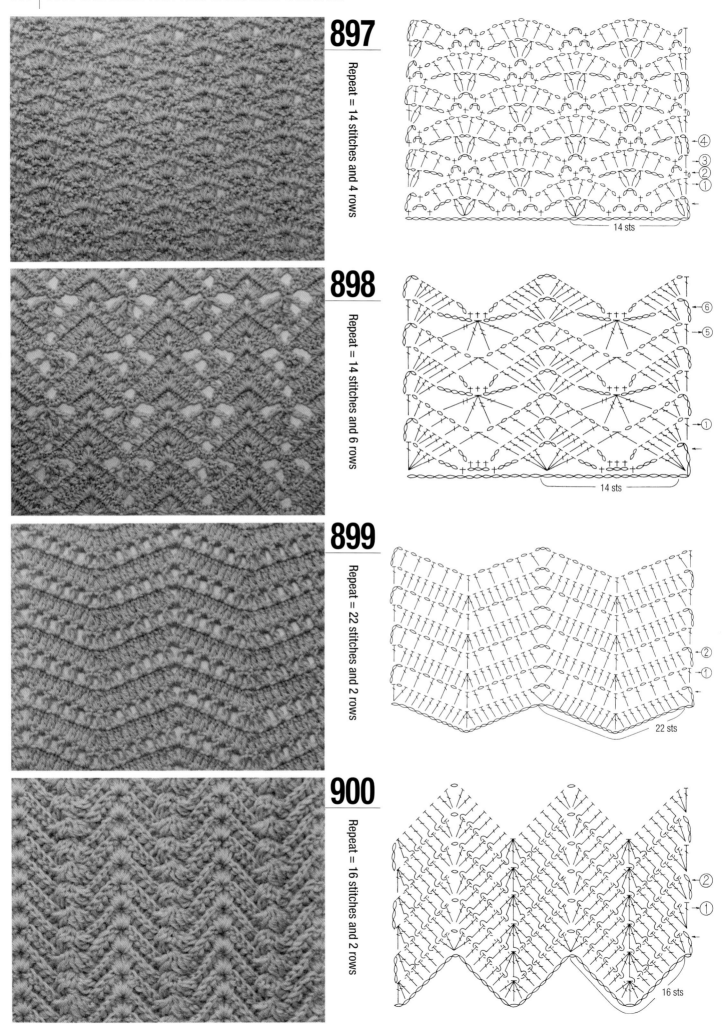

897

Repeat = 14 stitches and 4 rows

14 sts

898

Repeat = 14 stitches and 6 rows

14 sts

899

Repeat = 22 stitches and 2 rows

22 sts

900

Repeat = 16 stitches and 2 rows

16 sts

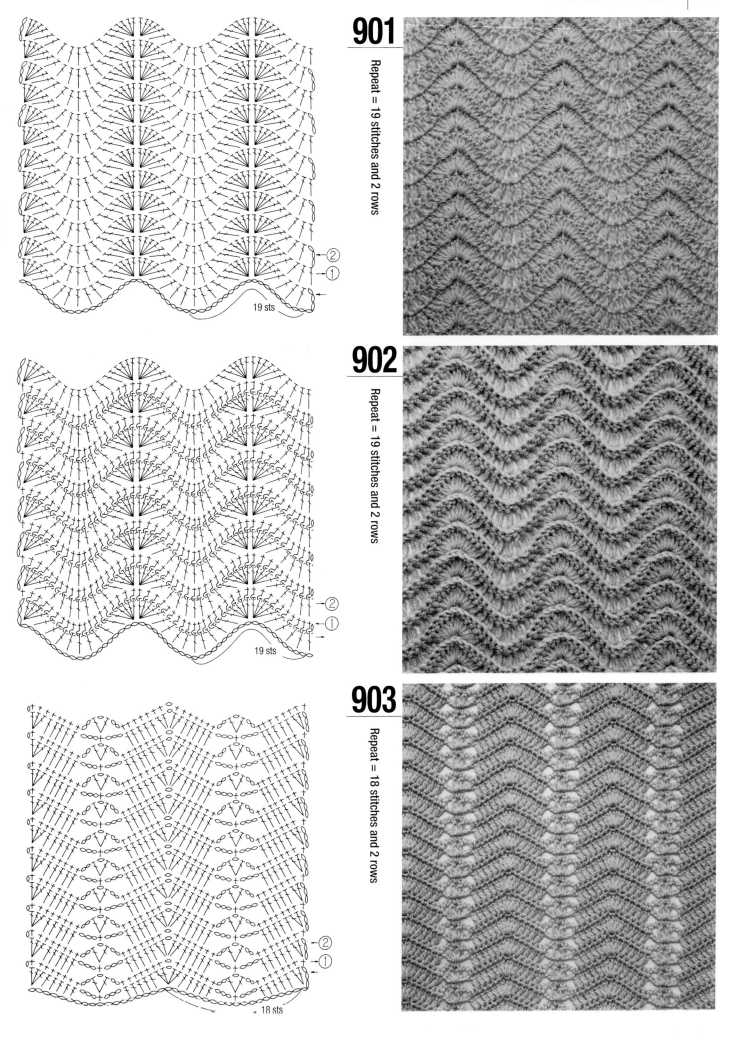

901

Repeat = 19 stitches and 2 rows

19 sts

902

Repeat = 19 stitches and 2 rows

19 sts

903

Repeat = 18 stitches and 2 rows

18 sts

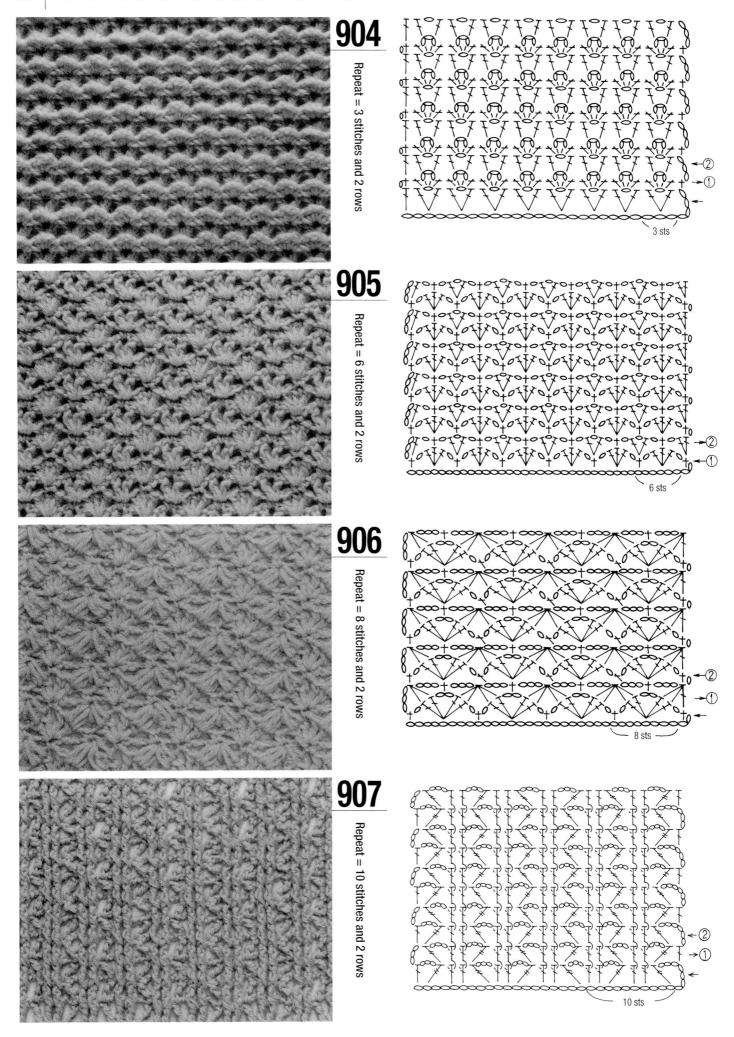

904

Repeat = 3 stitches and 2 rows

3 sts

905

Repeat = 6 stitches and 2 rows

6 sts

906

Repeat = 8 stitches and 2 rows

8 sts

907

Repeat = 10 stitches and 2 rows

10 sts

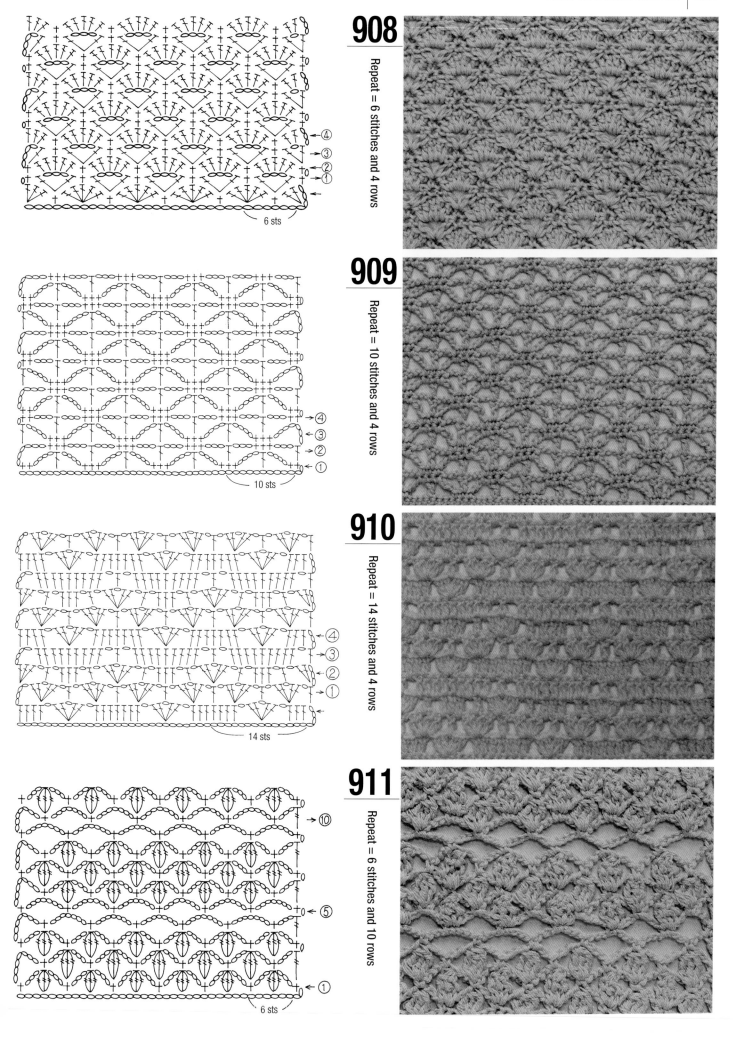

908
Repeat = 6 stitches and 4 rows

6 sts
④ ③ ② ①

909
Repeat = 10 stitches and 4 rows

10 sts
④ ③ ② ①

910
Repeat = 14 stitches and 4 rows

14 sts
④ ③ ② ①

911
Repeat = 6 stitches and 10 rows

6 sts
⑩ ⑤ ①

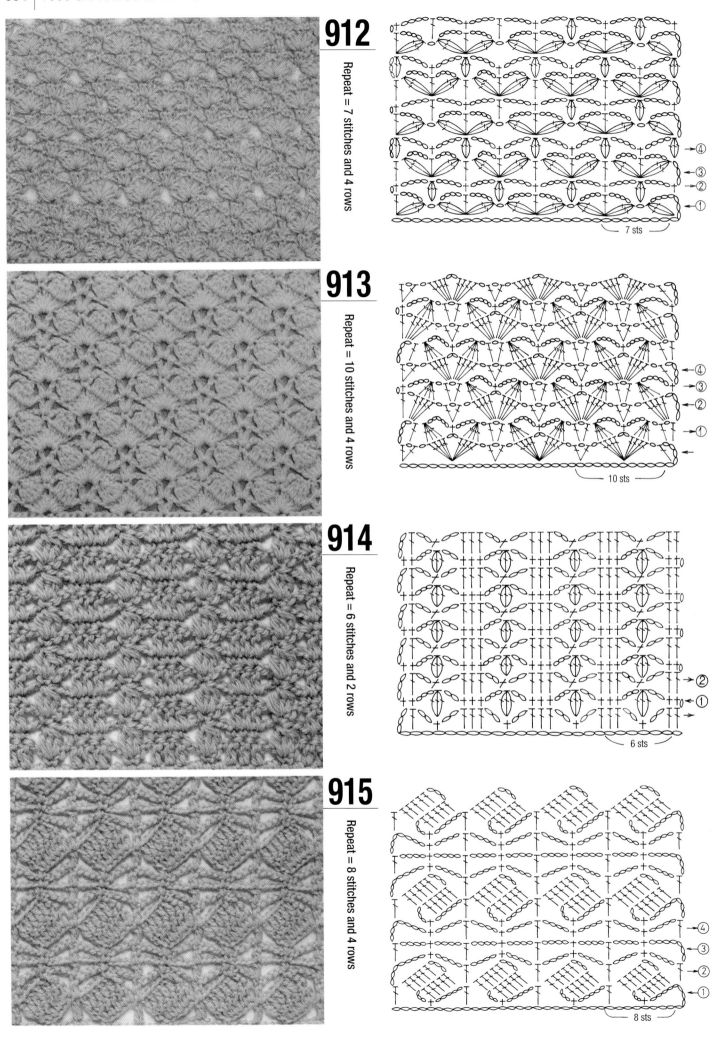

912
Repeat = 7 stitches and 4 rows

7 sts

913
Repeat = 10 stitches and 4 rows

10 sts

914
Repeat = 6 stitches and 2 rows

6 sts

915
Repeat = 8 stitches and 4 rows

8 sts

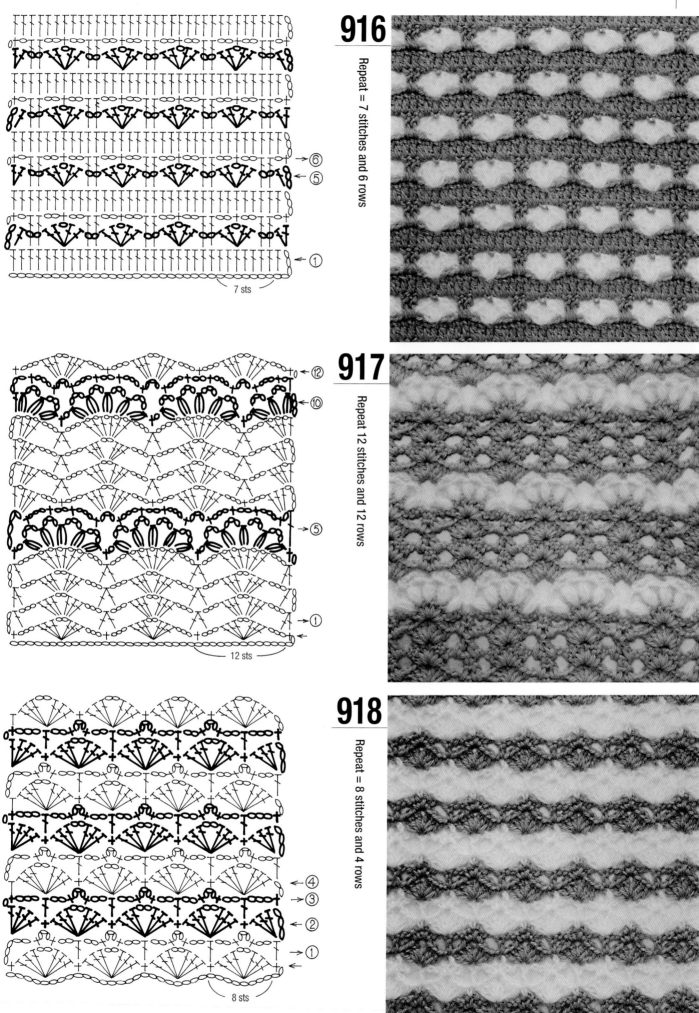

916

Repeat = 7 stitches and 6 rows

7 sts

917

Repeat 12 stitches and 12 rows

12 sts

918

Repeat = 8 stitches and 4 rows

8 sts

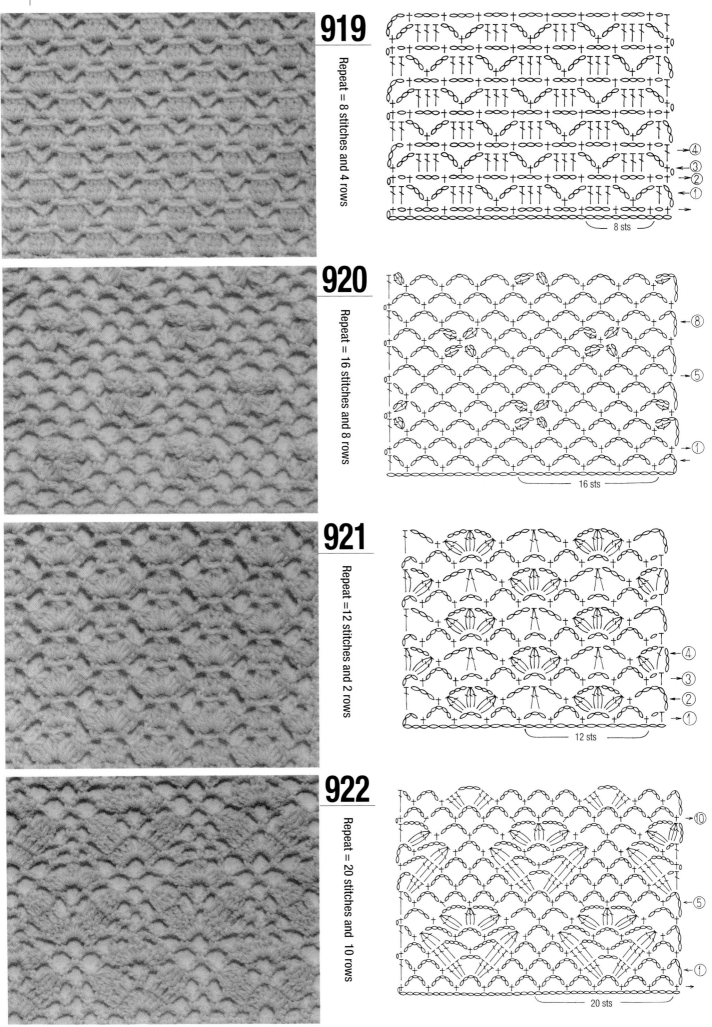

919

Repeat = 8 stitches and 4 rows

8 sts

920

Repeat = 16 stitches and 8 rows

16 sts

921

Repeat = 12 stitches and 2 rows

12 sts

922

Repeat = 20 stitches and 10 rows

20 sts

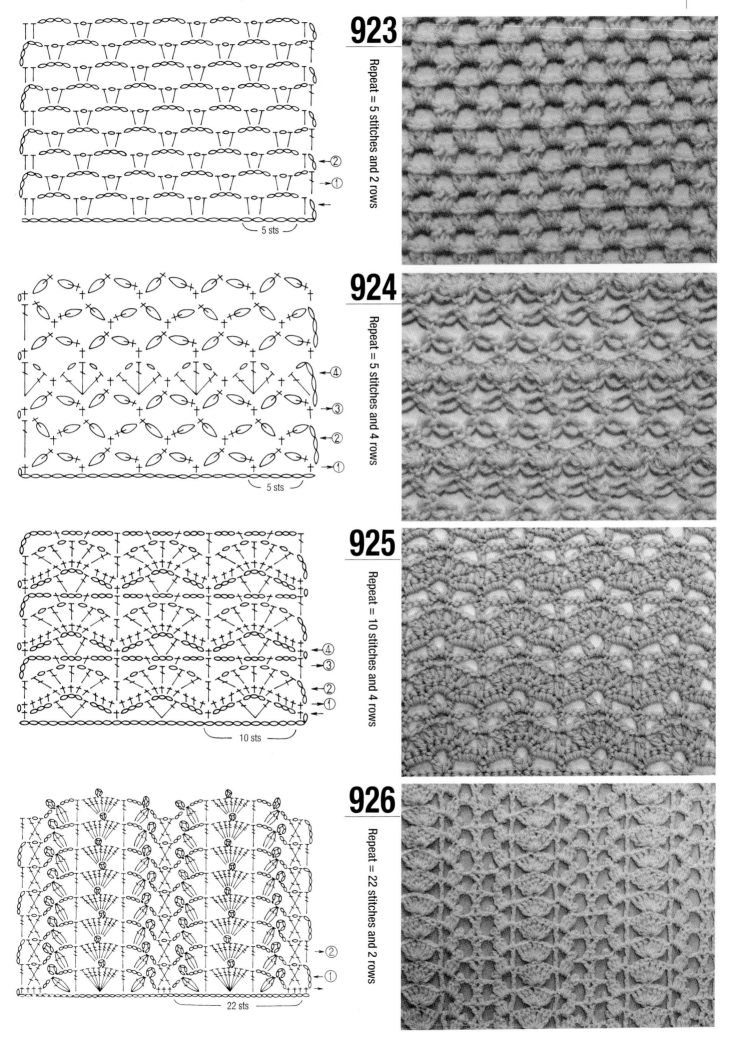

923

Repeat = 5 stitches and 2 rows

5 sts

924

Repeat = 5 stitches and 4 rows

5 sts

925

Repeat = 10 stitches and 4 rows

10 sts

926

Repeat = 22 stitches and 2 rows

22 sts

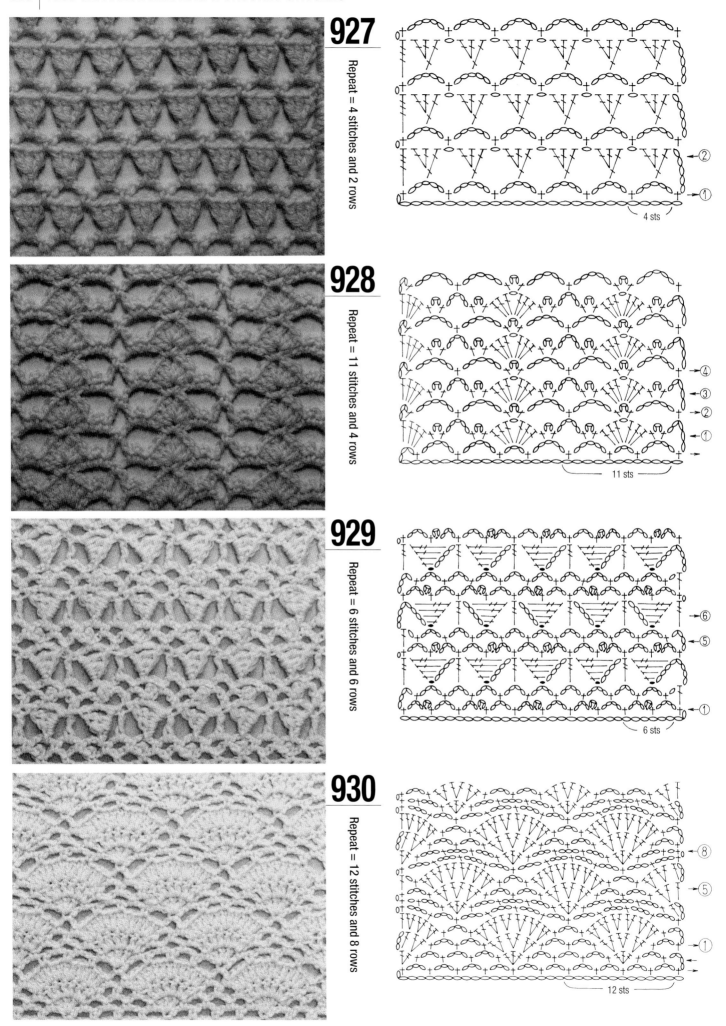

927

Repeat = 4 stitches and 2 rows

4 sts

928

Repeat = 11 stitches and 4 rows

11 sts

929

Repeat = 6 stitches and 6 rows

6 sts

930

Repeat = 12 stitches and 8 rows

12 sts

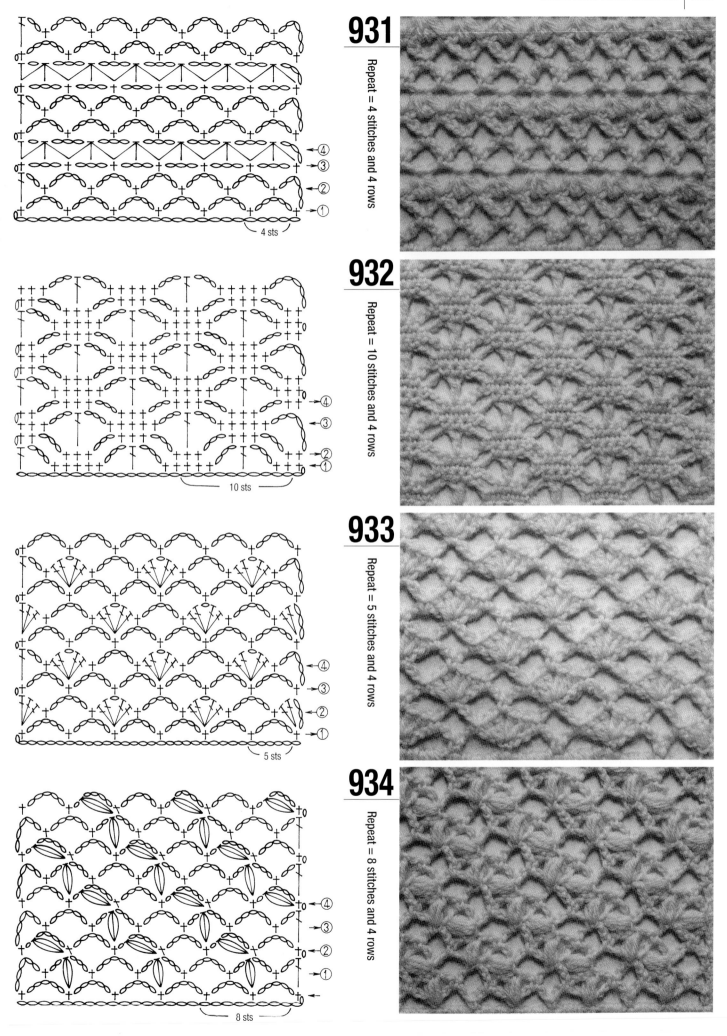

931

Repeat = 4 stitches and 4 rows

4 sts

932

Repeat = 10 stitches and 4 rows

10 sts

933

Repeat = 5 stitches and 4 rows

5 sts

934

Repeat = 8 stitches and 4 rows

8 sts

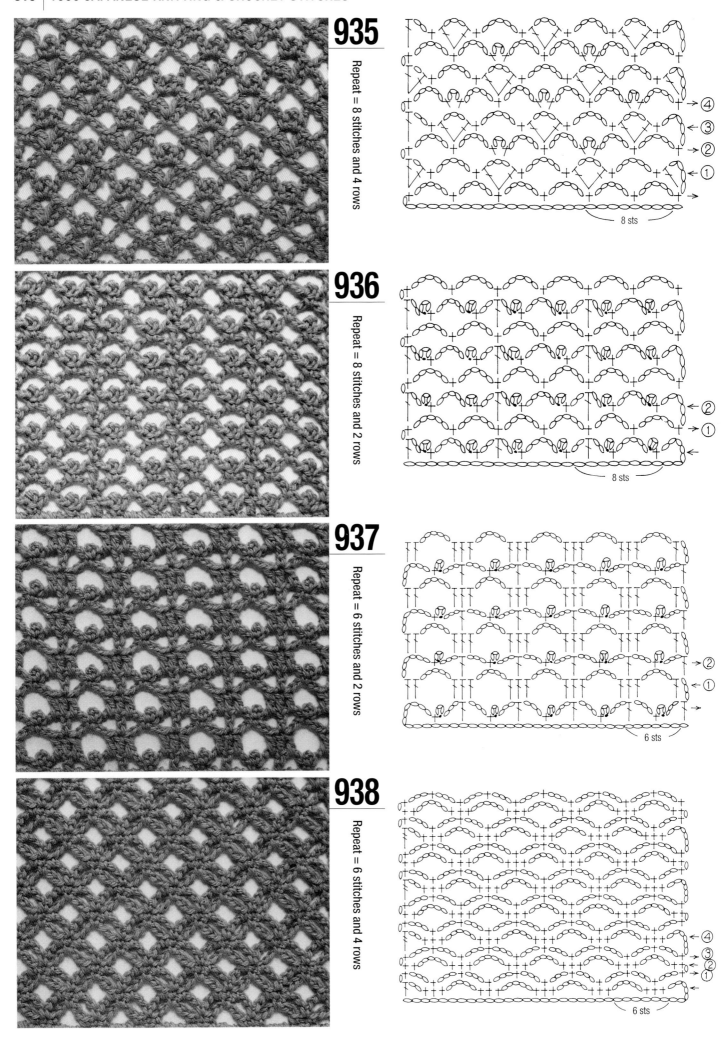

935

Repeat = 8 stitches and 4 rows

8 sts

936

Repeat = 8 stitches and 2 rows

8 sts

937

Repeat = 6 stitches and 2 rows

6 sts

938

Repeat = 6 stitches and 4 rows

6 sts

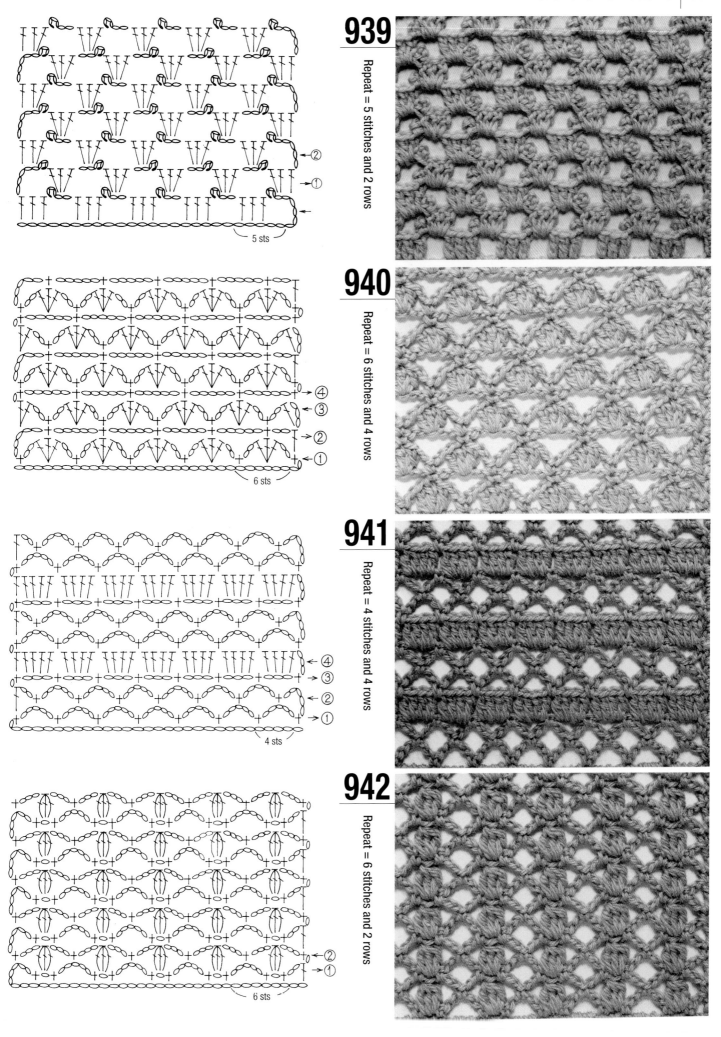

939

Repeat = 5 stitches and 2 rows

5 sts

940

Repeat = 6 stitches and 4 rows

6 sts

941

Repeat = 4 stitches and 4 rows

4 sts

942

Repeat = 6 stitches and 2 rows

6 sts

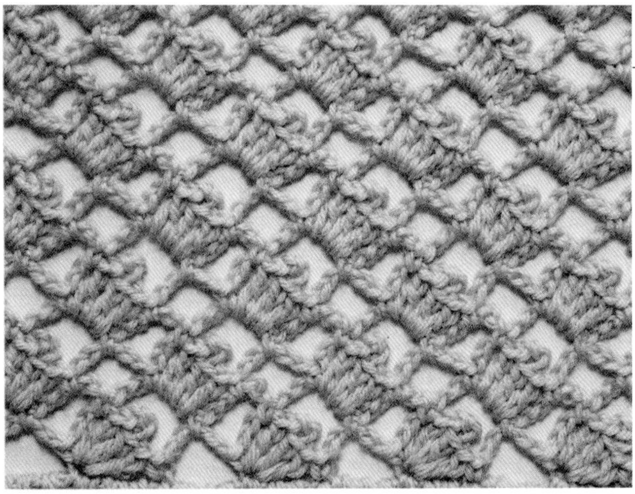

943

Repeat = 9 stitches and 4 rows

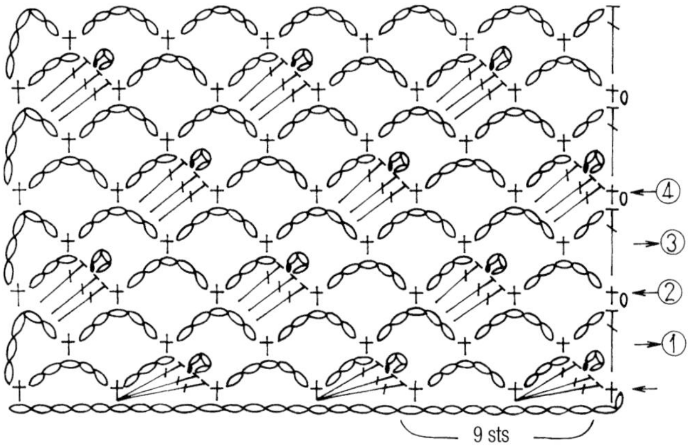

9 sts

944

Repeat = 6 stitches and 2 rows

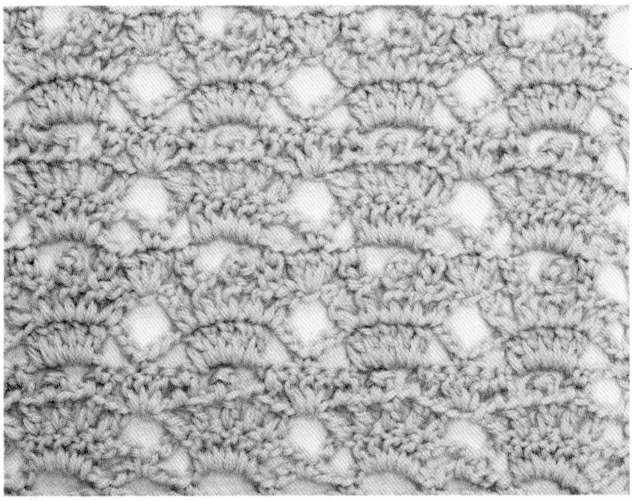

6 sts

945

Repeat = 10 stitches and 6 rows

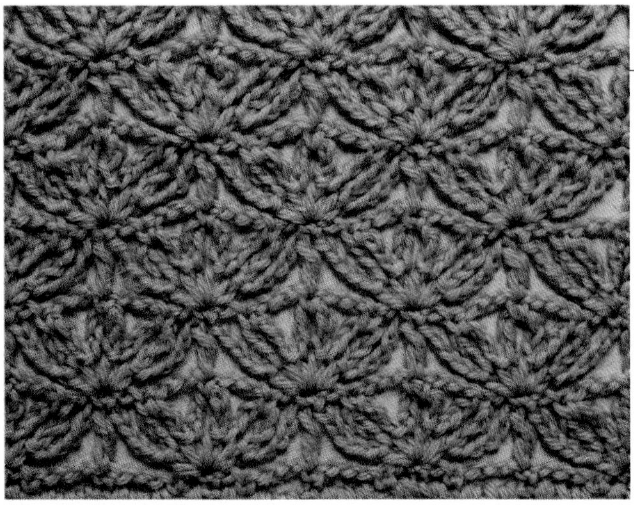

10 sts

946

Repeat = 12 stitches and 4 rows

12 sts

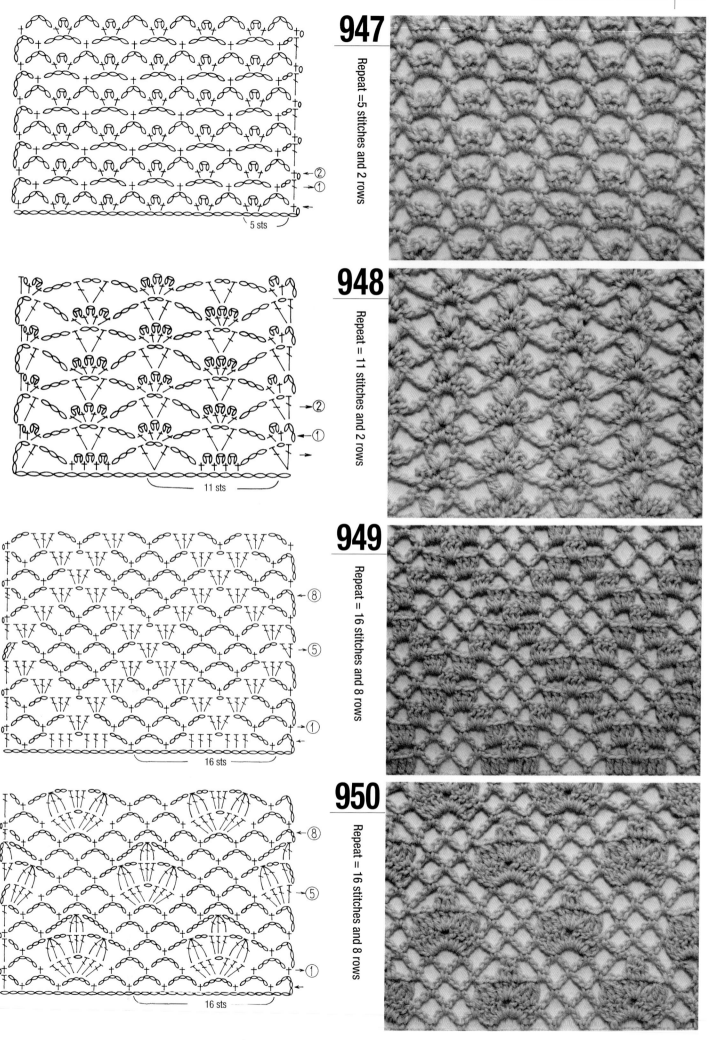

947

Repeat = 5 stitches and 2 rows

5 sts

948

Repeat = 11 stitches and 2 rows

11 sts

949

Repeat = 16 stitches and 8 rows

16 sts

950

Repeat = 16 stitches and 8 rows

16 sts

EDGINGS

These stitch patterns create edges, hems and decoration. When you add an ornamental edging, the garment looks gorgeous and polished. There is no end to the way you can change and combine stitches to enhance the finished product.

Note each edging has a fixed number of rows, so there is no row repeat given.

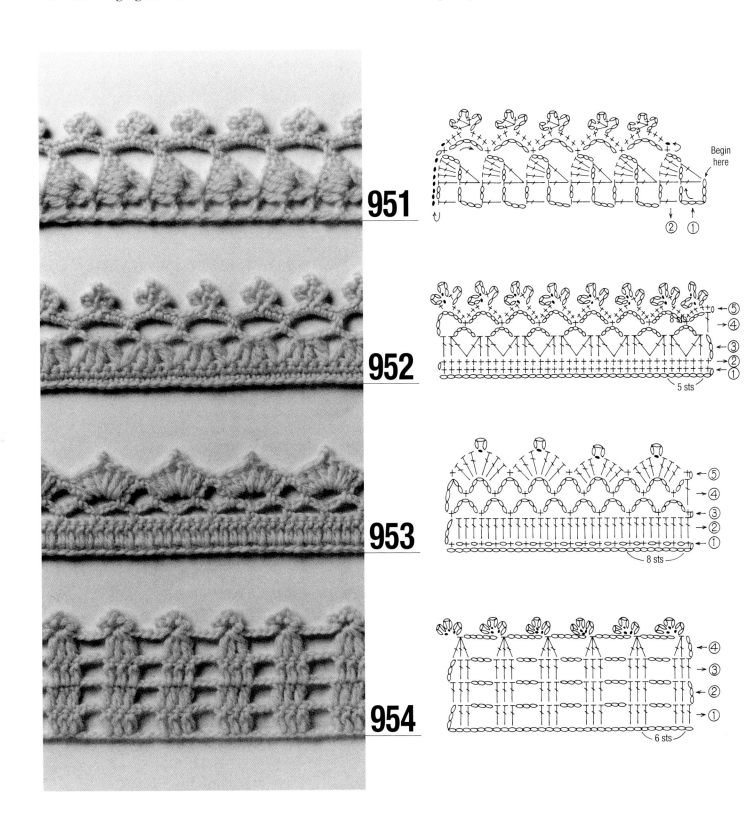

951

952

953

954

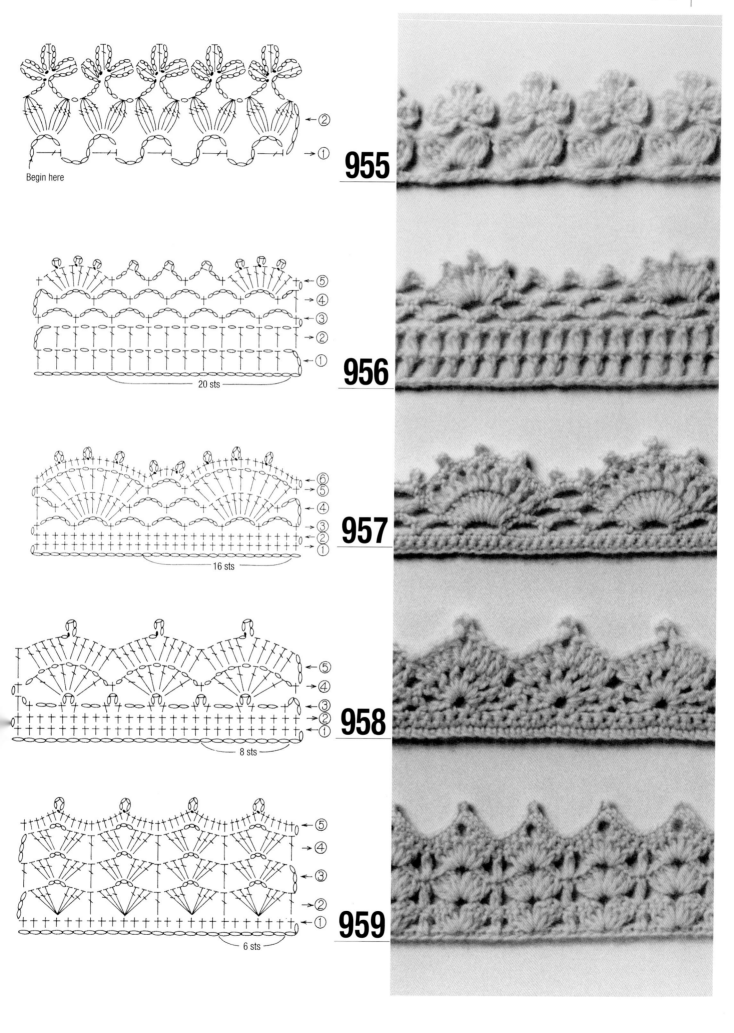

Begin here

955

20 sts

956

16 sts

957

8 sts

958

6 sts

959

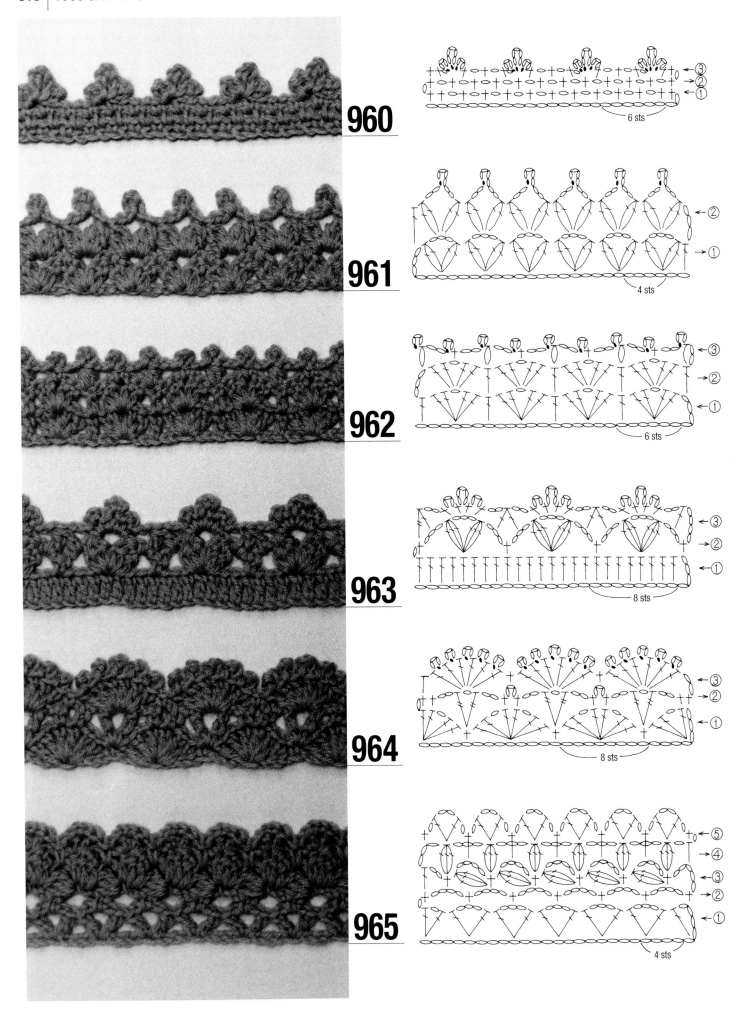

960

961

962

963

964

965

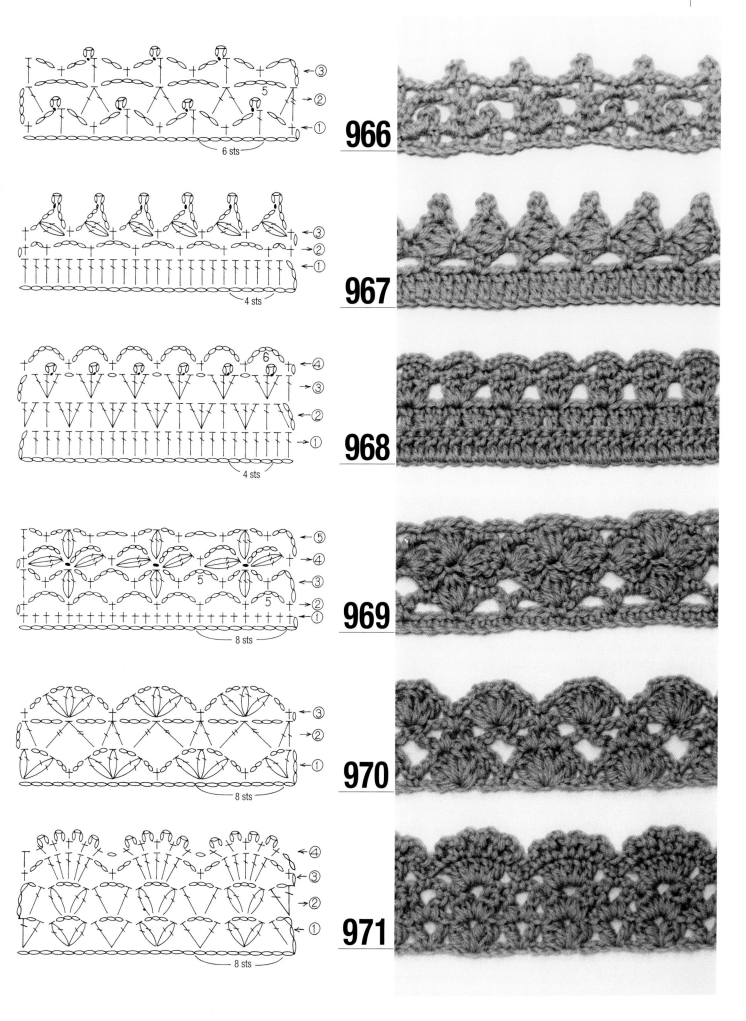

966

967

968

969

970

971

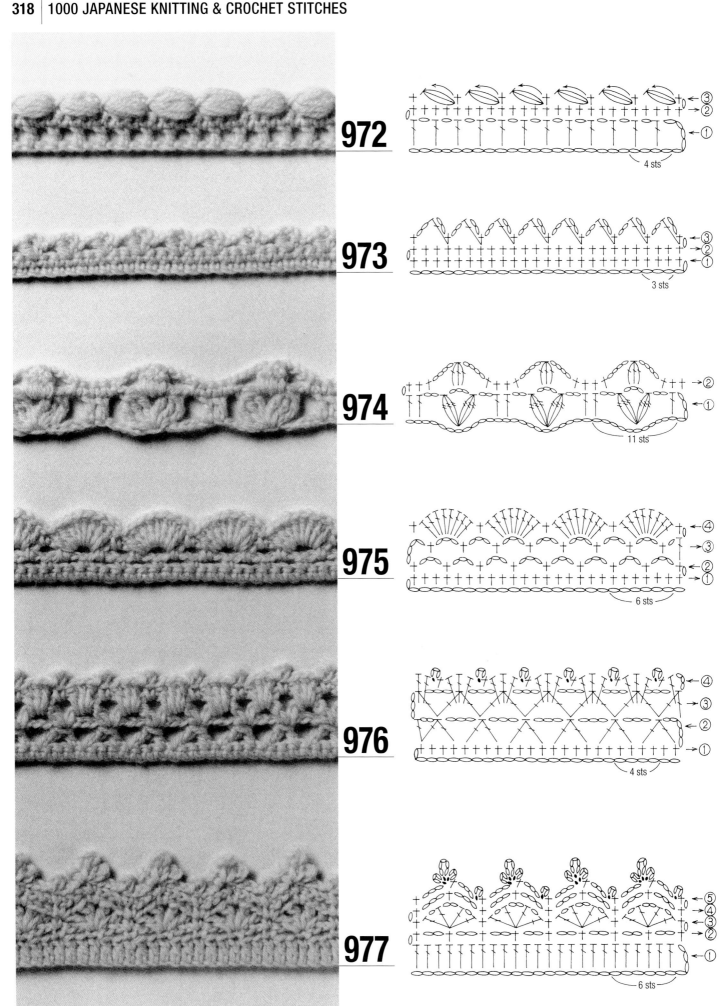

972

973

974

975

976

977

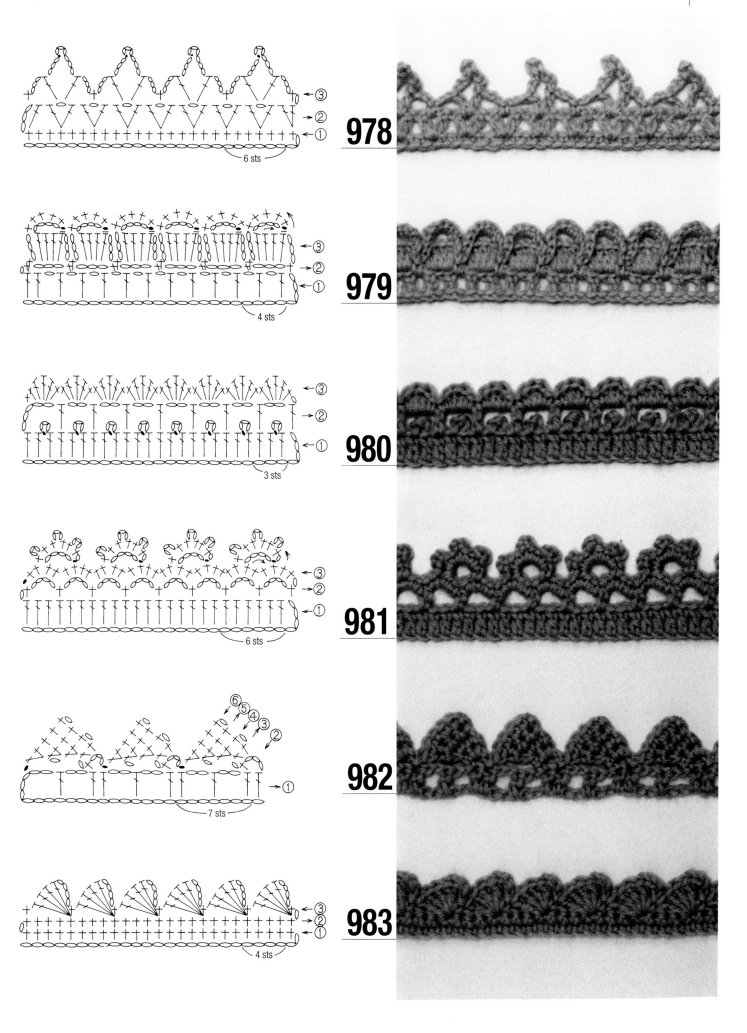

978

979

980

981

982

983

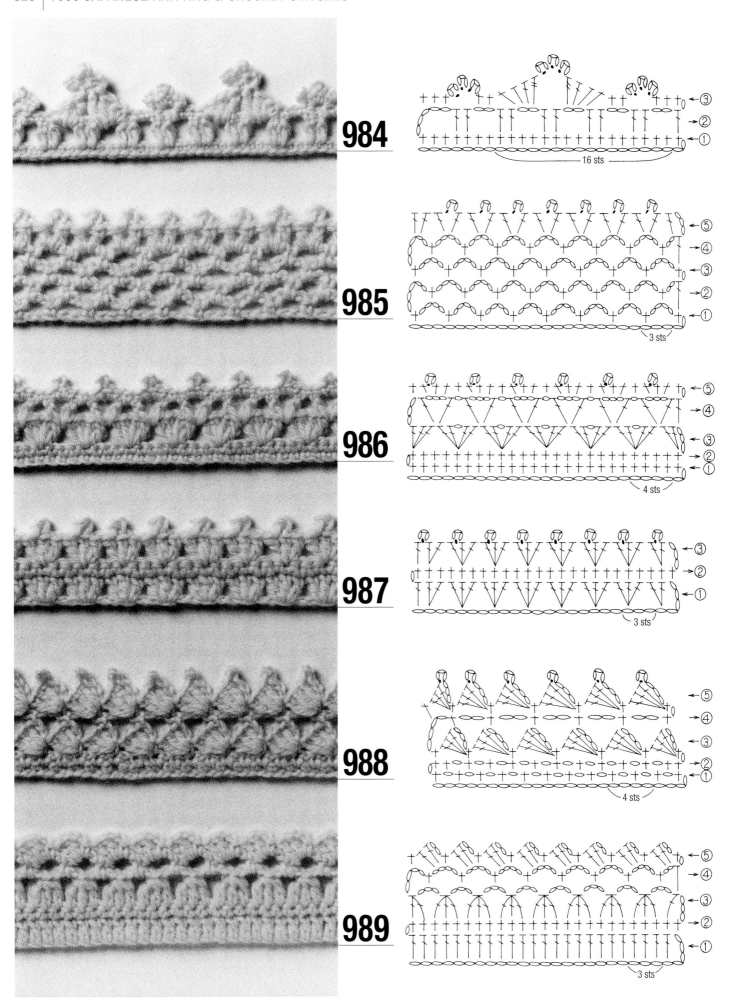

984

985

986

987

988

989

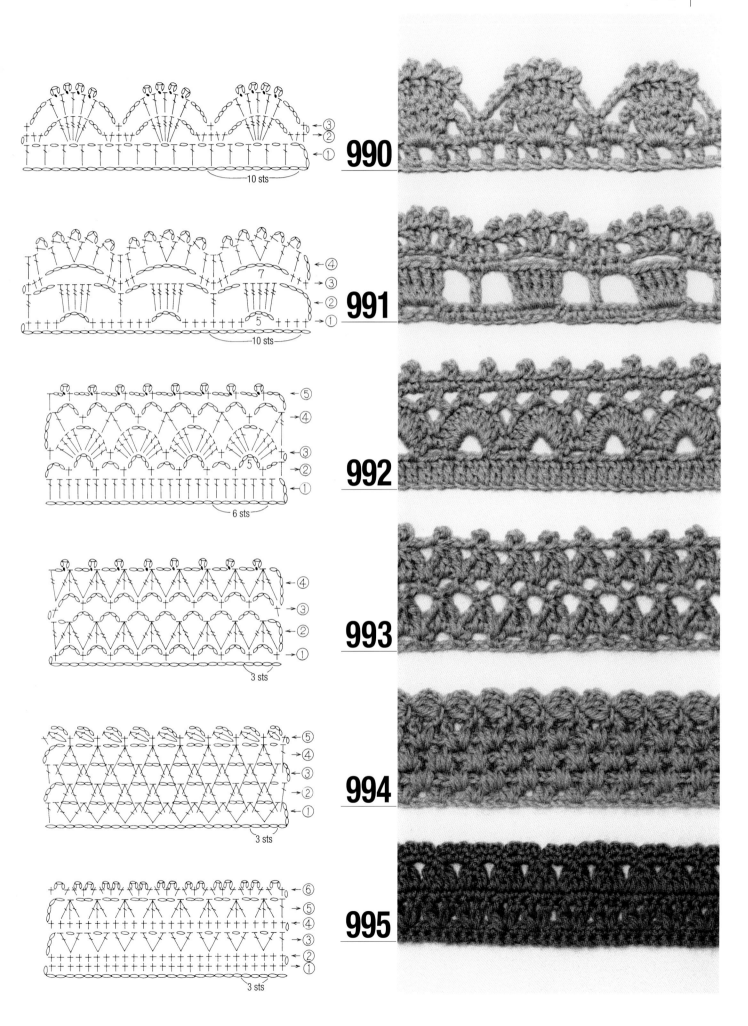

990

991

992

993

994

995

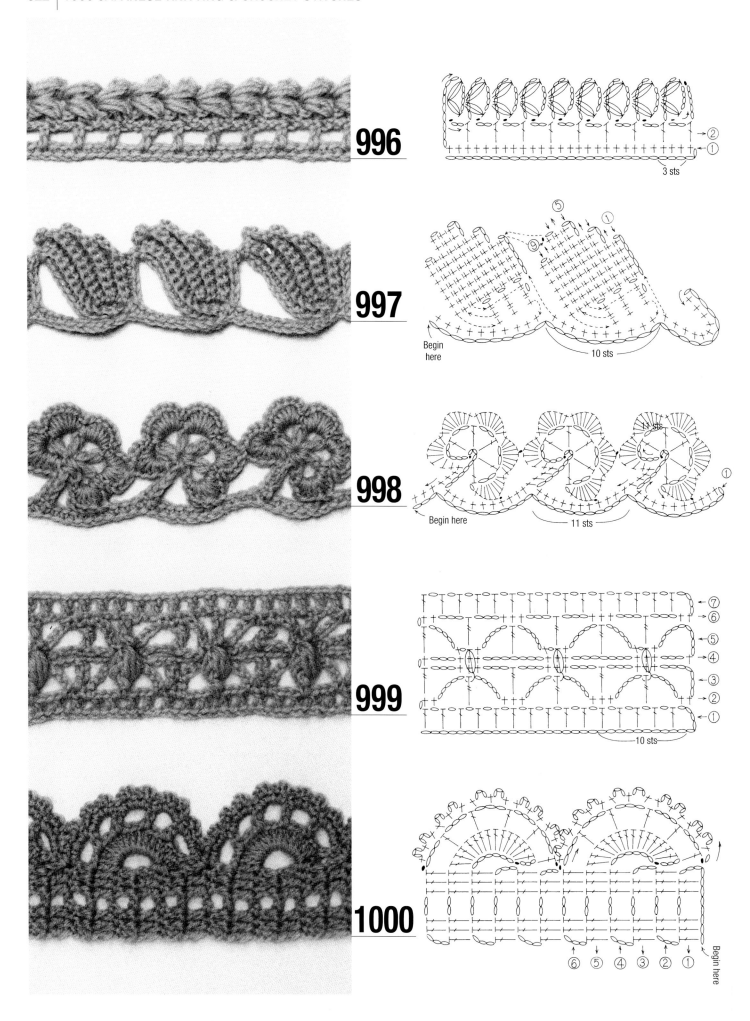

996

997

Begin here

10 sts

998

Begin here

11 sts

999

10 sts

1000

Begin here

ADDITIONAL KNITTING SYMBOLS

The additional symbols in this table are not illustrated in the technique section. However, most of them appear more than once throughout the charts, so definitions are included as a convenience.

SYMBOL	DEFINITION
Increases	
	M1 increase: Make one: with tip of RN, pick up the strand of yarn before the next stitch on LN and ktbl (or ptbl if picking up in purl)
7	k, yo, k, yo, k, yo, k into same st (1 st becomes 7)
5	3-to-5 increase: work a CDD: sl 2 tog knitwise, k1, p2sso but do not remove st from LN; then yo, k, yo, k into the same sts
Decreases	
	P3tog
	RS: k5tog WS: p5tog
	Centered quadruple dec: sl 3 sts tog knitwise, k2tog, p3sso This st may also appear elongated:
Two-stitch crosses	
	With RN, go behind first st and p second st without removing it from LN; ktbl first st and slip both off LN
	With RN, go in front of first st and ktbl second st without removing it from LN; p first st and slip both off LN
	With RN, go in front of first st and ktbl second st without removing it from LN; ktbl first st and slip both off LN
	With RN, go behind first st and ktbl second st without removing it from LN; ktbl first st and slip both off LN
Three-stitch crosses	
	Place 2 sts on CN and hold to back; k1; place 2nd st from CN on LN and k1; k1 from CN
	Place 1 st on CN and hold to front; place 2nd st on CN and hold to back; k1; k1 from back CN, then k1 from front CN
	Place 1 st on CN and hold to back; place 2nd st on CN and hold to front; k1; k1 from front CN, then k1 from back CN
	Place 2 sts on CN, hold to front, p1; k2 from CN WS (chart #475): Place 1 st on CN, hold to front; p2; k1 from CN
	Place 1 st on CN, hold to back, k2; p1 from CN WS (chart #475): Place 2 sts on CN, hold to back; k1; p2 from CN
	Place 1 st on CN, hold to back, k2; k1 from CN
	Place 2 sts on CN, hold to front, k1; k2 from CN
	Place 2 sts on CN and hold to back; k1; place 2nd st from CN on LN and p1; k1 from CN
	Place stitch 1 on CN, hold to front, k2; k1 from CN
	Place 2 sts on CN, hold to back, k1; k2 from CN

	Slip 3 sts to RN purlwise. Use tip of LN to lift the first over the second and third (without dropping them). Replace all sts on LN, then k in their new positions.
	With tip of LN, lift 3rd st over first and second sts on LN (without dropping them). K all 3 sts in their new positions.
	Place 1 st on CN, hold to front, p2; ktbl from CN
	Place 2 sts on CN, hold to back; ktbl, p2 from CN
	Place 1 st on CN, hold to front; place 1 st on another CN, hold to back, ktbl; p1 from back CN; ktbl from front CN
	Place 1 st on CN, hold to back; place 1 st on another CN, hold to back, ktbl; p1 from second CN; ktbl from first CN
	Place 2 sts on CN, hold to front, ktbl; k2 from CN
	Place 1 st on CN, hold to back, k2; ktbl from CN
	Place 2 sts on CN, hold to front, p1; ktbl2 from CN
	Place 1 st on CN, hold to back, ktbl2; p1 from CN

Four-stitch crosses

	Place 2 sts on CN, hold to front, k2; k2 from CN
	Place 2 sts on CN, hold to back, k2; k2 from CN WS (chart #236): Place 2 sts on CN, hold to back, p2; p2 from CN
	Place 2 sts on CN, hold to back, k2; p2 from CN
	Place 2 sts on CN, hold to front, p2; k2 from CN
	Place 1 st on CN, hold to back, k3; k1 from CN
	Place 3 st on CN, hold to front; k1; k3 from CN
	Place 1 st on CN, hold to back, k3; p1 from CN
	Place 3 sts on CN, hold to front, p1; k3 from CN
	Place 1 st on CN, hold to front, k3; k1 from CN
	Place 3 sts on CN, hold to back, k1; k3 from CN
	Place 1 st on CN, hold to front; place 2 sts on CN, hold to back; k1; p2 from back CN, k1 from front CN
	Place 1 st on CN, hold to back; place 2 sts on CN, hold to back; k1; p2 from second CN, k1 from first CN
	Place 2 sts on CN, hold to front, ktbl 2; ktbl 2 from CN

Five-stitch crosses

	Place 2 st on CN, hold to front; place 1 st on another CN, hold to back; k2; k1 from back CN; k2 from front CN
	Place 2 st on CN, hold to back; place 1 st on another CN, hold to back; k2; k1 from second CN; k2 from first CN
	Place 2 st on CN, hold to back; place 1 st on another CN, hold to back; k2; p1 from second CN; k2 from first CN

	Place 2 st on CN, hold to front; place 1 st on another CN, hold to back; k2; p1 from back CN; k2 from front CN
	Place 1 st on CN, hold to front; place 3 sts on another CN, hold to back; k1; k3 from back CN, k1 from front CN
	Place 1 st on CN, hold to back; place 3 sts on another CN, hold to back; k1; k3 from back CN, k1 from second back CN
	Place 3 sts on CN, hold to back; k2, k3 from CN
	Place 3 sts on CN, hold to back; k2, p3 from CN
	Place 1 sts on CN, hold to front; k4, k1 from CN
	Place 4 sts on CN, hold to back; k1, k4 from CN
	Place 2 sts on CN, hold to front; place 1 st on another CN, hold to back; ktbl 2; p1 from back CN; ktbl 2 from front CN
	Place 3 sts on CN, hold to front, p2; k3 from CN
	Place 2 sts on CN, hold to back, k3; p2 from CN
	Place 2 sts on CN, hold to back, ktbl, k1, ktbl; p2 from CN
	Place 3 sts on CN, hold to front, p2; ktbl, k1, ktbl from CN
	Place 2 sts on CN, hold to front; k3, k2 from CN
	Place 3 sts on CN, hold to back; k2, k3 from CN
	Place 2 sts on CN, hold to back, k3; k1, p1 from CN
	Place 2 sts on CN, hold to back, k3; p1, k1 from CN

Six-stitch crosses

	Place 3 sts on CN, hold to front, k3; k3 from CN
	Place 3 sts on CN, hold to back, k3; k3 from CN
	Place 2 sts on CN, hold to front, k4; k2 from CN
	Place 2 st on CN, hold to front; place 2 st on another CN, hold to back; k2; p2 from second CN; k2 from first CN
	Place 4 sts on CN, hold to back; k2; k1, p2, k1 from CN
	Place 2 sts on CN, hold to front, k1, p2, k1; k2 from CN

-stitch cross

	Place 3 sts on CN, hold to front; k4; k3 from CN

stitch crosses

	Place 4 sts on CN, hold to front, k4; k4 from CN
	Place 4 sts on CN, hold to back, k4; k4 from CN

Bobbles

Row 1 (RS): k, yo, k into same st; turn.
Row 2 (WS): p3; turn.
Row 3 (RS): CDD (sl 2 tog knitwise, k1, p2sso)

Variations:

= same as above, but complete on row 3 with sk2p

= K, p, k into the same st; then CDD those 3 sts

= same as above, but with 2 additional rows of stockinette

= same as above, but with 2 additional rows of stockinette, completed with sk2p

---

Row 1 (RS): k, double yo, k into the same st. Turn.
Row 2 (WS): p, ptbl 2, p. Turn.
Row 3: k 4. Turn.
Row 4: p4. Turn.
Row 5: ssk, k2tog.

Row 1 (RS): yo, k, yo, k into the same st. Turn.
Row 2 (WS): p4. Turn.
Row 3: k4. Turn.
Row 4: [p2tog] twice. Turn.
Row 5: k2tog.

Row 1 (RS): k, yo, k, yo, k into same st; turn
Row 2 (WS): p5; turn
Row 3 (RS): LQD (sl 4, k1, p4sso)

Variations:

= same as above, but complete on row 3 with sl 3 tog knitwise, k2tog, p3sso

= same as above, but with 3 rows of stockinette

= same as above, but with 5 rows of stockinette, and completed with sl 3 tog knitwise, k2tog, p3sso

= same as above, but with 5 rows of garter st, and completed with sl 3 tog knitwise, k2tog, p3sso

	[Yo, k] 4 times into the same st. Sl 1 st back to LN, then pass 7 sts over it

het bobbles

	3DC bobble See p. 29 for illustration Chart 476 uses ch2 rather than ch3 to begin Variations: = 2DC bobble (omit one DC) = 4DC bobble (make one additional DC) = 5 DC bobble (ch up 4 and make 5 DCs, then ch 1)
	2HDC bobble: ch3, [yarn over hook, draw up a loop] twice, yarn over hook, draw through all loops Variations: = work as above, but begin with draw up a loop instead of ch3 = 3HDC bobble: work as above, but begin with ch2 and make 3 HDCs

"Books to Span the East and West"

Tuttle Publishing was founded in 1832 in the small New England town of Rutland, Vermont [USA]. Our core values remain as strong today as they were then—to publish best-in-class books which bring people together one page at a time. In 1948, we established a publishing office in Japan—and Tuttle is now a leader in publishing English-language books about the arts, languages and cultures of Asia. The world has become a much smaller place today and Asia's economic and cultural influence has grown. Yet the need for meaningful dialogue and information about this diverse region has never been greater. Over the past seven decades, Tuttle has published thousands of books on subjects ranging from martial arts and paper crafts to language learning and literature—and our talented authors, illustrators, designers and photographers have won many prestigious awards. We welcome you to explore the wealth of oinformation available on Asia at **www.tuttlepublishing.com.**

Published by Tuttle Publishing, an imprint of Periplus Editions (HK) Ltd.

www.tuttlepublishing.com

MOYOUAMI 1000 BOUBARIAMI KAGIBARIAMI (NV 70183)
Copyright © NIHON-VOGUE-SHA 1992

English translation rights arranged with NIHON VOGUE, Corp. through Japan UNI Agency, Inc., Tokyo
English Translation © 2020 by Periplus Editions (HK) Ltd.
Translated from Japanese by Gayle Roehm

ISBN 978-4-8053-1519-4

Original Japanese edition
Photograph Suzuki Nobuo
Layout Terayama Fumie

Distributed by
North America, Latin America & Europe
Tuttle Publishing
364 Innovation Drive, North Clarendon, VT 05759-9436 U.S.A.
Tel: 1 (802) 773-8930
Fax: 1 (802) 773-6993
info@tuttlepublishing.com
www.tuttlepublishing.com

Japan
Tuttle Publishing
Yaekari Building 3rd Floor, 5-4-12 Osaki, Shinagawa-ku,
Tokyo 141-0032
Tel: (81) 3 5437-0171
Fax: (81) 3 5437-0755
sales@tuttle.co.jp
www.tuttle.co.jp

Asia Pacific
Berkeley Books Pte. Ltd.
3 Kallang Sector #04-01/02, Singapore 349278
Tel: (65) 6741 2178
Fax: (65) 6741 2179
inquiries@periplus.com.sg
www.tuttlepublishing.com

24 23 22   7 6 5 4 3
Printed in Singapore   2203TP